Poverty and Health

Poverty and Health

A Crisis among America's Most Vulnerable

Volume 2

The Importance of Place in Determining Their Future

Kevin M. Fitzpatrick, Editor

PRAEGER

AN IMPRINT OF ABC-CLIO, LLC
Santa Barbara, California • Denver, Colorado • Oxford, England

Library of Congress Cataloging-in-Publication Data

Poverty and health : a crisis among America's most vulnerable / Kevin M. Fitzpatrick, editor.

pages cm

Includes bibliographical references and index.

ISBN 978–1–4408–0263–8 (hardcopy : alk. paper) — ISBN 978–1–4408–0264–5 (ebook) 1. Poor—Medical care—United States. 2. Medically underserved areas—United States. 3. Health services accessibility—United States. 4. Poor—Health and hygiene—United States. 5. Medical policy—United States. I. Fitzpatrick, Kevin M., editor of compilation.

RA418.5.P6P682 2013

362.1086'942—dc23   2013013129

ISBN: 978–1–4408–0263–8
EISBN: 978–1–4408–0264–5

17 16 15 14 13   1 2 3 4 5

This book is also available on the World Wide Web as an eBook.
Visit www.abc-clio.com for details.

Praeger
An Imprint of ABC-CLIO, LLC

ABC-CLIO, LLC
130 Cremona Drive, P.O. Box 1911
Santa Barbara, California 93116-1911

This book is printed on acid-free paper ∞

Manufactured in the United States of America

These volumes are dedicated to the millions of Americans who are underserved and overlooked. Their daily struggles are my inspiration to be a catalyst for change.

Contents

Acknowledgments

These volumes represent an outgrowth of my recent book, *Unhealthy Cities*, which continued my long-standing interest and work on health-related issues among the "least of these." I acknowledge the support, assistance, insight, and thoughtful reflection of colleagues and staff in the development of the project. I would like to thank the University of Arkansas, Fulbright College of Arts and Sciences, and the Department of Sociology and Criminal Justice for creating the intellectual environment that affords me the opportunity to do these kinds of projects.

I would like to extend special thanks to my graduate assistants, Don Willis and Gail O'Connor, whose work throughout this project was vital to its completion. In addition to them, my review team, which included Kristen Kelley and Dave Woodring, did a fantastic job of carefully overseeing the review process with careful and constructive criticism that improved these manuscripts and the overall organization of these volumes. Thanks to Anna Zajicek-Wagemann for her review of one of the chapters and the comments that were provided to improve it. Finally, volumes like these just cannot happen without outstanding editorial advice, direction, and expertise. My editorial assistant, Jocelyn Bailey, did a wonderful job of keeping the process moving forward. Jocelyn made sure that all the authors were marching to the beat of the same drum and expertly provided editorial guidance to both the authors and the editor. I would also like to express my gratitude to Debbie Carvalko, my acquisitions editor at Praeger/ABC-CLIO, for providing expert guidance through this project.

As with all of my past work, I want to acknowledge my family and their support—particularly my wife Mary, who continues to be a sounding board, a critic, and my biggest fan. A final thank you goes to my parents, William and Evelyn, who have always been behind me and supported me in everything I ever did. They both passed away during this project, and they will be embedded in my memory of this work forever.

Abbreviations

ABCD: asset-based community development

ACA: Affordable Care Act

BMI: body mass index

CBPR: community-based participatory research

CDC: Centers for Disease Control and Prevention

COPD: chronic obstructive pulmonary disease

EPA: United States Environmental Protection Agency

GIS: geographic information system

MSA: metropolitan statistical area

MTO: Moving to Opportunity project

PRWORA: Personal Responsibility and Work Opportunity Reconciliation Act (1996)

PTSD: post-traumatic stress disorder

SES: socioeconomic status

Chapter 1

Introduction: Place, Health, and America's Disadvantaged

Kevin M. Fitzpatrick

Where we live determines so much about our living experiences, health trajectories, social development, and overall life satisfaction. Over the last several decades a plethora of research studies has determined that *place matters*, albeit not in the same way for everyone. The most recent report published by the National Survey of Children's Health (2012) clearly demonstrates that place matters for America's youth. Countless examples in this report provide a telling story of how the social, economic, and political climates of states can make a difference in health outcomes; nearly a 20% margin separates states with the highest rates of childhood obesity from those with the lowest rates of childhood obesity. These penetrating health differences are found at all levels of geography and suggest that our understanding of health, particularly among the poorest populations, is in part related to the places they live, work, and go to school.

Regardless of where we live, there is a certain amount of risk or hazard associated with the physical, cultural, social, and economic structures of places; whether neighborhoods in cities or villages in counties, how this risk is distributed across these landscapes impacts the mental and physical health outcomes of its residents. The ecological conditions present in some places influence the health beliefs and practices of residents, their health lifestyles, their access to health resources, and the social capital they use to cope with stressful circumstances. These same ecological conditions can intensify the disadvantages experienced by some groups and improve the advantages enjoyed by other groups. Because risk is spatially structured and unevenly distributed, places become mosaics of risk and protection that are not the same for everyone. This distribution is particularly telling when looking at differences across socioeconomic groups.

With recent research evidence beginning to pile up regarding the importance of place in determining health trajectories, the challenge ahead of us is to begin to develop and implement place-based strategies for health promotion. No longer can we develop a generic placeless health initiative and expect it to work for everyone or everywhere. The second volume in this set articulates the depth of struggle for so many different groups living in a variety of locations throughout the United States. Of course, there are geographic locations, specific subgroups, and challenges not included in this volume. Regardless, this volume provides some important substance, both theoretical and empirical, to a growing line of inquiry examining the nexus of health and place, particularly for poor people.

This volume begins with a comprehensive discussion of both theoretical and empirical works examining the relationship of place and health across a wide range of scholarly disciplines. Jokinen-Gordon takes on the formidable task of introducing the role of place in understanding health among America's most vulnerable. Her excellent chapter provides a strong framework for the volume to examine specific places and groups within this larger context of approaches to place-based health. Gillespie and Bostean's chapter focuses on residential mobility among the disadvantaged, considering how that constant flux affects their well-being. They explore the multilevel effects of mobility and examine the role of social capital as mediating the negative effects of mobility on health outcomes. The third chapter in this volume, by Lewis and colleagues, looks at a particularly vulnerable group whose members are subject to increased health risks and hazards because of their social and economic status—immigrants and refugees. These authors provide a number of very poignant examples from their work with this population in impoverished rural areas of North Carolina, putting a face to an often-faceless group at risk for significant negative health outcomes. Lachica and colleagues discuss one of the more controversial locations in the United States—the border towns between the United States and Mexico. Understanding these places is of particular importance not only because of their strategic locations, but also because they are very special places confronting very unique health problems. Dulin Keita and Hannon focus on one of the most important health problems facing low-income Americans today—obesity. This chapter supports the claim made earlier—namely, that place is important to determining health, but not all places have the same type of impact; urban neighborhoods in large metropolitan areas are of particular concern to the health of segregated subgroups like African-Americans and other racial and ethnic subgroups.

The next several chapters in this volume concentrate on specific place-based conditions and their role in exacerbating the negative health circumstances of those living in poverty. London and Frazier focus on household crowding and its impact on the health and well-being of persons living in poverty. Their analysis is one of several in this volume that is of particular importance to scholars interested in the role of place on childhood and youth well-being. Likewise, scholars have noted the critical role of exposure to violence in high-risk neighborhoods and its impact on child health and well-being. Hardy and colleagues examine both short- and long-term effects of violence exposure on health outcomes among both children and adults. Focusing on a particularly high health risk region of the country in the Mississippi delta, Green and Mitra explore the role of intersectional space on the health of residents, particularly low-income, minority women. This approach directs attention to specific initiatives and health outcomes that are distributed unequally. In part, their thesis calls our attention to this unequal distribution and its impact on policy and planning in high-risk areas such as the Mississippi Delta. As a follow-up to the previous chapter, Van Gundy and Mills elaborate on the health risks and hazards of rural America. Examining both mental and physical health outcomes among rural residents, they discuss the stress process and its significant variation between rural and nonrural locations.

The remaining two chapters in this second volume are programmatically focused on how we can lower or minimize disparities across groups by addressing specific elements of places and their role in mitigating negative health outcomes. Grimm and colleagues discuss the importance of shifting our way of thinking about disease and poverty and what that looks like in specific places. By focusing on neighborhood and human assets, these authors argue that health and health lifestyles can be redirected to grassroots and community-focused movements that can produce very different outcomes. The last chapter in this volume appropriately focuses on place-based initiatives for addressing health disparities. Zappia and Puntenney examine a large and comprehensive body of literature that points to the critical role of improving neighborhood/community health by specifically addressing the physical, structural, and political challenges ever present in communities, particularly in low-income ones, across the United States.

The chapters in this volume do a wonderful job of outlining for us exactly why place matters and for whom it matters most. From birth to death—across racial and ethnic, gender, and socioeconomic boundaries—health and place are inextricably linked. The work of this interdisciplinary group of authors helps sharpen our understanding of the health-place relationship while providing important insights into programming and policy that can make a difference in the lives of the most disadvantaged persons living in the United States. I am encouraged by the studies in this volume and in others like it, yet realize that we must be cautiously optimistic about their role in changing the way policymakers address the problems of health at the national, regional, and local levels. It is my hope that this and other volumes like it will begin to move the needle and force decision makers to consider how ZIP code soon may be the most important variable for us to consider in the health equation.

Chapter 2

Neighborhoods and Health

Hanna Jokinen-Gordon

Social conditions are fundamental causes of health and well-being (Link & Phelan, 1995). Our position in the social hierarchy determines our exposure to stress, as well as our access to health-related resources and information. However, as ecological models point out, development occurs within multiple interconnected domains. While individual social position is one domain, the conditions present in the community environment are equally important for healthy development. Our individual residential history and current geographic location are integral aspects of our identities (Fitzpatrick & LaGory, 2000). Place determines our access to tangible resources, such as schools and health services, but also the psychosocial environments to which we are exposed. The communities we belong to determine the way we think about the social world and our understanding of ourselves in relation to others. Thus the attributes of our spatial location shape our attitudes, beliefs, and actions in ways that matter for our individual and collective well-being.

The goal of social science research is to examine how human life is affected by social relationships and the communal environment. The geographic patterning of human society is determined not only by the physical landscape, but also by the formation of social relationships. Studies in sociology have demonstrated that changes in the community economic and social environment influence individual and family well-being

(Caplow & Forman, 1950; Chapin, 1940; Cressey, 1949). Early studies examined the spatial patterning of physical and mental health outcomes and found that individuals living in deteriorating and poor urban centers had higher rates of mental illness and infectious diseases (Faris & Dunham, 1939; Porter, 1998). Since these early studies, research on the ways that place and health are related have proliferated. When we consider place, we often think mainly of geographic location, yet every community is unique. The structural characteristics, the infrastructure and availability of resources, the social organization, and the physical environment are all attributes of place that matter for health and well-being.

As evidenced by the *Healthy People 2020* initiative, there is a growing recognition among policymakers of the importance of identifying and remedying national social inequalities in health and well-being. A continuation of the ambitious *Healthy People 2010* initiative, the *2020* project outlines multiple goals that work toward a future in which all U.S. residents have access to equitable health resources. New to the *2020* initiative is a focus on the social determinants of health with the specific goal of "[Creating] social and physical environments that promote good health for all" (Secretary's Advisory Committee on Health Promotion and Disease Prevention Objectives for 2020). Without acknowledging the importance of the neighborhood context and the way in which it conditions exposure to "risky or protective" health environments, it will not be possible to overcome existing social inequities in health and well-being (Fitzpatrick & LaGory, 2000). Policymakers and health researchers must continue to build on the existing body of social science research that strives to understand why, and how, neighborhoods and communities shape well-being, net of individual characteristics.

The aim of this chapter is to provide the reader with a general understanding of the relationship between neighborhoods and health, as well as a basic discussion of the methodological and theoretical challenges facing this type of research. To achieve this goal, the chapter considers (1) how neighborhoods are conceptualized and studied, (2) which theoretical mechanisms link neighborhood conditions to health outcomes, and (3) how social inequalities such as poverty, socioeconomic status, and race/ethnicity contribute to the relationship. The review concludes by presenting a theoretical model of the neighborhood-health relationship and discussing the potential future of scholarship on neighborhoods and health.

Neighborhoods and Health: Measurement and Methodology

Our social positions and geographic locations are closely intertwined. We are both producers and products of the contexts within which we exist. Our residential history is a selective process that is the result of both personal biography and structural position. At the same time, where we live can both promote and constrain our opportunities and life chances through the physical and social environments to which we are exposed. Thus it is challenging to determine the independent influence of the neighborhood contexts on health and well-being, net of individual characteristics. The following section provides a basic discussion of some of the ways place and health can be conceptualized and studied. (For a more detailed description, see Diez Roux, 2003.)

Defining Neighborhoods and Health

Neighborhoods are geographic areas bounded by both formal and informal borders (Diez Roux, 2001). The borders of a neighborhood house not only the objective attributes of the places we live—such the types of businesses and amenities available and the physical landscape—but also the social environment, such as the social networks we belong to and the social relationships we maintain. In health research, the way a neighborhood is conceptualized depends largely on discipline and the topic of interest. There exists a degree of ambiguity and limited conceptual consistency in the way that neighborhoods are operationalized, making it challenging to compare findings across studies. Often in research, the terms *neighborhood* and *community* are used interchangeably to describe area-level health affects (Diez Roux, 2001), yet both terms can be used to describe very different geographic localities.

A common practice in neighborhood research is to rely on census tracts as the main geographic unit of analysis. The use of census tracts began in 1906 as a way for researchers and policymakers to examine and plan for public health services, but it was not until the year 2000 that census tracts were defined for the entire United States (Krieger, 2006). The U.S. Census Bureau defines a census tract as a "small, relatively permanent statistical subdivision of a county." On average, a census tract contains between 2,500 and 8,000 individuals, and the tracts are designed based on the characteristics of the population and are meant to be fairly homogenous (U.S. Census Bureau). Aggregate-level compositional indicators of the sociodemographic features of a census tract can be appended to national-level data sets, thereby enabling researchers to examine how community-level characteristics are associated with individual-level health outcomes.

While using a census tract as a proxy for neighborhood is both efficient and straightforward, there are some limitations. For example, because census tracts are fairly large geographic areas, they face the problems of the possible loss of pertinent health-related information (Diez Roux, 2001, 2003) and the "obfuscation of local-level variability" (Weiss, Ompad, Galea, & Vlahov, 2007, p. S158). The boundaries of communities and neighborhoods are fluid and dynamic. As they grow and change demographically, the social, cultural, and economic climate of neighborhoods evolve, as do the boundaries. A single census tract may include parts of several neighborhoods, making it difficult to isolate exactly which aspects of the social and built environment matter most for health. Despite these limitations, research finds that census tracts tend to be reliable and efficient indicators of the neighborhood-health relationship, and it supports the continued use of such measures in health research (Messer, Vinikoor-Imler, & Laraia, 2012).

In addition to official boundaries, informal and symbolic boundaries are produced through residents' perceptions and definitions of what they consider to be part of their community. The social boundaries of neighborhoods are created and maintained through the formation of social relationships that are grounded in geographic proximity, but often extend beyond official borders. As a consequence, it is important to consider the qualitative aspects that define a neighborhood. Examining residents' perceptions of what they consider to be their neighborhood will improve our understanding of the unique ways that place and well-being are related (O'Campo, 2003; Weiss et al., 2007). Interviews find that people typically consider their neighborhoods to be the small geographic area in the immediate proximity of their home, typically a block or less, but also as slightly larger areas that correspond to historic and municipal boundaries (Altschuler, Somkin, & Adler, 2004). While the structural characteristics of a census tract have important implications for health, the relationships that are maintained within what residents consider their immediate neighborhood or community can buffer the consequences of structural disadvantage through mechanisms of social support (Umberson, Crosnoe, & Reczek, 2010).

Broadly speaking, we can think of health as both the physical condition of the body and psychological or emotional well-being. Past work on place and health has examined both individual—as well as group-level—health patterns in both physical and mental health, along with the behaviors associated with health outcomes. For example, place has been associated with life expectancy, mortality rates, birth outcomes, chronic diseases, weight and body mass, alcohol consumption, smoking, sleep quality, mental health, and the like (Burdette & Hill, 2008; Fitzpatrick & LaGory, 2000; Hill, Burdette, & Hale, 2009; Kramer, Cooper, Drews-Botsch, Waller, & Hogue, 2010; Leclere, Rogers, & Peters, 1997; Meijer, Röhl, Bloomfield, & Grittner, 2012; Subramanian, Kawachi, & Kennedy, 2001; Yen & Kaplan, 1999).

Characteristics of the Neighborhood Environment. Aspects of the neighborhood environment can be described at both the aggregate level and the individual level. Contextual variables are aggregate-level constructs that can be classified in two ways: (1) those that summarize the structure of the neighborhood, such as the percentage of residents living in poverty, the racial composition, or mean education level, and (2) those that are not derived from the group, but reflect characteristics of the neighborhood, such as the presence of substandard housing or health services (Diez Roux, 2003). Contextual-level variables are most often indicators of the social and demographic structure of a neighborhood and are measured at the group level, rather than individual level. Examples of contextual indicators of the neighborhood environment include the percentage of residents living in poverty, the percentage living in single-headed households, and the availability of health services. In contrast, questions that ask residents about their subjective experience of their community, including how they perceive social and physical characteristics, are typically measured at the individual level. However, contextual attributes of the neighborhood can also be included as individual-level data that describe the neighborhood context in which one resides.

Modeling Neighborhood Effects.   Because the spatial distribution of a community is not random, it is important to keep in mind the distinct levels at which neighborhood processes operate. With advances in methodology and statistical modeling, researchers are now able to distinguish between individual- and neighborhood-level effects. There are several ways of modeling the relationship between health and place, and the method chosen depends in large part on the availability of data and the health outcome of interest.

Some studies focus only on group-level associations. Such studies are used when the group, or community, is the unit of analysis and are useful when detailed individual-level data are unavailable or limited. This method is useful in large-scale epidemiologic studies interested in understanding population-level health trends. For example, researchers might examine how rates of infectious disease vary between high- and low-poverty neighborhoods. A second type of model, a multilevel model, combines two sampling units, the individual and the neighborhood, to examine the independent effect of individual- and group-level characteristics on health. Such models are particularly useful because they allow researchers to consider the impact of the neighborhood while simultaneously controlling for individual residents' characteristics. Other studies may include data on the neighborhood context, but the individual remains the primary sampling unit. For example, census tract data on the racial composition of the respondent's neighborhood can be linked to national data sets to address the influence of the neighborhood context on individual outcomes. Finally, purely individual-level studies focus on a respondent's individual evaluation or perception of the neighborhood as it pertains to health outcomes.

One of the biggest challenges to understanding how neighborhoods influence health is selection. Is it the case that living in an impoverished neighborhood worsens health, or are those persons living in impoverished neighborhoods already in worse health? Causal inference is particularly challenging in research attempting to link geography to health (Acevedo-Garcia & Osypuk, 2008; Oakes, 2004). Without complete information on residential and personal biography, determining whether the neighborhood-health relationship is one of causation or selection remains difficult. Further advances in methodology and longitudinal data collection are necessary to advance understanding of the complex relationship of humans and their environment.

Why Neighborhoods Matter: The Theoretical Pathways between Place and Health

The association of neighborhoods and health is well established (Diez Roux & Mair, 2010; Fitzpatrick & LaGory, 2000; Robert, 1999; Sampson, Morenoff, & Gannon-Rowley, 2002). Explanations for the association focus primarily on the objective conditions, subjective conditions, or some combination of the two. Objective conditions highlight the availability of material resources and indicators of the structural conditions of the community. The availability of health services, access to health-enhancing activities, and the physical landscape are aspects of the material composition of a neighborhood. We can think of the structural aspects of a neighborhood as aggregate indicators of the composition of the population, measured using variables such as the percentage living in poverty or the racial-ethnic composition. Finally, subjective characteristics include psychosocial evaluations and the residents' perceptions of the neighborhood. It is important to note that the objective and subjective characteristics of communities are not mutually exclusive, but rather interact to create the neighborhood environment. The following section presents a basic conceptual model useful for understanding the neighborhood-health relationship and discusses the supporting literature.

Conceptual Model

Figure 2.1 presents a basic summary of the way that the neighborhood context contributes to health and well-being. Individual social position influences health and well-being, but also determines the types of neighborhoods and communities we are likely to live in. The structural conditions of a neighborhood influence health and well-being indirectly through material resources and the psychosocial environment. However, the material conditions and psychosocial characteristics are interrelated. The neighborhood environment conditions health behaviors and exposure to stress, which in

Figure 2.1
Conceptual model of the contributions of neighborhood environment to health and well-being.

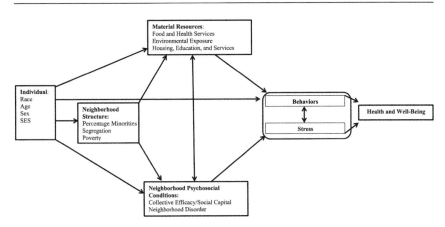

turn have direct effects on health and well-being. The rest of this subsection more thoroughly describes the mechanisms through which neighborhoods influence health outcomes.

Individual Characteristics and Neighborhood Context. Individual sociodemographic characteristics are fundamental causes of health (Link & Phelan 1995; Williams & Sternhal, 2010). The types of neighborhoods we live in and have access to, the communities in which we feel comfortable, and the ability to relocate when necessary all depend on both our social position and our residential history (Schwirian, 1983; South, Pais, and Crowder, 2011). Likewise, the community we live in determines the schools we attend and the social networks within which we are embedded, thereby influencing our health via the choices and constraints we face as they relate to our geographic location.

Neighborhood Structure. The structure of a neighborhood is measured by examining contextual indicators of the demographic and behavioral characteristics of residents. Measures such as the racial and ethnic composition, percentage of households living in poverty, mean level of education, and residential instability (often measured as housing tenure) are some examples of structural characteristics. Disadvantaged neighborhoods are characterized by a high level of residential instability, concentrated poverty, high unemployment, and a low mean level of education. When neighborhoods are structurally disadvantaged, important social and economic resources essential for maintenance of the public order are lacking (Ross, 2000). Living in a disadvantaged neighborhood increases experiences of daily stress and strain, but limits the formation of supportive social relationships—thus exerting a toll on both mental and physical functioning (Hill & Maimon, 2013; Ross & Mirowsky, 2009). The consequences of neighborhood disadvantage are amplified when neighborhoods are segregated. Massey and Denton (1989) observed the multiple dimensions of residential segregation, including the distribution of the neighborhood, the clustering of neighborhoods, and the level of contact residents have with other community members. As residential segregation increases, a neighborhood becomes increasingly isolated from the rest of the population and social problems intensify. Both disadvantage and residential segregation play roles in determining the availability of material and social resources present in a community.

Material Mechanisms.   The ability to access needed health services, to safely move about without fear of physical harm, and to purchase nutritious foods are some of the ways that the material conditions of a neighborhood contribute to health outcomes. Racially segregated and impoverished neighborhoods are more likely to be medically underserved, more likely to have a greater density of fast-food restaurants and liquor stores, and less likely to contain green space. Regardless of a person's individual resources, living in a poor neighborhood constrains health via the availability of resources within a reasonable proximity of one's residential location. Individuals with greater material resources are better equipped to navigate the geographic obstacles between themselves and good health, whereas the most marginalized face the combined effect of individual and neighborhood deprivation.

One topic that has attracted considerable academic and popular interest in recent years is the spatial distribution of food sources. Most studies have focused primarily on how the types of food outlets available in a community influence body mass index (BMI) or risk of being overweight or obese. Neighborhoods characterized by a high concentration of poor households and a greater percentage of racial minorities tend to contain a greater quantity of small grocery stores, but the foods sold tend to be of lower quality and are more costly (Moore & Diez Roux, 2006). As a consequence, residents are left to pay higher prices for nutritionally lacking foods and are often blocked from access to large supermarket chains that offer a greater variety of choices at lower cost (Walker, Keane, & Burke, 2010). Qualitative interviews with African-American women from low-income urban neighborhoods reveal that in addition to limited availability, other environmental and social factors influence their ability to acquire food (Zenk et al., 2011). For example, such women have reported concerns regarding sanitation and hygiene in the stores, poor treatment from store owners, and feelings that their safety was compromised in certain locations. Without access to affordable nutrition options, families living in poor communities are constrained by the neighborhood environment in their ability to secure basic needs as well as to alter or improve their dietary habits.

Findings from studies of the relationship between food availability and body mass vary. In one study, researchers found that the number and type of food establishments present in a census tract were associated with the prevalence of obesity (Morland & Evenson, 2009). Greater availability of convenience stores and a larger number of fast-food restaurants were associated with a significantly higher prevalence of obese residents. However, another study by Block and colleagues (2011) examined the association of BMI and food availability over a 30-year period and found no relationship. These authors' findings revealed no consistent or significant association between food outlet proximity and residential BMI. Therefore, while increasing community access to nutrition may enhance some aspects of well-being, it is likely that other structural and social characteristics are more robust predictors of health outcomes.

Individuals who live in poor and disadvantaged neighborhoods are more likely to report that they have unmet medical needs and are less likely to have received important preventive health services (Kirby & Kaneda, 2005, 2006). While there have been considerable improvements in access to general health care in underserved communities, the types of services available still vary. For example, neighborhoods characterized by a high degree of concentrated poverty tend to have fewer pharmacies, and the existing pharmacies are limited in the availability of certain medications (Morrison, Wallenstein, Natale, Senzel, & Huang, 2000). When residents are unable to access prescribed treatments and preventive health care, their existing health problems are intensified and they may become frustrated and stressed in their dealings with health care providers. Low-income and predominately racial-minority neighborhoods typically have the fewest retail health clinic options, such that residents may instead rely on emergency care (Pollack & Armstrong, 2009). In poor communities, certain cancer screening options may be less available compared to more affluent areas (Pruitt, Shim, Mullen, Vernon, & Amick, 2009). The ability to access care for acute conditions and preventive measures are both necessary for good health, yet residents of disadvantaged and poor neighborhoods have difficulty accessing both.

Like other basic needs, access to a safe and clean environment is integral to health and well-being. Communities with high concentrations of racial-ethnic minorities and poverty are more likely to be located near, or in, hazardous environmental conditions (Crowder & Downey, 2010; Evans & Kantrowitz, 2002; Fitzpatrick & LaGory, 2000). Exposure to hazardous waste, air and water pollution, ambient noise, and substandard or crowded residential living conditions has consequences for long-term physical and mental health outcomes (Morello-Frosch & Shenassa, 2006; O'Neill et al., 2003). In addition to the physical risks of living near industrial activity, simply living in the proximity of industrial production is detrimental for residents' mental health, as it increases psychological distress, particularly for women (Downey & Van Willigen, 2005, Boardman et al., 2008).

Many of the challenges faced by members of low-income neighborhoods are related to the availability of opportunities for upward social mobility (or lack thereof). Businesses and developers are wary of opening new facilities in neighborhoods perceived as disadvantaged and declining, which in turn limits further economic growth (Sampson & Raudenbush, 2004). Other aspects of the neighborhood environment also condition the way that residents seek and view employment opportunities. In disadvantaged neighborhoods, fewer options and norms regarding the use of public services limit the ways residents seek out employment (Casciano & Massey, 2008). Inadequate employment and educational opportunities constrain upward social mobility in poor communities. Without tax revenues from local businesses and property values, schools suffer and local infrastructures are weakened, further undermining the stability of the community. Underfunded schools contribute to lifelong inequalities by blocking access to the quality education that is integral to upward social mobility and good health.

Psychosocial Mechanisms: Collective Efficacy, Social Capital, and Neighborhood Disorder

In stable and supportive communities, residents often experience a sense of cohesion and are able to form beneficial supportive social ties with other community members. When residents feel that they can depend on their community and feel a sense of belonging, they act in ways that enhance the health of themselves and others. Like the material environment, the degree of social order, cohesion, and support is a function of the structure of a community. In structurally disadvantaged neighborhoods, aspects of the social and physical environment are eroded through processes of residential segregation and the social isolation of community members (Massey & Denton, 1989). When communities become isolated, they experience a breakdown of social control and social cohesion as well as an increase in deviant behavior (Sampson, Raudenbush, & Earls, 1997). These processes intensify existing social inequalities and increase the degree of instability and disorder perceived by residents, thereby increasing stress and strain. Concepts such as collective efficacy and neighborhood social capital are used to describe the health-enhancing feelings of cooperative ability and social cohesion characterized by relationships and reciprocity. At the other end of the spectrum, feeling that one's community is unsafe, unstable, and in state of general disorder leads to feelings of mistrust, suspicion, and isolation.

Thus the psychosocial attributes of communities can either improve or —more often—exacerbate existing health risks and inhibit the promotion of a beneficial health milieu. This section reviews scholarship on three key psychosocial mechanisms that underlie the neighborhood-health relationship: collective efficacy, neighborhood social capital, and neighborhood disorder.

Collective Efficacy and Social Capital

Collective efficacy and social capital are related concepts that form one theoretical bridge between neighborhoods and individual health outcomes. In many instances the terms are used interchangeably, but more often collective efficacy is considered to be one component of social capital (Kawachi, Kennedy, & Glass, 1999; Lochner, Kawachi, & Kennedy, 1999). However, their conceptual meanings differ. *Collective efficacy* refers to the beliefs held by members of a group about their abilities to perform as a collective. It can be measured as an individual's perceptions of the group's ability, or it may refer to the aggregate capabilities of members to act effectively as a cohesive whole (Bandura, 2000). When a community has a high degree of collective efficacy, it reflects a sense of social control, mutual trust, and the willingness of community members to intervene and act on behalf of one another (Browning, Dietz, & Feinberg, 2004).

Individuals who report high levels of efficacy are more likely to report that they are in better health (Browning & Cagney, 2002). In Browning and Cagney's study, the authors found that the structural conditions of the neighborhood were not related to self-rated health, net of individual characteristics. However, even when individual and structural characteristics were controlled using multilevel models, neighborhood-level collective efficacy had a positive and significant influence on self-rated health. Thus individuals who live in communities in which they perceive a high level of mutual trust and support are more likely to be in better health.

In another study, Cohen and colleagues (2006) use multilevel models to examine the influence of collective efficacy on adolescent BMI. Net of individual characteristics and neighborhood disadvantage, adolescents living in neighborhoods with the highest level of collective efficacy had BMIs one unit lower than adolescents in neighborhoods with the mean level. Compared to youth residing in the average level neighborhood, youth in the lowest collective efficacy had 52% higher odds of being overweight.

These findings highlight the importance of the subjective experience of the neighborhood environment for health outcomes. When individuals sense a high degree of efficacy, they are more likely to foster high levels of mastery and beliefs in their personal ability (Bandura, 2000). Likewise, when communities are empowered by feelings of efficacy, they are more likely to act in ways that improve the material and social conditions of their community. Yet, the structural aspects of the neighborhood create an environment in which collective efficacy either thrives or declines (Sampson et al., 1997). Communities that might most benefit from collective efficacy are those in which it is least likely to flourish (Cohen, Inagami, & Finch, 2008).

Compared to collective efficacy, social capital has received far more attention from health researchers. In general, *neighborhood social capital* can be thought of as a form of social cohesion that measures the neighborhood-level stocks of interpersonal trust, norms of reciprocity, and civic participation (Kawachi & Berkman, 2000). It is a collective indicator of the quantity and quality of social relationships, both formal and informal, and the norms of trust and reciprocity typical of a community (Putnam, 2001). At the neighborhood level, social capital influences the health of residents through three primary mechanisms (Kawachi & Berkman, 2000). First, using mechanisms of social control and social learning, neighborhoods with high levels of social capital promote positive health behaviors (Mohnen, Volker, Flap, & Groenewegen, 2012). Residents exercise both informal and formal mechanisms of social control to prevent negative or harmful health actions, spread important health-related information, and encourage positive change. Second, neighborhood social capital increases the number of available health-related services and amenities. Communities that foster high levels of social capital are more effective at promoting policies and programs that bring funding and resources to health-deprived areas (Altschuler et al., 2004). Third, social capital influences health via psychosocial processes by increasing social support. When residents have a sense of trust in their fellow community members, they are more prepared to handle the consequences of stressful and adverse living conditions (Umberson et al., 2010).

There is a long history of research on the relationship between individual social capital and health (Stephens, 2008). Notably, scholars have examined the role of aggregate measures of social capital as means of understanding the relationship between neighborhood conditions and health (Carpiano, 2006). In a study of Chicago neighborhoods, Lochner and colleagues (2003) found that higher neighborhood social capital is associated with significantly lower mortality rates among adults 45–64 years of age, net of neighborhood disadvantage. Specifically, their analysis found a robust relationship between neighborhood social capital and total mortality and mortality from heart disease among White residents. However, the results for other causes of death and for Black individuals were less consistent. Yet, when Hutchinson and colleagues (2009) examined Black all-cause mortality, they found that Black mortality is lower in neighborhoods that exhibit high social capital, particularly in neighborhoods with a higher percentage of Black residents (p. 1862). These studies and others (see, for example, Caughy, O'Campo, & Muntaner, 2003; Cramm, Van Dijk, & Nieboer, 2012) demonstrate the importance of considering how neighborhood structure, individual characteristics, and social capital interact to influence health and well-being.

One way that social capital impacts health is by influencing health behaviors. However, if the normative social interaction in a community centers on negative beliefs and behaviors, greater social capital can have consequences for well-being. Carpiano (2006) found that some aspects of neighborhood social capital are associated with a greater likelihood of engaging in negative behaviors. In this study, the author examined several aspects of neighborhood social capital: social cohesion, informal social control, civic participation, social leverage, and social support. While higher neighborhood social cohesion and social control were associated with lower rates of smoking and binge drinking, higher social support was associated with higher rates of smoking and drinking. Further, the influence of neighborhood social capital on health is contingent upon the structure of the neighborhood itself. Caughy and colleagues (2003) found that in low-poverty communities, neighborhood social capital is beneficial for children's behavioral health, yet in high-poverty communities, high social capital is associated with worse behavioral health.

Both collective efficacy and social capital are indicators of the degree of social cohesion and the collective nature of social relationships in a neighborhood. However, as noted previously, a high degree of social capital can also be associated with negative health behaviors. The inconsistencies in the neighborhood social capital and health relationship may be attributable to variations in the context in which the social ties are formed. If a neighborhood is characterized by a high level of social disorder and a breakdown of social control, such attributes may overshadow the supportive elements of social capital or encourage problematic behaviors.

Neighborhood Disorder

In all neighborhoods, social and physical cues communicate to both outsiders and residents information about the degree of social control and economic conditions of the community (Ross & Mirowsky, 1999). Physical signs that there is a breakdown of order include conditions such as graffiti, evidence of vandalism, and the presence of trash and litter. Signs of physical deterioration, along with cues of social disorder such as reports of loitering, drug and alcohol use, crime, and the general untrustworthiness of one's neighbors, are perceived and interpreted by residents as signs of *neighborhood disorder*. Neighborhood disorder is typically measured using an index that asks residents questions about their perception of the neighborhood. The measure includes both assessments of the physical environment and questions about social cohesion and relationships, not unlike some measures of collective efficacy or social capital. Because assessment of neighborhood disorder asks residents about their interpretation of the neighborhood environment, this concept differs from other aggregate psychosocial measures.

Neighborhood disadvantage and high residential instability are commonly associated with reports of perceived neighborhood disorder (Ross, Reynolds, & Geis, 2000). The combination of socioeconomic depression and frequent residential relocation creates an environment in which fear and suspicion inhibit the formation of positive social ties within the community and increase the stress of everyday living (Ross, 2011). How perceptions of disorder are formed depends on both neighborhood structure and individual experience. Despite the level of observed disorder, in neighborhoods with higher a percentage of racial minority residents and concentrated poverty, both residents and outsiders are more likely to perceive the neighborhood as disordered (Sampson & Raudenbush, 2004). Nevertheless, while certain structural characteristics may increase the likelihood of perceived neighborhood disorder, even within disadvantaged neighborhoods there is considerable variation in the degree of perceived disorder.

Neighborhood disorder influences health via complex psychological and physiological processes that are triggered by high rates of stress (Boardman, 2004; Hill, Ross, & Angel, 2005). Research on the perceptive component of the stress response has observed that neighborhood disorder is associated with high levels of mistrust and feelings of personal powerlessness that are manifested in feelings of anger, agitation, depression, and anxiety (Ross & Mirowsky, 2009). When individuals feel that their neighborhood environment is highly disordered, they are more likely to become socially isolated and to be suspicious of other social actors in their environment (Ross, 2010). Not surprisingly, when residents report higher perceived neighborhood disorder, they are more likely to have worse mental health in general, along with higher rates of depression, anxiety, and psychological distress (Hill & Maimon, 2013).

In disadvantaged and disordered neighborhoods, residents are more likely to be in worse health. When residents feel that their residential environment is disordered, that perception triggers a psychological and physiological stress response (Hill et al., 2005). Over time, chronic stress and strain increase the cumulative wear and tear on the body's regulatory systems, resulting in biological aging via increased allostatic load (Crimmins, Vasunilashorn, Kim, & Alley, 2008; Finch et al., 2010; Piazza et al., 2010). The health consequences of increased allostatic load may not be immediately noticeable, but over time they contribute to cumulative inequalities in health. Further, when residents perceive that their neighborhood is disordered, other basic physiological functions such as sleep are disrupted—thereby increasing feelings of mental agitation and compromising physical health (Hill et al., 2009).

The way individuals choose to cope with stress is largely dependent on the options available in their environment and the ways they choose can influence health. Access to positive means of coping is less available when disorder is high and social support is low. In such a scenario, residents are more likely to turn to negative behavioral means of coping with psychological distress (Burdette & Hill, 2008). Research has noted that when residents' perceptions of disorder increase, they are more likely engage in heavy alcohol consumption (Hill & Angel, 2005). Further, living in a disordered neighborhood increases residents' likelihood of smoking. Miles (2006) observed that individuals who live in high-disorder neighborhoods have 64% higher odds of smoking, particularly among men. Thus neighborhood disorder not only influences health through the physiological stress response, but also increases the probability of engaging in negative health behaviors.

The psychosocial and subjective experiences of the neighborhood environment are mechanisms through which neighborhoods influence health and well-being. Psychosocial processes that stimulate the psychological and physiological stress response and increase the likelihood of engaging in negative health behaviors compound the health consequences of living in a materially disadvantaged community, further entrenching existing social inequalities in health and well-being.

Landscapes of Inequality: Socioeconomic Status, Race and Ethnicity, and Health

Not all of society's groups are equally likely to reside in a disadvantaged or disordered neighborhood. Individuals with low socioeconomic status (SES), and racial-ethnic minorities in particular, are most likely to live in materially and socially impoverished neighborhoods. This section takes a closer look at the relationship of socioeconomic status, race and ethnicity, and neighborhoods in the context of health and well-being research.

Socioeconomic Status, Neighborhoods, and Health

An individual's position in the social hierarchy contributes to his or her ability to access health-related information and resources. Neighborhood socioeconomic status indicates the degree of structural disadvantage present within a community. Poor neighborhoods are characterized by limited access to basic services and amenities, lower-quality housing options, and little opportunity for upward economic social mobility (Robert, 1999). Through greater exposure to environmental hazards and social risks (such as neighborhood disorder), living in a poor neighborhood has an independent influence on residents' health, net of individual socioeconomic status (Robert, 1998). Communities with a higher percentage of residents who receive public assistance, higher percentage of adult unemployment, and higher scores on an Economic Disadvantage Index were associated with a larger number of chronic conditions that residents experienced when controlling for both individual and family SES (Robert, 1998, p. 31). While individual SES is a more robust indicator of health (Browning & Cagney, 2002; Meijer et al., 2012), low-SES individuals who also live in poor and disadvantaged communities face the added health compromise of residing in a risky physical and social environment.

In addition to having greater access to material resources, residents of more affluent neighborhoods are better equipped to utilize the psychosocial resources present in their community. Residents of higher-SES neighborhoods not only report lower neighborhood disorder, but are also more likely to effectively mobilize and employ strategies that involve the use of social capital and collective effort to improve living conditions. Wealthier neighborhoods typically have higher levels of reciprocated and intergenerational exchange (Sampson, Morenoff, & Earls, 1999). This is not to say that residents of lower-income communities do not utilize and build social capital, but rather that residents mobilize their neighborhood social capital for different goals depending on the neighborhood context. Higher-income neighborhoods are able to focus on quality of life issues, whereas lower-SES residents typically focus on meeting more immediate and basic needs (Altschuler et al., 2004). In poor communities, residents are more likely to spend their collective resources trying to ensure basic safety protections and resources for schools, whereas residents of wealthier neighborhoods are able to focus on enhancing the neighborhood quality of life.

Individual characteristics and neighborhood SES work together in ways that stratify health outcomes. Some research has found that living in a low-educated and disadvantaged neighborhood is associated with a higher allostatic load regardless of individual-level SES, yet higher-SES individuals who live in affluent communities receive cumulative benefits to their health (Finch et al., 2010). Similarly, in an analysis of the risk of premature mortality among older adults, neighborhood SES was not significant for those in fair/poor health, but for those who reported good/excellent health, living in a poor neighborhood was associated with an increased risk of death (Doubeni et al., 2012). Thus the influence of neighborhood socioeconomic status is conditioned by individual social position and experience. Individuals with higher SES are better equipped to take advantage of the health-enhancing opportunities present in their neighborhood, whereas in disadvantaged neighborhoods all residents are constrained by the social and material environment.

One of the ways that the neighborhood socioeconomic context contributes to individual health is by promoting or constraining upward social mobility. Of particular interest to researchers and policymakers is how the neighborhood environment influences individual attainment. One of the goals of the Moving to Opportunity (MTO) project introduced by the Department of Housing and Urban Development in the mid-1990s and early 2000s was to examine how communities influenced a range of individual outcomes. Participants in the MTO project were primarily residents of public housing in five large urban cities in the United States who were offered Section 8 housing vouchers to move to low-poverty neighborhoods in which fewer than 10% of residents lived below the federal poverty line (for a more detailed review of the MTO study, see Clampet-Lundquist & Massey, 2008). The outcomes of participants who received vouchers were compared to those in one of two control groups: individuals who received vouchers but no requirement in regard to relocation, and those who remained in public housing.

A number of studies have been published regarding the MTO study, and there remains scholarly debate regarding the efficacy of the intervention for upward social mobility (Clampet-Lundquist & Massey, 2008; Ludwig et al., 2008). However, there did appear to be benefits for the families who moved into, and stayed in, low-poverty communities. The children of families who relocated to nonpoor areas had better mental health outcomes and exhibited fewer risky behaviors during adolescence (Leventhal & Dupéré, 2011). Further, participants who relocated reported lower neighborhood disorder and felt that the living conditions of their families had improved (Rosenbaum & Harris, 2001). Other work has also found significant mental health benefits and a reduction in obesity for those who moved (Kling, Liebman, Katz, & Sanbonmatsu, 2004; Leventhal & Brooks-Gunn, 2003; Williams, Costa, Odunlami, & Mohammed, 2008). Few, if any, benefits have been noted concerning the physical health of study participants. This may be because the long-term consequences to physical health of living in poverty outweigh the short-term benefits of stress reduction. However, the benefits of reduced stress, increased feelings of safety, and lower rates of violent crime victimization will likely improve the overall health and well-being in the long term (Clampet-Lundquist & Massey, 2008).

Race, Ethnicity, Neighborhoods, and Health

Like socioeconomic status, an individual's race and ethnicity influence that person's likelihood of exposure to unhealthy social and physical environments (Williams & Sternhal, 2010). Black-White inequalities in health are well documented and continue to persist despite improvements in overall race relations (Williams et al., 2008). Perhaps one of the clearest examples of the relationship between place and health is demonstrated by examining the historical residential discrimination and segregation of African-Americans in the United States. A detailed discussion of the history of racial discrimination in the United States is not appropriate here, but it is important to point out the ways that the continuation of institutional racism has contributed to the spatial patterning of inequalities in African-American and minority health.

The post-Civil War increase in industrial production prompted many African-Americans to migrate from the rural South to urban centers in the North and Midwest in search of employment and economic opportunities. The mass suburbanization after World War II propelled many White residents into the outlying suburbs, leaving many African-Americans secluded in declining urban communities. The institutionalization of discriminatory real estate and lending practices excluded many Black Americans from the benefits of home ownership—leaving them in socially and economically isolated communities and stifling upward social mobility through intergenerational wealth accumulation via home ownership. While there have been major improvements in race relations in the United States, the vestiges of institutional racism and residential segregation continue to shape the health outcomes of racial and ethnic minorities. Research consistently demonstrates that African-Americans, Hispanics, and other racial minorities reside in overall worse conditions than their White counterparts (Williams, Mohammed, Leavell, & Collins, 2010).

African-Americans in particular are more likely to live in highly racially segregated communities—more so nationally than any other racial or ethnic minority group (Williams & Collins, 2001). Residential segregation at the most basic level can be thought of as the racial and ethnic composition of a neighborhood. Yet, more precise measures of segregation include other aspects of the degree to which a community is segregated, such as the spatial distribution of groups, isolation, concentration, centralization, and clustering (Massey & Denton, 1989). The mechanisms that link residential segregation to health are analogous to those associated with concentrated poverty. Williams and colleagues (2010) outline multiple ways that residential segregation contributes to racial disparities in health. In particular, the lack of basic health amenities, constrained upward social mobility due to poor-quality schools and few employment opportunities, the spatial patterning of chronic stress and strain, and exposure to environmental toxins and pollutants plague highly segregated and impoverished neighborhoods alike.

The relationship of health and racial residential segregation depends on the level to which the community is segregated. The most extreme form of residential segregation is "hypersegregation" (Massey & Denton, 1989). Hypersegregated communities are disadvantaged not only by their structural characteristics, but also by their spatial and social isolation.

Research demonstrates a consistent association between the degree of residential segregation and outcomes such as all-cause mortality, birth outcomes, mental health, and chronic conditions (Bell, Zimmerman, Almgren, Mayer, & Huebner, 2006; Rosenbaum and Harris, 2001; Jackson, Anderson, Johnson, & Sorlie, 2000; Williams & Collins, 2010). Subramanain and colleagues (2005) note that Blacks living in racially isolated areas are more likely to report that they are in worse physical health compared to those in more diverse communities. In hypersegregated communities, Black mothers are more likely to give birth to a preterm infant compared to Black mothers in nonhypersegregated areas (Bell et al., 2006; Osypuk & Acevedo-Garcia, 2008); moreover, in the most segregated metropolitan areas, Black women have the highest infant mortality rates (Poldenak, 1991).

However, living in a predominately minority neighborhood can also be protective for health and well-being. Minority neighborhoods characterized by a positive social environment and connectedness to the larger community promote a positive health environment. In a study of Philadelphia neighborhoods, researchers found that in predominately Black neighborhoods that also exhibit a high level of neighborhood social capital, all-cause Black mortality is lower than for African-Americans living in predominately White neighborhoods (Hutchinson et al., 2009). Among older Mexican-Americans, living in a neighborhood with a higher density of other Mexican-Americans is associated with lower mortality and fewer health problems (Eschbach, Ostir, Patel, Markides, & Goodwin, 2004) as well as fewer depressive symptoms among men (Gerst et al., 2011). Osypuk and colleagues (2009) note that a higher density of Hispanic or Chinese populations is associated with lower consumption of fats and increased availability of healthy foods, but also with fewer exercise resources and less community engagement, social cohesion, and safety.

Improving Health by Investing in Neighborhoods

Improving the social and physical environment in impoverished and disadvantaged neighborhoods will reduce health inequalities. While individual interventions are a direct means of improving health, interventions at the community level are more efficient and cost-effective. Investing in the quality of our neighborhoods can improve health through direct and indirect means. Building a cohesive environment and reducing sources of neighborhood disorder will make communities more attractive to outside investment. To improve health indirectly through upward social mobility, investments in infrastructure and education are necessary. The processes that lead to disadvantage and disorder are interrelated, so interventions aimed at increasing community health cannot focus on only one dimension of the neighborhood-health relationship. Instead, policymakers must address neighborhood health holistically.

When residents of poor and disadvantaged neighborhoods relocate to nonpoor communities, their health is benefited via reduced stress and better overall well-being (Leventhal & Brooks-Gunn, 2000; Leventhal & Dupéré, 2011). Thus one way of improving health is by increasing the availability of mixed-income and nonpoor neighborhoods. A broader income base increases investment in infrastructure and education. However, as income inequality in the United States has continued to increase, the level of economic segregation across communities has also risen (Fry & Taylor, 2012). With the foreclosure crisis, many U.S. neighborhoods have become increasingly unstable. Owing to this trend, the concentration of very poor communities has increased while the number of affluent neighborhoods has shifted upward. As a result of the economic downturn, many communities have seen considerable reductions in the availability of public funds for education and infrastructure. Government officials and policymakers should consider investing in improving the living conditions of declining and disadvantaged communities as a means of improving the health of all residents.

In addition to improving economic diversity, community health may be improved by reducing the effects of racial residential segregation. The long history of discriminatory real estate practices, lingering concerns regarding racism, and fear of social isolation may combine to discourage minority group members from relocating to predominately White areas. One way of reducing the consequences of residential segregation is by building social cohesion and social relationships within and between neighboring communities. Some research finds that communities characterized by significant racial heterogeneity may discourage social cohesion and are more likely to foster feelings of mistrust (Stolle, Soroka, & Johnston, 2008). Thus understanding which factors promote social ties between community subgroups is essential.

In large part, the response to residential diversity depends on the attributes of the community itself. Nyden and colleagues (1998) reported findings from a multiple-city research project of stable diverse communities and contended that there are certain aspects of a community that foster a positive sense of diversity. The authors noted two pathways to residential diversity: communities that diversified intentionally as a response to the civil rights movement and those that diversified over time, organically. In both types of neighborhoods, community organizations and social relationships played a key role in fostering connections between groups—highlighting the importance of promoting sources of neighborhood social capital and an overall positive social environment. Further, improving the social dynamics within primarily minority neighborhoods would improve the health of all residents (Hutchinson et al., 2009).

To reduce place-based social inequalities in health, policymakers and advocates must consider both individual- and group-level interventions.

Increasing the economic and racial diversity of neighborhoods is a means of improving both individual and community health. Yet, it is equally important to invest in community infrastructure that facilitates a health-enhancing environment. When residents and institutions are invested in maintaining and building a diverse social environment, individual economic and social conditions are improved.

Areas for Future Research and Advancement

This chapter examined the relationship between neighborhoods and health. First, it addressed the definition, measurement, and methodological considerations necessary to study neighborhoods. It then presented a basic schematic model useful for understanding how the structural conditions, material resources, and psychosocial environment of a neighborhood influence health outcomes. Finally, the chapter looked more closely at how socioeconomic status and race/ethnicity shape the neighborhood-health relationship. While there is much we know about how and why place matters for health, there is still need for further methodological, theoretical, and empirical work.

Continued advances in the conceptualization and definition of "neighborhood" will improve our understanding of how place influences physical and mental health. Current practice in most neighborhood and health research is to rely on census tract boundaries to measure neighborhoods. Such delineations are convenient and useful in demonstrating structural associations, but it is less clear how the social environment correlates to census tract boundaries. The psychosocial and subjective elements are what form the crux of the neighborhood and health relationship. Moving forward, it will be essential to look more closely at the subjective definition of neighborhoods and to understand the elements that matter most to residents' perceptions of their communities and, therefore, to their health and well-being.

Furthermore, research must embrace a long view of the neighborhood-health relationship. Individual biography and residential history unfold in tandem; without better understanding the role of timing, duration, and age in the neighborhood-health relationship, it will be difficult to move forward. Without detailed longitudinal data on individual and neighborhood characteristics, issues of selection will continue to plague research. Are there critical periods in which living in a disadvantaged neighborhood prove to be particularly harmful to well-being? Or is it the case that duration in a disadvantaged context is most predictive of health outcomes? With better conceptual definitions and advances in methodology, researchers will be better prepared to collect and analyze data on the longitudinal effects of neighborhood conditions on health and well-being.

One way of improving health via neighborhood interventions is by facilitating a cohesive and positive social environment. Considerable research has documented the association of social capital and collective efficacy with health. Yet, beyond structural explanations, there is little work that seeks to understand how efficacious and cohesive neighborhoods are formed and maintained. Further research is needed that looks more closely at how disadvantaged neighborhoods can overcome structural obstacles to facilitate the creation and maintenance of positive social bonds and thereby improve health and reduce disorder. In addition, we need similar improvements in understanding of the aspects of neighborhoods that contribute to the perception of neighborhood disorder.

Finally, as many scholars have pointed out (Diez Roux & Mair, 2010; Hill & Maimon, 2013), there is a great need for the development and empirical testing of theoretical models of the neighborhood-health relationship. Work on the mechanisms through which neighborhoods contribute to mental health has made progress (Hill & Maimon, 2013; Ross & Mirowsky, 2009), yet models that specify mechanisms through which neighborhoods influence physical health are sorely lacking. In addition, available research suggests that there are subgroup differences in the way that neighborhood environment influences health and well-being, yet we know little about the reasons for such variation. For example, why is living in a predominately minority neighborhood deleterious for the mental health of some groups, but not others? Without specification of the mediating and moderating mechanisms through which neighborhood processes influence health, it will be difficult to identify points of intervention.

Conclusion

There are clear documented associations between neighborhood characteristics and multiple health outcomes, ranging from general all-cause mortality to specific chronic conditions. Advances in methodology and data collection as well as the growing recognition of the importance of looking beyond the individual have led to important developments in describing how and why neighborhoods contribute to our health. In general, research suggests that neighborhood conditions influence health via the spatial patterning of material resources, the psychosocial environment, and perceptions of the neighborhood context. It is important to continue expanding methodological and theoretical models that improve our understanding of the causal ordering of the neighborhood and health relationship and address issues of selectivity. Better understanding of the degree to which individual-level covariates and selection effects contribute to the neighborhood-health association will improve our ability to address continued health inequalities.

References

Acevedo-Garcia, D. & Osypuk, T. (2008). Invited commentary: Residential segregation and health—The complexity of modeling separate social contexts. *American Journal of Epidemiology, 168*(11): 1255–1258.

Altschuler, A., Somkin, C. P., & Adler, N. E. (2004). Local services and amenities, neighborhood social capital, and health. *Social Science & Medicine, 59*(6), 1219–1229.

Bandura, A. (2000). Exercise of human agency through collective efficacy. *Current Directions in Psychological Science, 9*(3), 75–78.

Bell, J. F., Zimmerman, F. J., Almgren, G. R., Mayer, J. D., & Huebner, C. E. (2006). Birth outcomes among urban African-American women: A multilevel analysis of the role of racial residential segregation. *Social Science & Medicine, 63*(12), 3030–3045.

Block, J. P., Christakis, N. A., O'Malley, A. J., & Subramanian, S. V. (2011). Proximity to food establishments and body mass index in the Framingham Heart Study Offspring Cohort over 30 years. *American Journal of Epidemiology, 174*(10), 1108–1114.

Boardman, J. D., Downey, L., Jackson, J. S., Merrill, J. B., Onge, J. M. S., & Williams, D. R. (2008). Proximate industrial activity and psychological distress. *Population and Environment, 30*(1–2), 3–25.

Boardman, J. D. (2004). Stress and physical health: The role of neighborhoods as mediating and moderating mechanisms. *Social Science & Medicine, 58*(12), 2473–2483.

Browning, C. R., & Cagney, K. A. (2002). Neighborhood structural disadvantage, collective efficacy, and self-rated physical health in an urban setting. *Journal of Health and Social Behavior, 43*(4), 383–399.

Browning, C. R., Dietz, R. D., & Feinberg, S. L. (2004). The paradox of social organization: Networks, collective efficacy, and violent crime in urban neighborhoods. *Social Forces, 83*(2), 503–534.

Burdette, A. M., & Hill, T. D. (2008). An examination of processes linking perceived neighborhood disorder and obesity. *Social Science & Medicine, 67*(1), 38–46.

Caplow, T., & Forman, R. (1950). Neighborhood interaction in a homogeneous community. *American Sociological Review, 15*(3), 357–366.

Carpiano, R. M. (2006). Toward a neighborhood resource-based theory of social capital for health: Can Bourdieu and sociology help? *Social Science & Medicine, 62*(1), 165–175.

Casciano, R., & Massey, D. S. (2008). Neighborhoods, employment, and welfare use: Assessing the influence of neighborhood socioeconomic composition. *Social Science Research, 37*(2), 544–558.

Caughy, M. O., O'Campo, P. J., & Muntaner, C. (2003). When being alone might be better: Neighborhood poverty, social capital, and child mental health. *Social Science & Medicine, 57*(2), 227–237

Chapin, F. S. (1940). An experiment on the social effects of good housing. *American Sociological Review, 5*(6), 868–879.

Clampet-Lundquist, S., & Massey, D. S. (2008). Neighborhood effects on economic self-sufficiency: A reconsideration of the moving to opportunity experiment. *American Journal of Sociology, 114*(1), 107–143.

Cohen, D. A., Finch, B. K., Bower, A., & Sastry, N. (2006). Collective efficacy and obesity: The potential influence of social factors on health. *Social Science & Medicine, 62*(3), 769–778.

Cohen, D. A., Inagami, S., & Finch, B. (2008). The built environment and collective efficacy. *Health & Place, 14*(2), 198–208.

Cramm, J. M., Van Dijk, H. M., & Nieboer, A. P. (2012). The importance of neighborhood social cohesion and social capital for the well being of older adults in the community. *The Gerontologist.* http://www.erasmusmc.nl/cs-research/subsidies/3600331/thegerontologist030512

Cressey, P. F. (1949). Social disorganization and reorganization in Harlan County, Kentucky. *American Sociological Review, 14*(3), 389–394.

Crimmins, E., Vasunilashorn, S., Kim, J. K., & Alley, D. (2008). Biomarkers related to aging in human populations. In G. S. Makowski (Ed.), *Advances in clinical chemistry* (Vol. 46, pp. 161–216). San Diego, CA: Academic Press.

Crowder, K., & Downey, L. (2010). Inter-neighborhood migration, race, and environmental hazards: Modeling micro-level processes of environmental inequality. *American Journal of Sociology, 115*(4), 1110–1149.

Diez Roux, A. V. (2001). Investigating neighborhood and area effects on health. *American Journal of Public Health, 91*(11), 1783–1789.

Diez Roux, A. (2003). The examination of neighborhood effects of health: Conceptual and methodological issues related to the presence of multiple levels of organization. In I. Kawachi & L. F. Berkman (Eds.), *Neighborhoods and health* (pp. 45–64). Oxford, UK: Oxford University Press.

Diez Roux, A. V., & Mair, C. (2010). Neighborhoods and health. *Annals of the New York Academy of Sciences, 1186*(1), 125–145.

Downey, L., & Willigen, M. V. (2005). Environmental stressors: The mental health impacts of living near industrial activity. *Journal of Health and Social Behavior, 46*(3), 289–305.

Doubeni, C. A., Schootman, M., Major, J. M., Stone, R. A. T., Laiyemo, A. O., Park, Y., . . . Schatzkin, A. (2012). Health status, neighborhood socioeconomic context, and premature mortality in the United States: The National Institutes of Health-AARP Diet and Health Study. *American Journal of Public Health, 102*(4), 680–688.

Eschbach, K., Ostir, G. V., Patel, K. V., Markides, K. S., & Goodwin, J. S. (2004). Neighborhood context and mortality among older Mexican Americans: Is there a barrio advantage? *American Journal of Public Health, 94*(10), 1807–1812.

Evans, G. W., & Kantrowitz, E. (2002). Socioeconomic status and health: The potential role of environmental risk exposure. *Annual Review of Public Health, 23*(1), 303–331.

Faris, R. E. L., & Dunham, H. W. (1939). *Mental disorders in urban areas: An ecological study of schizophrenia and other psychoses.* Chicago, IL: University of Chicago Press.

Finch, B. K., Phuong Do, D., Heron, M., Bird, C., Seeman, T., & Lurie, N. (2010). Neighborhood effects on health: Concentrated advantage and disadvantage. *Health & Place, 16*(5), 1058–1060.

Fitzpatrick, K., & LaGory, M. (2000). *Unhealthy places: The ecology of risk in the urban landscape.* New York, NY: Routledge.

Fry, R., & Taylor, P. (2012). The rise of residential segregation by income. *Pew Social & Demographic Trends.* http://www.pewsocialtrends.org/2012/08/01/the-rise-of-residential-segregation-by-income/

Gerst, K., Miranda, P. Y., Eschbach, K., Sheffield, K. M., Peek, M. K., & Markides, K. S. (2011). Protective neighborhoods: Neighborhood proportion of Mexican Americans and depressive symptoms in very old Mexican Americans. *Journal of the American Geriatrics Society, 59*(2), 353–358.

Hill, T. D., Burdette, A. M., & Hale, L. (2009). Neighborhood disorder, sleep quality, and psychological distress: Testing a model of structural amplification. *Health & Place, 15*(4), 1006–1013.

Hill, T. D., Ross, C. E., & Angel, R. J. (2005). Neighborhood disorder, psycho-physiological distress, and health. *Journal of Health and Social Behavior, 46*(2), 170–186.

Hill, T. D., & Maimon, D. (2013). Neighborhood context and mental health. In C. S. Aneshensel, J. C. Phelan, & A. Bierman (Eds.), *Handbook of the Sociology of Mental Health* (pp. 479–501). Springer (e-book).

Hill, T. D., & Angel, R. J. (2005). Neighborhood disorder, psychological distress, and heavy drinking. *Social Science & Medicine, 61*(5), 965–975.

Hutchinson, R. N., Putt, M. A., Dean, L. T., Long, J. A., Montagnet, C. A., & Armstrong, K. (2009). Neighborhood racial composition, social capital and black all-cause mortality in Philadelphia. *Social Science & Medicine, 68*(10), 1859–1865.

Jackson, S. A., Anderson, R. T., Johnson, N. J., & Sorlie, P. D. (2000). The relation of residential segregation to all-cause mortality: A study in black and white. *American Journal of Public Health, 90*(4), 615–617.

Kawachi, I., & Berkman, L. (2000). Social cohesion, social capital, and health. *Social epidemiology,* 174–190.

Kawachi, I., Kennedy, B. P., & Glass, R. (1999). Social capital and self-rated health: A contextual analysis. *American Journal of Public Health, 89*(8), 1187–1193.

Kirby, J. B., & Kaneda, T. (2005). Neighborhood socioeconomic disadvantage and access to health care. *Journal of Health and Social Behavior, 46*(1), 15–31.

Kirby, J. B., & Kaneda, T. (2006). Access to health care: Does neighborhood residential instability matter? *Journal of Health and Social Behavior, 47*(2), 142–155.

Kling, J. R., Liebman, J. B., Katz, L. F., & Sanbonmatsu, L. (2004). Moving to opportunity and tranquility: Neighborhood effects on adult economic self-sufficiency and health from a randomized housing voucher experiment. *SSRN eLibrary.* http://0-www.irs.princeton.edu.library.uark.edu/pubs/pdfs/481.pdf

Kramer, M. R., Cooper, H. L., Drews-Botsch, C. D., Waller, L. A., & Hogue, C. R. (2010). Metropolitan isolation segregation and Black-White disparities in very preterm birth: A test of mediating pathways and variance explained. *Social science & medicine (1982), 71*(12), 2108–2116.

Krieger, N. (2006). A century of census tracts: Health and the body politic (1906–2006). *Journal of Urban Health, 83*(3), 355–361.

Leclere, F. B., Rogers, R. G., & Peters, K. D. (1997). Ethnicity and mortality in the United States: Individual and community correlates. *Social Forces, 76*(1), 169–198.

Leventhal, T., & Brooks-Gunn, J. (2000). The neighborhoods they live in: The effects of neighborhood residence on child and adolescent outcomes. *Psychological Bulletin, 126*(2), 309–337.

Leventhal, T., & Dupéré, V. (2011). Moving to Opportunity: Does long-term exposure to "low-poverty" neighborhoods make a difference for adolescents? *Social Science & Medicine, 73*(5), 737–743.

Link, B. G., & Phelan, J. (1995). Social conditions as fundamental causes of disease. *Journal of Health and Social Behavior, 35*, 80–94. Lochner, K. A., Kawachi, I., Brennan, R. T., & Buka, S. L. (2003). Social capital and neighborhood mortality rates in Chicago. *Social Science & Medicine, 56*(8), 1797–1805.

Lochner, K., Kawachi, I., & Kennedy, B. P. (1999). Social capital: A guide to its measurement. *Health & Place, 5*(4), 259–270.

Ludwig, J., Liebman, J. B., Kling, J. R., Duncan, G. J., Katz, L. F., Kessler, R. C., & Sanbonmatsu, L. (2008). What can we learn about neighborhood effects from the Moving to Opportunity experiment? *American Journal of Sociology, 114*(1), 144–188.

Massey, D., & Denton, N. (1989). Hypersegregation in U.S. metropolitan areas: Black and Hispanic segregation along five dimensions. *Demography, 26*(3), 373–391.

Meijer, M., Röhl, J., Bloomfield, K., & Grittner, U. (2012). Do neighborhoods affect individual mortality? A systematic review and meta-analysis of multilevel studies. *Social Science & Medicine, 74*(8), 1204–1212.

Messer, L. C., Vinikoor-Imler, L. C., & Laraia, B. A. (2012). Conceptualizing neighborhood space: Consistency and variation of associations for neighborhood factors and pregnancy health across multiple neighborhood units. *Health & Place, 18*(4), 805–813.

Miles, R. (2006). Neighborhood disorder and smoking: Findings of a European urban survey. *Social Science & Medicine, 63*(9), 2464–2475.

Mohnen, S. M., Völker, B., Flap, H., & Groenewegen, P. P. (2012). Health-related behavior as a mechanism behind the relationship between neighborhood social capital and individual health-a multilevel analysis. *BMC public health, 12*(1), 116.

Moore, L. V., & Diez Roux, A. V. (2006). Associations of neighborhood characteristics with the location and type of food stores. *American Journal of Public Health, 96*(2), 325–331.

Morello-Frosch, R., & Shenassa, E. D. (2006). The environmental "riskscape" and social inequality: Implications for explaining maternal and child health disparities. *Environmental Health Perspectives, 114*(8), 1150–1153.

Morland, K. B., & Evenson, K. R. (2009). Obesity prevalence and the local food environment. *Health & Place, 15*(2), 491–495.

Morrison, R. S., Wallenstein, S., Natale, D. K., Senzel, R. S., & Huang, L. L. (2000). "We don't carry that": Failure of pharmacies in predominantly nonwhite neighborhoods to stock opioid analgesics. *New England Journal of Medicine, 342*(14), 1023–1026.

Nyden, P., Lukehart, J., & Maly, M. (1998). Neighborhood racial and ethnic diversity in U.S. cities. *SSRN eLibrary.* http://papers.ssrn.com/sol3/papers.cfm?abstract_id=149389

Oakes, J. M. (2004). The (mis)estimation of neighborhood effects: Causal inference for a practicable social epidemiology. *Social Science & Medicine, 58*(10), 1929–1952.

O'Campo, P. (2003). Invited commentary: Advancing theory and methods for multilevel models of residential neighborhoods and health. *American Journal of Epidemiology, 157*(1), 9–13.

O'Neill, M. S., Jerrett, M., Kawachi, I., Levy, J. I., Cohen, A. J., Gouveia, N., Schwartz, J. (2003). Health, wealth, and air pollution: Advancing theory and methods. *Environmental Health Perspectives, 111*(16), 1861–1870.

Osypuk, T. L., & Acevedo-Garcia, D. (2008). Are racial disparities in preterm birth larger in hypersegregated areas? *American Journal of Epidemiology, 167*(11), 1295–1304.

Osypuk, T. L., Roux, A. V. D., Hadley, C., & Kandula, N. (2009). Are Immigrant Enclaves Healthy Places to Live? The Multi-ethnic Study of Atherosclerosis. *Social science & medicine (1982), 69*(1), 110–120.

Piazza, J. R., Almeida, D. M., Dmitrieva, N. O., & Klein, L. C. (2010). Frontiers in the use of biomarkers of health in research on stress and aging. *The Journals of Gerontology Series B: Psychological Sciences and Social Sciences, 65B*(5), 513–525.

Poldenak, Anthony P. 1991. Black-White Differences in Infant Mortality in 38 Standard Metropolitan Statistical Areas. American Journal of Public Health 81: 1480–1482.

Pollack, C. E., & Armstrong, K. (2009). The geographic accessibility of retail clinics for underserved populations. *Archives of Internal Medicine, 169*(10), 945–949.

Porter, D. (1998). *Health, Civilization and the State: A History of Public Health from Ancient to Modern Times.* London: Routledge.

Pruitt, S. L., Shim, M. J., Mullen, P. D., Vernon, S. W., & Amick, B. C. (2009). Association of area socioeconomic status and breast, cervical, and colorectal cancer screening: A systematic review. *Cancer Epidemiology Biomarkers & Prevention, 18*(10), 2579–2599.

Putnam, R. D. (2001). *Bowling Alone.* New York, NY: Simon and Schuster.

Robert, S. A. (1998). Community-level socioeconomic status effects on adult health. *Journal of Health and Social Behavior, 39*(1), 18–37.

Robert, S. A. (1999). Socioeconomic position and health: The independent contribution of community socioeconomic context. *Annual Review of Sociology, 25*(1), 489–516.

Rosenbaum, E., & Harris, L. E. (2001). Residential mobility and opportunities: Early impacts of the Moving to Opportunity demonstration program in Chicago. *Housing Policy Debate, 12*(2), 321–346.

Ross, C. E. (2000). Neighborhood disadvantage and adult depression. *Journal of Health and Social Behavior, 41*(2), 177–187.

Ross, C. E. (2011). Collective threat, trust, and the sense of personal control. *Journal of Health and Social Behavior, 52*(3), 287–296.

Ross, C. E., & Mirowsky, J. (1999). Disorder and decay: The concept and measurement of perceived neighborhood disorder. *Urban Affairs Review, 34*(3), 412–432.

Ross, C. E., & Mirowsky, J. (2009). Neighborhood disorder, subjective alienation, and distress. *Journal of Health and Social Behavior, 50*(1), 49–64.

Ross, C. E., Reynolds, J. R., & Geis, K. J. (2000). The contingent meaning of neighborhood stability for residents' psychological well-being. *American Sociological Review, 65*(4), 581–597.

Sampson, R. J., & Raudenbush, S. W. (2004). Seeing disorder: Neighborhood stigma and the social construction of "broken windows." *Social Psychology Quarterly, 67*(4), 319–342.

Sampson, R. J., Morenoff, J. D., & Gannon-Rowley, T. (2002). Assessing "Neighborhood Effects": Social processes and new directions in research. *Annual Review of Sociology, 28*, 443–478.

Sampson, R. J., Raudenbush, S. W., & Earls, F. (1997). Neighborhoods and violent crime: A multilevel study of collective efficacy. *Science, 277*(5328), 918–924.

Sampson, R. J., Morenoff, J. D., & Earls, F. (1999). Beyond Social Capital: Spatial Dynamics of Collective Efficacy for Children. *American Sociological Review, 64*(5), 633–660.

Schwirian, K. P. (1983). Models of Neighborhood Change. *Annual Review of Sociology, 9*, 83–102.

Secretary's Advisory Committee on Health Promotion and Disease Prevention Objectives for 2020. (2010, July 26). Healthy people 2020: An opportunity to address the societal determinants of health in the United States. http://www.healthypeople.gov/2010/hp2020/advisory/SocietalDeterminants Health.htm

South, S. J., Pais, J., & Crowder, K. (2011). Metropolitan influences on migration into poor and nonpoor neighborhoods. *Social Science Research, 40*(3), 950–964.

Stephens, C. (2008). Social capital in its place: Using social theory to understand social capital and inequalities in health. *Social Science & Medicine, 66*(5), 1174–1184.

Stolle, D., Soroka, S., & Johnston, R. (2008). When Does Diversity Erode Trust? Neighborhood Diversity, Interpersonal Trust and the Mediating Effect of Social Interactions. *Political Studies, 56*(1), 57–75.

Subramanian, S., Kawachi, I., & Kennedy, B. P. (2001). Does the state you live in make a difference? Multilevel analysis of self-rated health in the US. *Social Science & Medicine, 53*(1), 9–19.

Subramanian, S. V., Acevedo-Garcia, D., & Osypuk, T. L. (2005). Racial residential segregation and geographic heterogeneity in black/white disparity in poor self-rated health in the US: a multilevel statistical analysis. *Social Science & Medicine, 60*(8), 1667–1679.

Umberson, D., Crosnoe, R., & Reczek, C. (2010). Social relationships and health behavior across life course. *Annual review of sociology, 36*, 139–157.

Walker, R. E., Keane, C. R., & Burke, J. G. (2010). Disparities and access to healthy food in the United States: A review of food deserts literature. *Health & Place, 16*(5), 876–884.

Weiss, L., Ompad, D., Galea, S., & Vlahov, D. (2007). Defining neighborhood boundaries for urban health research. *American Journal of Preventive Medicine, 32*(suppl 6), S154–S159.

Williams, D. R., & Collins, C. (2001). Racial residential segregation: A fundamental cause of racial disparities in health. *Public Health Reports, 116*(5), 404–416.

Williams, D. R., Costa, M. V., Odunlami, A. O., & Mohammed, S. A. (2008). Moving upstream: How interventions that address the social determinants of health can improve health and reduce disparities. *Journal of public health management and practice: JPHMP, 14*(Suppl), S8–17.

Williams, D. R., & Sternthal, M. (2010). Understanding racial-ethnic disparities in health sociological contributions. *Journal of Health and Social Behavior, 51*(1 suppl), S15–S27.

Williams, D. R., Mohammed, S. A., Leavell, J., & Collins, C. (2010). Race, socioeconomic status, and health: Complexities, ongoing challenges, and research opportunities. *Annals of the New York Academy of Sciences, 1186*(1), 69–101.

Yen, I. H., & Kaplan, G. A. (1999). Neighborhood Social Environment and Risk of Death: Multilevel Evidence from the Alameda County Study. *American Journal of Epidemiology, 149*(10), 898–907.

Zenk, S. N., Odoms-Young, A. M., Dallas, C., Hardy, E., Watkins, A., Hoskins-Wroten, J., & Holland, L. (2011). "You have to hunt for the fruits, the vegetables": Environmental barriers and adaptive strategies to acquire food in a low-income African American neighborhood. *Health Education & Behavior, 38*(3), 282–292.

Chapter 3

Socioeconomic Status, Residential Mobility, and Health

Brian Joseph Gillespie and Georgiana Bostean

Social conditions, particularly socioeconomic status, are essential determinants of health (Marmot, 1996) and can be considered "fundamental causes" of disease (Link & Phelan, 1995). Residential mobility is a main characteristic of the socioeconomically disadvantaged and is arguably an important determinant of health and disease because it embodies access to important resources and shapes multiple aspects of health through a complex set of mechanisms (Link & Phelan, 1995, p. 80). Drawing on a social perspective on health, this review contextualizes residential mobility to understand its role in shaping socioeconomic health disparities in the United States. Specifically, we suggest that social capital can explain the link between mobility and health.

Residential mobility has historically been more common in the United States than in other Western nations. For instance, the average 18-year-old American has moved four times—nearly the lifetime average in Ireland (Long, 1992b). The housing destabilization caused by the recent economic downturn of the 2000s has led to tighter housing budgets and higher rates of refinancing and foreclosure in the United States, particularly for low- and middle-income groups. Although declining overall in the United States, residential mobility still disproportionately affects the economically vulnerable segments of society (Frey, 2009). Nevertheless, in the context of increasing evictions and job relocations, approximately 35 million Americans—12% of the population—moved to a different household between 2010 and 2011 (U.S. Census Bureau, 2012). Moreover, in 2010, more than 40% of the U.S. population lived in a state other than the one in which they were born (Ren, 2011). Even in the best economic times, residential mobility in the United States is high, particularly among impoverished families. Those from disadvantaged socioeconomic backgrounds, such as poor and single-parent homes, are particularly prone to moving, especially forced moving (Geist & McManus, 2008; Schachter, 2004).

Considering the large proportion of the United States population that is residentially mobile in a given year (U.S. Census Bureau, 2012) and the relatively high rates of mobility in the United States (Long, 1992a), it is important to understand the impacts of moving on individuals and families at various stages of the life cycle. The effects of moving on mental health and health behaviors are well documented (Magdol, 2002; Simpson & Fowler, 1994). Much less research has examined the impact of mobility on other health aspects such as physical health outcomes, although some notable exceptions exist (Fowler, Simpson, & Schoendorf, 1993; Knudson-Cooper & Leuchtag, 1982; Larson, Bell, & Young, 2004; Schluter, Ford, Mitchell, & Taylor, 1998). Yet many of these studies have lacked adequate theoretization of the relationship between moving and health. Moreover, there have been few attempts to synthesize the evidence on the relationship between moving and health across disciplines or across health and well-being measures. Therefore, the portrait of health of the mobile population, and of health disparities between the mobile and non-mobile, remains segmented.

Chapter Aims, Approach, and Organization

This chapter contributes to the understanding of how residential mobility and health are related by (1) contextualizing residential mobility, (2) proposing a conceptual approach—social capital—to understanding the relationship, and (3) discussing how mobility and health, particularly physical health, are related across life-cycle stages.

Throughout the chapter, we focus on internal migration, meaning changes of permanent residence within the United States (regardless of distance). We use the following terms interchangeably to refer to this type of move: *internal migration, residential mobility, relocation,* and *moving.* We chose to focus on internal migration, rather than international migration, because a large and separate body of literature addresses international migration and health (see, for example, Evans, 1987) and suggests that international migrants differ along many sociodemographic and some health characteristics (Bostean, 2012; Feliciano, 2005). For example, unlike internal migrants, international immigrants tend to have lower mortality and better health outcomes than expected based on their socioeconomic positions, but the reasons underlying this relationship are not well understood (for a review, see Markides & Eschbach, 2005). For these reasons, rather than reiterate findings from this well-developed research area, we will instead briefly discuss international migration as a type of moving and focus on internal U.S. migration for the remainder of the chapter. Finally, in keeping with the theme of this volume, we pay more attention to the effects of mobility on the socioeconomically disadvantaged, although residential moves can be undertaken for upward mobility (Keels, DeLuca, Duncan, Mendenhall, & Rosenbaum, 2005; Sharkey & Sampson, 2010).

The chapter is organized as follows. First, we begin by discussing the reasons for moving and types of residential mobility. Next, we describe the characteristics of the residentially mobile. Following, we propose social capital as a useful concept in understanding how mobility might impact health. We then turn to the relationship between residential mobility and health, reviewing the literature linking mobility and health at various life stages—specifically, childhood, adulthood, and later life. We discuss some of the limitations of the residential mobility research to date and provide suggestions for advancing this area of study. Finally, we present empirical data on the relationship between residential mobility and several health and well-being measures from the National Longitudinal Survey of Youth 1997. We conclude with a summary of our findings and implications for policy and future research.

"Contextualizing" Residential Mobility

Reasons for and Types of Residential Mobility

Research examining the rationale behind residential mobility largely focuses on the decision to move *to* a new residence *from* an old residence. This is broken down into "push and pull" factors (the former usually negative and the latter positive). In his research on the push and pull factors associated with residential mobility, Sell (1983) categorized residential mobility as being either forced, imposed, or preference dominated.

Forced mobility applies to the individual or household that is required to vacate. This type of move could occur for any number of reasons, including natural disaster, eviction, and "tied movers" (individuals who follow partners on whom they are dependent). Evidence from mobility research has suggested that individuals who are forced to move are usually poor, and their moves take place locally (within the same county) (Long,

1992a). *Imposed mobility* usually occurs because of a change in marital status, an expanding family, or other factors in the life cycle and transition to adulthood, such as leaving the parental home to go to college. *Preference-dominated* moves are based on a gradual decision-making process based mostly on household or neighborhood satisfaction.

The type of residential mobility that occurs—often categorized as local, long distance, or international—is closely linked to the reasons driving mobility (Fischer, 2002; Long, Tucker, & Urton, 1998). Local residential mobility is defined as a move that occurs within the same county or neighborhood and is often a result of personal preference, family changes, and other housing considerations (Frey, 2003; Long, 1988; Rossi, 1980). A long-distance move is usually defined as relocation across city, county, or state lines (U.S. Census Bureau, 2012). This type of move is typically made for employment- or health-related reasons and macroeconomic conditions, such as job transfers or shifts in labor market demand (Kilborn, 2009; Schachter, 2004). International migration occurs across national boundaries. While only 3% of the world's population comprises international migrants (International Organization for Migration, 2012), 13% of the U.S. population is foreign born (Grieco et al., 2012). Importantly, immigration affects rates of internal migration among the native-born population (Frey, 1995), and many international migrants subsequently migrate internally, meaning that they make several additional moves after migrating to the United States.

These distinctions between types of mobility are important with regard to the consequences of moving on health and other aspects of peoples' lives. The reasons for moving and the type of move are associated with different magnitudes of, for example, control, stress, and responsibility; therefore, they likely have varying consequences on health. For example, there are often greater consequences of mobility for those individuals who are pushed out of their homes (Fischer et al., 1977)—sometimes compounded by job loss and extreme financial burden. In turn, the negative behavioral and health effects of mobility on individuals who are forced to move are worsened. In addition, a long-distance move may be more stressful than a local move, involving more planning and loss of social ties. We elaborate on these issues in subsequent sections.

Who Moves?

Mobile and nonmobile individuals and households differ along many characteristics that are related to the desire and ability to move—socioeconomic status, age, housing tenure and satisfaction, marital status, and household size, for instance. Household income is an important predictor of residential mobility for the rich and poor alike. Poor adults move more than nonpoor adults at every stage of life (Geist & McManus, 2008;

Schachter, 2004). Long (1992a) found that local moves are more common among families in poverty and that these families are also more likely to be hypermobile, meaning they move more than once during a five-year period. In his analyses, households that moved with above-average frequency were also disproportionately headed by a single parent who was unemployed or did not graduate high school (Long 1992a). Lower-income households are also more often renters and less tied to their homes and neighborhoods and, therefore, are more prone to moving (South & Deane, 1993).

Age is among the most important predictors of whether someone makes a residential move, either local or long distance. Long (1992a) found that the highest rates of mobility for Americans were among those persons in their 20s. Recent estimates of mobility rates from 2010 and 2011 Current Population Survey data are similar to Long's (1992a) estimates, finding the highest mobility among the population aged 20 to 29 (U.S. Census Bureau, 2012). Mobility rates decline substantially when people reach their 30s and 40s and then taper off as individuals approach old age until the retirement years, when there is a slight upturn (U.S. Census Bureau, 2012). Regardless of age, the poor are more likely than the nonpoor to move (Geist & McManus, 2008; Schachter, 2004).

Social Capital, Residential Mobility, and Health

Social capital may be a useful concept to understand the links between residential mobility and health outcomes at the individual, household, and community levels. Social capital, broadly construed, has been described as "the ability of actors to secure benefits by virtue of memberships in social networks or other social structures" (Portes, 1998, p. 6). This concept can be used to explain which types of individuals move and why they might do so—but it also provides a plausible link between mobility and health. The definition of social capital has evolved to include both individual assets and collective attributes. Kawachi and colleagues (1997) argued that social capital—which includes features of social organization that facilitate cooperation for mutual benefit (e.g., civic participation and trust)—is a community-level variable whose individual-level analog is social networks. Research on both community-level and individual-level measures of social capital have yielded findings that may speak to the relationship between mobility and health. Coleman's (1988) work on social capital has inspired scholars to view information networks within a community as promoting the formation and maintenance of social ties and relationships that are paramount to individuals' well-being. Coleman argues that interactions within and outside of the household (e.g., among children, parents, teachers, schools, and community) are resources that afford individuals, especially children, assets that increase their general welfare.

Subsequent work supports the importance of social networks in affecting health (Valente, 2010). Social interactions among members of a community provide opportunities for social support, socialization, social control, information and resource sharing, and establishing and reinforcing norms—all factors that contribute to individuals' health. Thus social capital serves as a developmental resource based on one's sense of community and social support network. Community support influences emotional well-being and reduces the stress of day-to-day events. Cooper, Arber, Fee, and Ginn (1999) suggest that social capital mediates the relationship between a stressful neighborhood environment and poor health.

Social and community ties are broken when a family relocates, resulting in a loss of social capital (Coleman, 1988; Pettit & McLanahan, 2003; Pribesh & Downey, 1999; Stack, 1994), which may have health consequences. For hypermobile families, the negative effects of mobility may be even more prominent. Coleman notes that, "for families that have moved often, the social relations that constitute social capital are broken at each move" (1988, p. 113).

Social capital and community social cohesion have also been linked to overall health (Kawachi, Kennedy, & Glass, 1999) and decreased mortality (Kawachi et al., 1997) as well as positive health outcomes for children (Waterston, Alperstein, & Stewart-Brown, 2004). Thus the loss of social capital associated with a move affects the health and well-being of movers as well those communities marked by high rates of mobility.

As a heuristic, consider the example of a residentially mobile family who must move, for any number of reasons. Along with the stress of moving, and irrespective of the characteristics of the place they are leaving or those of the place to which they are moving, the family members no longer have a trustworthy community of friends to whom they can turn for friendly assistance or support. They are less likely to volunteer at community and school functions, and they no longer have a working knowledge of the local community environment, such as where to find health clinics. Oftentimes, relations with neighbors are distant and possibly untrustworthy. All in all, they face a great increase in powerlessness associated with a great loss of social capital. Intuitively, most would agree that this situation would be unhealthy for children and families.

This anecdote demonstrates how the loss of social capital associated with a move might have deleterious health effects for children and families. Moving often reduces (or at least weakens) one's social network ties and the reciprocal support and exchange that may be tied to it, leading to poorer health outcomes for mobile families. In fact, studies have shown a connection between social capital and health outcomes such as decreased risk of heart disease (Orth-Gomér, Rosengren, & Wilhelmsen, 1993), cancer (Reynolds & Kaplan, 1990), mortality (Hemingway & Marmot, 1999), and child abuse (Garbarino & Kostelny, 1992).

At the same time, *not having* social capital—to some degree—is associated with coming from a poor, urban area because these areas have fewer opportunities and resources to foster social/community ties in the first place. Thus impoverished families are less likely to have social capital to start with (i.e., they are just moving from one "social capital limited" place to another). These persons and families may even be less likely to adapt to their new (possibly unreceptive, even hostile) environment. This context illustrates the complex relationships that must be conceptually disentangled.

While the literature on social capital and health is abundant, some have criticized its usefulness, noting important limitations such as the multitude of ways that these concepts are defined and operationalized across studies (Pitkin Derose & Varda, 2009; Portes, 2000). Detailing the conceptual gaps in the social capital literature goes beyond the scope of this review. However, with careful consideration, the concept of social capital may prove useful in uncovering links between residential mobility and health.

Mobility and Health across the Life Cycle

A reciprocal relationship exists between residential mobility and health. In other words, an individual's health may influence whether he or she moves and, in turn, moving may impact health. Some literature has examined how health may influence the decision to move, mostly at older ages, yet scholars have given less attention to how residential mobility affects health. Considering the sociodemographic differences between movers and nonmovers, residential self-selection bias likely contributes to some of the health differences between the groups. In other words, preexisting differences between mobile and nonmobile individuals and households may explain part of the association between mobility and health. For example, persons from lower-socioeconomic backgrounds have poorer health outcomes and are more likely to be mobile. However, the way in which selection impacts this relationship is not necessarily straightforward; it may, in fact, bias estimates toward the null hypothesis (Boone-Heinonen, Guilkey, Evenson, & Gordon-Larsen, 2010). While selective migration likely does not fully account for the mobility-health relationship, it is an important methodological issue to consider.

Mechanisms Linking Mobility and Health

Beyond the impact of selective migration, residential mobility may impact health through a number of mechanisms, and social capital plays an important role in these relationships. First, moving may be related to changes in health behaviors, such as preventive health checkups.

Especially in the short term after a move, there may be gaps in health care, or at least a period in which one must find a new health care provider for regular care. This may lead to delays in health care, especially preventive care, and especially among the poor.

Second, the stress associated with moving may have health ramifications. Moving is among life's most stressful events (Holmes & Rahe, 1967). In one survey, respondents weighted the life-change impact of a change of residence as being almost as significant as a child leaving home and slightly more significant than "trouble with in-laws" (Miller & Rahe, 1997). Residential relocation may increase tension and distress because of separation from supportive ties; the diversion of time, energy, and resources; and the uncertainties of a new, perhaps unknown environment. Research documenting the influence of stressful life experiences on physical health has shown a strong connection, as stressful events have been linked to substance abuse (Brady & Sonne, 1999) and physical/emotional abuse (Aneshensel, 1992; Seltzer & Kalmuss, 1988) in households. Moreover, researchers have shown a link between psychological distress and physical outcomes such as immune function (Kiecolt-Glaser, Glaser, Gravenstein, Malarkey, & Sheridan, 1996). Thus the disruptive and stressful act of moving may have potentially detrimental effects on individual health that vary across life-cycle stages.

Third, internal migration may affect individuals' health and well-being through their social relationships (see Oishi, 2010, for a review). Social relationships are consistently related to health, in both positive and negative ways. Relationships are important sources of social support and social control (for a review, see House, Landis, & Umberson, 1988), which can impact health behaviors. Social ties can also determine health care utilization (Pescosolido, Wright, Alegria, & Vera, 1998). Insofar as social relationships provide coping resources, access to health information, social control, and other resources beneficial to health, they may buffer an individual against the potentially deleterious physical and mental health effects of stress.

Childhood and Adolescence

Being among the most vulnerable segments of U.S. society, children have the highest poverty rates in the country, estimated at more than 20% (Macartney, 2011). In families with children, decisions surrounding moving, such as whether and where to move, are made almost completely by parents, although many times keeping in mind children's interests. Nevertheless, these decisions have health consequences for all family members, including (and perhaps especially) children and adolescents (Jelleyman & Spencer, 2008).

As noted previously, there is a shortage of social science research examining the relationship between residential mobility and physical health. In fact, with the notable exception of the work done by Fowler and colleagues (1993), little research exists on residential mobility and child physical health outcomes. Using data from the National Health Interview on Child Health, Fowler et al. found high rates of residential mobility to be associated with visits to the emergency room for pediatric health. These authors also found that children whose families moved more than twice in their lifetime were three times more likely to lack a regular source of health care compared with children who did not move. Recent relocation was also associated with lack of a regular source for pediatric care. Fowler et al. argue that multiple relocations are associated with a "chaos factor"— disorganized families might be more likely to move, plus they might also take a while to locate health care providers in their new residence.

Social sciences research has focused on the behavioral effects of moving on children. Compared with nonmobile children, mobile children experience significantly more behavioral problems (Haynie, South, & Bose, 2006; Simpson & Fowler, 1994) and, therefore, engage in health-risky behaviors that have deleterious long-term consequences for health and well-being. For example, residentially mobile adolescents are more likely to be teen parents (Crowder & Teachman, 2004); to drink, smoke, and use drugs (DeWit, 1998); to experience depression (Gilman, Kawachi, Fitzmaurice, & Buka, 2003); to associate with delinquent peers (South & Haynie, 2004); and to commit suicide (Beautrais, Joyce, & Mulder, 1996). In their longitudinal study, Oishi and Schimmack (2010) found that residential mobility was associated with lower emotional well-being and increased mortality. Highly mobile introverted children in their study were more likely to have died before the 10-year adult follow-up. Conversely, residential stability in childhood has been linked to significantly greater self-reported health in adulthood (Bures, 2003). Thus the negative effects of residential mobility are not just acute (lasting only for a short period after moving); in fact, in some cases mobility in childhood leads to later-life health effects.

Adulthood

Despite the fact that residential mobility is common in adulthood, mid-life individuals are relatively understudied in mobility research (Wulff, Champion, & Lobo, 2010). Consequently, very little research exists on how mobility and health are related among middle-aged populations. However, some evidence suggests that mobility may negatively impact the psychological well-being of adults. For example, research has shown that moving is related to increased depression in adult women (Magdol, 2002).

At this life-cycle stage, people are usually mobile for employment reasons. When considered in the context of an economy in recession with limited health care for individuals and families, these employment-related moves are unavoidable yet necessary. At the same time, "tied mobility" is important in explaining behavioral outcomes for individuals who move with their partners (Brett, 1982). These "tied movers"—mostly adult women—have increased depression and anxiety (Boyle, Kulu, Cooke, Gayle, & Mulder, 2008) as a result of the reduced employment rates and personal income (Jacobsen & Levin, 1997) associated with moving.

Mobility at middle age is also related to health behaviors. Larson et al. (2004) found that mobility, both local and long distance, was associated with smoking and long-term chronic health problems among adult Australian women, even after controlling for SES and marital status. Other research shows a more direct link between mobility and physical health. Stokols, Shumaker, and Martinez (1983) found that high mobility is associated with having more illness-related symptoms and greater health problems in adults. Therefore, mobility indirectly impacts physical health through its effect on health-risky behaviors.

Later Life

Among older adults, moving is often a response to health needs. For instance, older adults who have suffered a fall are nearly 50% more likely to report plans to relocate within the next two years (Stoeckel & Porell, 2010). Litwak and Longino (1987) suggest that residential mobility among older adults is associated with major life events, such as illness, disability, retirement, and widowhood. As such, moving in later life encompasses much more than a move earlier in life. It sometimes involves moving from a lifelong residence, developing reliance on other family members, and downsizing of personal belongings (Ekerdt & Sergeant, 2006). In turn, older individuals need to consider whether to move closer to family or other sources of support (Bradley & Willigen, 2010; Silverstein & Angelelli, 1998), a more pleasant climate (Walters, 2002), or more formal institutional care (Sergeant, Ekerdt, & Chapin, 2010). Of course, the availability of these options depends on family characteristics, such as size and solidarity, and economic ability to do so (Walters, 2002).

Chen and Wilmoth (2004) found that residential mobility was associated with an increase in activity limitations for older adults, even after controlling for social support, social integration, and demographic characteristics; however, this was only the case for those who reported moving for a subjective health reason. This finding highlights the importance of considering individuals' reasons for moving.

The negative health effects of moving are compounded for economically disadvantaged older adults, who often move to low-cost housing and poorly maintained nursing or retirement facilities. Older individuals could move to a place where formal institutional health care services are more adequate. However, this is only an option for individuals with the means to do so, and poverty in later life may lead to constraints in receiving adequate care for the elderly (Walters, 2002). Considering that more than 9% of older adults in the United States live in poverty (Carr, 2010), a better understanding of how moves affect health and well-being in this vulnerable population is needed.

Multilevel Effects of Residential Mobility

Thus far, we have reviewed the literature on the negative effects of residential mobility as they occur at different stages of the life cycle. However, the life-cycle organizational framework we have adopted does not adequately reflect the effects of mobility as they operate at the family, household, neighborhood, and community levels. Just as social capital operates at the individual, household, and community level (Portes, 2000), so, too, does residential mobility. Moving is often a family and household decision, and mobile individuals and families are often geographically concentrated; therefore, the impact of mobility goes beyond the individual level and should be considered from a multilevel perspective.

Household and Family

Moving imposes considerable strain on not only mobile individuals, but the entire family. The family is the primary agent of socialization and support for children and adolescents, making it a particularly important unit for mobility research. Families are negatively affected by the act of mobility through the disruption of the household and through the loss of ties to extended family (Mulder & Cooke, 2009). Household characteristics that predict selection into migration can complicate the picture, as moves can be instigated by family disruptions, such as divorce (Astone & McLanahan, 1994; Norford & Medway, 2002; Tucker, Marx, & Long, 1998) and employment changes (Brett, 1982) that independently affect behavioral and health outcomes. The majority of residential mobility research on the family suggests that negative effects result from the loss of community ties and social support because of the move (Coleman, 1988). This finding raises an important issue: how do the origins and destination communities of the residentially mobile affect their health outcomes?

Neighborhood and Community

One of the more widely accepted views in the social sciences is that individuals' behaviors and attitudes are shaped by the broader social environment (e.g., neighborhood context) in which they live (Sampson, Morenoff, & Gannon-Rowley, 2002). Much research has documented that residential areas are patterned by socioeconomic status, with economically disadvantaged subpopulations being concentrated in less desirable neighborhoods (Wilson, 1987). Because the poor move more frequently (Long, 1992a), the neighborhoods in which they live are often marked with high turnover and lack the social organization and regulation that stayer-communities have (Sampson & Groves, 1989). Moreover, neighborhoods with high levels of residential mobility have below-average property values (Sampson & Laub, 1994), poor maternal and child health outcomes (Crowder & Teachman, 2004), and high crime rates (Sampson & Groves, 1989). Thus, not only are the poor more mobile, but they also move into and within neighborhoods characterized by high rates of residential mobility that perpetuate social disorganization and poverty concentration and negatively impact their residents' health above and beyond the individual effects of moving.

A recent theme in some mobility research is the notion that certain types of moves can be undertaken as a pathway to upward mobility—for example, through better jobs and neighborhood environments. A unique social experiment, Moving to Opportunity (MTO), revealed that individuals and families fare better when moving from a poor, inner-city neighborhood to a suburban location. In the mid-1990s, MTO enrolled more than 4,600 low-income public housing families living in extremely high-poverty neighborhoods in Los Angeles, Baltimore, New York, Boston, and Chicago. The families involved in MTO were randomized into three "treatment" groups to examine behavioral and health outcomes of impoverished individuals and families and compare them to a control group of similar nonmovers. The low-poverty voucher group received Section 8 housing vouchers that subsidized rent for use in census tracts with poverty rates below 10% (according to the 1990 Census). The comparison group received housing vouchers without any MTO relocation constraint. Members of the control group received no rental subsidy through MTO. This quasi-experimental design allowed for high-poverty households to be integrated into more economically advantaged areas, thereby overcoming the selection issue prevalent in many studies of community effects and residential mobility.

Baseline surveys indicated that the experimental group consisted mostly of single-parent, low-educated (less than high school) households headed by African-American or Hispanic females. Moreover, while the program moved low-income families into low-poverty areas, most individuals—but particularly the poor—relocated within their counties and remained in economically underprivileged areas (Long, 1992a; South & Crowder, 1997; U.S. Census Bureau, 2012). Therefore, these results are not generalizable to the broader U.S. population because the MTO programs did not reflect the empirical realities of demographic and mobility patterns.

Nevertheless, the MTO study provides unique insight into the potential effects of migration from impoverished areas to more socioeconomically advantaged neighborhoods, among poor families. Some evidence from MTO suggests that moving from neighborhoods with concentrated poverty into more affluent, suburban areas may lead to positive behavioral and physical health benefits (Keels et al., 2005; Ludwig et al., 2011). With regard to physical health outcomes, Rosenbaum and Harris (2001) made an indirect connection between upward residential mobility and physical health. They found that significantly fewer MTO mothers reported that they or a family member had been victimized after the move when compared to their premove baseline report. More recent research examining the MTO program has shown a decreased likelihood of obesity and diabetes in young women who moved to more affluent areas (Ludwig et al., 2011). Specifically, the group receiving low-poverty vouchers had between 3.4% and 4.6% lower prevalence of severe or morbid obesity and 4.3% lower prevalence of diabetes than the control group in the 15-year follow-up (Ludwig et al., 2011).

Overall, the evidence reviewed here about the health effects of residential mobility suggests that, in many cases, moving has deleterious health effects. Movers tend to be impoverished and to move into and within socioeconomically disadvantaged areas. For many, moving is related to psychological distress, which can have physical health consequences. It is also associated with a loss of social capital. The combined effects of these contexts on the health of movers often lead to mental, behavioral, and physical health problems. Yet social programs such as MTO show that moving out of impoverished areas and into nonpoor areas may have health benefits. Therefore, the health effects of residential mobility are linked to the context in which the move occurs, with the origin and destination communities being among the important contextual factors.

Empirical Evidence for the Mobility-Health Relationship

To provide preliminary support, based on empirical data, for the association between residential mobility and health, we examined a sample of young adults in the United States, surveyed in 2009. We compared several health-related measures on the basis of the number and types of residential moves in the 12 months prior to the survey (between 2008 and 2009). A major limitation of data on the topic is the lack of data sources that adequately address, across all ages, both residential mobility and health; therefore we chose to examine the most mobile group, those in their 20s.

We utilized data from the National Longitudinal Survey of Youth 1997 (NLSY97), which sampled 8,984 respondents who were adolescents in

1997, and interviewed them yearly on a range of topics, including child and family interactions and relationships, residential mobility, health, and other environmental characteristics. We drew on data from the 13th round of the survey, which took place in 2009, when the respondents were between the ages of 24 and 30.

Figures 3.1 and 3.2 present the percentage of respondents who, at the time of interview, had no health coverage, did not have a routine checkup in the prior year, did not visit the doctor when they were injured or ill in the prior year, were limited in the amount or kind of work they could do because health, or reported having fair or poor self-rated health. As previously mentioned, the type of move and the number of moves that occur within a defined period of time are important correlates of socioeconomic status and health indicators. Figure 3.1 presents health outcomes by number of moves in the year prior to the interview (none, one, more than one), and Figure 3.2 presents outcomes by type of move (did not move, local move, or distance move).

These data illustrate that mobility and health-related factors are associated. There were clear trends in most health measures when assessed based on the number of moves (Figure 3.1). Respondents who moved in the year prior to the interview had higher rates of uninsurance, and they were more likely to have not visited a doctor despite having been injured or ill in the prior year. In terms of health outcomes, movers were more likely to have an activity limitation and to report fair or poor health

Figure 3.1

Health coverage, doctor visits, and health outcomes by number of moves in past 12 months.

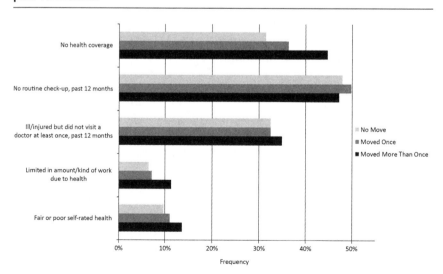

Figure 3.2
Health coverage, doctor visits, and health outcomes by type of move in past 12 months.

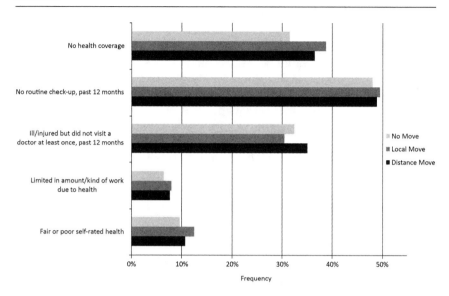

(versus excellent, very good, or good health). Those who had moved more than once generally had worse outcomes than those who moved only once, with the exception of routine checkups. Notably, more than 45% of those persons who moved multiple times were uninsured, compared to approximately 32% of nonmovers and to the national average of 21% among those aged 18–64 in 2009 (National Health Interview Survey, 2011).

Health outcomes also differed by the type of move (Figure 3.2). In most cases, local movers had worse health-related outcomes than both long-distance movers and nonmovers, with the exception of doctor visits when ill; those who moved locally were less likely than nonmovers and distance movers to not visit a doctor when they were injured or ill in the past year. The fact that distance movers fared better may reflect the trend of upward mobility being associated with distance moving (Frey, 2009).

These statistics on the differences in various health-related measures by residential mobility status hint at the importance of considering how various aspects of internal migration are associated with multiple facets of health and well-being. Although they do not account for the sociodemographic differences between movers and nonmovers, they illustrate several health measures that are related to mobility. For example, the fact that movers were less likely to have had a routine checkup in the last year was likely due to both their lack of health coverage and the difficulty in maintaining a routine care schedule with a primary care physician. Thus residential mobility may be an important facet of the socioeconomic status-health relationship.

To account for the sociodemographic differences between movers and nonmovers that may confound the relationship with our health measures, we conducted multivariate regression analyses. Table 3.1 presents the results of multivariate logistic regression analyses of several health outcomes on different measures of residential mobility. After controlling for a host of theoretically important variables, compared with nonmobile households, individuals who moved locally were 1.3 times as likely to report being in fair or poor health following the move. Residentially mobile individuals were also 1.3 times more likely to report having health limitations that impeded the kind and amount of work they can do. Highly mobile families (those who moved more than once between 2008 and 2009) were more than twice as likely to report work limitations as a result of health problems. Those who moved locally were 1.4 times more likely to have health limitations for work.

Residentially mobile individuals at every dimension of relocation were more likely to report that they had no health insurance coverage. Specifically, mobile individuals in the sample were 1.3 times as likely to report no health insurance. Moving once, compared to not moving at all, was associated with reporting no health insurance. Moving more than once, compared to not moving at all, was associated with being 2.3 times more likely to report no health insurance coverage. Moving locally, compared to not moving at all, was associated with reporting no health insurance. Distance moving, compared to not moving, was associated with being more than twice as likely to report no insurance. Interestingly, residential mobility was not significantly associated with whether an individual had received a routine checkup in the past 12 months.

Challenges and Future Research Directions

Our review points to areas that future research can build upon. First, greater theoretization of the mobility-health relationship is needed. A starting point is to agree on a conventional conceptualization of "residential mobility" that accounts for the multiple facets of mobility. For instance, existing research has often studied distance and local mobility together, despite the very different forces driving them.

We have suggested that social capital may be a useful concept in understanding the mobility-health relationship, but the literature on social capital is similarly limited by inadequate theoretization and vague definition of the concept. More careful consideration of the theoretical meaning, operationalization of the concept, and analytic approach is needed. Our broad discussion of social capital, in addition to the review of household- and

Table 3.1
Logistic Regression (Odds Ratios) Predicting Health-Related Outcomes for Adults Ages 24-30: Poverty and Residential Mobility

	Fair or Poor Health			Health Limits Work			No Health Insurance Coverage			No Routine Checkup		
Family Income, Poverty Ratio	2.1***	2.1***	2.1***	3.0***	3.0***	3.0***	2.6***	2.6***	2.6***	.93	.93	.93
Moved	1.2			1.3*			1.3**			1.0		
Move Number												
No Move (omitted)												
Moved Once		1.1			1.2			1.2**			1.0	
Moved 1+		1.4			2.1**			2.3***			.86	
Move Type												
No Move (omitted)												
Local Move			1.3*			1.4*			1.4*			1.1
Distance Move			1.1			1.3			2.2***			.96

Note: Data come from National Longitudinal Survey of Youth 1997 (Wave 13: 2009). N = 4,511.

+ p < .10; * p < .05; ** p <.01; *** p < .001 (two-tailed tests).

All models control for race, age in 2009, and urbanicity in 2009. Models 1, 2, and 4 control for health insurance coverage. To control for the number of family members when looking at income, the "poverty ratio" in 2009 is the ratio of the family's income to the 2009 poverty line for the family, which controls for the number of and age of the individuals in the household. The ratio of the resources to the threshold determines the poverty status. A ratio less than 1.0 implies the youth's family is "in poverty." The measure was dichotomized to denote poverty = 1 (19.1%), else = 0(88.9%).

Poverty ratio in 2009; Moving measures are between 2008 and 2009.

NLSY selected random household member to interview.

neighborhood-level effects of mobility, suggests that a multilevel approach is best suited to addressing how social capital, residential mobility, and health might be associated.

This area of research can also be improved by addressing some of the methodological limitations of the current research on residential mobility. First, residentially mobile households suffer attrition in longitudinal studies more often than nonmobile households. In fact, mobility is the major source of panel attrition in most longitudinal studies (Call, Otto, & Spenner, 1982). Future studies will need to address the challenge of collecting longitudinal survey data with adequate measures of both mobility and health, and successfully following mobile individuals to prevent attrition, so as to move this area of research forward.

Second, qualitative research on residential mobility would help to elucidate some of the mechanisms by which mobility may impact health. For instance, open-ended, in-depth interviews would be useful in identifying the complex reasons underlying the decision to move as well as the challenges in preparing for and undergoing the move, and then subsequently adjusting to the new locale. A consistent pitfall of the qualitative research design in mobility research is that retrospective accounts are often unreliable (see, for example, Stokols et al., 1983).

Lastly, as mentioned earlier, data are not available for a wide age range so as to study mobility across the various life stages. As such, most studies focus only on a specific life-cycle stage, such as adolescence (Haynie & South, 2005), young adulthood (Gasper, DeLuca, & Estacion, 2010), middle age (Wulff et al., 2010), or later life (Bloem, van Tilburg, & Thomese, 2008; Bures, 2009). These studies typically use divergent measures, making cross-cohort comparisons difficult. For practical reasons, we have organized our chapter in the same fashion (while also considering the effects at other levels), but future research should incorporate data from a wider age range to augment the understanding of residential mobility at different stages of life.

Military personnel may serve as a useful case study for understanding how residential mobility and health are associated. A Population Reference Bureau report characterized the military as unique compared to other employers in that it expects even rank-and-file workers, as opposed to only higher-level employees, to relocate (Segal & Segal, 2004), and it relocates personnel over longer distances. Many military personnel, of all ranks and branches, are subject to frequent moving. Estimates from the U.S. Census Bureau are that 37% of military personnel moved between 2000 and 2001, compared to 15% of civilians (Segal & Segal, 2004). Many military personnel can be considered hypermobile, as the military often moves its personnel every three years. Additionally, military personnel are nine times more likely than civilians to move to another state (Segal & Segal, 2004, p. 7). Military moves have some distinctive characteristics that make them a useful case. For example, while military personnel are highly selected, once in the military they have access to many institutional resources. Additionally, military moves usually occur to a discrete set of areas, usually to or near military installations. These and other characteristics may make the effects of residential mobility on military personnel and their families an area worthy of further exploration.

Discussion

The present review has contextualized residential mobility to provide insight into its potential role in shaping socioeconomic health disparities in the United States. The evidence presented here suggests that the health consequences of residential mobility are not uniform, but rather depend on the social context. Poor individuals are more prone to mobility, especially forced mobility and hypermobility, which in turn has largely detrimental effects on their behavior and physical health. Moreover, poor people who move usually have more negative outcomes than poor people who do not move and the more socioeconomically advantaged, regardless of their mobility. Moving affects children, adolescents, adults, and the elderly in multifaceted ways, but research has not adequately explained how or why this is the case, and especially how these factors may differ across life stages. We have identified several pathways linking mobility and health: (1) distress related to moving may directly influence health; (2) health behaviors may change as a result of moving, especially the use of preventive health services; and (3) the loss of social capital due to moving may lead to decreased well-being and lesser access to health resources.

The health of the residentially mobile population—a vulnerable and underserved group—is of particular relevance to poverty and public health researchers. A more nuanced understanding of the pathways between mobility and health outcomes might facilitate the development of policies that address the unique health needs of residentially mobile individuals and families. Such policies would not be aimed at decreasing residential mobility, but rather at buffering the negative effects of moving on individual, family, and community health and well-being. For example, when equipped with this information, public health practitioners could assist internal migrants by increasing access to adequate low-income health care agencies. Furthermore, the high prevalence of moving, especially forced moves, among the poor suggests the need to target housing assistance and social services to mobile and highly mobile individuals. Neighborhood-level policies can be put into place to facilitate community well-being and social capital among the mobile and nonmobile alike. More attention from policymakers and practitioners in these areas might help offset the negative health and behavioral effects of moving on individuals, families, and communities. Hence, it is necessary for researchers and practitioners to consider the pronounced effects of mobility on an already vulnerable population prone to moving—the poor.

Conclusion

Taken together, high residential mobility rates and an economy in which many individuals and families lack health insurance make it important to understand how socioeconomic status, residential mobility, and health are related. Future research should examine the health consequences of mobility and explore how and why residential mobility is associated with behavioral and physical health outcomes across different life stages. Public health researchers should consider mobility as a potential contributor to socioeconomic and other health disparities, and should aim to identify the mechanisms at the individual, family, and community levels through which this relationship operates. This information may ultimately lead to policies that help reduce the negative impact of moving. People will never stop moving—but helping to integrate mobile families into their destination communities represents a good start at alleviating the negative health and behavioral effects of residential mobility on children and families. Ultimately, to improve the health of the impoverished, we must improve their social conditions.

References

Aneshensel, C. S. (1992). Social stress: Theory and research. *Annual Review of Sociology, 18*(1), 15–38.

Astone, N. M., & McLanahan, S. S. (1994). Family structure, residential mobility, and school dropout: A research note. *Demography, 31*(4), 575–584.

Beautrais, A. L., Joyce, P. R., & Mulder, R. T. (1996). Risk factors for serious suicide attempts among youth aged 13 through 24 years. *Journal of the American Academy of Child and Adolescent Psychiatry, 35*(9), 1174–1182.

Bloem, B., van Tilburg, T., & Thomese, F. (2008). Residential mobility in older Dutch adults: Influence of later life events. *International Journal of Ageing and Later Life, 1*(3), 21–44.

Boone-Heinonen, J., Guilkey, D. K., Evenson, K. R., & Gordon-Larsen, P. (2010). Residential self-selection bias in the estimation of built environment effects on physical activity between adolescence and young adulthood. *International Journal of Behavioral Nutrition and Physical Activity, 7*, 70.

Bostean, G. (2012). Does selective migration explain the Hispanic paradox? A comparative analysis of Mexicans in the U.S. and Mexico. *Journal of Immigrant and Minority Health*, Advance online publication May 23, 2012.

Boyle, P. J., Kulu, H., Cooke, T., Gayle, V., & Mulder, C. H. (2008). Moving and union dissolution. *Demography, 45*(1), 209–222.

Bradley, D. E., & Willigen, M. V. (2010). Migration and psychological well-being among older-adults: A growth curve analysis based on panel data from the Health and Retirement Study, 1996–2006. *Journal of Aging and Health, 22* (7), 882–913.

Brady, K. T., & Sonne, S. C. (1999). The role of stress in alcohol use, alcoholism treatment, and relapse. *Alcohol Research & Health, 23*(4), 263–271.

Brett, J. M. (1982). Job transfer and well-being. *Journal of Applied Psychology, 67*(4), 450–463.

Bures, R. M. (2003). Childhood residential stability and health at midlife. *American Journal of Public Health, 93*(7), 1144–1148.

Bures, R. M. (2009). Moving the nest: The impact of coresidential children on mobility in later midlife. *Journal of Family Issues, 30*(6), 837–851.

Call, V. R. A., Otto, L. B., & Spenner, K. I. (1982). *Tracking respondents: A multi-method approach.* Lexington, MA: Lexington Books.

Carr, D. (2010). Golden years? Poverty among older Americans. *Contexts, 9*(1), 62–63.

Chen, P. C., & Wilmoth, J. A. (2004). The effects of residential mobility on ADL and IADL limitations among the very old living in the community. *Journals of Gerontology Series B—Psychological Sciences and Social Sciences, 59*(3), S164–S172.

Coleman, J. S. (1988). Social capital in the creation of human capital. *American Journal of Sociology, 94*, S95–S120.

Cooper, H., Arber, S., Fee, L., & Ginn, J. (1999). *The influence of social support and social capital on health: A review and analysis of British data.* London, UK: Health Education Authority.

Crowder, K. D., & Teachman, J. (2004). Do residential conditions explain the relationship between living arrangements and adolescent behavior? *Journal of Marriage and Family, 66*(3), 721–738.

DeWit, D. J. (1998). Frequent childhood geographic relocation: Its impact on drug use initiation and the development of alcohol and other drug-related problems among adolescents and young adults. *Addictive Behaviors, 23*(5), 623–634.

Ekerdt, D. J., & Sergeant, J. F. (2006). Family things: Attending the household disbandment of elders. *Journal of Aging Studies, 20*(3), 193–205.

Evans, J. (1987). Introduction: Migration and health. *International Migration Review, 21*(3), v–xiv.

Feliciano, C. (2005). Educational selectivity in U.S. immigration: How do immigrants compare to those left behind? *Demography, 42*(1), 131–152.

Fischer, C. S. (2002). Ever-more rooted Americans. *City and Community, 1*(2), 177–198.

Fischer, C. S., Jackson, R. M., Stueve, C. A., Gerson, K., Jones, L. M., & Baldassare, M. (1977). *Networks and places: Social relations in the urban setting.* New York, NY: Free Press.

Fowler, M. G., Simpson, G. A., & Schoendorf, K. C. (1993). Families on the move and children's health care. *Pediatrics, 91*(5), 934–940.

Frey, W. H. (1995). Immigration impacts on internal migration of the poor: 1990 Census evidence for U.S. states. *International Journal of Population Geography, 1*(1), 51–67.

Frey, W. H. (2003). *Who moves where: A 2000 Census survey.* Washington, DC: Population Reference Bureau.

Frey, W. H. (2009). *The great American migration slowdown: Regional and metropolitan dimensions. Metropolitan Policy Program.* Washington, DC: Brookings Institute.

Garbarino, J., & Kostelny, K. (1992). Child maltreatment as a community problem. *Child Abuse and Neglect, 16*(4), 455–464.

Gasper, J., DeLuca, S. A., & Estacion, A. (2010). Coming and going: Explaining the effects of residential and school mobility on adolescent delinquency. *Social Science Research, 39*(3), 459–476.

Geist, C., & McManus, P. A. (2008). Geographical mobility over the life course: Motivations and implications. *Population, Space and Place, 14*, 283–303.

Gilman, S. E., Kawachi, I., Fitzmaurice, G. M., & Buka, S. L. (2003). Socio-economic status, family disruption and residential stability in childhood: Relation to onset, recurrence and remission of major depression. *Psychological Medicine, 33*(8), 1341–1355.

Grieco, E. M., Acosta, Y. D., de la Cruz, G. P., Gambino, C., Gryn, T., Larsen, L., . . . Walters, N. P. (2012). The foreign-born population in the United States: 2010. U.S. Census Bureau. http://www.census.gov/prod/2012pubs/acs-19.pdf

Haynie, D. L., & South, S. J. (2005). Residential mobility and adolescent violence. *Social Forces, 84*(1), 361–374.

Haynie, D. L., South, S. J., & Bose, S. (2006). The company you keep: Adolescent mobility and peer behavior. *Sociological Inquiry, 76*(3), 397–426.

Hemingway, H., & Marmot, M. (1999). Psychosocial factors in the aetiology and prognosis of coronary heart disease: Systematic review of prospective cohort studies. *British Medical Journal, 318*, 1460–1467.

Holmes, T. H., & Rahe, R. H. (1967). The Social Readjustment Rating Scale. *Journal of Psychosomatic Research, 11*(2), 213–218.

House, J. S., Landis, K. R., & Umberson, D. (1988). Social relationships and health. *Science, 241*, 540–545.

International Organization for Migration. (2012). Facts and figures: Global estimates and trends. http://www.iom.int/jahia/Jahia/about-migration/facts-and-figures/lang/en/

Jacobsen, J. P., & Levin, L. M. (1997). Marriage and migration: Comparing gains and losses from migration for couples and singles. *Social Science Quarterly, 78*(3), 688–709.

Jelleyman, T., & Spencer, N. (2008). Residential mobility in childhood and health outcomes: A systematic review. *Journal of Epidemiology and Community Health, 62*(7), 584–592.

Kawachi, I., Kennedy, B. P., & Glass, R. (1999). Social capital and self-rated health: A contextual analysis. *American Journal of Public Health, 89*(8), 1187–1193.

Kawachi, I., Kennedy, B. P., Lochner, K., & Prothrow-Stith, D. (1997). Social capital, income inequality, and mortality. *American Journal of Public Health, 87*(9), 1491–1498.

Keels, M., DeLuca, S., Duncan, G. J., Mendenhall, R., & Rosenbaum, J. (2005). Fifteen years later: Can residential mobility programs provide a long-term escape from neighborhood segregation, crime and poverty? *Demography, 42*(1), 51–73.

Kiecolt-Glaser, J. K., Glaser, R., Gravenstein, S., Malarkey, W. B., & Sheridan, J. (1996). Chronic stress alters the immune response to influenza virus vaccine in older adults. *Proceedings of the National Academy of Sciences, 93*(7), 3043–3047.

Kilborn, P. T. (2009). *Next stop, Reloville: Life inside America's new rootless professional class*. New York, NY: Henry Holt and Company.

Knudson-Cooper, M. S., & Leuchtag, A. K. (1982). The stress of a family move as a precipitating factor in children's burn accidents. *Journal of Human Stress, 8*(2), 32–38.

Larson, A., Bell, M., & Young, A. F. (2004). Clarifying the relationships between health and residential mobility. *Social Science & Medicine, 59*(10), 2149–2160.

Link, B. G., & Phelan, J. C. (1995). Social conditions as fundamental causes of disease. *Journal of Health and Social Behavior, 36*, 80–94.

Litwak, E., & Longino, C. F. (1987). Migration patterns among the elderly: A developmental perspective. *The Gerontologist, 27*(3), 266–272.

Long, L. H. (1988). *Migration and residential mobility in the United States*. New York, NY: Russell Sage Foundation.

Long, L. H. (1992a). Changing residence: Comparative perspectives on its relationship to age, sex, and marital status. *Population Studies, 46*(1), 141–158.

Long, L. H. (1992b). International perspectives on the residential mobility of America's children. *Journal of Marriage and Family, 54*(4), 861–869.

Long, L., Tucker, C. J., & Urton, W. L. (1988). Migration distances: An international comparison. *Demography, 25*(4), 633–640.

Ludwig, J., Sanbonmatsu, L., Gennetian, L., Adam, E., Duncan, G. J., Katz, L. F., ... McDade, T. W. (2011). Neighborhoods, obesity, and diabetes: A randomized social experiment. *New England Journal of Medicine, 365*(16), 1509–1519.

Macartney, S. (2011). *Child poverty in the United States in 2009 and 2010: Selected race groups and Hispanic origin. American Community Survey Briefs* (ACSBR/10-05). Washington, DC: U.S. Census Bureau.

Magdol, L. (2002). Is moving gendered? The effects of residential mobility on the psychological well-being of men and women. *Sex Roles, 47*(11/12), 553–560.

Markides, K. S., & Eschbach, K. (2005). Aging, migration, and mortality: Current status of research on the Hispanic paradox. *Journals of Gerontology B: Psychological and Social Sciences, 60*(2), S68–S75.

Marmot, M. G. (1996). The social pattern of health and disease. In D. Blane, E. Brunner, & R. Wilkinson (Eds.), *Health and social organization: Towards a health policy for the 21st century* (pp. 42–67). London, UK: Routledge.

Miller, M. A., & Rahe, R. H. (1997). Life changes scaling for the 1990's. *Journal of Psychosomatic Research, 43*(3), 279–292.

Mulder, C. H., & Cooke, T. J. (2009). Family ties and residential locations. *Population, Space and Place, 14*(4), 299–304.

National Health Interview Survey. (2011). Lack of health insurance and type of coverage. Table 1.1b: Percentage of persons without health insurance coverage at time of interview, 1997–2010. Centers for Disease Control. http://www.cdc.gov/nchs/data/nhis/earlyrelease/201109_01.pdf

Norford, B. C., & Medway, F. J. (2002). Adolescents' mobility histories and present social adjustment. *Psychology in the Schools, 39*(1), 51–62.

Oishi, S. (2010). The psychology of residential mobility: Implications for the self, social relationships, and well-being. *Perspectives on Psychological Science, 5*(1), 5–21.

Oishi, S., & Schimmack, U. (2010). Residential mobility, well-being, and mortality. *Journal of Personality and Social Psychology, 98*(6), 980–994.

Orth-Gomér, K., Rosengren, A., & Wilhelmsen, L. (1993). Lack of social support and incidence of coronary heart disease in middle-aged Swedish men. *Psychosomatic Medicine, 55*(1), 37–43.

Pescosolido, B. A., Wright, E. R., Alegria, M., & Vera, M. (1998). Social networks and patterns of use among the poor with mental health problems in Puerto Rico. *Medical Care, 36*(7), 1057–1072.

Pettit, B., & McLanahan, S. (2003). Residential mobility and children's social capital: Evidence from an experiment. *Social Science Quarterly, 84*(3), 632–649.

Pitkin Derose, K., & Varda, D. M. (2009). Social capital and health care access: A systematic review. *Medical Care Research and Review, 66*(3), 272–306.

Portes, A. (1998). Social capital: Its origins and applications in modern sociology. *Annual Review of Sociology, 24*(1), 1–24.

Portes, A. (2000). The two meanings of social capital. *Sociological Forum, 15*(1), 1–12.

Pribesh, S., & Downey, D. B. (1999). Why are residential and school moves associated with poor school performance? *Demography, 36*(4), 521–534.

Ren, P. (2011). *Lifetime mobility in the United States: 2010. American Community Survey Briefs*. Washington, DC: U.S. Census Bureau.

Reynolds, P., & Kaplan, G. A. (1990). Social connections and risk for cancer: Prospective evidence from the Alameda County study. *Behavioral Medicine, 16* (3), 101–110.

Rosenbaum, E., & Harris, L. E. (2001). Low-income families in their new neighborhoods: The short-term effects of moving from Chicago's public housing. *Journal of Family Issues, 22*(2), 183–210.

Rossi, P. H. (1980). *Why families move*. Beverly Hills, CA: Sage.

Sampson, R. J., & Groves, W. B. (1989). Community structure and crime: Testing social-disorganization theory. *American Journal of Sociology, 94*(4), 774–802.

Sampson, R. J., & Laub, J. H. (1994). Urban poverty and the family context of delinquency: A new look at structure and process in a classic study. *Child Development, 65*(2), 523–540.

Sampson, R. J., Morenoff, J. D., & Gannon-Rowley, T. (2002). Assessing "neighborhood effects": Social processes and new directions in research. *Annual Review of Sociology, 28*(1), 443–478.

Schachter, J. P. (2004). *Geographic mobility: March 2002 to March 2003*. (U.S. Census Bureau, No. P20–549). Washington, DC: U.S. Department of Commerce.

Schluter, P. J., Ford, R. P. K., Mitchell, E. A., & Taylor, B. (1998). Residential mobility and sudden infant death syndrome. *Journal of Pediatrics and Child Health, 34*(5), 432–437.

Segal, D. R., & Segal, M. W. (2004). America's military population. *Population Bulletin, 59*(4), 3–40.

Sell, R. R. (1983). Analyzing migration decisions: The first step—whose decisions? *Demography, 20*(3), 299–311.

Seltzer, J. A., & Kalmuss, D. (1988). Socialization and stress explanations for spouse abuse. *Social Forces, 67*(2), 473–491.

Sergeant, J. F., Ekerdt, D. J., & Chapin, R. K. (2010). Older adults' expectations to move: Do they predict actual community-based or nursing facility moves within 2 years? *Journal of Aging and Health, 22*(7), 1029–1053.

Sharkey, P., & Sampson, R. J. (2010). Destination effects: Residential mobility and trajectories of adolescent violence in a stratified metropolis. *Criminology, 48*(3), 639–681.

Silverstein, M., & Angelelli, J. J. (1998). Older parents' expectations of moving closer to their children. *Journal of Gerontology, 53*(3), S153–S163.

Simpson, G. A., & Fowler, M. G. (1994). Geographic mobility and children's emotional/behavioral adjustment and school functioning. *Pediatrics, 93*(2), 303–309.

South, S. J., & Crowder, K. D. (1997). Residential mobility between cities and suburbs: Race, suburbanization, and back-to-the-city moves. *Demography, 34*(4), 525–538.

South, S. J., & Deane, G. D. (1993). Race and residential mobility: Individual determinants and structural constraints. *Social Forces, 72*(1), 147–167.

South, S. J., & Haynie, D. L. (2004). Friendship networks of mobile adolescents. *Social Forces, 83*(1), 315–350.

Stack, S. (1994). The effect of geographic mobility on premarital sex. *Journal of Marriage and the Family, 56*(1), 204–208.

Stoeckel, K. J., & Porell, F. (2010). Do older adults anticipate relocating? The relationship between housing relocation expectations and falls. *Journal of Applied Gerontology, 29*(2), 231–250.

Stokols, D., Shumaker, S. A., & Martinez, J. (1983). Residential mobility and personal well-being. *Journal of Environmental Psychology, 3*(1), 5–19.

Tucker, C. J., Marx, J., & Long, L. (1998). "Moving on": Residential mobility and children's school lives. *Sociology of Education, 71*(2), 111–129.

U.S. Census Bureau. (2012). *Geographic mobility: March 2010 to March 2011. Current Population Reports.* Washington, DC: U.S. Government Printing Office.

Valente, T. W. (2010). *Social networks and health: Models, methods, and applications.* New York, NY: Oxford University Press.

Walters, W. H. (2002). Place characteristics and later-life migration. *Research on Aging, 24*(2), 243–277.

Waterston, T., Alperstein, G., & Stewart-Brown, S. (2004). Social capital: A key factor in child health inequalities. *Archives of Disease in Childhood, 89*(5), 456–459.

Wilson, W. J. (1987). *The truly disadvantaged: The inner city, the underclass, and public policy.* Chicago, IL: University of Chicago Press.

Wulff, M., Champion, A., & Lobo, M. (2010). Household diversity and migration in mid-life: Understanding residential mobility among 45–64 year olds in Melbourne, Australia. *Population, Space and Place, 16*(4), 307–321.

Chapter 4

Examining the Complexity of the Nexus of Poverty and Health: Impact on Immigrants and Refugees

Mary T. Lewis, Maura Nsonwu, Sharon Warren Cook,
Raleigh Bailey, and A. B. Mayfield-Clarke

Introduction

The purpose of this chapter is to examine the complexity of the nexus of poverty and health and to consider how it affects the United States' disenfranchised group of immigrants and refugees through the use of a modified social systems framework perspective that targets nine components influenced by the World Health Organization (WHO, 2010). According to Anderson and Johnson (1997), a "[social] system is a group of interacting, interrelated or interdependent components that form a complex and unified whole" (p. 23). This type of a theoretical framework is designed to identify and understand the many elements that need to be considered to comprehend large, complex issues or concerns, such as those regarding poverty, health, immigrants, and refugees (Kotwani & Danis, 2007). Current literature is presented in this chapter within each of the nine components of the nexus of poverty and health system. These components are the disparities or barriers that negatively impact the nexus of poverty and health. Much of the research in this area not only explores the effects of various interacting elements of the system, but also presents suggested best practices to enhance the effectiveness of the system. These best practices, which are geared toward offering culturally sensitive health care to the immigrant and refugee population, are explored in this chapter as well. Three case studies—involving a legal immigrant family, an undocumented immigrant, and a refugee family—are utilized to enliven the theory and statistics. The case studies are composites based on the experiences of social workers who work with the University of North Carolina at Greensboro's Center for New North Carolinians (CNNC), whose mission is to support, advocate for, and assist those who have migrated to Guilford County, North Carolina.

In American society, poverty is concentrated in four overlapping groups: racial minorities; families headed by females; children; and the elderly, disabled, and those who have recently migrated to the United States. Within the last group are recent migrants including individuals and families who are legal immigrants, undocumented immigrants, and refugees. According to a recent study by Camarota (2012), the number of immigrants in the United States hit a new high in 2010 at 40 million, which represents a 23% increase in this population over the last decade. Immigrants make up 12% of the total U.S. population (Grantmakers Concerned with Immigrants and Refugees, 2010). Table 4.1 indicates how the

Table 4.1
Number of Immigrants (Legal and Undocumented) and Refugees at the National, State, and Local Levels

Level/Year	Legal Immigrants	Undocumented Immigrants	Refugees
National			
2009	12,400,000	10,000,000	74,602
2010	12,600,000	11,600,000	73,293
2011	13,100,000	11,500,000	56,384
North Carolina			
2009	NA	275,000	2,235
2010	150,000	440,000	2,342
2011	150,000	325,000	2,120
Guilford County			
2009	1,398		
2010	2,302		
2011	1,398		

Notes: On the national and state levels, the numbers are estimates, especially for undocumented immigrants. The numbers are rounded to the nearest million/thousand. Numbers for Guilford County also need to be viewed with caution and represent immigrants (legal and undocumented) and refugees. Information was gathered from the U.S. Census's (2011) Mobility Survey and Population Survey.

numbers of immigrants and refugees have changed from 2009 until 2011 at the national, state, and county levels.

Terms and Concepts

In hopes of creating a shared understanding, several concepts need to be described. Immigrants (legal and undocumented) and refugees are entering the United States, which is not their country of origin. The reality is that these groups overlap. On rare occasions, one person may belong to all of these categories, and some families are a mixture of legal or undocumented immigrants and refugees. The children may be U.S. citizens, but because they are members of an immigrant or refugee family, they live within the confines of the immigrant nexus. Refugees may sponsor family members through reunification, but these new arrivals might arrive as immigrants, not refugees. Nevertheless, for the purposes of this chapter, each category of migration is presented separately here.

Immigrants

Immigrants (legal and undocumented) share similarities such as suffering loss, enduring the stress of relocation, and adjusting to a new culture with a set of different beliefs, values, and language. Immigrants and refugees are foreigners in their new country and must endure the prejudices that come with being different (Difference Between, 2009).

Each group has a unique set of characteristics that differentiates its circumstances. A person who has voluntarily and legally migrated to the United States is an immigrant. Poor economic conditions may have pushed the immigrant to move to a new country. However, if the new country offers more opportunities, it also increases the pull on the immigrant toward moving to that country. Under U.S. law, immigrants must apply to enter the country, which requires complex paperwork and long waits while the documents are being processed. Once they move to the United States, immigrants are expected to support themselves and are not eligible for federal- and state-funded support services for the first five years of residency. Immigrants must explore or rely on their sponsor in the United States to assist them with resettlement issues.

Undocumented Immigrants

According to the Department of Homeland Security's (2011) population estimates, 11.5 million unauthorized immigrants were living in the United States in 2011. This number decreased from the 11.6 million estimated in 2010. The Department of Homeland Security recommends caution when interpreting these numbers, as the annual estimates of the undocumented immigrant population are subject to error. Undocumented immigrants are defined as foreign-born noncitizens who are not legal residents. Undocumented immigrants either entered the country without inspection or were granted temporary status and overstayed their leave date. The Personal Responsibility and Work Opportunity Reconciliation Act (PRWORA) of 1996 makes it clear that undocumented immigrants are ineligible to receive government resources. This includes retirement, welfare, health, disability, or any other monetary benefits provided by a state or local government or by appropriated funds of a state or local government. The exceptions are emergency medical care and public health immunizations with respect to communicable diseases. PRWORA of 1996 also allowed provision of public benefits to undocumented immigrants, if states enact legislation providing such eligibility or if the U.S. Attorney General declares additional services to be exempt from the law's restriction (Kullgren, 2003).

Undocumented immigrants enter the United States with a disproportionate burden of undiagnosed illnesses and frequently lack basic preventive care. The adverse circumstances that some may have experienced when they are traveling to the country, in addition to the substandard conditions in which many live after their arrival, intensify their poor health. These health concerns are exacerbated by language barriers, lack of health literacy concerning the U.S. health care system, and fear of detection by immigration authorities. These factors limit undocumented immigrants' ability to access health care services. Most undocumented immigrants work in low-paying jobs, which do not offer insurance or offer sufficient financial resources to pay for health care (Kullgren, 2003).

Refugees

Refugees leave their country due to their fear of persecution and flee to another country before eventually arriving in the United States. They may fear being detained, injured, or killed in their country of origin. Refugees are more likely to have suffered trauma and post-traumatic stress disorder (PTSD) due to violence and/or natural disasters (Silove, Steel, McGorry, & Mohan, 1998). According to a study by Hollifield et al. (2002), refugees experience multiple stressful events that are associated with adverse health outcomes. They may have increased morbidity, vulnerability to medical illnesses, and in time, poor health habits, as do other traumatized populations. Refugees receive specific immigrant status after the determination that they meet the definition of the 1951 Refugee Convention, which states that refugees have "a well-founded fear of being persecuted due to their race, religion, nationality, membership of a particular social group or political group" (United Nations High Commissioner for Refugees, 2012, p. 1).

The 1967 Protocol Relating to the Statute of Refugees Policy governs the protection of refugees. Before they are resettled in the United States, the individual or family live in a refugee camp located in the respective country or another safe haven. This is where they can receive basic health care and are provided with rudimentary amenities. When they enter the United States, resettlement services funded by the federal government provide them with housing, employment services, access to language courses, and psychological and medical care. Health care coverage, food stamps, and, on occasion, cash payments are also made available. This support can be extended up to eight months. Refugees are allowed to obtain a work permit and to attend school (Refugee Council, 2012). After one year, a refugee is required by the statue to apply for legal permanent residency. If it is granted, then the applicant may apply for citizenship five years after the individual's admission date (Department of Homeland Security, 2011). In many cases, they cannot leave the new country for five years (Refugee Council, 2012).

Poverty

Poverty has been described in multiple ways: the lack of material resources; the lack of access to health resources including healthy food, life-supporting employment, and safe housing; and the inability to participate in common activities such as education. People living in poverty are described as excluded, marginalized, and deprived. The complexity of poverty is due to the lack of material resources, which stems from a variety of causes, and from the consequences that this lack brings to those who are financially marginalized (Murali & Oyebode, 2004; Whelan & Whelan, 1995).

In the United States, poverty can be defined as either having decreased assets when compared to the middle class or lacking adequate housing, food, medical care, and clothing. Reasons for poverty have generally stemmed from the dichotomy between individual origins and social structural foundations, often referred to as economic causes (Wright, 1993). Americans have traditionally favored and shown strong support for the individual explanations of poverty. The individual rationalization of poverty often confuses the effect that poverty has on families, as it portrays poverty as a linear series of events rather than a multileveled, interconnected, and interactive process of influencing events. The chairperson of the Subcommittee on Primary Health and Aging for the U.S. Senate stated that poverty "is the single biggest factor contributing to poor health outcomes and as poverty becomes more severe, health outcomes become worse" (Sanders, 2011, p. 1). Among the top immigrant- and refugee-receiving states, North Carolina has the second highest percentage of immigrants and their families living in poverty, estimated at 36% (Camarota, 2012).

Figure 4.1 presents the disparities or barriers that affect the poverty and health care access that the disenfranchised immigrants and refugees

Figure 4.1
**Comparison between native-born in U.S. and foreign-born on rate of poverty
and absence of access to health care.**

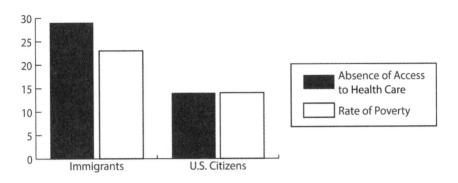

experience as compared to native-born U.S. citizens. The reasons for these
disparities involve a number of complex and interrelated issues that create a causal relationship between the nine components of the social system
framework.

If rates of poverty were the only factor that influenced lack of access to
health care, then the immigrant and U.S. native-born population groups
would share similar characteristics. Figure 4.1 shows the existence of other
influencing factors that cause an increased lack of access to health care for
the immigrant population. Those factors are identified as the barrier components that compose the nexus of poverty and the health social system,
as presented later in the chapter.

Health

The definition of health is equally multidimensional. The understanding of health has developed over the years from the concept of being without disease and abnormality to today's more positive conceptualization
that emphasizes social and personal resources as well as physical
capacities (Nordquvist, 2009). For most people, there are two broad
aspects of health: physical and mental. According to WHO (2010), good
health depends on a variety of elements, most of which are out of the individual's control. Those elements interact with each other depending on
the context of the person's life. The elements that are identified within
the nexus of poverty and the health system, as presented in the next section, are the gaps or disparities that are recognized by WHO. They include
(1) cultural awareness; (2) access to medical care and unmet needs;
(3) education and training; (4) job prospects and employment conditions;
(5) physical environment and world environment; (6) relationships with

family and friends; (7) genetics including gender; (8) life events such as deprivation and trauma; and (9) health literacy. All of these barriers or disparities are influenced by socioeconomic conditions.

Conceptual Framework of the Nexus of Poverty and the Health System

The graphic model in Figure 4.2 is a modified visual representation of the complexity of the nexus of poverty and the health system. The model identifies the various elements that affect the refugee and immigrant population. The diagram shows the interconnections of the barrier or disparity components that make up the nexus of poverty and the health social system, as it impacts the disenfranchised group of the immigrant and refugee population.

Figure 4.2
Nexus of poverty and health social system framework. The World Health Organization influenced the selection of the components. (Modified by M. T. Lewis, 2012.)

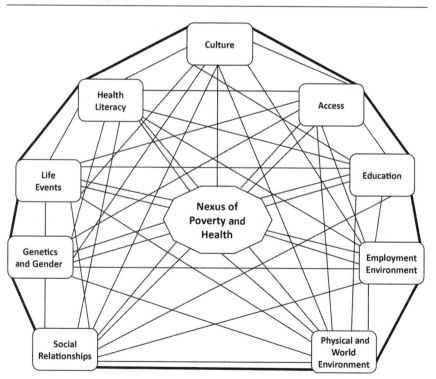

The delimiting factors of poverty and health are at the center of the system. Surrounding these factors are the nine components that serve as the barriers or disparities that impact and interact with the nexus of poverty and health. The lines indicate the connections and interconnections as they form the complex network of components that need to be examined within this system. An important tenet in a system's functioning is that changing one part of the system, while impacting the overall system, will not change the whole system if a transformation of that system is needed. When a whole-system alteration is required, then all parts of the system need to be realigned in the goal direction (Anderson & Johnson, 1997).

While health and poverty are concerns that affect a large portion of Americans, the impact is felt most severely by members of minority groups, who are overrepresented in those populations living below or just above the poverty threshold (Sanders, 2011). As members of minority groups, immigrants and refugees are more likely to be affected by risk factors that produce negative health outcomes. Health and poverty concerns for the immigrant and refugee population vary greatly depending on the person's or family's nationality of origin, education, documentation, duration in the country, and ability to speak and understand English, as well as the size and acculturation of the surrounding community. The Kaiser Commission on Medicaid and the Uninsured study (2003) found that "regardless of national origin, immigrants are much more likely than U.S.-born residents to be poor, even though they are equally likely to participate in the labor force" (as cited in Fennelly, 2005, p. 2).

Literature Review of the Nine Component Barriers within the Nexus of Poverty and the Health System

This section of the chapter is a summary review of the literature as it pertains to each of the nine barrier components of the poverty and health system. Three case studies are provided as examples of how the various elements interact and impact the designated immigrants and refugee families. The first portion of each of the case studies presents the immigrant's (legal and undocumented) or refugee's story. The case studies were written by one of the authors based on her experience working at the University of North Carolina at Greensboro's Center for New North Carolinians. Following each of the presentations is a response from the Director of CNNC that identifies the gap or disparities that impact the immigrant or refugee and resources that the CNNC can offer. A number designates the gap that was presented in Figure 4.2.

Case Study 1: Sophal

Sophal is an eight-year-old girl from Thailand who was diagnosed as a young child with a terminal, chronic, genetic disease. She and her family of six migrated to the United States. Sophal received health screenings and well-baby checks in her homeland. Once in the United States, her mother continued bringing Sophal and her siblings to the local child health clinic and was compliant with maintaining their childhood immunizations. Medical access was provided through the employment of Sophal's father—a job provided by his uncle, who was the family's sponsor. After Sophal's medical condition was diagnosed, her family continued to utilize the health care system. Both family and child were well known to hospital staff and home health care nurses, who visited weekly. Sophal and her siblings spoke English very well and often had to interpret for their parents, who primarily spoke their native language. For the most part, Sophal was happy and well adjusted. She was able to attend school on a regular basis and participated in daily activities.

Sophal had lived longer than her physicians had expected, considering her diagnosis. Her family had a very limited understanding of her diagnosis or the Western prognosis and treatment plan. However, the family readily accepted support from the medical team. As devout Buddhists, Sophal's parents relied mainly on their spiritual beliefs to find meaning and comfort. They were very involved in their local temple and were leaders in their Southeast Asian community. After five years in the country, Sophal's parents became U.S. citizens. Despite receiving all available governmental assistance, they were barely managing to cover their daily costs.

Medical tragedy struck Sophal's family once again when her mother was diagnosed with stage IV breast cancer. After this heartbreaking diagnosis, Sophal's family traveled out of the state to consult with a Buddhist monk, whom they revered as a traditional healer. In an elaborate healing ceremony, the monk used a reed to burn a circular pattern into Sophal's abdomen to bring out the "bad blood" and restore her health. He also performed curing rituals to heal her mother. The family returned home with hope that their religious beliefs would prevail over Western medicine and that Sophal and her mother would overcome their fateful diagnoses in restoration of their good health. Unfortunately, Sophal's mother died within the year and Sophal died the following year. Due to a medical insurance cap, medical bills continued to negatively impact the family.

Response to Case Study 1

According to the case study, Sophal often had to interpret for her family. This is a violation of Title VI of the 1964 Civil Rights Act, which assures culturally and linguistically appropriate services if an agency receives federal funds (gaps 1 and 2).

The use of the Buddhist temple is a culturally appropriate intervention. In fact, the Buddhist temple in Greensboro, North Carolina, was founded in 1986 to provide culturally appropriate mental health interventions. The Buddhist temple and the monk provide rituals and security to help members of the community deal with their grief and stress due to migration and to mitigate other stressors due to a history that contains violence and war. The temple and the monk offer spiritual support to help the community members begin to rebuild their lives (1, 6, and 8). The monk and his assistants regularly counsel Southeast Asian community members and others on spiritual and health/wellness-related problems from a Buddhist perspective. However, the monk also recommends the use of Western medicine (1, 2, 6, 8, and 9).

Beginning in the mid-1990s, the temple monk, as well as several of the younger Southeast Asian members of the community, participated in the AmeriCorps ACCESS Project. They were trained in Cross-Cultural Human Services, a certificate program of the CNNC in Greensboro that recommends the use of both paths to wellness (1, 2, 3, 6, 8, and 9). In addition, they were trained as professional medical interpreters (1 and 2). In that capacity, they had a culture-broker role of explaining to the physician the traditional beliefs and practices of the culture and explaining the role of Western medicine to the client's family (9).

However, none of the Western or traditional interventions saved Sophal or her mother. Presumably, the Buddhist temple performed the appropriate funeral rituals for the family (1, 6, and 8). The local hospice has been a resource for several refugee and immigrant families and has consulted with CNNC for interpretation and for advice in appropriate cultural practices in the grieving and healing practices and beliefs of newcomer client families (1 and 9).

This case study indicates that Sophal's family had medical insurance, provided by her father's employment, but it is likely that it was not adequate to cover the family's exceptional medical bills. This is an ongoing issue for immigrants and refugees (2). This case study does not discuss the issue of food stability. A significant portion of this population suffers from food insecurity, as families skip meals on a regular basis to pay bills for housing and health care (2). The CNNC and partner organizations are pursuing strategies to address this issue. The CNNC has brought on two extra AmeriCorps members to serve as lay health advisors (2). These lay health advisors have medical training and medical care experience gained from their home countries, even though they cannot find medical work in the United States (2 and 9). They are helping in their new home communities by assisting with emergency care, providing transportation, engaging in interpretation for clients, and linking clients to special food banks and community gardens. When necessary, the CNNC's employees take clients to hospital emergency rooms (1, 2, and 9).

Case Study 2: Juan

Juan Rodriquez experienced several of the concerns depicted as components of the poverty and health social system framework (see Figure 4.2). The numbers show how the various components of system have impacted Juan—namely, (1) culture, (2) access to health care, (3) education, (4) employment, (6) social relationships, (7) gender and genetics, (8) life events, and (9) health literacy.

Thirty-year-old Juan arrived to the United States, with undocumented status, after a torturous three-day journey in 110-degree desert heat with only the clothes on his back. He was taken advantage of by the "coyote" who promised to deliver him safely to the border. During Juan's journey, thieves, who preyed on the travelers, robbed him. Juan was physically exhausted and dehydrated because he had not eaten in two days. He was emotionally drained by the thought that he might be deported and would not succeed in accomplishing his goal of financially providing for his family. Juan left his wife, their three children (all younger than age 10), and aging parents in Mexico to search for steady employment so that he could send money home. This income would be the primary financial support to provide for his nuclear and extended family. Juan had been out of work for almost a year after farming opportunities had literally dried up related to the changes in North America Free Trade Agreement (NAFTA) regulations. Juan was told that if he was able to make his way to the United States, he would be guaranteed a construction job paying more than $10 per hour. Additionally, he would have the opportunity to work 12-hour days, six days a week, weather permitting.

Juan moved into an apartment with a group of men from his hometown and began work the following day. He accompanied his friends to the work site and was told to begin clearing debris from the construction site where new townhomes were being built. As the day continued, Juan assisted other workers with foundation and roofing work. He had never seen—much less used—some of the electric nail guns used at the work site, nor had he worked with any other complex machinery that the crew leader supplied.

Juan was a hard, efficient worker who hardly took any breaks. At the end of the week, his crew leader was impressed with Juan's skills and his ability to quickly learn new tasks. He was "promoted" to laying concrete, as most of the foundation work had been completed. Juan was still unfamiliar with the machinery, but eager to continue working because he wanted to earn as much money as possible to send home after his first week. Juan and another worker labored with managing the bulky machine that mixed the concrete. It was during this exchange that he accidently had his hand pulled into the equipment, causing the flesh and bones of his thumb to be torn apart. Juan was bleeding profusely and in a great deal of physical pain. Notwithstanding, he was terrified of going to the hospital for assessment and treatment of his wound. He was fearful that he would be identified as an undocumented immigrant and possibly deported. Instead, Juan and his coworkers decided to provide home-care solutions and indigenous remedies to alleviate the pain that would save his extremity. This decision cost Juan two weeks of pay from being off the work site, as well as the future use of his thumb. He suffered nerve damage and his thumb was permanently disfigured. Juan continued to work in the construction industry because the pay provided maximum benefits for his family, albeit ultimately costing him physically.

Response to Case Study 2

Juan's arrival story is very similar to that of many new arrivals from Mexico and other Central American countries. He is living in overcrowded housing that is most likely in poor condition (4). Construction, roofing, and landscaping are by far the primary building industry labor source in North Carolina for the Latino population (5). Many of the jobs do not offer medical coverage, sick leave, or training on the use of equipment. Training of this nature is not open and available to undocumented immigrants (5).

Juan's belief that he would be deported if he went to the emergency room is most likely unfounded. At this point, North Carolina law does not require medical workers to report undocumented patients (1 and 2). In fact, emergency Medicaid reimbursement for treatment of undocumented immigrant patients is an allowable hospital expense. The lack of trained medical intervention for his injury probably led to Juan's disability (3).

Juan will likely continue to work in construction for as long as he is able, despite the painful disability. He sees this as the only way to care for his family. Single men in his situation, struggling to support families back home, are highly susceptible to alcoholism and hypertension, as well as poor nutrition (2).

The CNNC does not have many resources to assist Juan (2). The widespread hostility toward undocumented immigrants overshadows human services in his case. If his wife and children were here, the CNNC and other organizations would be able to address some of their needs. The men remain isolated from their home villages, except for their work connections and nearby neighbors. Life is not easy for men living in isolation and with limited English skills. If Juan becomes active in a church, then he may have the opportunity to learn the English language through a health fair that the CNNC hosts in cooperation with a congregational nurse program in some churches. Otherwise, another major accident or health crisis may again thrust him into the health care system.

Case Study 3: Patience

Patience experienced many of the concerns presented as components of the poverty and health social system framework (see Figure 4.2). The numbers show how the various components of the system have affected Patience: (1) culture, (2) access to health care, (3) education, (4) employment, (6) social relationships, (7) gender and genetics, (8) life events, and (9) health literacy.

Patience, a widowed 40-year-old West African refugee, arrived in the United States three years before she suffered a debilitating stroke. She had experienced extreme suffering, having fled her homeland in chaos amidst a raging civil war that left many of her family, friends, and community members tortured, raped, and killed. Patience witnessed the brutal murder of her parents, her husband, and their youngest child by rebel forces who had invaded their small village. Patience and her four other children were able to hide in the fields, thereby evading their ultimate demise. Together they trekked to a neighboring country, only to find that the war had followed them and spilled into this area. This led to yet another harrowing escape that separated her from her eldest child. Patience and three of her children—ages five, eight, and nine—made it safely to a refugee camp in a third West African country, where they spent five years struggling to survive on the meager rationings of bulgur wheat. After the time-consuming process of filing documents and verifying their refugee status, the paperwork for Patience and her children was approved and they were eventually sent to the United States for resettlement.

In the United States, a local refugee resettlement agency assisted Patience with employment by providing her with a minimum-wage position without health care benefits. This employment opportunity barely allowed her to provide for her family. Having no formal education or literacy in her own language, Patience had no transferable skills with which to secure a higher-paying position. She applied for governmental assistance and was able to receive food stamps for her family and Medicaid for her children. However, due to her income level, Patience did not qualify for health care benefits for herself. This lack of coverage meant that Patience did not receive preventive health care services beyond her initial refugee Medicaid time period.

Although Patience reports being given medication in the refugee camp as well as in the refugee health clinic when she first arrived to the United States, she was not aware that it was to treat high blood pressure. Furthermore, she did not attribute her "stroke" to a medical condition. Instead,

she felt that it was a result of a curse called African juju. Her subsequent
dreams of snakes, spiders, and ghosts validated her suspicion that an evil
curse was placed upon her. Medication was not the solution to address
her suffering and bad fortune. She felt spiritual intervention was the only
way to dispel the hex that had haunted her throughout her last eight years
of hardship.

Patience was rushed to the local hospital via ambulance with com-
plaints of a violent headache, paralysis on one side of her body, and an
inability to communicate verbally. At the emergency room, a physician
informed Patience's family that the diagnosis was a severe stroke. Immediate surgery was needed and her prognosis was poor. Remarkably,
Patience came through the surgery and was admitted to the intensive care
unit (ICU), where the medical staff monitored and evaluated her dubious
progress.

Response to Case Study 3

As refugees, Patience and her family were eligible for refugee health
screenings and refugee Medicaid on her arrival. However, once employed
in her low-paying job, Patience had no insurance (2). Her children were
eligible for Medicaid for up to six to eight months, but then lost that coverage based on the PRWORA of 1996 regulations (2). This case study indicates that Patience may have received some medical care in Africa, but it
is clear that she was not aware of her hypertension (9). In addition, her
health condition was not adequately addressed either overseas or upon
her arrival to the United States (2). Clearly, the economic and cultural challenges that Patience faced after resettlement added to her hypertension (4,
5, 6, 7, 8, and 9). Her family's extreme hardships and poverty contributed
to her health crisis (1, 2, 3, 4, 6, 7, and 8). There was no process in the refugee resettlement program or upon her arrival in the United States to
address the extreme traumas and losses that she faced (2, 7, 8, and 9).
Due to her lack of medical insurance, Patience did not receive preventive
screenings or early intervention therapies. Notwithstanding, she did not
understand the role of the health care system, which may have addressed
her hypertension (2, 4, 8, and 9). She had to adjust to the loss of her husband and eldest son, who would have helped support and make decisions
for the family. There was a major role change for her as she moved from
one culture to another (1 and 7).

Patience was illiterate in her own language and not fluent in English. It
is unclear if she had access to language schools or any other types of training that could have possibly enhanced her job pay (2, 3, and 4). It is likely
that not just her country of origin, but also her tribal identity and gender
would have isolated her (1, 6, and 7). Probably others shared her folk
beliefs about African juju and avoided her so as not to be exposed to her

curse. These cultural beliefs can be very strong. While faith communities are strong among African refugees, both Christian and Muslim, Patience did not appear to be affiliated with a group who could counter her belief in the curse (6).

Culture (1)

The first component of the nexus of poverty and the health system is the importance of cultural awareness. The National Center for Cultural Competence (2012) defines culture as an interrelated set of behaviors including values; assumptions; thoughts; patterns of communication (verbal and nonverbal); customs; ritual practices; roles that are influenced by gender, age, or social status; and ways that members of the culture make meaning about the history of their society. Culture is transmitted from one generation to another. It is a multilevel construct that is in a constant state of change. The elements of culture help to define who we are, how we define right and wrong, and how we relate to others around us. Culture also influences expectations about health care and how to participate in the care.

A Robert Wood Johnson Foundation study (2006), which was based on data gathered from focus-group conversations with immigrants and refugees from across the United States, determined that the major issues they faced were language barriers and cultural misunderstandings, especially in health care. Numerous studies (Buki, Garces, Kogan, & Hinestrosa, 2008; Gany, Herrera, Avallone, & Changrani, 2006; Kwong & Mak, 2009; Lin, Finlay, Tu, & Gany, 2005; Nguyen, Tran, Kagawa-Singer, & Foo, 2011) point to cultural barriers that prevent access to and engagement with health care. These barriers include language difficulties and the lack of appropriate interpretation services, which result in difficulty setting up appointments, receiving explanations of illness symptoms, and understanding treatment options. Even though Title VI of the 1964 Civil Rights Act requires health providers receiving federal funds to provide interpreters, this provision has been unevenly addressed (Derose, Escarce, & Lurie, 2007). Prescreening appointments are often missed due to misunderstanding of their importance in health care. Many immigrants and refugees come from countries where they relied on traditional health care practices and spiritual healers. These relationships are more personal than the professional, more objective stance practiced in the United States. Numerous studies, such as those identified earlier in this section, have found that refugees and immigrants often have a fatalistic view of many diseases such as cancer, heart disease, and other ailments, which causes them to be less compliant with Western practices. Another cultural barrier is privacy of the human body, which makes physical examinations difficult, especially for women. These barriers lead to misunderstanding and lack of trust between the health practitioner and the immigrant/refugee. The recommendations from these studies have impressed the need for culturally sensitive medical care that includes educating both the practitioners in the United States and the immigrant/refugee communities that they serve.

Access to Health Care, Healthy Resources, and Impact of Unmet Needs (2)

The second gap component of the health and poverty social system framework is related to cultural barriers. Immigrants have been found to have less access to health care than the general population: "29% of immigrants and their U.S. born children (under 18) [lack] health insurance, compared to 13.8% of native born and their children" (Camarota, 2012, p. 2). The number of uncovered immigrants is high, in large part due to the 1996 Personal Responsibility and Work Opportunity Reconciliation Act, which made most legal immigrants ineligible for publicly funded programs such as Medicare and Medicaid for the first five years of residency. Undocumented immigrants were already ineligible for these programs. The act also extended the number of years that a sponsor's income would be considered a part of the immigrant's income, thus making many immigrants ineligible for coverage due to the income restrictions on eligibility. PRWORA 1996 has contributed to the stigmatization of some immigrant groups, and those who are eligible for coverage are often fearful that using government-funded insurance will impact their ability to stay in the United States. The high number of uninsured immigrants is also attributable to fact that many within this population work in low-paying jobs with no insurance coverage (Derose et al., 2007).

Food insecurity is a health concern among the immigrant and refugee groups. According to Dharod, Drewette-Card, and Crawford (2011), food insecurity is defined as lack of access to food of sufficient quantity and quality for all members of a household all of the time. Members of immigrant and refugee communities experience food insecurity more often than members of the native-born population. Again, this disparity is typically due to low income and these individuals' immigration status, which limits access to food stamps. Fennelly (2005) cited findings that highlighted the deteriorating nutritional status of U.S. immigrants over time. In addition, this study found that 39% of 6,637 foreign-born participants had increased their intake of junk food and meat, which resulted in higher body mass indices, and decreased their intake of fruits, vegetables, fish, and rice since their arrival in the United States. This is only one study in the growing body of evidence related to the "healthy immigrant phenomenon."

Immigrants and refugees have a significantly higher level of unmet social needs than the general population. Unmet social needs are linked to poor health, according to the Robert Wood Johnson Foundation's (2011) national survey of doctors. Eighty-five percent of doctors surveyed noted that while patients from all income levels experience many unmet needs, low-income and immigrant households carry a heavier burden. These unmet needs include more exercise (i.e., a fitness program), nutritional food, housing assistance, transportation assistance, employment assistance, adult education, and healthy support networks. According to this report, there is "strong evidence linking social needs to health and life expectancy. Health care itself plays a surprisingly small role (10% of contributing factors) in life expectancy. Social circumstances, environmental exposure, and behaviors are estimated [to account] for 60% of the risk for premature death" (Robert Wood Johnson Foundation, 2011, p. 1).

Education (3)

Education is the third component gap in the health and poverty social system framework. Within the general population, there is a strong connection between education and health, which has been documented in many countries and for a wide variety of health measures. A literature review that completed a statistical analysis on the relationship between education and health found that better-educated people have a lower rate of death from common acute and chronic diseases. Life expectancy is increasing among all sectors of the U.S. population, yet the gap between people with and without college education continues to expand. This gap cannot be explained based solely on healthy behaviors, which have been noted to increase as a person's education increases (Cutler & Llerasp-Muney, 2007).

Few studies have directly connected the impact of immigrants' and refugees' health with educational attainment. Some statistics do demonstrate the impact of a lack of education on income levels and poverty, however. For example, Camarota (2012) found that "While immigrants comprise 16% of the total adult workforce, they comprise more than 44% of adults in the labor force who have not completed high school" (p. 12). A lack of education influences the types of employment that are available to immigrants, as does the level of written and verbal English skill that immigrants have attained. Lower-paying jobs often do not have insurance coverage for employees, and if health care is needed, the individual or family is frequently unable to pay for it.

Environmental Issues (4)

The fourth component gap of the health and poverty social system framework is environmental considerations. This component includes housing, space to exercise, quality of air and water, and safety. In the United States, overcrowding is an issue for many immigrants. Camarota

(2012) found that immigrants account for half of all overcrowded house-holds. In 2010, 13% of immigrant households were overcrowded com-pared to 2% of native-born households. Forum presentations sponsored by the New York Immigration Coalition (2011) suggest a major cause for overcrowding is the cost of housing when compared to the immigrants' income level. Most immigrants are unable to pay the cost of rent, so dou-bling up is required. Immigrants are also unable to access housing vouch-ers and housing subsidies, as these are federal- and state-funded programs. Due to these factors, the immigrant population is more likely to be living in unsafe and illegal housing (Waters & Bach, 2011). Evans, Well, and Moch (2003) found an association between housing and mental health concerns. For many immigrants, the loss of housing due to migra-tion increases stress and a loss of identity. The loss of a home represents more than the loss of material possessions; it leads to the loss of status, community, identity, and a sense of safety (Brun, 2005). Overcrowding and inadequate housing are associated with a wide range of health con-cerns, including respiratory infections, asthma, lead poisoning, injuries, and mental health problems (Krieger & Higgins, 2002).

Additional environmental concerns include the air we breathe, the water we drink, and the safety of the community. Studies performed on the impact of pollution have found that low-income and minority neigh-borhoods, inclusive of immigrant communities, are most often located nearer to industrial areas and highways than are more affluent neighbor-hoods. Similar findings apply to communities located near or on top of old landfills. These neighborhoods have increased pollution and difficul-ties that negatively affect childhood health outcomes, which may have a lifelong impact on adult health (Nilsen, 2007). The lack of open and safe space plays a major role in lack of physical activity and other obesity-related behaviors that could lead to higher rates of health-related diseases and conditions (Gordon-Larsen, Nelson, Page, & Popkin, 2006).

Job Prospects and Employment Conditions (5)

The fifth gap component to consider is employment and employment conditions. Employment is directly related to one's level of poverty and is influenced by immigration status, education, and English commu-nication ability (Capps, Fix, Passel, Ost, & Perez-Lopez, 2003). As of March 2011, the percentage of immigrants who were working aged was the same as the percentage of native-born Americans who were working aged—that is, 68%. Immigrant men had a higher rate of employment than native-born citizens, while immigrant women had lower rates of employ-ment. Immigrants tend to be concentrated in certain jobs, including clean-ing personnel, construction laborers, and day-labor workers. In most job categories, however, there is a higher percentage of native-born workers than foreign-born immigrant workers. It is important to note that of adult immigrants between ages 25 and 65, 28% have not completed high school, compared to only 7% of native-born U.S. citizens. Most job training programs require that attendees have at least a ninth-grade education, which eliminates many immigrants and refugees from participation. The majority of immigrants have little education, which constitutes one of the primary reasons for their lower socioeconomic status—not their legal status or unwillingness to work (Camarota, 2012).

As has been mentioned, many low-paying jobs do not offer health insurance coverage. The U.S. Department of Labor reports that the working underprivileged are less likely to be covered by health insurance. Without coverage, many immigrants with low incomes are unable to pay health care costs and are more likely to access only emergency care as opposed to preventive care. The lack of access owing to financial considerations is compounded by other barriers such as language, cultural differences, and unmet needs (transportation and the ability to take time off from work).

A study conducted in the late 1960s and replicated over the next 30 years found that health symptoms were worst in participants with a low socioeconomic status and low-paying jobs. The differences noted to be more prevalent among this population included health risk-taking behaviors such as smoking, poor diet, lack of exercise, and work environment concerns (monotonous work). Low socioeconomic status and low-paying jobs appeared to lead to low job satisfaction, sexual harassment, lack of self-development, and lack of social support, all of which impact physical and mental health (Marmot et al., 1991).

Genetics and Gender (6)

The sixth gap component to consider comprises predisposing genetic concerns of the immigrant population and the impact migration has on gender-based health. A study by Dunn and Dyck (2000) found that health care genetic issues were not the most important factors in determining immigrants' long-term health in the new country, nor were the immigrants' current health behavioral practices. Instead, the economic and social characteristics that the immigrant population encountered in their new country were the elements responsible for decreased health status. Another study by Jasso, Massey, Rosenzweig, and Smith (2004) identified genetic patterns of diseases within various cultures, but also identified the stress of the immigrants' adjustment to the new country and the social and economic situations they encountered as likely triggers of the onset of disease.

Displacement is difficult for all refugees and immigrants, but women are often the most seriously affected. Women are more vulnerable to physical assault, sexual harassment, and rape. Their experiences and fears are often not taken seriously. Women may have to take on new roles and responsibilities in their new country, including being the head of the disrupted household. Training and education programming, which are two important cultural adaptation supports, are often targeted to male heads of households. When they do not understand the new culture or learn the new country's language, women are in a weaker position to care for themselves and their families. Stress due to acculturation and employment difficulties can cause increased domestic violence, as it adds to women's lack of self-efficacy. Moreover, due to cultural roles within the women's home culture, they may not be able to advocate for themselves and their needs may go unmet and unaddressed (Burnett & Peel, 2001).

Acculturation can also cause mental health concerns for the immigrant, refugee, and undocumented person. Commonly experienced problems include stress, loss, depression, and a sense of helplessness, especially among the financially marginalized and elderly populations. These problems may arise due to barriers of employment, training, isolation, discrimination, and the Americanization and alienation of children as they adapt to their new country (Fennelly, 2005).

Supportive Relationships (7)

The seventh barrier component of the poverty and health social system framework examines the importance of supportive relationships. House, Landis, and Umberson (1988) conducted a significant study based on the general population that found both a theoretical basis and strong empirical evidence for a solid connection between social relationships and health. The researchers reported an increased risk of death and poor health outcomes for people with low quality of relationships. Over the next several decades, numerous studies (Newbold & Filice, 2006; Simich, Beiser, Stewart, & Mwakarimba, 2005; Simich, Scott, & Agic, 2005) continued to report similar findings. Relationships have costs and benefits for health; they shape health outcomes and are cumulative throughout the life course (Umberson & Montez, 2010). For the immigrant and refugee population, the quality of the emotional adjustment to the new home is heavily dependent on resolving interpersonal stressors such as leaving the family and the community, the breakup of one's social network from their home country, and replacement of those ties in the new country. This process is influenced by the reasons for migration, reception, and opportunities that are available in the new country, and whether the migration occurred with a family, with a group, or individually (Vega, Kolody, Valle, & Weir, 1991).

Traumatic Life Experience (8)

The eighth barrier component of the poverty and health social system framework focuses on how traumatic life experience affects the mental and physical health of immigrants. The migration path to the United States is filled with risks and stressors that are unique to the events taking place in the home country, the process or journey to the new country, and the acculturation process encountered upon arrival. For all immigrants, the process of migration can lead to increased risk for emotional and traumatic events. For refugees, their country of origin has become an unsafe place where violence and war may have torn their families apart. Children and adults may have witnessed the death and torture of loved ones. Detention in refugee camps for long periods of time and the journey of illegal immigration also increase the risk of violence and abuse. Once the individual or family arrives the receiving country, they may face the stress of poverty, lack of education, underemployment or unemployment, lack of supportive relationships, a sense of isolation due to cultural and language barriers, a complete change in living conditions (i.e., overcrowded housing in unsafe neighborhoods), lack of familiar foods, and spiritual support. Discrimination and prejudice are also major stressors that the newcomers encounter (Beiser, Hou, Hyman, & Tousignant, 2002; Finch, Kolody, & Vega, 2000; Pumariega, Rothe, & Pumariega, 2005).

Traumatic life events in the immigrant populations are common and are associated with psychiatric disorders, including PTSD. Other disorders may include depression, anxiety, and anger management. Mental health impairments may lessen motivation, increase fear, negatively impact relationships and learning, and decrease work functions. These mental health conditions and issues are strongly associated with poor physical health and higher rates of morbidity (Holman, Siver, & Waitzkin, 2000).

Health Literacy (9)

The ninth gap component in the health and poverty social system framework examines health literacy and its impact on the immigrant population. WHO (2010) has defined health literacy as cognitive and social skills that determine the motivation and ability of individuals to gain access to, understand, and use information in ways that promote and maintain good health. The health literacy process includes the integration of cultural assumptions and Western health care. Currently, immigrants and refugees suffer disproportionally from diabetes, stroke, cancer, and heart attacks, as well as HIV/AIDS (Kreps & Sparks, 2008). Some of these diseases can be treated if preventive health screening occurs, or if immigrants and refugees have access to health information that might influence risk-taking behaviors. Barriers to accessing this information include written and oral language, lack of cultural understanding of how to access health care, spiritual belief in herbal treatments, and concern over body privacy when a physical exam is needed. In addition, confusion about and mistrust of treatment practice in Western medicine are often apparent (Zanchetta & Poureslami, 2006).

Implications for Culturally Responsive Health Care

An examination of the recent strides made toward achieving culturally responsive health care must address the ongoing disparities or barrier components in the poverty and health social system framework. There is a realization that the social, financial, and policy barriers must be addressed. Furthermore, there is a need to educate medical personnel on how to provide culturally sensitive medical care and simultaneously educate the immigrant population on how the health care system works. Fortier (2010) indicated that medical services will not work effectively until clinical, service, and administrative personnel begin to understand and value the unique health and social needs of the immigrant and refugee population. This requires developing the knowledge and skills needed to offer culturally competent interventions. Campinha-Bacote (2002) views the development of culturally competent health care as an ongoing process of learning about the culture of the people served and coming to value and understand the context of their lives. This process integrates cultural awareness, cultural knowledge, and cultural skills while the medical professional learns from cultural encounters. The literature suggests that this training should be done in conjunction with health literacy training for the immigrant and refugee communities (Fortier, 2010).

There is also a strong push to encourage the use of community when defining evidence to assure appropriate culturally sensitive interventions. Community-defined evidence is a set of practices that communities use to identify positive results as determined by community consensus over time. It is meant to complement evidence-based practices and treatments, which emphasize empirical testing and rarely consider cultural appropriateness in their development or application (Martinez, Callejas, & Hernandez, 2010). The practice of adopting community-defined evidence allows the voices, beliefs, and needs of the migrant population to be at the center of the health care plan and influences delivery of care.

An example of this combination of addressing the medical, physical, psychosocial, and financial needs of the immigrant and refugee population, while educating the immigrant community on health care needs, can be found at the University of North Carolina in Greensboro's Center for New North Carolinians. In the case studies presented earlier in this chapter, the numbers representing the gaps and barrier components of the poverty and health social system framework were presented in parentheses following the exemplars of CNNC outreach programs. Examples of the services offered include locating, identifying, training, and advocating for availability of interpreters for culture and language issues in health and service care areas (1 and 2); providing health and nutritional education to immigrant and refugee communities (1 and 2); working with medical personnel to educate and assist new immigrants in signing up for special programs that can offer access to prescreening and preventive care, access to food pantries, community gardens, and shops that have similar food products from their homeland (this also includes providing information on social, educational, spiritual, and other resources; 1, 2, 3, and 5); providing transportation to appointments (4); and creating and supporting community centers in the immigrant and refugee communities that offer language programs, job training, support groups, tutoring for the children, activities for children and teens, and programs intended to help the communities develop a supportive and safe environment (1, 2, 3, 4, 5, 6, 7, 8, and 9).

The CNNC has also worked to support the development of a religious temple and centers that can advocate for the immigrant and refugee spiritual practices. These spiritual centers provide healing to those who have experienced loss, trauma, or difficulty with acculturation, and they offer a place to practice important rituals that celebrate special events (1 and 8). In addition, the CNNC conducts community-based research with and in the immigrant communities. The continued working goal is that these community sites will serve as community-based, evidence-based practice laboratories where researchers and practitioners can test a project and collect data in cooperation with participating community members. The goal is for community members to be involved in analyzing and understanding the findings to ensure that the outcomes are culturally appropriate.

Finally, the CNNC has been working with hospitals used by the immigrant community in Guilford County to determine how immigrant doctors and healers can work together to cocreate culturally sensitive health care (1, 2, 5, 6, 7, 8, and 9).

Future Considerations for Possible Solutions to the Nexus of Poverty and Health

According to WHO (2010), economic, environmental, and social conditions have increased migration movement on a worldwide basis. With such movement, there is a growing need to generate data and disseminate evidence on the costs and benefits of migration. The WHO report suggests that there is a potentially cost-effective return from paying for health care services that help build an economically productive workforce. By providing public access to health care, people are able to engage in preventive and early intervention care, which is less expensive than is the cost of treatment at a later stage of disease.

The WHO (2010) report also examines the concept of access to health care as a human right. This recognition would allow public health care services to be extended to refugees as well as legal and undocumented immigrants. The report points out that disease and illness do not know national and international boundaries, so it is economically productive to offer health care both locally and globally. Such a system would allow the immigrant and refugee population groups to be in good health and ultimately allow them to better contribute to social and economic development in both their country of origin and their new country of residence. When viewed in this manner, the cost of health care is seen as an investment rather than a burden.

Conclusion

This chapter has explored the nexus of poverty and health as it impacts a select group of disenfranchised immigrants and refugees. A social system framework was used to present a summary examination of the current literature dealing with the nexus of poverty and health. Influenced by the work of the World Health Organization and current literature, nine barrier components within the social system were chosen to create an understanding of the complexity of the nexus of poverty and health. These barriers are interrelated, and they interact to negatively impact immigrants and refugees throughout their migration journeys and acculturation processes. Understanding the barriers, the protective factors, and the ways that they interact to affect immigrant and refugee population is fundamental to understanding the nexus of poverty and health and its impact on this select population.

The elimination of any one of the barriers, while helpful, will not eradicate the poverty and health problems faced by this population. By comparison, engaging the whole system and addressing all of the identified components can help move the system to a more positive place. Current best practices were presented in this chapter, along with suggested future considerations. Case studies were offered as examples of the impact of the identified barriers and current service attempts to address them by one immigrant and refugee service agency.

Immigrants are survivors. Their will to survive makes them sound investments for our communities for the future. Their children, who are educated in the United States, will be the basis for the economy of the next generation. They have or are acquiring cultural competency skills—which are invaluable skills for the diverse communities in which all people live. Immigrants represent wise investments as we all learn to live in a global economy. Their transnational networks expand our economic potential.

While research strives to identify and apply the best practices that might multiply the protective factors, improved health care will mitigate the risk factors as well as add to the common good, both globally and locally.

References

Anderson, V., & Johnson, L. (1997). *Systems thinking basics: From concepts to causal loops*. Waltham, MA: Pegasus Communications.

Beiser, M., Hou, F., Hyman, I., & Tousignant, M. (2002). Poverty, family process and mental health of immigrant children in Canada. *American Journal of Public Health, 92*(2), 220–227.

Brun, C. (2005). *House: Loss, refuge and belonging*. Norwegian University of Science and Technology. http://www.fmreview.org/sites/fmr/files/FMRdownloads/en/FMRpdfs/Supplements/House.pdf

Buki, L. P., Garces, D. M., Kogan, L., & Hinestrosa, M. C. (2008). Latina breast cancer survivors lived experiences: Diagnosis, treatment and beyond. *Cultural Diversity and Ethnic Minority Psychology, 14*(2), 163–167.

Burnett, A., & Peel, M. (2001). Health needs of asylum seekers and refugees. *British Medical Journal, 322*(7285), 544–547.

Camarota, S. A. (2012). Immigrants in the United States: A profile of America's foreign born population. Center for Immigration Studies. http://cis.org/node/3876#poverty

Campinha-Bacote, J. (2002). The process of cultural competence in the delivery of healthcare service: A model of care. *Journal of Transcultural Nursing, 13*(3), 181–184.

Capps, R., Fix, M. E., Passel, J. S., Ost, J., & Perez-Lopez, D. (2003). *A profile of the low-wage immigrant workforce*. Washington, DC: Urban Institute. http://www.urban.org/UploadedPDF/310880_lowwage_immig_wkfc.pdf

Cutler, D. M., & Llerasp-Muney, A. (2007). *Policy brief #9: Education and health*. Ann Arbor, MI: National Poverty Center. http://www.npc.umich.edu/publications/policy_briefs/brief9/

Department of Homeland Security. (2011). Yearbook of immigration statistics. http://www.dhs.gov/yearbook-immigration-statistics

Derose, K. P., Escarce, J. J., & Lurie, N. (2007). Immigrant and health care: Sources of vulnerability. *Health Affairs, 26*(5), 1258–1268.

Dharod, J. M., Drewette-Card, R., & Crawford, D. (2011). Development of the Oxford Hills Healthy Mom Project using a social marketing process: A community-based physical activity and nutrition intervention for low-socioeconomic-status mothers in a rural area in Maine. *Health Promotion Practice, 12*(2), 312–321.

Difference Between. (2009). Difference between immigrants and refugees. http://www.differencebetween.net/miscellaneous/difference-between-immigrants-and-refugees/

Dunn, J. R., & Dyck, I. (2000). Social determinants of health in Canada's immigrant population: Result from the national population health survey. *Social Science & Medicine, 51*(11), 1573–1593.

Evans, G. W., Wells, N. M., & Moch, A. (2003). Housing and mental health: A review of the literature and a conceptual and methodological critique. *Journal of Social Issues, 59*(3), 474–500.

Fennelly, K. (2005). The "healthy migrant" effect. *Healthy Generations, 5*(3). Minneapolis, MN: University of Minnesota. http://www.epi.umn.edu/mch/resources/hg/hg_immi.pdf

Finch, B. K., Kolody, B., & Vega, W. A. (2000). Perceived discrimination and depression among Mexican-origin adults in California. *Journal of Health and Social Behavior, 41*(3), 295–313.

Fortier, J. P. (2010). Migrant-sensitive health systems. In *Health of migrants: The way forward: Report of a global consultation* (pp. 61–70). http://www.who.int/hac/events/consultation_report_health_migrants_colour_web.pdf

Gany, F. M., Herrera, A. P., Avallone, M., & Changrani, J. (2006). Attitudes, knowledge and health seeking behaviors for five immigrant minority communities in the prevention and screening of cancer: A focus group approach. *Ethnicity and Health, 11*(1), 19–39.

Gordon-Larsen, P., Nelson, M. C., Page, P., & Popkin, B. M. (2006). Inequality in the built environment underlies key health disparities in physical activity and obesity. *Pediatrics, 117*(2), 417–424.

Grantmakers Concerned with Immigrants and Refugees. (2010). *U.S. immigration statistics*. Sebastopol, CA: Author. http://www.gcir.org/immigration/facts/statistics

Hollifield, M., Warner, T. D., Lian, N., Krakow, B., Jenkins, J. H., Kesler, J., & Westermeyer, J. (2002). Measuring trauma and health status in refugees: A critical review. *Journal of the American Medical Association, 288*(5), 611–621.

Holman, E. A., Siver, R. C., & Waitzkin, H. (2000). Traumatic life events in primary care patients: A study in an ethnically diverse sample. *Archives of Family Medicine, 9*(9), 802–810.

House, J. S., Landis, K. R., & Umberson, D. (1988). Social relationships and health. *American Association for the Advancement of Science: New Series, 241*(4865), 540–545.

Jasso, G., Massey, D. S., Rosenzweig, M. R., & Smith, J. P. (2004). Immigrant health: Selectivity and acculturation. In N. B. Anderson, R. A. Bulatao, & B. Cohen (Eds.), *Critical perspectives on racial and ethnic differences in health in late life* (pp. 227–266). Washington, DC: National Academy Press.

Kotwani, N., & Danis, M. (2007). Tracking the health-poverty nexus: Primary care medicine and intersectional health action. *Journal of General Internal Medicine, 22*(11), 1632–1633.

Kreps, G. L., & Sparks, L. (2008). Meeting the health literacy needs of immigrant populations. *Patient Education and Counseling, 71*(3), 328–332.

Krieger, J., & Higgins, D. (2002). Housing and health: Time again for public health action. *Public Health, 92*(5), 758–768.

Kullgren, J. T. (2003). Restrictions on undocumented immigrants' access to health services: The public health implication of welfare reform. *American Journal of Public Health, 93*(10), 1630–1633.

Kwong, K., & Mak, A. (2009). Health care and cancer screening experience of Chinese immigrants in New York City: A qualitative study. *Social Work and Health Care, 48*(3), 321–347.

Lin, J. S., Finlay, A., Tu, A., & Gany, F. M. (2005). Understanding immigrant Chinese Americans' participation in cancer screening and clinical trials. *Journal of Community Health, 30*(6), 451–466.

Marmot, M. G., Smith, G. D., Stansfeld, S., Patel, C., North, F., Head, J., . . . Feeney, A. (1991). Health inequalities among British civil servants: The Whitehall study (abstract). *Lancet, 337*, 1387–1393.

Martinez, K. J., Callejas, L., & Hernandez, M. (2010). Community-defined evidence: A bottom-up behavioral health approach to measure what works in communities of color. *Emotional & Behavioral Disorders in Youth, 10*(1), 11–16.

Murali, V., & Oyebode, F. (2004). Poverty, social inequality and mental health. *Advances in Psychiatric Treatment, 10*, 216–224.

National Center for Culture Competence. (2012). Conceptual frameworks/models, guiding values and principles. http://nccc.georgetown.edu/foundations/frameworks.html#ccdefinition

Newbold, K. B., & Filice, J. (2006). Health status of older immigrants to Canada. *Canadian Journal of Aging, 25*(3), 305–319.

New York Immigration Coalition. (2011). Forum on many immigrant groups are vulnerable to high rent burdens. http://www.thenyic.org/CSS-March30-11event

Nguyen, T. U. N., Tran, J. H., Kagawa-Singer, M., & Foo, M. A. (2011). A qualitative assessment of community based breast health navigation services for Southeast Asian women in southern California: Recommendations for developing a navigator-training curriculum. *American Journal of Public Health, 101*(1), 87–93.

Nilsen, S. R. (2007). Poverty in America: Consequences for individuals and the economy. United States Government Accountability Office. http://www.gao.gov/new.items/d07343t.pdf

Nordquist, C. (2009, May 21). What is health? What does good health mean? *Medical News Today.* http://www.medicalnewstoday.com/articles/150999.php

Pumariega, A. J., Rothe, E., & Pumariega, J. B. (2005). Mental health of immigrants and refugees. *Community Mental Health Journal, 41*(5), 581–597.

Refugee Council. (2012). Post arrival assistance and benefits. http://www.rcusa.org/index.php?page=post-arrival-assistance-and-benefits

Robert Wood Johnson Foundation. (2006). Living in America: Challenges facing new immigrants and refugees. http://www.policyarchive.org/handle/10207/bitstreams/21623.pdf

Robert Wood Johnson Foundation. (2011). Health care's blind side: The overlooked connection between social needs and good health. http://www.rwjf.org/content/rwjf/en/research-publications/find-rwjf-research/2011/12/health-care-s-blind-side.html

Sanders, B. (2011). Is poverty a death sentence? The human cost of socioeconomic disparities. A report from Chairman Bernie Sanders, Subcommittee on Primary Health and Aging. http://www.sanders.senate.gov/imo/media/doc/IsPovertyADeathSentence.pdf

Silove, D., Steel, Z., McGorry, P., & Mohan, P. (1998). Trauma exposure, post migration stressors, and symptoms of anxiety, depression and post-traumatic stress in Tamil asylum-seekers: Comparison with refugees and immigrants. *Acta Psychiatrica Scandinavica, 97*(3), 175–181.

Simich, L., Beiser, M., Stewart, M., & Mwakarimba, E. (2005). Providing social support for immigrants and refugees in Canada: Challenges and directions. *Journal of Immigrant Health, 7*(4), 259–268.

Simich, L., Scott, J., & Agic, B. (2005). Alone in Canada: A case study of multi-lingual mental health promotion. *International Journal of Mental Health Promotion, 7*(2), 15–23.

Umberson, D., & Montez, J. K. (2010). Social relationships and health: A flashpoint for health policy. *Journal of Health and Social Behavior, 51*(suppl 1), 54–66.

United Nations High Commissioner for Refugees. (2012). Flowing across borders. http://www.unhcr.org/pages/49c3646c125.html

Vega, W. A., Kolody, B., Valle, R, & Weir, J. (1991). Social networks, social support and their relationship to depression among immigrant Mexican women [Abstract]. *Society of Applied Anthology, 50*(2), 154–162.

Waters, T., & Bach, V. (2011). Housing the city of immigrants. Community Service Society Policy Brief. http://www.cssny.org/publications/entry/housing-the-city-of-immigrantsMarch2011

Whelan, B., & Whelan, C. T. (1995). In what sense is poverty multidimensional? In G. Room (Ed.), *The measurement and analysis of social exclusion: Beyond the threshold* (pp. 29–48). Bristol, UK: Policy Press.

World Health Organization (WHO). (2010). Health of migrants: The way forward: Report of a global consultation. http://www.who.int/hac/events/consultation_report_health_migrants_colour_web.pdf

Wright, S. E. (1993). Blaming the victim, blaming society or blaming the discipline: Fixing responsibility for poverty and homelessness. *Sociological Quarterly, 34*(1), 1–16.

Zanchetta, M. S., & Poureslami, I. J. (2006). Health literacy within the reality of immigrants' culture and language. *Canadian Journal of Public Health, 97* (suppl 2), 26–29.

Chapter 5

Poverty, Place, and Health along the United States-Mexico Border

Josué Gilberto Lachica, Ernesto Castañeda, and
Yolanda McDonald

This chapter discusses the relationships among poverty, migration, housing, homelessness, and health on the U.S.-Mexico border. The border is a region where poor Hispanics experience a disproportionate burden of exposure to health risks. This chapter uses environmental justice as a framework to discover where health disparities are prevalent among border populations. The Centers for Disease Control and Prevention (CDC) defines health disparities as follows:

> [P]reventable differences in the burden of disease, injury, violence, or opportunities to achieve optimal health that are experienced by socially disadvantaged populations. Populations can be defined by factors such as race or ethnicity, gender, education or income, disability, geographic location (e.g., rural or urban), or sexual orientation. Health disparities are inequitable and are directly related to the historical and current unequal distribution of social, political, economic, and environmental resources. (CDC, 2012)

The disparities around poverty, inadequate housing, and poor health along the U.S-Mexico border must continue to be addressed for a higher quality of life to be shared by all. Yet things have worsened for the poor since the economic crisis that began in 2008; according to the U.S. Census Bureau (2010a), in 2009 the poverty rate of the U.S. counties along the borders was 20.12%. This is more than twice the national poverty rate, which averaged 13.8% between 2006 and 2010 (U.S. Census Bureau, 2012a).

Numerous cases of disproportionate negative environmental impacts on the socially marginalized have been documented (Brulle & Pellow, 2006; Chakraborty, 2009; Grineski & Collins, 2010; Mohai, Pellow, & Roberts, 2009), and a growing body of research has focused particularly on environmental justice along the U.S.-Mexico border (Collins, Grineski, Chakraborty, & McDonald, 2011; Grineski & Collins, 2010; Grineski, Collins, de Lourdes Romo Aguilar, & Aldouri, 2010). Environmental justice (EJ) is defined by the United States Environmental Protection Agency (EPA) as follows:

> The fair treatment and meaningful involvement of all people regardless of race, color, national origin, or income with respect to the development, implementation, and enforcement of environmental laws, regulations, and policies. Fair treatment means that no group of people, including racial, ethnic, or socio-economic groups, should bear a disproportionate share of the negative environmental consequences resulting from industrial, municipal, and commercial operations or the execution of federal, state, local, and tribal programs and policies. (Bullard, 2005, p. 4)

The U.S.-Mexico border region has a high percentage of Hispanics and Native-Americans, many of whom are vulnerable to a variety of social and contextual factors that contribute to poor health. The region has a high prevalence of noncommunicable diseases, communicable diseases, infections, environmental health hazards (water and air quality), and substandard housing, as well as high rates of poverty and unemployment, low rates of literacy, and limited access to affordable health care (Grineski & Juárez-Carrillo, 2012).

The significant disparities in terms of wealth and development—on both sides of the border, as well as between and within respective border cities— have created a social and physical landscape that is conducive to socially marginalized people being exposed to environmental injustices (Grineski & Juárez-Carrillo, 2012). In El Paso County, an intracategorical analysis between non-Hispanic Whites and Hispanics found that ethnicity (i.e., being Hispanic, even when having higher socioeconomic status than another White non-Hispanic group) had a greater influence on cancer risks from air toxicities than did social class (Collins et al., 2011). Many unplanned semirural subdivisions, called *colonias*, are located along the U.S.-Mexico border and are mainly inhabited by socially marginalized residents, predominantly Hispanics with a yearly household income below the poverty line. Residents living in *colonias* are subjected to poor water quality. A 2012 study found that residents living in El Paso County *colonias* without access to water from a public water supplier had increased predicted odds for diarrhea, stomach cramps, stomach pain, and bloated stomach—all conditions that were associated with their water supply not meeting the free residual chlorine EPA Safe Drinking Water Act (SDWA) standard (McDonald, 2012).

The border has a high concentration of non-White populations living below the poverty line, especially among Native-Americans and Hispanics. Hispanics share a larger burden of health problems and higher cancer risks due to air pollution in El Paso (Collins et al., 2011). Studies have consistently shown a high concentration of air pollutants in and around international bridges linking the U.S.-Mexico border (Olvera, Li, & Garcia, 2012; Olvera, Lopez, Guerrero, Garcia, & Li, 2013). Yet some health risks are not as high as one could initially expect for the border region in comparison to other regions—for example, border rates of diabetes or obesity among adults are not the highest in their respective nations (Ogden, Lamb, Carroll, & Flegal, 2010; SINAIS, 2011). Nevertheless, at both national and local levels, there is an upward trend among minors developing diabetes at an early age.

A contested issue in the literature delves into the "Hispanic health paradox" and its potential application to Latinos along the border. The Hispanic health paradox comprises the empirical puzzle that, despite living in poverty and having grown up in Latin America, many Latino immigrants have better health upon arrival and as they age compared to U.S.-born Latinos (Jasso, Massey, Rosenzweig, & Smith, 2004; Turra & Goldman, 2007). The causes of this puzzle have not been fully attributed, and many nonconclusive hypotheses remain in need of further research.

This chapter begins with a general overview of geographic, ethnic, and cultural life on the U.S.-Mexico border. Through the lens of environmental justice, this chapter addresses variations in ethnicity, language, health practices, migration generation, and other variables that lead to socioeconomic and health inequalities along the U.S.-Mexico border. This chapter then moves on to discuss communicable and noncommunicable diseases prevalent in the region. Later, it considers how the increase of violence amidst the "war on drugs"[*] in Mexico has affected the physical and mental health of border residents.

---

[*]On December 12, 2006, former Mexican President Felipe Calderon ordered thousands of troops to the state of Michoacán to combat increased rates of drug-related violence. This move was regarded by many as the beginning of the "war on drugs" that has affected many regions of Mexico, including Ciudad Juárez. Although accounts as to how many acts of violence and murder vary between government and watchdog sources, it is estimated that approximately 10,000 people have been murdered in Ciudad Juárez since the "war on drugs" began.

General Demographics

The U.S.-Mexico border is more than 2,000 miles long, stretching from the Pacific Ocean to the Gulf of Mexico. The landscape ranges from rural to semirural to urban settings, creating important differences among the 44 contiguous U.S. counties and 80 municipalities in Mexico. The counties along the U.S. side of the border have more than 7,589,980 million inhabitants; of these people, more than 60% are Hispanic, 6.34% are Black, and 6.99% are Asian (La Fe Policy and Advocacy Center, 2006). The U.S. border is also home to 881,070 Native-Americans, who belong to 154 Native-American tribes and 25 Native-American Nations (EPA, 2012; U.S. Census Bureau, 2010b). The diversity of ethnicities, income, education, culture, languages, health practices, and immigrant generations, among many other characteristics, makes for a complex and multidimensional reality along the U.S.-Mexico border. Acknowledging the particularities found in each county along the border, this chapter addresses key issues shared by the four U.S. states along the U.S.-Mexico border: California, Arizona, New Mexico, and Texas. It hones in on the largest border cities, where most of the population resides and upon which most of the research has focused.

In 1983, federal environmental authorities in the United States and Mexico signed a cooperative initiative to implement a multiyear plan to protect the environment and the public's health in the U.S.-Mexico border region. This collaboration, known as the La Paz Agreement, defines the U.S.-Mexico border region as all the land area straddling approximately 63 miles on either side of the border, stretching from the Pacific Ocean to the Gulf of Mexico (EPA, 2012). This definition has become a common spatial designation used in public health and social sciences literature.

The EPA (2012) estimates that the population of this strip of land on both sides of the U.S.-Mexico border exceeds 12 million people, with this population expected to keep growing at higher rates than other areas in either country. According to the 2010 U.S. Census, the border states of Texas, New Mexico, Arizona, and California have a combined population of 70,850,713, representing 22.9% of the total U.S. population (U.S. Census Bureau, 2010b). The estimated combined population of the six Mexican border states in 2010 was 19,894,418 (INEGI, 2010). The population of the Mexican and American border undoubtedly exceeds 90 million people, as many scholars recognize that the U.S. Census historically undercounts populations: most notably minorities, the socially marginalized, the poor, the undocumented, people doubling-up, and the homeless—all groups prevalent in the border.

The population of the border states nearly matches the overall population of all of Mexico: 112.3 million (INEGI, 2010). Thus, if the border states were to form a country, it would be the 15th largest in the world in terms of population. These comparisons do not reflect a political reality or an aspiration, but rather indicate the important population size in a largely mountainous and desert region that only 100 years ago was sparsely populated. In 1900, "only about 36,000 persons lived along the entire border" (Brandon, Crespin, Levy, & Reyna, 1997). Due to recent internal and international immigration, the U.S.-Mexico border states are young and dynamic and have some of the highest economic and population growth rates found in both Mexico and the United States. Approximately 31% of the border population is younger than the age of 19 (La Fe Policy and Advocacy Center, 2006).

Two of the 10 fastest-growing metropolitan areas in the United States—Laredo and McAllen—are located on the Texas-Mexico border. The U.S. border also has some of the safest cities in the United States. Homicide rates in border cities are much lower than in nonborder cities (Castañeda & Heyman, 2012). In 2010 and 2011, El Paso, Texas, was ranked the safest city in the United States with a population of more than 500,000 (CQ Press, 2011). Since 1997, El Paso has been ranked among the top three of the nation's safest largest cities.

The border area could be seen as a binational, multistate network of cities. Fourteen twin cities are on both sides of the international boundary, and they are where the majority of the population lives. Some of the twin cities (city in the United States/city in Mexico) are San Diego, California/Tijuana, Baja California; El Paso, Texas/Ciudad Juárez, Chihuahua; Laredo, Texas/Nuevo Laredo, Tamaulipas; and Del Rio, Texas/Ciudad Acuña, Coahuila. These international twin-city regions are among the busiest border crossings in the world. More than half a million people move legally in both directions each day in pursuit of activities such as employment, visiting family, commerce, housing, and health care (Flores & Kaplan, 2009).

Ethnicity and Immigration

It would be incorrect to say that the border counties are the main destination for new immigrants or that these areas are overrun by undocumented immigrants. American citizens constitute approximately 78% of the border population, with a significant portion of the population consisting of permanent legal residents or visa holders. Hispanics account for more than 54% of the border population. Yet the Hispanic population in the border areas is a very diverse group. Except in California, the majority of Hispanics in the border states are U.S.-born Americans. Many of them have lived in the area for more than five generations. International immigrants represent only 22% of the border population—a share that, although approximately twice the national immigration rate of 13% (which is obtained by adding the noncitizen and the naturalized citizen columns in Table 5.1), does not represent the majority of Hispanics. What differentiates the border areas and the Southwest in general from the rest of the United States is the more than 100-year-old history of migration from Mexico into the area (Jiménez, 2010; Massey, Durand, & Malone, 2002), along with the Mexican and Native-American populations already living in the Southwest prior to the ceding of the Southwest territory to the United States at the end of the Mexican-American war of 1848. Not surprisingly, the border states and counties show the largest concentrations of Mexican- or Hispanic-origin populations in the nation. For example, El Paso is more than 82% Hispanic (U.S. Census Bureau, 2010b; Washington Valdez, 2011). The highest new-immigrant concentrations are also found in border counties, in agricultural areas, and in California. Southern California has a larger percentage of first-generation migrants than the other border states, which have a majority of people who are second- or later-generation immigrants (U.S. Census Bureau, 2012b).

GIS Methodology

California, Arizona, New Mexico, and Arizona are the four states that border Mexico. For our analysis, we selected counties along the U.S.-Mexico border states that are contiguous with northern Mexico, as well as a cluster of southwestern border Texas counties. The two border counties in California are Imperial and San Diego. The four Arizona border counties are Cochise, Pima, Santa Cruz, and Yuma. In New Mexico, there are seven border counties: Doña Ana, Eddy, Grant, Hidalgo, Lea, Luna, and Otero. The 22 Texas border counties are Brewster, Brooks, Cameron, Culberson, Dimmit, El Paso, Hidalgo, Hudspeth, Jeff Davis, Jim Hogg, Kenedy, Kinney, Maverick, Pecos, Presidio, Reeves, Starr, Terrell, Val Verde, Webb, Willacy, and Zapata. Census 2010 data at the county level were used to estimate the total population and to construct the percentage represented by Hispanic populations (self-selected ethnicity or Latin American or Spanish origin). American Community Survey (ACS) five-year estimates (2006–2010) at the county level were used to construct the percentage of the population below the poverty line, the percentage of the population represented by naturalized citizens, and the percentage of the population who are not U.S. citizens. Census and ACS sociodemographics variables were mapped using the ArcMap10 geographic information system (GIS) software and are shown as quantiles in Table 5.1.

As Table 5.1 shows, the percentage of the population below the poverty level in U.S. border counties (20.12%) is much higher than the national average (13.82%), particularly for New Mexico (21.37%) and Texas (30.91%) (U.S. Census Bureau, 2012a). The GIS map included in Figure 5.1 provides a more nuanced and graphical display of the population

Table 5.1
Population, Poverty, and Citizenship Status at the U.S., Border State, and County Levels

Area	TTL Population[2]	Percent Hispanic[2]	Percent below Poverty[3]	Percent Naturalized U.S. Citizen[3]	Percent Not a U.S. Citizen[3]
United States (US)	308,745,538	15.36%	13.82%	5.48%	7.24%
States along the border[1]	70,850,713	37.15%	15.05%	8.77%	12.84%
Border Counties	7,589,980	54.24%	20.12%	8.89%	13.87%
California (CA)	37,253,956	37.62%	13.71%	12.21%	14.99%
Border Counties CA	3,269,841	34.61%	12.79%	10.78%	12.79%
Arizona (AZ)	6,392,017	29.65%	15.27%	4.64%	9.53%
Border Counties AZ	1,354,780	39.67%	17.30%	5.94%	9.67%
New Mexico (NM)	2,059,179	46.30%	18.36%	3.09%	6.64%
Border Counties NM	451,089	55.15%	21.37%	4.59%	9.30%
Texas (TX)	25,145,561	37.62%	16.75%	8.77%	12.84%
Border Counties TX	2,514,270	87.46%	30.91%	8.79%	18.42%

[1]Border states along the U.S.-Mexico border are California, Arizona, New Mexico, and Texas.

[2]Source: U.S. Census, 2010.

[3]Percentage of population. Source: American Community Survey, 2006–2010.

below the poverty level in the counties in the border states. Texas shows the strongest spatial correlations of poverty and large Hispanic populations at the county level (see Figures 5.1 and 5.2).

Access to Health Care

In Mexico, more than 34% of the population has no health care coverage. Of those persons who do have some form of coverage, approximately 65% have health coverage through government programs, and only 2.8% through private insurance (INEGI, 2010). Access to health care is an ongoing issue on many parts of the U.S.-Mexico border. In the northern Mexican border states, 37.3% of all individuals have no health insurance, 58.7% are insured by the state social security system, and 4% are considered unspecified. The situation was much worse before 2002, when the so-called Seguro Popular was implemented. As of April 2012, 52.6 million people were enrolled in this Mexican government-run program (Secretaría de Salud, 2012). Seguro Popular was designed to provide medical help to low-income families. Anyone enrolled in this program has medical coverage for 284 medical interventions and more than 500,000 illnesses as described in the program's catalogue (*Catalago Universal de Servicios de Salud*). To qualify for the program, a family should not have an annual income higher than 11,378.86 pesos. Seguro Popular is funded by the

Figure 5.1
Population below poverty level (percent).

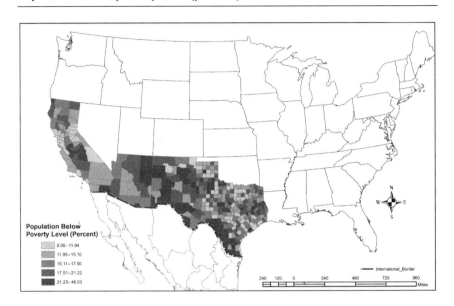

Figure 5.2
Hispanic population (percent).

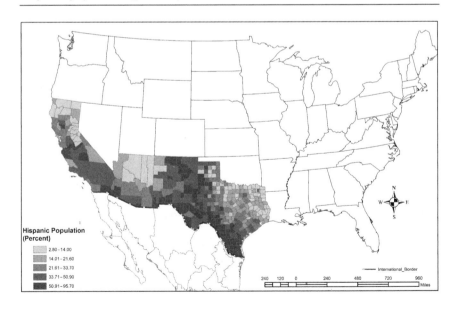

federal government and the states, and the percentage every family or individual pays as their share is determined by their annual income. In 2012, the federal government paid 880.19 pesos per individual enrolled in the program; the states paid 440.10 per individual enrolled in the program; and the rest of the funding came from the percentage each individual enrolled in Seguro Popular has to pay (Seguro Popular, 2012). In 2009, more than 9 million families were enrolled in the program, yet the states next to the U.S. border have some of the lowest enrollment numbers, leaving many Mexican citizens uninsured (INEGI, 2010).

The border region of Texas has a 30% rate of uninsured people, and approximately 14% of California county populations along the U.S.-Mexico border are uninsured (United States-Mexico Border Health Commission, 2010). Some border residents from Mexico and the United States (insured and uninsured) access both traditional and alternative forms of medicine, such as herbs or massages, more frequently than the national rate (Rivera, Ortiz, Lawson, & Verma, 2002).

Although populations in border communities along the U.S.-Mexico border region have some of the highest uninsured rates in the United States, the proximity to medical care in neighboring Mexican border cities may offer more alternative forms of health care to the uninsured than communities farther away from the border. It is important to note that the number of people seeking medical care in Mexico has dropped significantly since the "drug war" violence began in Ciudad Juárez. In a recent study of 1,091 border residents surveyed in El Paso, Castañeda and Lachica found that 55.6% of respondents did not have medical insurance. Among the uninsured, 31% cross the border into Ciudad Juárez for health care. Reflecting the toll taken by the ongoing violence, 40% of the sample surveyed reported going to Mexico for medical care before 2008; today 26% still go to Mexico for medical care, but 14% no longer seek affordable care in that country due to safety concerns.

Some border residents living alone or in relative poverty do not have access to convenient and extensive public transportation systems that might enable them to seek health services. Preliminary research by Castañeda and Lachica revealed that more than 12% of their respondents were kept from seeking health care because of transportation issues, while more than 34% reported that financial problems kept them from seeking health care.

Health on the U.S.-Mexico Border: Transnational Approaches

Traditional approaches to understanding disease and health care as either local, regional, or national problems are particularly inadequate to describe disease and health in this binational border region. Social sciences research specifically related to border health can be divided into two equally substantive research and intervention approaches and bodies of literature (Collins-Dogrul, 2006). The first deals with the transnational approaches of people, patients, pathogens, and diseases crossing borders (Collins-Dogrul, 2006). For example, research by Grineski (2011) describes how parents of children with asthma navigate transnational medical fields to take advantage of the best health care practices and prices on each side of the border. Parents on both sides of the U.S.-Mexico border cross the border for their children's health care, unless constrained by a lack of documentation or various other barriers, such as lack of transportation (Heyman, Nunez, & Talavera, 2009). The second body of literature addresses collaboration across geopolitical borders (Collins-Dogrul, 2006), as seen with ongoing research by the Pan American Health Organization (PAHO) and the Border Health Commission, which are binational collaborations designed to address health and environmental issues in border regions shared by the United States and Mexico. Diseases and environmental degradation are blind to geopolitical boundaries—hence the need for increased collaborative partnership between countries.

Noncommunicable Diseases

The predominant diseases among the U.S.-Mexico border region population include cardiovascular disease, diabetes mellitus, and cancer— more specifically, prostate, breast, cervical, and uterine cancers (United States-Mexico Border Health Commission, 2010). The United States and Mexico share similar health concerns. In the United States in 2009 and 2010, heart disease was the leading cause of death, with lesser causes including malignant neoplasms (second), cerebrovascular diseases (fourth), and diabetes mellitus (seventh) (Kochanek, Xu, Murphy, Miniño, & Kung, 2011; Murphy, Xu, & Kochanek, 2012). For Mexico in 2008, the leading cause of death was diabetes mellitus, followed by ischemic diseases of the heart, cerebrovascular diseases, and hypertension (SINAIS, 2011). Not surprisingly, then, type 2 diabetes is one of the priority objectives in the Healthy Border 2010 Program (United States-Mexico Border Health Commission, 2010). According to the literature, the high rates of diabetes among Hispanics and the high percentage of Hispanics living along the U.S.-Mexico border region have collectively resulted in a disproportionate number of cases of diabetes occurring in the border states compared to the rest of the United States (Diaz-Kenney et al., 2010).

According to the Latino Coalition for Healthy Californians (2006), the relationship between diabetes and obesity in Latinos is rooted in communities that may both unknowingly and knowingly encourage unhealthy food choices. Some theorize that limited choices within communities regarding where one can eat and the availability and pricing of healthy food (such as fresh produce) can impact one's caloric intake and influence the probability of a person being obese. Predominantly poor communities may also be "healthy food deserts," which are defined by the United States Department of Agriculture (USDA) as follows:

> [U]rban neighborhoods and rural towns without ready access to fresh, healthy, and affordable food. Instead of supermarkets and grocery stores, these communities may have no food access or are served only by fast food restaurants and convenience stores that offer few healthy, affordable food options. The lack of access contributes to a poor diet and can lead to higher levels of obesity and other diet-related diseases, such as diabetes and heart disease. (USDA, 2012)

The landscape of food deserts can be seen as going hand in hand with communities that are predominantly poor, like many of those found in the U.S-Mexico border regions. Yet due the proximity to Mexico, to agricultural lands, and to large chain stores and small ethnic businesses catering to Hispanics, this does not seem to be the case in the border (Anchondo, 2013).

The Pan American Health Organization (2005) reported that among the 7.5 million adults living on the U.S.-Mexico border, approximately 1.2 million adults have diabetes, with approximately 500,000 living on the Mexican side of the border and 700,000 living on the U.S. side. The diabetes border study also showed that the level of obesity on both sides of the U.S.-Mexico border is between 33% and 41%. The report estimated that 5.3 million adults in these areas are overweight or obese. Obese individuals are at increased risk of diabetes mellitus, cardiovascular disease, hypertension, and certain cancers, among other conditions. The study also indicated that people on the U.S. side of the border who are obese have a 2.8 times greater risk of having diabetes than people of normal weight (PAHO, 2005).

Interestingly, a study by CDC researchers found that most obese adults are not classified as "low income," warranting questions as to reasons for obesity among poor border residents (Ogden et al., 2010). Yet other researchers point directly at poverty being an indicator of obesity (Foreyt, 2003). The difference may not be so much the incidence of diabetes among Hispanics as the higher mortality rates among Hispanics at the border (La Fe Policy and Advocacy Center, 2006). The increasing size of the Hispanic population in the southwestern United States as well as throughout all parts of the United States calls for more research to begin to understand and prevent the growing issues of obesity and diabetes among all Hispanic populations, including those who live on the border.

Communicable Diseases

From an epidemiological perspective, twin cities such as El Paso and Ciudad Juárez should be seen as one metropolitan area. Although the two entities are separated by the U.S.-Mexico border, the "sister cities" (as they are often called) should be recognized as one region insofar as pathogens do not recognize geopolitical boundaries. Preliminary results of an analysis commissioned by PAHO show that HIV/AIDS on the border is a critical issue, with rates ranging from 10 to 15 per 100,000 population in the U.S. border states and from 2 to 5 per 100,000 population in the Mexico border states. According to the Texas Department of State Health Services (2011), tuberculosis rates are higher in border regions than in interior parts of Texas. This may be due in part to the higher numbers of foreign-born individuals passing through border regions (Texas Department of State Health Services, 2011). It is important to note that although transmission of tuberculosis (TB) across the U.S.-Mexico border is widespread, a similar phenomenon can be seen in many borders and ports of entry around the world (Salaam-Blyther, 2008). The Texas border with Mexico has one of the highest incidences of TB in the United States, estimated at 9.9 per 100,000 (2011). Tuberculosis disproportionately affects poor communities. The national TB rate for Mexico in 2007 was 21%, while the Mexican border states were home to 31% of the total cases in Mexico in 2007 (Moya & Lusk, 2009). The Texas Department of State and Health Services (2010b) also reported a higher prevalence rate of hepatitis C concentrated around the U.S.-Mexico border, with the upper level nearing 2.63% in 2010.

Violence and Mental Health

Along with tuberculosis, cancer, and diabetes, "violence, mental illness, psychosocial problems, suicide, depression and substance abuse . . . are major contributors to the burden of disease and disability for the U.S.-Mexico Border communities" (PAHO, 2012). An increasing body of literature describes violence as a public health issue (Krug, Dahlberg, Mercy, Zwi, & Lozano, 2002). Since 2008, northern Mexico has seen an unprecedented deployment of the Mexican Federal Police and Mexican military. Campbell (2009) describes the northern Mexican border as a "drug war zone," indicating the warlike, violent atmosphere found there. With a current count of 47,515 murders (Cave, 2012) and an ongoing fear of federal, military, and local police officers and cartel members alike, citizens on the Mexican side of the border increasingly have to deal with stress and trauma. Some of the residents of northern Mexico who have American citizenship or visas, or the few who have been given asylum, come to the United States and may suffer from different levels of post-traumatic stress disorder (PTSD).

Although research on the effects of the ongoing violence in northern Mexico is limited (in part due to the continuous nature of the violence, which makes for a lack of long-term analysis on the outcomes of such violence), one can deduce that the widespread murder, kidnapping, and extortion found on the Mexico side of the U.S.-Mexico border have ongoing implications for the mental health of both Mexican and United States residents of the border. Despite the low levels of violence and crime on the U.S. side, the effects of violence in Mexico are felt: if the local culture can be binational, so, too, can the mental health effects of violence, even for those persons who do not cross into Mexican border cities. Ongoing research will allow us to better understand the effects of increased violence on people's health.

Upper-middle-class immigrants—including asylum seekers, U.S. citizens previously living in Mexican border cities, and, to a much smaller extent, undocumented Mexican citizens fleeing the violence in Mexican border cities—face a lack of mental health professionals trained to deal with this type of trauma once they arrive in the United States. According to a local clinical social worker, another barrier to searching for health care treatment is the paranoia observed among people escaping extortion attempts in Ciudad Juárez; patients even fear that the organized crime elements there may find out that they are talking about them to their therapists.

Although border cities such as El Paso have always maintained services for migrants (such as the Annunciation House migrant shelter), the mental health infrastructure in cities such as El Paso is not set up to assist the increased wave of trauma-stricken migrants fleeing the violence experienced since 2007. Amid the rise of this violence, the Greater El Paso Chamber of Commerce Community Mental Health Survey in 2008 found that a number of factors make service delivery difficult in El Paso, including stigma regarding mental health within the community culture, a lack of funding, a large number of indigent or uninsured patients, and limited licensed mental health professionals (Tomaka, Caire, & Soden, 2008). Despite the immigrant reality of the area, mental health services cannot adequately deal with the stressors brought about by migration itself (Castañeda & Buck, 2011).

Drug and Alcohol Use

Drug and alcohol smuggling have played a significant role in the culture and economy of many regions along the U.S.-Mexico border. Since the days of alcohol prohibition in the 1920s, through the growth of the Mexican heroin trade, and now due to the U.S. countercultural demand for marijuana, the border has been a major port of entry of illegal substances (Campbell, 2009). According to Moya and Shedlin (2008), "While new immigrants are less likely to engage in drug use than the U.S.-born population, those living in the United States for 10 years or longer report drug use that does not differ statistically from that of native born populations" (p. 1748).

The constant availability of drugs along the U.S.-Mexico border has increasingly become a public health issue. The increased prevalence of smoking and injecting methamphetamines and crack, plus the continued preferred method of injecting Mexican tar heroin, leads to high-risk, drug-influenced behaviors including shared syringes (Maxwell et al., 2006). Clean syringes can help reduce the spread of blood-borne diseases such as HIV and hepatitis C. Scott Comar's (2010) memoir illustrates the common practice of Ciudad Juárez law enforcement regularly rounding up injection drug users and anyone else who might look transient, confiscating their needles and drug paraphernalia, and then putting them in prison when the suspects do not have enough money to pay off the arresting officers. Drug addicts go through terrible withdrawal symptoms in prison and are desperate for a fix when they come out after 48 hours. After leaving detention, because of the chemical need to "get well," they may use other people's syringes. This behavior is poses a high risk for spreading HIV and hepatitis C.

Health Disparities Survey Findings

Here we present the results from a survey of a purposive sample of 1,091 residents of El Paso, Texas, of whom 223 were homeless people of any race or ethnicity. The survey focused on Hispanics and mobile populations. It oversampled the undocumented and homeless subpopulations, but also included housed people and citizens. The survey includes information on Hispanics of different generations and legal statuses.

The following figures are from a subsample of 884 Hispanics. Fifty-three percent of respondents had no medical insurance. Seventeen percent said they needed general health care services in the last 12 months but could not get them. Fifteen percent said they needed, but could not access, dental care. Ten percent said they needed, but could not access, eye care. Another 3.4% said they needed mental care but could not access it; 2.5% said they needed substance abuse counseling but could not access it. As a point of comparison, 14% said they needed help finding a job. Out of those who were declined health care in the last 12 months, 25% reported having been victims of discrimination in the past 5 years. In turn, of those who were declined health care in the last 12 months, 35% had at one point been convicted of a crime. Of the 17% who said they lacked access to health care in the United States, 34% of those denied health care in the United States were able to obtain it in Ciudad Juárez. The question remains as to what happens to the other 66% of those without access to health care.

Conclusion

The proximity to Mexico and the relatively low cost of living in the U.S.-Mexico border region can make poverty and disease more bearable in some ways, yet poverty on the border presents particular challenges to some of the area's inhabitants—especially those disenfranchised without citizenship, those without residency papers or visas, and those living in *colonias*. What can be stated without hesitation is that there is a need for more culturally sensitive (i.e., Mexican-American), linguistically appropriate, class-sensitive, and place-informed (i.e., U.S.-Mexico border region) research and analysis. Although the communities along the U.S.-Mexico border do share demographic, cultural, and socioeconomic similarities, further studies taking into consideration the many variables that distinguish the border communities are needed. The increasing population of Hispanics in the southwestern United States as well as throughout all parts of the United States calls for more research to better understand and prevent the growing issues of obesity, diabetes, mental health, and poverty among all Hispanic populations, including those who live on the border.

Acknowledgments

Krystal Martinez, RN, MPH, provided useful research assistance. Lesley Buck helped with editing. Holly Mata provided important help with language and content. Sara Grineski provided pointers to the literature. All the errors remain the authors'. The projects "El Paso County *Colonias* and Health Study" (primary investigator: McDonald), "Social Determinants of Physical and Mental Health of Migrant, and Transient Homeless Populations" (primary investigator: Castañeda), and "Health Disparities among the Hispanic Homeless Populations" (primary investigator: Lachica) were supported by Award Number P20MD002287 (primary investigator: Provencio-Vazquez) from the National Institute on Minority Health and Health Disparities. The content of this chapter is solely the responsibility of the authors and does not necessarily represent the official views of the National Institute on Minority Health and Health Disparities or the National Institutes of Health.

References

American Community Survey. (2006–2010). *American community survey.* Washington, DC: U.S. Census Bureau.

Anchondo, T. M. (2013). *Neighborhood deprivation and the retail food environment in a U.S.-Mexico border urban area.* Paper presented at the Society of Behavioral Medicine, San Francisco, CA. http://newsuc.utep.edu/index.php/research-news/767-students-to-present-behavioral-medicine-research

Brulle, R., & Pellow, D. (2006). Environmental justice: Human health and environmental inequalities. *Annual Review of Public Health, 27,* 103–124.

Bullard, R. D. (2005). *The quest for environmental justice: Human rights and the politics of pollution.* San Francisco, CA: Sierra Club Books.

Brandon, J. E., Crespin, F., Levy, C., Reyna, D. M., Bruhn, J., & Brandon, J. (1997). Border health issues. *Border Health: Challenges Along the US-Mexico Border*. New York, NY: Garland Press.

Campbell, H. (2009). *Drug war zone: Frontline dispatches from the streets of El Paso and Juárez*. Austin, TX: University of Texas Press.

Castañeda, E., & Heyman, J. (2012). *Is the Southwestern border really unsafe?* Cambridge, UK: Scholars Strategy Network.

Castaneda, E., & Buck, L. (2011). Remittances, Transnational Parenting, and the Children Left Behind: Economic and Psychological Implications. *The Latin Americanist*, 55(4), 85–110.

Cave, D. (2012, January 11). Mexico updates death toll in drug war to 47,515, but critics dispute the data. *New York Times*, p. A4.

Centers for Disease Control and Prevention (CDC). (2012). Adolescent and school health: Health disparities. http://www.cdc.gov/healthyyouth/disparities/index.htm

Chakraborty, J. (2009). Automobiles, air toxics, and adverse health risks: Environmental inequities in Tampa Bay, Florida. *Annals of the Association of American Geographers*, 99(4), 674–697.

Collins, T. W., Grineski, S. E., Chakraborty, J., & McDonald, Y. J. (2011). Understanding environmental health inequalities through comparative intracategorical analysis: Racial/ethnic disparities in cancer risks from air toxics in El Paso County, Texas. *Health and Place*, 17(1), 335–344.

Collins-Dogrul, J. (2006). Managing US-Mexico "border health": An organizational field approach. *Social Science and Medication*, 63(12), 3199–3211.

Comar, S. (2010). *Border junkie*. Austin, TX: University of Texas Press.

CQ Press. (2011). City crime rankings by population. http://os.cqpress.com/citycrime/2010/City_Crime_Rankings_bypop_2011-2011.pdf

Diaz-Kenney, R. V., Ruiz-Holguin, R., de Cosio, F., Ramos, R., Rodriguez, B., Beckles, G. L., . . . Thompson-Reid, P. (2010). A historical overview of the United States-Mexico border prevention and control projects. *Pan American Journal*, 28(3), 143–150.

Environmental Protection Agency (EPA). (2012, May 17). U.S.-Mexico border 2012. www.epa.gov: http://www.epa.gov/border2012/framework/background.html

Flores, L., & Kaplan, A. (2009). *Addressing the mental health problems of border and immigrant youth*. Los Angeles, CA: National Child Traumatic Stress Network, Substance Abuse and Mental Health Services Administration.

Foreyt, J. P. (2003). Cultural competence in the prevention and treatment of obesity: Latino Americans. In *Weight management and obesity symposium* (pp. 42–45). Portland, OR: Permanente Journal.

Grineski, S. (2011). Why parents cross for children's health: Transnational cultural capital in the United States-Mexico border region. *Social Theory & Health*, 9, 256–274.

Grineski, S. E., & Collins, T. W. (2010). Environmental injustices in transnational context: Urbanization and industrial hazards in El Paso/Ciudad Juárez. *Environment and Planning*, 42(6), 1308–1327.

Grineski, S. E., Collins, T. W., de Lourdes Romo Aguilar, M., & Aldouri, R. (2010). No safe place: Environmental hazards and injustices along Mexico's northern border. *Social Forces*, 88(5), 2241–2266.

Grineski, S. E., & Juárez-Carrillo, P. M. (2012). Environmental injustice in the U.S.-Mexico border region. In M. Lusk, K. Staudt, & E. Moya (Eds.), *Social justice in the U.S.-Mexico border region* (pp. 179–198). Dordrecht, Netherlands: Springer (e-book).

Heyman, J. M., Nunez, G. G., & Talavera, V. (2009). Healthcare access and barriers for unauthorized immigrants in El Paso County, Texas. *Family & Community Health, 32*(1), 4–21.

INEGI. (2010). Mexico City: Instituto Nacional de Estadística y Geografía.

Jasso, G., Massey, D. S., Rosenzweig, M. R., & Smith, J. P. (2004). Immigrant health: Selectivity and acculturation. *National Academy of Science Conference on Racial and Ethnic Disparities in Health,* 2–48.

Jiménez, T. R. (2010). *Replenished Ethnicity: Mexican Americans, Immigration, and Identity.* Berkeley, CA: University of California Press.

Kochanek, K. D., Xu, J., Murphy, S. L., Miniño, A. M., & Kung, H. (2011). Deaths: Preliminary Data for 2009. *National Vital Statistics Reports, 59*(4), 1–51.

Krug, E. G., Dahlberg, L. L., Mercy, J. A., Zwi, A. B., & Lozano, R. (2002). *World report on violence and health.* Geneva, Switzerland: World Health Organization. http://www.who.int/violence_injury_prevention/violence/world_report/en/introduction.pdf.

La Fe Policy and Advocacy Center (2006). The U.S./Mexico Border: Demographic, Socio-Economic, and Health Issues Profile1. San Antonio, TX: La Fe Policy and Advocacy Center.

Latino Coalition for Healthy Californians. (2006). *Obesity in Latino communities.* Sacramento, CA: Author.

Massey, D. S., Durand, J., & Malone, N. J. (2002). Beyond smoke and mirrors mexican immigration in an era of economic integration.

Maxwell, J. C., Cravioto, P., Galván, F., Ramírez, M. C., Wallisch, L., & Spence, R. T. (2006). Drug use and risk of HIV/AIDS on the Mexico-USA border: A comparison of treatment admissions in both countries. *Drug and Alcohol Dependence, 82*(suppl 1), 85–93.

McDonald, Y. (2012). *Lacking a connection to a community water system: Water quality and human health impacts in El Paso colonias.* Doctoral dissertation, University of Texas at El Paso. http://digitalcommons.utep.edu/dissertations/AAI1512587

Mohai, P., Pellow, D., & Roberts, J. (2009). Environmental justice. *Annual Review of Environment and Resources, 34*(1), 405–430.

Moya, E. M., & Lusk, M. (2009). Two case studies in El Paso, Texas, and Ciudad Juárez, Mexico. *Professional Development, 12*(3), 48–58.

Moya, E., & Shedlin, M. (2008). Policies and laws affecting Mexican-origin immigrant access and utilization of substance abuse treatment: Obstacles to recovery and immigrant health. *Substance Use & Misuse, 43*(12–13), 1747–1769.

Murphy, S. L., Xu, J., & Kochanek, K. D. (2012). Deaths: Preliminary Data for 2010. Hyattsville: United States Department of Health and Human Services.

Ogden, C. L., Lamb, M. M., Carroll, M. D., & Flegal, K. M. (2010). *Obesity and socio-economic status in adults: United States 2005–2008.* Atlanta, GA: Centers for Disease Control and Prevention.

Olvera, H. A., Li, W. W., & Garcia, H. (2012). *Air quality characterization at the Mexican customs inspection area at the International Bridge of the Americas.* Under review.

Olvera, H., Lopez, M., Guerrero, V., Garcia, H., & Li, W. W. (2013). Ultrafine particle levels at an international port of entry between the U.S. and Mexico: Exposure implications for users, workers, and neighbors. *Journal of Exposure Science and Environmental Epidemiology* (advance online publication).

Pan American Health Organization (PAHO). (2005). The U.S. Mexico Border Diabetes Prevention and Control Project: First report of results. http://www.dshs.state.tx.us/WorkArea/DownloadAsset.aspx?id=21327

Pan American Health Organization (PAHO). (2012, May 21). Situation analysis issues and challenges. http://new.paho.org/fep/index.php?option=com_joomlabook&Itemid=259&task=display&id=88

Rivera, J. O., Ortiz, M., Lawson, M. E., & Verma, K. M. (2002). Evaluation of the use of complementary and alternative medicine in the largest United States-Mexico border city. *Pharmacotherapy, 22*(2), 256–264.

Salaam-Blyther, T. (2008). *Tuberculosis: International efforts and issues for Congress.* Washington, DC: Congressional Research Service. http://www.fas.org/sgp/crs/misc/RL34246.pdf

Secretaría de Salud (2012). Seguro Popular. Comisión Nacional de Protección Social en Salud. Retrieved from http://www.seguro-popular.salud.gob.mx/index.php?option=com_content&view=article&id=272&Itemid=286.

SINAIS. (2011). *Causas de mortalidad 2008 Mexico City: Sistema Nacional de Informacion de Sauld, Secretaria de Salud.* Secretaria de Salud.

Texas Department of State and Health Services. (2010b). *Hepatitis C plan: Report to the 82nd Legislature.* Austin, TX: Author. http://www.dshs.state.tx.us/hivstd/reports/HCVBiannualReport.pdf

Texas Department of State Health Services. (2011). *Tuberculosis in Texas.* Austin, TX: Author. http://www.dshs.state.tx.us/WorkArea/linkit.aspx?LinkIdentifier=id&ItemID=8589974032

Tomaka, L., Caire, M., & Soden, D. L. (2008). *Greater El Paso Chamber of Commerce community mental health survey.* El Paso, TX: IPED Technical Reports.

Turra, C. M., & Goldman, N. (2007) Socioeconomic differences in mortality among U.S. adults: Insights into the Hispanic paradox. *Journal of Gerontology: Social Sciences, 62*(3), S184–S192.

United States Census Bureau. (2010a). County populations. http://quickfacts.census.gov/qfd/index.html.

United States Census Bureau. (2010b). Interactive population map. http://www.census.gov/2010census/popmap/

United States Census Bureau. (2012a). 2006-2010 5-year American Community Survey. Washington, DC: United States Census Bureau.

United States Census Bureau. (2012b). Census Bureau: Quickfacts. http://quickfacts.census.gov/qfd/states/00000.html

United States Department of Agriculture (USDA). (2012). Home: Creating access to healthy, affordable food: Food deserts. http://apps.ams.usda.gov/food deserts/foodDeserts.aspx

United States-Mexico Border Health Commission. (2010). *Healthy border 2010.* El Paso, TX: United States-Mexico Border Health Commission.

Washington Valdez, D. (2011). Hispanics grow to 82 percent of county population, *El Paso Times.* Retrieved from http://www.elpasotimes.com/news/ci_17418626.

Chapter 6

Neighborhood Effects on Obesity among Racial-Ethnic Minorities: A Lifespan Approach

Akilah Dulin Keita and Lonnie Hannon

While the etiology of racial-ethnic disparities in obesity is complex, the scientific evidence clearly supports a link between neighborhood context and obesity among racial-ethnic minority groups. Although overweight and obesity prevalence have increased for all racial-ethnic groups, the rate of overweight and obesity among racial-ethnic minorities is disproportionately larger than that among non-Hispanic Whites (Ogden, Carroll, Kit, & Flegal, 2012; Schell & Gallo, 2012). This disparity may be due in part to the neighborhood contexts in which racial-ethnic minorities reside (Frank, Kerr, Sallis, Miles, & Chapman, 2008).

There are several plausible mechanisms through which neighborhood context contributes to the disproportionate prevalence of obesity among racial ethnic minorities. Prominent among them are neighborhood economic viability, built environment barriers, and social contexts. Often, racial-ethnic minorities are concentrated in racially segregated urban areas characterized by a large percentage of residents living below the poverty line (Subramanian, Chen, Rehkopf, Waterman, & Krieger, 2005; Williams & Collins, 2001; Wilson, 1987, 1996). This concentration of urban poverty resulted from the exodus of middle-class Blacks, Whites, and the working class to suburban areas, and the concomitant declines in inner-city industries (Wilson, 1987, 1996). With the out-migration of the economic base, small retailers and stores also shifted their resources to suburban areas (Dreier, Mollenkopf, & Swanstrom, 2001; Wilson, 1996). The resulting patterns of racial and economic residential segregation impeded access to essential obesity-preventing resources such as access to quality neighborhoods with environmental designs facilitative of physical activity, healthy food resources, and fewer neighborhood-based stressors (Pabayo, Belsky, Gauvin, & Curtis, 2011; Williams & Collins, 2001).

Low neighborhood-level and individual-level socioeconomic status may interact to amplify obesity risk for racial-ethnic minorities. Individuals in lower socioeconomic status contexts report greater exposure to chronic social stressors, greater severity of stressors, and more daily hassles (Bak, Tanggaard Andersen, Bacher, & Draghiciu Bancila, 2012; Gruenewald, Cohen, Matthews, Tracy, & Seeman, 2009; McEwen, 1998; Muennig, Sohler, & Mahato, 2007; Myers, 2009). Exposure to such stressors may lead to allostatic load—the chronic overactivity or underactivity of allostatic systems (i.e., the hypothalamic-pituitary-adrenal axis, the autonomic nervous system, insulin, the immune system, and the metabolic system's thyroid axis) that are responsible for maintenance of the body during times of stress (McEwen, 1998). Repeated activation of these systems results in prolonged circulation of stress hormones and inflammatory cytokines that may increase obesity (Bird et al., 2010; Diez Roux, 2003; Diez-Roux et al., 2001; Maes et al., 1998; McDade, Hawkley, & Cacioppo, 2006; McEwen, 1998; Nordstrom, Diez Roux, Jackson, & Gardin, 2004; Rod, Gronbaek, Schnohr, Prescott, & Kristensen, 2009; Smith, Hart, Watt, Hole, & Hawthorne, 1998; van Lenthe & Mackenbach, 2002). The mechanisms through which low neighborhood socioeconomic status creates barriers to health-promoting opportunities and increased stressor exposures may contribute to the disproportionately higher rates of obesity observed among racial-ethnic minorities.

The built environment, which refers to "human-formed, developed or structured areas" (Centers for Disease Control and Prevention, 2005), may impact attitudes toward health behaviors and obesity risk for racial-ethnic minorities (Gordon-Larsen, Nelson, Page, & Popkin, 2006). In impoverished areas, health-promoting infrastructures such as recreational facilities and parks are often underutilized whether due to safety concerns or absence of such facilities (Dreier et al., 2001; Heinrich et al., 2008; Motl et al., 2005; Powell, Slater, Mirtcheva, Bao, & Chaloupka, 2007; Romero, 2005). In addition to these factors, neighborhood design, presence and quality of sidewalks, and traffic density may affect participation in neighborhood-based physical activity. Neighborhoods that are more walkable may promote walking and physical activity, which help to maintain a healthy body weight (Franzini et al., 2010; Hannon, Sawyer, & Allman, 2012). However, research findings indicate that in racial-ethnic minority neighborhoods, many built environment barriers to physical activity exist. For example, one study indicated that predominantly African-American neighborhoods in St. Louis, Missouri, were more likely to have uneven and obstructed sidewalks and physical disorders (Kelly, Schootman, Baker, Barnidge, & Lemes, 2007). The absence of these health-promoting resources may lead to physical inactivity, which may become internalized as a collective lifestyle within neighborhoods (Boardman, Saint Onge, Rogers, & Denney, 2005).

Neighborhood-based food outlets function as resources for healthy dietary intake and are instrumental in preventing weight gain and obesity for racial-ethnic minorities. Research findings suggest that supermarkets stock twice the number of healthy foods found in neighborhood grocery stores and four times the average number of healthy foods found in convenience stores (Morland, Wing, Diez Roux, & Poole, 2002; Sallis, Nader, Rupp, Atkins, & Wilson, 1986). Most often, however, racial-ethnic minorities are concentrated in urban environments where supermarkets are less accessible than those available in higher-income, racially diverse, or White neighborhoods (Leung et al., 2011). When stores of the same type are located in economically depressed neighborhoods, there is less availability of foods, limited selection, and higher prices than those in more affluent neighborhoods (Zenk et al., 2005). In one study, Zenk and colleagues (2005) found that suburban store location was associated with reports of greater selection and quality of foods, whereas stores located in African-American neighborhoods were inferior to their suburban counterparts and tended to have poorer quality and selection. Another study found that supermarkets were four times more plentiful in White neighborhoods than in Black neighborhoods, a disparity that had significant consequences for dietary intake (Morland et al., 2002). Cumulatively, studies suggest that less access to supermarkets is associated with self-reported lower intakes of fruits and vegetables, lower levels of serum carotenoids (biomarkers of fruit and vegetable intake), higher intakes of meat, lower fish intakes, and poorer overall diet quality (Diez-Roux et al., 1999; Moore & Diez Roux, 2006; Stimpson, Nash, Ju, & Eschbach, 2007). The work of Morland and colleagues (2002) revealed that among Black adults, every additional supermarket available in the neighborhood is associated with a 32% increase in fruit and vegetable intake. These findings suggest that the protective effects of supermarket and healthy food availability and accessibility clearly operate to protect against poor diet quality and obesity among racial-ethnic minority adults.

The density of fast-food restaurants is another factor that may make it easier to consume excess calories, thereby increasing weight gain and obesity risk among racial-ethnic minorities (Cohen, Finch, Bower, &

Sastry, 2006). Although research suggests that on a national level, full-service and fast-food restaurants are more prevalent in ZIP codes with a larger proportion of White and suburban areas, there are some significant differences in access (Powell, Auld, Chaloupka, O'Malley, & Johnston, 2007). Within predominantly Black urban ZIP codes, there is a significantly higher proportion of fast-food restaurants compared to predominantly White urban neighborhoods (Powell, Auld, et al., 2007). However, there do not appear to be significant differences in the types of restaurants found in predominantly Hispanic and White ZIP codes (Powell, Auld, et al., 2007). Findings from the Atherosclerosis Risk in Communities study also suggest that food service places of all types are more common in predominantly White census tracts or racially mixed neighborhoods than in Black neighborhoods (Morland et al., 2002). Studies conducted in more geographically limited areas also suggest that there is increased density of fast-food restaurants in predominantly Black census tracts (Block, Scribner, & DeSalvo, 2004) and that communities of low socioeconomic status have 2.5 times more fast-food restaurants relative to the highest-socioeconomic-status communities (Reidpath, Burns, Garrard, Mahoney, & Townsend, 2002).

To compensate for the reduced levels of goods and resources in their neighborhoods, racial-ethnic minority inner-city residents often must travel outside of their neighborhoods to engage in leisure activity and to access quality stores and services (Wilson, 1996). These structural constraints may limit opportunities for increased fruit and vegetable intake and may contribute to the unhealthier diets that are associated with high obesity rates among racial-ethnic minorities.

The social milieu of the neighborhood may partially explain the increased risk of obesity among racial-ethnic minorities (Cohen et al., 2006; Fitzpatrick & LaGory, 2000). In neighborhoods with high levels of social and physical disorder, the resources that can promote healthy behaviors are mostly absent. Socially disordered neighborhoods are associated with characteristics such as fights, public drinking or drug use, crime, incivility, and physical characteristics such as decaying buildings, pervasive litter, graffiti, and vandalism (Cohen et al., 2000; Ross & Mirowsky, 1999; Sampson, Raudenbush, & Earls, 1997; Wilson & Kelling, 1989). When residents see cues of social and physical disorder, they perceive that crime rates are higher and fear for their own victimization (Ross & Mirowsky, 1999; Wilson & Kelling, 1989). In turn, residents may modify their behavior by refraining from navigating public spaces through measures such as avoiding public parks, keeping their children indoors, and isolating themselves from their neighbors to protect against victimization (Sampson, 2003; Villarreal & Silva, 2006; Wilson & Kelling, 1989). Crime and disruption are further allowed to flourish because the socially disordered neighborhood lacks collective efficacy, whereby people do not share strong social ties with their neighbors—thus reducing the likelihood that informal social controls will monitor and sanction any negative activities that might occur within the neighborhood (Cohen et al., 2006; Franzini et al., 2010; Wilson, 1987). This contributes to the development of subcultures and beliefs that are not conducive to healthy outcomes (Fitzpatrick & LaGory, 2000, 2010). Collectively, these factors indicate how the economic, physical, and social aspects of place have real consequences for health and may be significant drivers of the disproportionate obesity prevalence among racial ethnic minorities.

The Evidence for Neighborhood Effects on Obesity: A Lifespan Approach

Children

United States Census-level neighborhood characteristics such as socioeconomic status and residential racial segregation may be significant factors related to increased obesity prevalence for racial-ethnic minority children. Kimbro and Denney (2012) analyzed data from a nationally representative sample of 21,400 kindergarten students to examine whether neighborhood context was associated with increased odds of obesity. Their research findings indicated that Black, Hispanic, and Asian children lived in higher-poverty areas compared to White children (23.3%, 18.2%, and 13.0%, respectively, versus 8.7%), and Black and Hispanic children were more likely to reside in racially segregated areas. Among this sample of kindergarten children, individual-level characteristics explained the Black-White disparity in the odds of obesity; in contrast, among Hispanic children, some variance was left unexplained. Nevertheless, neighborhood socioeconomic status was not significantly associated with increased odds of obesity among kindergarten-age Hispanic children. While neighborhood socioeconomic status was not significant, living in a neighborhood with a high proportion of non-Hispanic Blacks was significantly associated with increased odds of obesity among kindergarteners regardless of race, whereas living in a neighborhood with a higher concentration of Hispanic and foreign-born residents was protective against obesity.

Merten (2010) examined the associations between community-level economic disadvantage and obesity among a racially diverse sample of 13,907 adolescent participants from Wave 1 of the National Longitudinal Study of Adolescent Health. Although no race-stratified analyses were conducted, the sample was 42% non-White (21% Black, 15% Hispanic, 6% Asian, and 1% Native-American). The findings suggested that in addition to African-American, Hispanic, and Native-American race/ethnicity, community economic disadvantage was significantly related to adolescent obesity. Wickrama and colleagues (2006) conducted race-stratified analyses of the effects of neighborhood-level poverty on obesity among 20,000 adolescent participants in the National Longitudinal Study of Adolescent Health. The study findings suggested that overweight and obesity prevalence were highest among Native-Americans, African-Americans, Hispanics, and Asians in poorer communities. Although the difference was significant, African-Americans in poor communities were only 5% more likely to be obese than African-Americans in nonpoor communities. Similar results were found among Hispanic children. Asian-American children had the lowest overall prevalence of obesity and were less likely to be obese despite community type. A different study examined the relative contribution of neighborhood socioeconomic status to adolescent body mass index (BMI) among a sample that included 42% African-American adolescents. The study findings suggested that neighborhood socioeconomic status predicted adolescent BMI even after controlling for individual-level measures of income and wealth (Chen & Paterson, 2006).

Racial-ethnic minority children may be more likely to engage in obesity-preventive behaviors such as physical activity if their neighborhood built environments are supportive of this type of activity. Research findings suggest that neighborhood design (e.g., better sidewalks, quality and access to recreational facilities, housing density, traffic safety, and neighborhood walkability) is a significant factor that affects children's participation in physical activity and their obesity risk (Carver, Timperio, & Crawford, 2008; Grafova, 2008; Kipke et al., 2007). However, these relationships operate differently among children and adolescents. Among preschool-age children, there is inconsistent support for the relationships among playground access, crime rates, and BMI (Burdette & Whitaker, 2004; Sturm & Datar, 2005). Among a sample of fifth-graders who participated in the Healthy Passages Study, the research findings suggested that there were no significant differences in accessibility of physical activity-promoting resources, residential density, and environment type in Black and Latino neighborhoods relative to White neighborhoods. However, Black and Latino neighborhoods were perceived as less safe by children residing in these areas, and the neighborhood sidewalks were in worse condition (Franzini et al., 2010). Evenson and colleagues (2007) examined the relationship between the built environment and physical activity among a sample of adolescent girls. Their study sample was racially and ethnically diverse (3.9% Asian, Native-Hawaiian or Pacific Islander, 21% Black, 0.7% Native-American, 7.2% multiracial, and 22% Hispanic) and included 1,554 sixth-grade girls who participated in the Trial of Activity in Adolescent Girls Study. The findings suggested that neighborhood built environment factors such as streetlights and recreational facility access were associated with greater non-school-related physical activity participation.

One study involving a nationally representative sample of adolescent participants in the Monitoring the Future Surveys (14% African-American, 14% Hispanic, 4% Asian, and 6% other race) indicated that low street connectivity and less physical disorder were inversely associated with overweight and obesity, whereas urban sprawl was positively associated with overweight and obesity (Slater et al., 2010). Norman and colleagues (2010) also examined the associations of the built environment with adolescent physical activity and obesity. Their study sample included adolescents who resided in San Diego County, California and was racially and ethnically diverse (13% Hispanic, 6% African-American, 3% Asian or Pacific Islander, and 20% multiracial/multiethnic). The study revealed that girls living in residential areas with cul-de-sacs were more physically active than girls in neighborhoods with more parks, vacant acreage, and high-density residential areas. There were no significant effects of the neighborhood built environment type on physical activity among boys. However, the proportion of obesity was highest among boys and girls residing in the areas of highest residential density.

Several studies that included nationally representative samples of children and longitudinal designs have examined relationships among the built environment, physical activity, and obesity. Among a nationally representative sample of children that included Black and Hispanic participants in the Child Development Supplement of the Panel Study of Income Dynamics (PSID), physical disorder and living in a neighborhood built after 1969 were associated with increased odds of overweight (Grafova, 2008). Using a longitudinal study design, Wolch and colleagues (2011) examined whether proximity to neighborhood parks and recreational facilities affected the incidence of childhood obesity among participants in the Southern California Children's Health Study. The participants in this study were racially and ethnically diverse and included Hispanic, Asian-American, and African-American children who were aged 9–10 years at baseline. After collecting data over an eight-year period, the researchers found that having access to a park within a 500-meter distance from the child's home was negatively associated with BMI at age 18. Additionally, having a recreational program within 10 kilometers (6.2 miles) from the child's home was inversely associated with BMI at age 18. Significant gender differences in these associations were observed, with access to recreational programs being more strongly associated with BMI for boys than for girls. The effect size of access to recreational programming translated into –0.19 lower BMI unit for males and –0.1 lower BMI unit for females. Ewing, Brownson, and Berrigan (2006) also examined the cross-sectional and longitudinal relationships between urban sprawl and obesity among adolescents who participated in the National Longitudinal Survey of Youth. Their sample was 26% non-Hispanic Black, 21.2% Hispanic, and 3.5% other race. Urban sprawl was measured by six

indicators of residential density and street accessibility. The study findings indicated significant cross-sectional associations between urban
sprawl and overweight and obesity. However, urban sprawl was not
associated with longitudinal changes in BMI.

The built environment also influences to some extent the degree to
which racial-ethnic minority children have access to healthy food options.
However, studies examining the link between resident proximity to food
outlets and obesity risk among children are inconclusive. Study findings
among racially/ethnically diverse samples of preschool-age children provide equivocal results for fast-food restaurant effects on BMI (Burdette &
Whitaker, 2004; Sturm & Datar, 2005). However, among a nationally
representative sample of children who participated in the Child Development Supplement of the PSID, density of convenience food stores was
associated with increased odds of overweight among children (Grafova,
2008). Galvez and colleagues (2009) examined the relationships between
neighborhood food store availability and childhood obesity among a
diverse sample of young Hispanic and Black children residing in East
Harlem, New York. While more than 65% of the children resided in census
blocks that did not have specialty stores, grocery stores, or restaurants,
these factors were not significantly related to obesity. However, children
in neighborhoods with one or more convenience stores were significantly
more likely to be classified into the 97th or greater BMI percentile (indicative of obesity). The research of Davis and Carpenter (2009) also identified
significant relationships between food outlet type and obesity for adolescents. Among adolescents in California, fast-food proximity to schools
was associated with obesity, and this relationship was particularly
marked for African-American adolescents. Another study suggested that
closer proximity to neighborhood supermarkets was protective against
obesity, particularly among African-American adolescents relative to their
White or Hispanic counterparts (Powell, Auld, et al., 2007). These age-
related differences are important and likely reflect differences in food
access and transportation; young children are typically more reliant on
their parents to provide food resources, whereas adolescents have greater
independence and decision making in regard to their food choices (Cardel
et al., 2012; Contento, Williams, Michela, & Franklin, 2006). However, adolescents experience geographic limitations in mobility and are likely to
depend on the local environment for food items, which may play a role
in the significant associations between the built food environment and
obesity among racial-ethnic minority adolescents (Cradock, Melly, Allen,
Morris, & Gortmaker, 2009).

Neighborhood social contexts such as perceptions of the social environment and collective efficacy—the ability of neighborhood residents to
establish and address collective goals—may contribute to declines in
physical activity and high levels of obesity among racial-ethnic minority

children (Burdette, Wadden, & Whitaker, 2006; Cohen et al., 2006; Sampson, 2003; Sampson et al., 1997). Racial-ethnic minorities are more likely to reside in low-income urban areas that are more socially disordered and include elements such as graffiti, crime, heightened feelings of insecurity (lack of safety), and lower levels of collective efficacy (Bishaw, 2005; Cubbin, Pedgregon, Egerter, & Braveman, 2008). Romero (2005) examined the relationship between neighborhood context and physical activity resources among a sample of predominantly Mexican-American adolescents in low-income neighborhoods. Findings from this particular study concluded that perceptions of feeling unsafe in the neighborhood and unsafe at the neighborhood recreational facilities were barriers to physical activity participation (Romero, 2005). Among a racially diverse sample of adolescent girls (approximately 40% African-American) who resided in South Carolina, perceived neighborhood safety was not associated with physical activity over a one-year period (Motl et al., 2005). However, this null finding may not represent true neighborhood effects, as the mean level of perceived neighborhood safety was high. It is possible that if there was more variation in perceptions of safety among this particular sample of adolescent girls, significant associations might have been identified (Motl et al., 2005). Other studies that have included objectively measured physical activity levels also indicate that neighborhood safety and disorder might not be associated with child and adolescent physical activity (Adkins, Sherwood, Story, & Davis, 2004). Evenson and colleagues (2007) assessed the relationship between neighborhood factors and BMI for adolescent girls who participated in the trial of Activity in Adolescent Girls Study. Their findings suggested that neighborhood factors such as reduced crime and seeing other children playing outside were associated with lower BMI. These results suggest that while perceived neighborhood social disorder may decrease feelings of safety and participation in physical activity, population density on the streets may provide a buffering effect against neighborhood disorder (Evenson et al., 2007). Although the findings of Evenson and colleagues indicate that the influence of neighborhood factors is minimal among adolescent girls, neighborhood effects are important and may operate to protect adolescent girls from increased obesity.

While many studies have examined perceptions of neighborhood safety and social order and the effects on obesity among racial-ethnic minority children, fewer studies have addressed the associations of neighborhood collective efficacy with physical activity and obesity. The available literature indicates that among a random sample that included Black and Hispanic children who participated in the Los Angeles Family and Neighborhood Survey, low-neighborhood collective efficacy was associated with 64% higher odds of overweight and 52% higher odds of obesity compared to adolescents residing in neighborhoods with average levels of collective efficacy (Cohen et al., 2006). Similar findings have been obtained in nationally representative samples. Grafova's (2008) work indicates that among a nationally representative sample of children (including Hispanic and Black children) who participated in the Child Development Supplement of the PSID, low levels of perceived neighborhood informal social controls (e.g., informal social surveillance by neighbors) were associated with increased odds of being overweight.

In summary, while some studies have not found significant relationships between neighborhood context and obesity among racial-ethnic minority children, the preponderance of the evidence underscores that neighborhood contexts—whether economic, demographic, built, or social—are associated with participation in physical activity, diet, and obesity. Although the neighborhood associations with obesity findings are overwhelmingly significant, these relationships are understudied among subsets of the population. Further research examining the effects of neighborhood context on obesity among Asian, Pacific Islander, Native-Hawaiian, Alaska Native, and American-Indian children and adolescents is warranted to fully understand the impact of neighborhood context among all racial-ethnic minority children.

Young and Middle-Aged Adults

There may be race/gender-specific differences in the relationship between neighborhood-level indicators of economic status (conceptually referred to as disadvantage, deprivation, income inequality, education, employment status, or socioeconomic status) and BMI among adults, yet the findings on this point are inconsistent. Study findings suggest that neighborhood effects on obesity tend to be stronger and more significant for women and either weak or not statistically significant for men (Chichlowska et al., 2008; Coogan et al., 2010; Robert & Reither, 2004; Rundle et al., 2008; van Lenthe & Mackenbach, 2002). Robert and Reither (2004) indicated that among Black and White women who participated in the Americans Changing Lives Study, community-level economic disadvantage and income inequality partially explained the Black/non-Black disparity in obesity among women. However, there was no evidence that community-level factors explained obesity differences between Black and White men, possibly because there were no statistically significant differences in BMI between Black and White men at baseline. A follow-up report analyzed longitudinal data from women participants in the American Changing Lives Study and indicated that while baseline community disadvantage was associated with baseline BMI among Black women, it did not predict changes in BMI over time (Ruel, Reither, Robert, & Lantz, 2010). Coogan, Cozier, and colleagues (2010) examined the longitudinal effects of neighborhood socioeconomic status on weight gain and

BMI among participants in the Black Women's Health Study. This study included more than 59,000 Black women who were aged 21–69 at baseline and who had BMI data at the 10-year follow-up. The findings suggested that for the overall sample there was an inverse relationship between neighborhood socioeconomic status and weight gain. Also, low neighborhood socioeconomic status was associated with increased 10-year incidence of obesity among Black women who were normal weight at baseline (BMI < 25 kg/m^2).

Studies that include samples of Latinos also suggest that there are racial/gender differences in the relationships between neighborhood socioeconomic status and obesity. One investigation that included Mexican-American participants in the San Antonio Heart Study indicated that among men, neighborhood socioeconomic status was not significantly associated with overweight or obesity. However, among women, neighborhood type was significant and linearly related to obesity: women who lived in low-income Mexican-American neighborhoods had a higher prevalence of overweight and obesity than women who lived in upper-income predominantly non-Hispanic White suburban areas (Hazuda, Mitchell, Haffner, & Stern, 1991). Wen and Maloney (2011) examined the relationship of neighborhood socioeconomic status on obesity among Latinos residing in Utah. Their findings indicated that neighborhood socioeconomic status was inversely associated with obesity among both men and women. While the evidence offers some support for race/gender-specific effects, the literature is largely inconclusive—which is perhaps due to differences in measurement of neighborhood-level socioeconomic status.

Findings from other nationally representative studies also provide conflicting evidence regarding the effects of neighborhood economic status on obesity among racial-ethnic minorities. Do and colleagues (2007) examined whether neighborhood socioeconomic status contexts were associated with obesity among a nationally representative sample of participants in the National Health and Nutrition Examination Survey. The research findings suggested that neighborhood disadvantage and neighborhood-level education were significantly associated with BMI among Mexican-American females and males. However, among Black females and males, these neighborhood factors were not significantly associated with BMI. Nationally representative data from the Atherosclerosis Risk in Communities study also supported these null findings and suggested that neighborhood-level socioeconomic status was not significantly associated with large waist circumference among Black men and women (Chichlowska et al., 2008).

While the previously mentioned studies used a cross-sectional design, longitudinal studies have also provided conflicting results. Mujahid and colleagues (2005) analyzed longitudinal data from the Atherosclerosis Risk in Communities study to examine neighborhood effects on BMI among Black males and females. Their findings indicated that among

Black women, neighborhood socioeconomic status was inversely associated with BMI. However, among Black men, neighborhood socioeconomic status was positively associated with BMI. Over time, BMI increased across all neighborhood socioeconomic status categories, and there did not appear to be clear and consistently significant longitudinal effects of neighborhood socioeconomic status on BMI.

Thus the general literature on neighborhood socioeconomic status and obesity among racial-ethnic minorities is inconsistent, and the relationships between neighborhood socioeconomic status and obesity do not always operate in the posited directions. Additional research is needed to understand these varying relationships and to examine the associations among racial and ethnic minority populations aside from Blacks and Hispanics.

Some research has sought to elucidate the reasons for the lack of significant associations or clear patterns of neighborhood-level socioeconomic status effects on obesity among racial-ethnic minority adults. The available evidence that attempts to disentangle these complex relationships has examined only samples of African-Americans. The work of Miles and colleagues (2008) sought to provide clarity to these relationships by examining whether rates of walking and obesity differed significantly between two African-American neighborhoods with different levels of neighborhood disadvantage and physical activity resources. The results suggested that there were no statistically significant differences in physical activity or obesity between the two neighborhoods. The researchers hypothesized that the expectations of a middle-class lifestyle and the resultant constraints on time may have been barriers to participation in obesity-preventing behaviors. Instead of a neighborhood comparative analysis, Laveist and colleagues (2011) conducted a review of neighborhood effects on obesity among a racially integrated low-income community in southwest Baltimore, Maryland. The community met the following select criteria: (1) the community was at least 35% African-American and 35% White; (2) the ratio of Black-to-White median incomes was 0.85 to 1.15; and (3) the ratio of Black-to-White high school graduation rates was 0.85 to 1.15. The study authors compared national data from the National Health Interview Survey with obesity data from Black and White women in southwest Baltimore. Their findings suggested that there were no appreciable differences in the odds of obesity between Black and White women residing in southwest Baltimore. However, additional research is needed to understand the lack of clear and consistent effects of neighborhood socioeconomic status on obesity among Latino and Black adults.

The majority of studies that examine neighborhood socioeconomic status and obesity employ a cross-sectional design and include exclusively Black and/or Latino populations. Black and Macinko (2010) attempted to address these limitations by examining neighborhood-level effects on obesity status among participants in the New York City Community Health Survey, which included 48,506 adults residing in 34 unique neighborhoods. The study sample was racially/ethnically diverse and included individuals who self-reported as Black/African (22.7%), Hispanic/Latino (24.83%), Asian/Pacific Islander (10.11%), or 3.4% other race/ethnicity. The study results suggested that neighborhood area income was associated with decreased obesity among women but not among men. Overall, the general findings from this investigation warrant further attention, as researchers need to build further evidence through longitudinal and population-based assessments of neighborhood socioeconomic status on obesity and should also oversample understudied racial-ethnic minority populations.

Research indicates that neighborhood race-based residential segregation (measured by isolation index, proportions of racial-ethnic minorities in the neighborhood, and concentration of immigrants) may be related to obesity (Wen & Maloney, 2011). Wen and Maloney (2011) found that after controlling for neighborhood built environment and socioeconomic status characteristics among Latino men and women residing in Utah, Latino racial residential isolation was positively associated with obesity, whereas immigrant concentration was inversely associated with obesity. Drenowski and colleagues (2007) examined the relationship between residential segregation and obesity among individuals in King County in Washington State. The researchers found that percentage of the total population that was Hispanic within a ZIP code was significantly associated with increased obesity. However, among a racially and ethnically diverse sample of low-income female participants in the WISEWOMAN Study, residential racial segregation—measured by the degree to which members of each racial-ethnic group in the community were exposed more to one another than to members of other racial-ethnic groups—was not significantly related to BMI for American-Indian, Asian, Hispanic, or Black women (Mobley et al., 2006).

Results from the work of Robert and Reither (2004) indicated that among a sample of Black and White women participants in the Americans Changing Lives Study, higher concentration of Black residents in the community was not significantly associated with obesity among women. In contrast, another study that assessed nationally representative data on Black adults in the United States suggested that residential segregation was significantly associated with obesity (Boardman et al., 2005). This investigation found that neighborhood characteristics were associated with higher rates of obesity among predominantly African-American neighborhoods than among non-African-American neighborhoods. Racial concentration among African-Americans was significantly associated with obesity, such that 20% of the race effect in obesity disparities was due to concentration of Blacks in the neighborhood. While this observed effect in part reflected the concentration of poverty among African-Americans in residential areas, rates of obesity remained high among nonpoor African-American neighborhoods even when compared to poor non-African-American communities.

Do and colleagues (2007) examined whether neighborhood-level proportion Black and proportion Hispanic measurements were associated with obesity among both Black and Hispanic adults. They found that both neighborhood-level proportion Black and proportion Hispanic were significantly associated with BMI among Mexican-American females. Among Mexican-American males, proportion Hispanic was associated with obesity but not proportion Black. For Black adults, these neighborhood indicators were not significantly associated with BMI among females and were marginally significant for males.

Chang (2006) analyzed data from the Centers for Disease Control and Prevention's 2000 Behavioral Risk Factor Surveillance System survey for Black and White adults. The findings concluded that among non-Hispanic Blacks, a one standard deviation increase in racial isolation increased BMI by 0.423 unit and led to a 14% increase in the odds of overweight. Another study conducted by Chang and colleagues (2009) that examined racial segregation and obesity further supported these relationships. The results from this cross-sectional study concluded that when neighborhood racial isolation was accounted for, the difference in BMI between Black women and White women was reduced by 26%, and the difference was reduced by 18% between Latina women and White women. However, there were no significant associations between Black racial isolation and BMI among men. These findings suggest that residential segregation plays a significant role in obesity among racial-ethnic minority adults, whereas concentration of immigrants in a community may protect against obesity.

In racial-ethnic minority neighborhoods, the built environment characteristics that facilitate physical activity and reduce obesity risk are often absent, limited, or of lower quality (Hannon et al., 2012; Lovasi, Hutson, Guerra, & Neckerman, 2009; Romero, 2005). Ainsworth and colleagues (2003) found that among a sample of 917 African-American women residing in South Carolina, the lack of sidewalks and high traffic density were barriers to participation in physical activity. Another study that included African-American, Latina, and American-Indian women participating in the Women's Cardiovascular Health Network Project suggested that the presence of sidewalks was significantly associated with meeting physical activity recommendations for African-American women but not for Latina or American-Indian women (Eyler et al., 2003). Duarte and colleagues (2010) examined whether urban physical environment characteristics (e.g., interviewer-observed indicators of graffiti; decay; boarded-up, vacant, and abandoned buildings) were associated with BMI among a racially and ethnically diverse sample of mother/child dyads. Across groups, the physical environment was associated with BMI among non-Hispanic Black mothers, but the association was not statistically significant for Hispanic mothers.

Studies that include samples of both men and women also suggest that built environment characteristics are associated with physical activity. The research of Fan et al. (2011) suggested that among a sample of predominantly Black and Hispanic adults in Chicago, every 1% increase in park acreage within the neighborhood was associated with a 0.024% increase in physical activity. Although the effect was modest, the findings suggested a direct association between neighborhood greenness (as measured by park acreage in the neighborhood) and physical activity, which is a key health-promoting strategy to maintain a healthy body weight. Among a sample of 900 Hispanic adults in low-income border communities in Texas, living in a less residential area was positively associated with BMI (Rutt & Coleman, 2005). However, among Black adults in metropolitan Atlanta, there was no association between urban design (i.e., street connectivity, net residential density, and land-use mix) and BMI (Frank, Andresen, & Schmid, 2004). For Black and Hispanic participants in the New York Cancer Project, built environment neighborhood characteristics such as population density and bus access were inversely associated with BMI for Black adults, whereas population density, public transit use, subway access, and bus access were inversely related to BMI for Hispanics (Lovasi, Neckerman, Quinn, Weiss, & Rundle, 2009). Mujahid et al. (2008) examined the relationships of neighborhood built environment features and obesity among Multi-ethnic Study of Atherosclerosis study participants. This study mostly enrolled racial-ethnic minorities (27.7% African-American, 11.8% Chinese American, and 22% Hispanic). The study findings indicated that a better walking environment was associated with lower BMI among women and men. However, these relationships were attenuated after accounting for individual-level health behaviors. Nevertheless, the results suggest that built environment impediments to physical activity are significant factors that affect obesity for racial-ethnic minorities.

Nationally representative studies also provide support for the relationship among physical activity, built environment characteristics, and obesity. Among a nationally representative sample of racially and ethnically diverse adults (29.4% Black, 2.1% Asian-American, 2.7% American-Indian, and 11.4% other), lack of walking trails and heavy neighborhood traffic were associated with increased odds of obesity (Joshu, Boehmer, Brownson, & Ewing, 2008). Analysis of data from the National Health and Nutrition Examination Survey (which included 11.7% Black and 13.4% Hispanic participants) also concluded that the built environment was significantly associated with obesity; however, these features did not explain racial-ethnic disparities between Whites, Blacks, and Hispanics (Wen & Kowaleski-Jones, 2012). While this study's conclusions were based on a racial comparative analysis between Whites and racial-ethnic minorities, the work of Miles et al. (2008) examined whether rates of walking and obesity significantly differed between two African-American neighborhoods with differing levels of neighborhood disadvantage and physical activity resources. The results suggested that there were no statistically significantly differences in leisure walking and physical activity. Among participants in both neighborhoods, the majority of participants were classified as sedentary. The researchers hypothesized that middle-class lifestyle and the resultant constraints on time may have been barriers to physical activity that prevented participation in physical activity despite the safer and cleaner neighborhood environment.

While some studies have examined participant-reported perceptions of the built environment and objective indicators, very few have investigated these outcomes concurrently. Boehmer and colleagues (2007) examined whether perceived and observed neighborhood characteristics were associated with obesity among urban adults residing in St. Louis, Missouri, and Savannah, Georgia. The research project included data from a sample that was 32% non-Hispanic Black. Although the researchers measured objective indicators such as the density of recreational facilities and nonresidential destinations, access to public transit, and street safety, these factors were not significantly related to obesity. In fact, the hypothesized inverse association between recreational facilities and obesity operated in the reverse direction for women. The indicators of observed neighborhood characteristics that were of significance suggested that observed indicators of poor sidewalk quality, physical disorder, and garbage were associated with obesity. The perceived indicators of poor aesthetics and perceptions of the lack of sidewalks were also associated with obesity. The overall findings from the built environment literature suggest that removing neighborhood built environment characteristics that are barriers to physical activity may result in significant increases in health-promoting behaviors that reduce obesity risk for racial-ethnic minority adults.

Additional built environment studies have examined whether neighborhood food environments explain the disproportionately higher prevalence of obesity among racial-ethnic minority adults. Rundle and colleagues (2009) examined the relationship between food outlet type and obesity among a sample of participants in the New York Cancer Project, which included a large percentage of racial-ethnic minority adults (20% Hispanic, 12% Asian, 19% Black, and 2% other). Their results suggested that the density of healthy food outlets that are protective against obesity was greater in affluent and majority-White neighborhoods, whereas there were lower densities of such food sources in majority-Black and majority-Latino neighborhoods. After adjustments were made for neighborhood sociodemographic characteristics and population density, density of BMI-healthy foods was found to be inversely associated with obesity.

Inagami and colleagues (2006) analyzed data from the Los Angeles Family and Neighborhood Study (58% Hispanic) to identify whether the interactions among grocery store location, neighborhood disadvantage, and car ownership affected weight status. Their findings indicated that frequenting grocery stores in disadvantaged neighborhoods and increased distance to grocery stores among car owners were both associated with higher BMI. Another study that analyzed participant data from the Los Angeles Family and Neighborhood Study identified significant associations between the concentration of restaurants and obesity (Inagami, Cohen, Brown, & Asch, 2009). Although fast-food restaurant density was not associated with obesity among the participants, there was a significant interactive effect between car ownership and neighborhood fast-food outlet density such that individuals who did not own cars and lived in areas with a high concentration of fast-food outlets had higher BMI relative to their counterparts who owned cars.

Mujahid et al. (2008) examined the relationship between the neighborhood food environment and obesity among Multi-ethnic Study of Atherosclerosis participants (27.7% African-American, 11.8% Chinese American, and 22% Hispanic). Their findings indicated that the availability of healthy foods was associated with a lower BMI among women and men. Another study examined the associations between neighborhood food environments and obesity among individuals in the southern region of the United States, where obesity prevalence is the highest among all U.S. regions (Morland & Evenson, 2009). The study sample was 38% African-American, and the results suggested that having at least one supermarket in the census tract was associated with a 0.73 lower prevalence of obesity. Conversely, access to small grocery stores or more than one fast-food restaurant in the area was associated with increased prevalence of obesity.

The primary evidence for neighborhood food environments' effects on obesity is cross-sectional in nature, and review articles specific to racial-ethnic minority populations are limited. The work of Black and Macinko (2010), however, examined longitudinal relationships among participants in the New York City Community Health Survey. Their results suggested that although neighborhood vulnerability (as measured by availability of small grocers, emergency food providers, violent crime, and percentage Black residents) was not significantly associated with obesity, greater availability of food stores (i.e., large supermarkets, smaller grocers, restaurants, beverage/snack stores, and emergency food providers) was associated with decreased obesity.

A comprehensive review of the literature on the roles of the built environment and obesity within racial-ethnic minority populations concluded that changing the neighborhood food environment, providing places to exercise, and improving safety would have the greatest impacts on reducing obesity among these populations (Lovasi, Hutson, et al., 2009). These findings suggest that multiple aspects of the built environment interact and amplify the propensity to become obese, and that improvements in the healthy food and physical activity environments are needed to induce substantial obesity reduction effects among racial-ethnic minority adults.

While the majority of the neighborhood research examines objective indicators of sociodemographic characteristics and the built environment, perceived social contexts may also significantly affect physical activity and obesity risk for racial-ethnic minority adults (Boslaugh, Luke, Brownson, Naleid, & Kreuter, 2004). Among a multiethnic sample of African-American, Latina, and American-Indian women who participated in the Women's Cardiovascular Health Network Project, it was found that seeing people exercising in the neighborhood was associated with physical activity participation for both American-Indian and African-American women, but not Latina women (Eyler et al., 2003). Ainsworth and colleagues (2003) also found that among a randomly selected sample of 917 African-American women residing in South Carolina, seeing people exercise in the neighborhood was associated with physical activity.

In addition to neighborhood-level social norms for physical activity, perceptions of neighborhood safety may affect physical activity. Perceptions of safety were associated with physical activity participation among a subsample of urban African-American women (Eyler et al., 2003). In contrast, the work of Ross (2000) found that although poorer people reported more neighborhood-related fears of victimization, they were more likely to walk in the neighborhood than people in wealthier neighborhoods; however, this tendency may also reflect their limited transportation means. These findings suggest that neighborhood perceptions may be significant barriers to participation in physical activity.

Additional research on perceived social contexts supports a relationship between these contexts and obesity for racial-ethnic minority adults. Among participants in the WISEWOMAN Study, increased crime rates were associated with higher BMI (Mobley et al., 2006). Burdette and colleagues (2006) examined these associations among women participants in the Fragile Families and Well Being Study; their sample was 52% non-Hispanic Black, 25% Hispanic, and 3% other race. The findings suggested that relative to women in the safest neighborhoods, obesity prevalence was 9 percentage points higher among women in the least safe neighborhoods. In contrast, neighborhood collective efficacy was not significantly associated with BMI or obesity prevalence in this sample.

Other studies have examined these relationships for both men and women. The research of Fish and colleagues (2010) supports a relationship between perceived neighborhood safety and obesity risk. These investigators examined data from the Los Angeles Family and Neighborhood Survey, which included a sample that was 73% non-White (55% Latino, 9% Black, 8% Asian or Pacific Islander, and 1% Native-American) and 54% first-generation immigrants. Among these individuals, perceived neighborhood safety was associated with a 2.81 kg/m^2 increase in BMI relative to participants who perceived their neighborhoods as safe.

Burdette and Hill (2008) tested a conceptual model that posited that the effects of perceived neighborhood disorder on obesity would be mediated by psychological and physiological distress, poorer diet quality, and irregular exercise. Their study sample included 19% Mexican/Mexican-American, 5% other Hispanic, 7% African-American, and 5% other racial-ethnic minority participants from the 2004 Survey of Texas adults. The results from this cross-sectional study suggested that neighborhood disorder was significantly associated with obesity, with this relationship being mediated by psychological and physiological distress and poor self-rated overall diet quality. However, irregular exercise did not appear to be a significant mediator of the relationship between perceived neighborhood disorder and obesity. These general study findings suggest that perceptions of the neighborhood environment are important factors that affect obesity risk among racial-ethnic minority adults.

Older Adults

Very few studies have assessed the relationships among neighborhood contexts, health behaviors, and obesity among older adults (King et al., 2011), and even fewer have examined these relationships among racial-ethnic minority older adults. The available literature provides conflicting evidence for the significance of neighborhood characteristics and obesity among racial-ethnic minority older adults. The research findings from King et al. (2011) suggested that among participants in the Senior Neighborhood Quality of Life Study (28% non-White), neighborhood-level income was associated with participation in moderate and vigorous physical activity and lower BMI. However, among participants in the Baltimore Memory Study (41% African-American), there were weak or nonsignificant associations between neighborhood economic deprivation and the odds of obesity for both Black and White older adults (Glass, Rasmussen, & Schwartz, 2006). In contrast, study results from a nationally representative sample of older adults who participated in the Health and Retirement Study (who included Hispanics and Blacks) indicated that after controlling for neighborhood-level disadvantage and high-density areas, neighborhood economic advantage was significantly associated with lower odds of obesity for both men and women (Grafova, Freedman, Kumar, & Rogowski, 2008).

Other studies have examined gender-specific associations of neighborhood economic context with physical activity and obesity. Dubowitz and colleagues (2012) examined the associations of neighborhood socioeconomic status and obesity among 68,132 participants in the Women's Health Initiative Clinical Trial who were aged 50–79 years at baseline (11% Black, 4.5% Hispanic, and 4.1% other). Neighborhood socioeconomic status was associated with BMI such that as neighborhood socioeconomic status increased from the 10th to 90th percentile of its distribution, BMI was lowered by 1.26 kg/m^2. Also, there is scant evidence for an association between neighborhood demographic characteristics and obesity among older adults. Only one study has addressed these relationships among a nationally representative sample of older adults. Among women participants in the Health and Retirement Study, no significant relationship was found between neighborhood-level immigrant concentration and obesity. For men, however, living in an area with a high concentration of immigrants was associated with increased odds of obesity (Grafova et al., 2008).

The effects of the built environment on participation in physical activity and obesity may be of greater significance for racial-ethnic minority older adults, as aging-related limitations in mobility and cognitive decline may significantly reduce the social space that they navigate (Li, Fisher, Brownson, & Bosworth, 2005; Yen, Michael, & Perdue, 2009). However, study findings are inconclusive, with some investigations suggesting that the built environment influences physical activity among older adults whereas others do not (Berke, Koepsell, Moudon, Hoskins, & Larson, 2007; Frank, Kerr, Rosenberg, & King, 2010; King et al., 2005). Frank et al. (2010) found that among older adults, built environment factors such as street block length, multiple route choices and destinations, neighborhood aesthetics, presence of sidewalks, and recreational facilities were associated with leisure-based walking activity among older adults.

Hannon and colleagues (2012) also examined the associations of the built environment and leisure-time physical activity among a large sample of older adults residing in the southern region of the United States. They conceptualized housing characteristics as a key component of the built environment. In a cross-sectional study of older adults, these researchers found a significant and independent positive association with housing characteristics such as homeownership and occupancy rate with leisure-time physical activity among rural African-Americans. However, this relationship was not significant among urban African-Americans. A possible explanation for this finding is the higher rate of renters in urban African-American communities, who tend to be more transient and as a result may be less connected to their neighborhood. Another explanation offered by Hannon et al. (2012) is that fewer homeownership opportunities exist for urban African-Americans given the historical and current economic inequality experienced by this group. Furthermore, a review article conducted by Yen et al. (2009) that summarized the evidence from cross-sectional studies strongly supports a role of neighborhood built environment characteristics on walking behavior.

Additional studies have sought to extend the research on physical activity-promoting elements of the built environment by examining this environment's associations with both physical activity and obesity. The work of Frank et al. (2010) revealed that highly walkable neighborhoods in the Atlanta metropolitan region were associated with more walking and lower odds of being overweight among older adults. Another study examined the neighborhood psychosocial hazards of the built environment—such as calls to city agencies about street problems and the number of off-site liquor licenses—and their relationship to obesity among Baltimore Memory Study participants (Glass et al., 2006). The findings indicated that these neighborhood psychosocial hazards were associated with 52% to 96% increased odds of obesity among participants in the Baltimore Memory Study.

Another study suggested, however, that the effects of the built environment on physical activity and obesity may be gender specific. Among a nationally representative sample of adults age 55 and older who participated in the Health and Retirement Study (including Hispanic and Black older adults), built environment features such as street connectivity were significant for women only, such that low street connectivity was associated with obesity (Grafova et al., 2008).

While many studies rely on self-reported levels of physical activity, King et al. (2011) included objectively measured assessments of physical activity in their work. They found that among participants in the Senior Neighborhood Quality of Life Study (28% non-White), neighborhood walkability was marginally associated with moderate-to-vigorous physical activity, was significantly associated with meeting the national recommendations for physical activity, and was significantly associated with lower BMI among older adults. There was, on average, a one-unit difference in BMI (equivalent to 6 pounds) between older adults in higher-walkable versus lower-walkable neighborhoods. A longitudinal study that included African-American older adults also lends support to these cross-sectional relationships. Li, Harmer, Cardinal, Bosworth, Johnson-Shelton, et al. (2009) assessed the relationship between neighborhood walkability, BMI, and waist circumference over a one-year period among participants in the Portland Neighborhood Environment and Health Study. Their findings indicated that neighborhood walkability was associated with a 1.2-kilogram decrease in weight and a 1.57-centimeter decrease in waist circumference.

Research studies of the built environment have also examined the relationships between food outlets and obesity among older adults. Li, Harmer, Cardinal, Bosworth, & Johnson-Shelton (2009) found that, net of neighborhood socioeconomic and demographic characteristics, fast-food restaurant density was associated with an increased likelihood of obesity among older non-Hispanic Black adults in Oregon. The findings from this study, which assessed these relationships over a one-year, suggested that a high density of fast-food outlets was associated with a 1.4-kilogram increase in weight and a 2.04-centimeter increase in waist circumference among residents who frequently visited fast-food restaurants. Dubowitz and colleagues (2012) examined the cross-sectional associations of grocery store/supermarket availability and neighborhood socioeconomic status on BMI among participants in the Women's Health Initiative Clinical Trial (11% Black, 4.5% Hispanic, and 4.1% other). Their findings suggested that as availability of grocery stores/supermarkets increased from the 10th to 90th percentile of their distribution, BMI was lowered by 0.30 kg/m^2. Similar, but opposite, relationships were found between fast-food outlet availability and BMI, such that as fast-food outlet availability increased from the 10th to 90th percentile of its distribution, BMI was increased by 0.28 kg/m^2. These findings suggest that the built environment may significantly affect obesity among older adults, particularly as they experience significant aging-related declines in mobility.

Few studies have examined the relationships of neighborhood context on obesity status among older adults. The available evidence suggests that neighborhoods appear to affect obesity among this population (Grafova et al., 2008). However, significantly more research on aspects of the different neighborhood contexts and obesity outcomes among racial-ethnic minority older adults needs to be conducted to examine how the aging process and neighborhood contexts interact to affect obesity.

Neighborhood-Level Interventions

A growing area of research interest seeks to understand whether neighborhood contexts moderate the effects of individual-level health behavior interventions or whether neighborhood-level interventions promote healthier behaviors and reduce obesity risk for racial-ethnic minorities. The majority of the evidence in this growing field examines the built environment aspects of neighborhoods. One study examined whether built environment factors moderated the effects of a walking intervention for a diverse sample of women (64% African-American and 36% Latina) (Lee, Mama, Medina, Ho, & Adamus, 2012). Among Latina and African-American women participating in the intervention, built environment characteristics significantly interacted with the walking intervention. Factors such as traffic control devices that favor walkability (e.g., stop signs, streetlights, and crossing aids) were significantly associated with adoption and maintenance of physical activity for women relative to the control group. Another study examined health behavior changes among women and men in San Diego County, California (approximately 30%

non-White), who were randomized into either a control group or a health behavior change group (increased walking and nutrition) (Kerr et al., 2010). In this study, low traffic safety was associated with decreased walking over time for women. However, neighborhood walkability was associated with changes in walking behaviors over time, such that men and women in the low-walkable neighborhoods actually increased their walking time more so than individuals in highly walkable areas did. These research findings suggest that individuals in low-walkable neighborhoods may have received more beneficial effects from the intervention and may have learned strategies that would help moderate neighborhood barriers to physical activity.

Additional studies have focused on how urban planning and changing the built environments to facilitate physical activity may promote the adoption of healthier behaviors and prevent obesity. Smart Growth Communities—which are based on the principles of compact building design (e.g., lower housing density), walkable neighborhoods (e.g., sidewalk requirements), sense of place (e.g., areas for interaction among residents), mixed land uses (e.g., commercial and residential), and open space—are well-established factors shown to be more favorable to physical activity promotion within neighborhoods (Dunton, Intille, Wolch, & Pentz, 2012). Dunton and colleagues (2012) examined whether Smart Growth Community design affected physical activity levels among a sample of children (32% Hispanic, 15% biracial, 9.5% Asian, 8.5% African-American, and 7.4% other race). They concluded that although the types of physical activity differed between children residing in Smart Growth Communities relative to the control group, increases in physical activity did not differ significantly between the two groups. While this evidence is contrary to the goals of Smart Growth Communities, the researchers suggest that the six-month study duration may not have allowed enough time for the Smart Growth Communities to directly impact children's physical activity levels. In contrast to these findings, a review study found that changes to the built environment—such as increasing access to physical activity resources including trails and bicycle paths—were associated with increased physical activity, which in turn was associated with lower obesity (Foster et al., 2006).

The research project known as Moving to Opportunity focused on the impacts of changing economic contexts and their potential influences on obesity among low-income women (Kling, Liebman, & Katz, 2004; Ludwig et al., 2011). Moving to Opportunity, which was sponsored by the U.S. Department of Housing and Urban Development, was a quasi-experimental study of 4,498 women with children who resided in public housing (approximately 65% Black, 28.1% other non-White, and 31.5% Hispanic in the low-poverty voucher group). The families were randomly selected to participate in one of three groups: (1) 1,788 families were assigned to receive Section 8 housing vouchers that could be redeemed only if the family moved to a low-poverty census tract (i.e., an area with a poverty rate of less than 10%) and received housing counseling; (2) 1,312 families received a Section 8 housing voucher where they could move to any neighborhood but did not receive counseling; and (3) 1,398 families were assigned to be an in-place control group who did not receive any vouchers or counseling. Compared to the control groups, the group who moved to low-poverty neighborhoods had a 20% reduction in the risk of being obese. Although the other families who received Section 8 vouchers had lower rates of obesity, they were not statistically different from the control group (Kling et al., 2004).

Ludwig and colleagues (2011) analyzed follow-up data from the Moving to Opportunity project and examined the obesity data from the follow-up survey (2008–2010). Their findings suggested that the prevalence of class 2 and class 3 obesity (BMI greater than 35 kg/m^2 or 40 kg/m^2, respectively) was significantly lower among women who received the low-poverty vouchers than women in the control group. There were no significant differences between the other families who received Section 8 vouchers and the control group. Collectively, these findings suggest that, as additional policy and urban planning strategies are implemented to modify neighborhood environments in favor of physical activity and healthy food intake, there may be significant reductions in the disproportionate prevalence of obesity among racial-ethnic minorities.

While significant neighborhood effects on obesity among racial-ethnic minorities have been identified in many studies, other studies have yielded null findings. This inconsistency in findings may be due to measurement issues at the neighborhood level. As many research studies suggest, the heterogeneity in measurement and definition of neighborhoods, the built environment, the social environment, and economic indicators may preclude agreement in the literature about the strength of neighborhood effects on obesity and health-promoting behaviors (Boone-Heinonen, Popkin, Song, & Gordon-Larsen, 2010; Carter & Dubois, 2010; Diez Roux & Mair, 2010; Ding & Gebel, 2012; Feng, Glass, Curriero, Stewart, & Schwartz, 2010; Papas et al., 2007). Thus, as future work assesses the effects of the neighborhood environment on physical activity, dietary context, and obesity status among racial-ethnic minorities, consensus as to the most appropriate neighborhood measurements is warranted.

References

Adkins, S., Sherwood, N. E., Story, M., & Davis, M. (2004). Physical activity among African-American girls: The role of parents and the home environment. *Obesity Research, 12*(suppl), 38S–45S.

Ainsworth, B. E., Wilcox, S., Thompson, W. W., Richter, D. L., & Henderson, K. A. (2003). Personal, social, and physical environmental correlates of physical activity in African-American women in South Carolina. *American Journal of Preventive Medicine, 25*(3 suppl 1), 23–29.

Bak, C. K., Tanggaard Andersen, P., Bacher, I., & Draghiciu Bancila, D. (2012). The association between socio-demographic characteristics and perceived stress among residents in a deprived neighbourhood in Denmark. *European Journal of Public Health, 22*(6), 787–792.

Berke, E. M., Koepsell, T. D., Moudon, A. V., Hoskins, R. E., & Larson, E. B. (2007). Association of the built environment with physical activity and obesity in older persons. *American Journal of Public Health, 97*(3), 486–492.

Bird, C. E., Seeman, T., Escarce, J. J., Basurto-Davila, R., Finch, B. K., Dubowitz, T., . . . Lurie, N. (2010). Neighbourhood socioeconomic status and biological "wear and tear" in a nationally representative sample of US adults. *Journal of Epidemiology and Community Health, 64*(10), 860–865.

Bishaw, A. (2005). Areas with concentrated poverty: 1999. http://www.census.gov/prod/2005pubs/censr-16.pdf

Black, J. L., & Macinko, J. (2010). The changing distribution and determinants of obesity in the neighborhoods of New York City, 2003–2007. *American Journal of Epidemiology, 171*(7), 765–775.

Block, J. P., Scribner, R. A., & DeSalvo, K. B. (2004). Fast food, race/ethnicity, and income: A geographic analysis. *American Journal of Preventive Medicine, 27*(3), 211–217.

Boardman, J. D., Saint Onge, J. M., Rogers, R. G., & Denney, J. T. (2005). Race differentials in obesity: The impact of place. *Journal of Health and Social Behavior, 46*(3), 229–243.

Boehmer, T. K., Hoehner, C. M., Deshpande, A. D., Brennan Ramirez, L. K., & Brownson, R. C. (2007). Perceived and observed neighborhood indicators of obesity among urban adults. *International Journal of Obesity, 31*(6), 968–977.

Boone-Heinonen, J., Popkin, B. M., Song, Y., & Gordon-Larsen, P. (2010). What neighborhood area captures built environment features related to adolescent physical activity? *Health Place, 16*(6), 1280–1286.

Boslaugh, S. E., Luke, D. A., Brownson, R. C., Naleid, K. S., & Kreuter, M. W. (2004). Perceptions of neighborhood environment for physical activity: Is it "who you are" or "where you live"? *Journal of Urban Health, 81*(4), 671–681.

Burdette, A. M., & Hill, T. D. (2008). An examination of processes linking perceived neighborhood disorder and obesity. *Social Science and Medicine, 67*(1), 38–46.

Burdette, H. L., Wadden, T. A., & Whitaker, R. C. (2006). Neighborhood safety, collective efficacy, and obesity in women with young children. *Obesity (Silver Spring), 14*(3), 518–525.

Burdette, H. L., & Whitaker, R. C. (2004). Neighborhood playgrounds, fast food restaurants, and crime: Relationships to overweight in low-income preschool children. *Preventive Medicine, 38*(1), 57–63.

Cardel, M., Willig, A. L., Dulin-Keita, A., Casazza, K., Beasley, T. M., & Fernandez, J. R. (2012). Parental feeding practices and socioeconomic status are associated with child adiposity in a multi-ethnic sample of children. *Appetite, 58*(1), 347–353.

Carter, M. A., & Dubois, L. (2010). Neighbourhoods and child adiposity: A critical appraisal of the literature. *Health Place, 16*(3), 616–628.

Carver, A., Timperio, A. F., & Crawford, D. A. (2008). Neighborhood road environments and physical activity among youth: The CLAN study. *Journal of Urban Health, 85*(4), 532–544.

Centers for Disease Control and Prevention. (2005). Perceptions of neighborhood characteristics and leisuretime physical inactivity—Austin/Travis County, Texas, 2004. *Morbidity and Mortality Weekly Report, 54*, 926–928.

Chang, V. W. (2006). Racial residential segregation and weight status among US adults. *Social Science and Medicine, 63*(5), 1289–1303.

Chang, V. W., Hillier, A. E., & Mehta, N. K. (2009). Neighborhood racial isolation, disorder and obesity. *Social Forces, 87*(4), 2063–2092.

Chen, E., & Paterson, L. Q. (2006). Neighborhood, family, and subjective socioeconomic status: How do they relate to adolescent health? *Health Psychology, 25*(6), 704–714.

Chichlowska, K. L., Rose, K. M., Diez-Roux, A. V., Golden, S. H., McNeill, A. M., & Heiss, G. (2008). Individual and neighborhood socioeconomic status characteristics and prevalence of metabolic syndrome: The Atherosclerosis Risk in Communities (ARIC) study. *Psychosomatic Medicine, 70*(9), 986–992.

Cohen, D. A., Finch, B. K., Bower, A., & Sastry, N. (2006). Collective efficacy and obesity: The potential influence of social factors on health. *Social Science and Medicine, 62*(3), 769–778.

Cohen, D., Spear, S., Scribner, R., Kissinger, P., Mason, K., & Wildgen, J. (2000). "Broken windows" and the risk of gonorrhea. *American Journal of Public Health, 90*(2), 230–236.

Contento, I. R., Williams, S. S., Michela, J. L., & Franklin, A. B. (2006). Understanding the food choice process of adolescents in the context of family and friends. *Journal of Adolescent Health, 38*(5), 575–582.

Coogan, P. F., Cozier, Y. C., Krishnan, S., Wise, L. A., Adams-Campbell, L. L., Rosenberg, L., & Palmer, J. R. (2010). Neighborhood socioeconomic status in relation to 10-year weight gain in the Black Women's Health Study. *Obesity (Silver Spring), 18*(10), 2064–2065.

Cradock, A. L., Melly, S. J., Allen, J. G., Morris, J. S., & Gortmaker, S. L. (2009). Youth destinations associated with objective measures of physical activity in adolescents. *Journal of Adolescent Health, 45*(3 suppl), S91–S98.

Cubbin, C., Pedgregon, V., Egerter, S., & Braveman, P. (2008). Where we live matters for our health: Neighborhoods and health. http://www.rwjf.org/files/research/commissionneighborhood102008.pdf

Davis, B., & Carpenter, C. (2009). Proximity of fast-food restaurants to schools and adolescent obesity. *American Journal of Public Health, 99*(3), 505–510.

Diez-Roux, A. V. (2003). Residential environments and cardiovascular risk. *Journal of Urban Health, 80*(4), 569–589.

Diez-Roux, A. V., Kiefe, C. I., Jacobs, D. R. Jr., Haan, M., Jackson, S. A., Nieto, F. J., . . . Schulz, R. (2001). Area characteristics and individual-level socioeconomic position indicators in three population-based epidemiologic studies. *Annals of Epidemiology, 11*(6), 395–405.

Diez-Roux, A. V., & Mair, C. (2010). Neighborhoods and health. *Annals of the New York Academy of Sciences, 1186*(1), 125–145.

Diez-Roux, A. V., Nieto, F. J., Caulfield, L., Tyroler, H. A., Watson, R. L., & Szklo, M. (1999). Neighbourhood differences in diet: The Atherosclerosis Risk in Communities (ARIC) study. *Journal of Epidemiology and Community Health, 53*(1), 55–63.

Ding, D., & Gebel, K. (2012). Built environment, physical activity, and obesity: What have we learned from reviewing the literature? *Health Place, 18*(1), 100–105.

Do, D. P., Dubowitz, T., Bird, C. E., Lurie, N., Escarce, J. J., & Finch, B. K. (2007). Neighborhood context and ethnicity differences in body mass index: A multilevel analysis using the NHANES III survey (1988–1994). *Economics & Human Biology, 5*(2), 179–203.

Dreier, P., Mollenkopf, J., & Swanstrom, T. (2001). *Place matters: Metropolitics for the twenty-first century.* Lawrence, KS: University Press of Kansas.

Drewnowski, A., Rehm, C. D., & Solet, D. (2007). Disparities in obesity rates: Analysis by ZIP code area. *Social Science and Medicine, 65*(12), 2458–2463.

Duarte, C. S., Chambers, E. C., Rundle, A., & Must, A. (2010). Physical characteristics of the environment and BMI of young urban children and their mothers. *Health Place, 16*(6), 1182–1187.

Dubowitz, T., Ghosh-Dastidar, M., Eibner, C., Slaughter, M. E., Fernandes, M., Whitsel, E. A., & Escarce, J. J. (2012). The Women's Health Initiative: The food environment, neighborhood socioeconomic status, BMI, and blood pressure. *Obesity (Silver Spring), 20*(4), 862–871.

Dunton, G. F., Intille, S. S., Wolch, J., & Pentz, M. A. (2012). Investigating the impact of a smart growth community on the contexts of children's physical activity using Ecological Momentary Assessment. *Health Place, 18*(1), 76–84.

Evenson, K. R., Scott, M. M., Cohen, D. A., & Voorhees, C. C. (2007). Girls' perception of neighborhood factors on physical activity, sedentary behavior, and BMI. *Obesity (Silver Spring), 15*(2), 430–445.

Ewing, R., Brownson, R. C., & Berrigan, D. (2006). Relationship between urban sprawl and weight of United States youth. *American Journal of Preventive Medicine, 31*(6), 464–474.

Eyler, A. A., Matson-Koffman, D., Young, D. R., Wilcox, S., Wilbur, J., Thompson, J. L., . . . Evenson, K. R. (2003). Quantitative study of correlates of physical activity in women from diverse racial/ethnic groups: The Women's Cardiovascular Health Network Project: Summary and conclusions. *American Journal of Preventive Medicine, 25*(3 suppl 1), 93–103.

Fan, Y., Das, K. V., & Chen, Q. (2011). Neighborhood green, social support, physical activity, and stress: Assessing the cumulative impact. *Health and Place, 17*(6), 1202–1211.

Feng, J., Glass, T. A., Curriero, F. C., Stewart, W. F., & Schwartz, B. S. (2010). The built environment and obesity: A systematic review of the epidemiologic evidence. *Health Place, 16*(2), 175–190.

Fish, J. S., Ettner, S., Ang, A., & Brown, A. F. (2010). Association of perceived neighborhood safety with [corrected] body mass index. *American Journal of Public Health, 100*(11), 2296–2303.

Fitzpatrick, K. M., & LaGory, M. (2000). *Unhealthy places: The ecology of risk in the urban landscape.* New York, NY: Routledge.

Fitzpatrick, K., & LaGory, M. (2010). *Unhealthy cities: Poverty, race, and place in America.* New York, NY: Routledge.

Foster, C., Hillsdon, M., Cavill, N., Bull, F. C., Buxton, K., & Crombie, H. (2006). Interventions that use the environment to encourage physical activity: Evidence review. National Institutes of Health and Clinical Excellence. http://www.nice.org.uk/niceMedia/pdf/Physical_activity_Evidence_Review _FINAL.pdf

Frank, L. D., Andresen, M. A., & Schmid, T. L. (2004). Obesity relationships with community design, physical activity, and time spent in cars. *American Journal of Preventive Medicine, 27*(2), 87–96.

Frank, L., Kerr, J., Rosenberg, D., & King, A. (2010). Healthy aging and where you live: Community design relationships with physical activity and body weight in older Americans. *Journal of Physical Activity and Health, 7*(suppl 1), S82–S90.

Frank, L. D., Kerr, J., Sallis, J. F., Miles, R., & Chapman, J. (2008). A hierarchy of sociodemographic and environmental correlates of walking and obesity. *Preventive Medicine, 47*(2), 172–178.

Franzini, L., Taylor, W., Elliott, M. N., Cuccaro, P., Tortolero, S. R., Janice Gilliland, M., . . . Schuster, M. A. (2010). Neighborhood characteristics favorable to outdoor physical activity: Disparities by socioeconomic and racial/ethnic composition. *Health Place, 16*(2), 267–274.

Galvez, M. P., Hong, L., Choi, E., Liao, L., Godbold, J., & Brenner, B. (2009). Childhood obesity and neighborhood food-store availability in an inner-city community. *Academic Pediatrics, 9*(5), 339–343.

Glass, T. A., Rasmussen, M. D., & Schwartz, B. S. (2006). Neighborhoods and obesity in older adults: The Baltimore Memory Study. *American Journal of Preventive Medicine, 31*(6), 455–463.

Gordon-Larsen, P., Nelson, M. C., Page, P., & Popkin, B. M. (2006). Inequality in the built environment underlies key health disparities in physical activity and obesity. *Pediatrics, 117*(2), 417–424.

Grafova, I. B. (2008). Overweight children: Assessing the contribution of the built environment. *Preventive Medicine, 47*(3), 304–308.

Grafova, I. B., Freedman, V. A., Kumar, R., & Rogowski, J. (2008). Neighborhoods and obesity in later life. *American Journal of Public Health, 98*(11), 2065–2071.

Gruenewald, T. L., Cohen, S., Matthews, K. A., Tracy, R., & Seeman, T. E. (2009). Association of socioeconomic status with inflammation markers in Black and White men and women in the Coronary Artery Risk Development in Young Adults (CARDIA) study. *Social Science and Medicine, 69*(3), 451–459.

Hannon, L. 3rd, Sawyer, P., & Allman, R. M. (2012). The influence of community and the built environment on physical activity. *Journal of Aging and Health, 24*(3), 384–406.

Hazuda, H. P., Mitchell, B. D., Haffner, S. M., & Stern, M. P. (1991). Obesity in Mexican American subgroups: Findings from the San Antonio Heart Study. *American Journal of Clinical Nutrition, 53*(6 suppl), 1529S–1534S.

Heinrich, K. M., Lee, R. E., Regan, G. R., Reese-Smith, J. Y., Howard, H. H., Haddock, C. K., . . . Ahluwalia, J. S. (2008). How does the built environment relate to body mass index and obesity prevalence among public housing residents? *American Journal of Health Promotion, 22*(3), 187–194.

Inagami, S., Cohen, D. A., Brown, A. F., & Asch, S. M. (2009). Body mass index, neighborhood fast food and restaurant concentration, and car ownership. *Journal of Urban Health, 86*(5), 683–695.

Inagami, S., Cohen, D. A., Finch, B. K., & Asch, S. M. (2006). You are where you shop: Grocery store locations, weight, and neighborhoods. *American Journal of Preventive Medicine, 31*(1), 10–17.

Joshu, C. E., Boehmer, T. K., Brownson, R. C., & Ewing, R. (2008). Personal, neighbourhood and urban factors associated with obesity in the United States. *Journal of Epidemiology and Community Health, 62*(3), 202–208.

Kelly, C. M., Schootman, M., Baker, E. A., Barnidge, E. K., & Lemes, A. (2007). The association of sidewalk walkability and physical disorder with area-level race and poverty. *Journal of Epidemiology and Community Health, 61*(11), 978–983.

Kerr, J., Norman, G. J., Adams, M. A., Ryan, S., Frank, L., Sallis, J. F., . . . Patrick, K. (2010). Do neighborhood environments moderate the effect of physical activity lifestyle interventions in adults? *Health Place, 16*(5), 903–908.

Kimbro, R. T., & Denney, J. T. (2012). Neighborhood context and racial/ethnic differences in young children's obesity: Structural barriers to interventions. *Social Science and Medicine,* [Epub ahead of print.]

King, A. C., Sallis, J. F., Frank, L. D., Saelens, B. E., Cain, K., Conway, T. L., . . . Kerr, J. (2011). Aging in neighborhoods differing in walkability and income: Associations with physical activity and obesity in older adults. *Social Science and Medicine, 73*(10), 1525–1533.

King, W. C., Belle, S. H., Brach, J. S., Simkin-Silverman, L. R., Soska, T., & Kriska, A. M. (2005). Objective measures of neighborhood environment and physical activity in older women. *American Journal of Preventive Medicine, 28*(5), 461–469.

Kipke, M. D., Iverson, E., Moore, D., Booker, C., Ruelas, V., Peters, A. L., & Kaufman, F. (2007). Food and park environments: Neighborhood-level risks for childhood obesity in east Los Angeles. *Journal of Adolescent Health, 40*(4), 325–333.

Kling, J. R., Liebman, J. B., & Katz, L. F. (2004). Moving to Opportunity and tranquility: Neighborhood effects on adult economic self-sufficiency and health from a randomized housing voucher experiment. In N. B. E. R. Inc. (Ed.), *NBER working papers* (pp. 1–56). Cambridge, MA: Harvard University, John F. Kennedy School of Government.

Laveist, T., Pollack, K., Thorpe, R. Jr., Fesahazion, R., & Gaskin, D. (2011). Place, not race: Disparities dissipate in southwest Baltimore when Blacks and Whites live under similar conditions. *Health Affairs (Millwood), 30*(10), 1880–1887.

Lee, R. E., Mama, S. K., Medina, A. V., Ho, A., & Adamus, H. J. (2012). Neighborhood factors influence physical activity among African American and Hispanic or Latina women. *Health Place, 18*(1), 63–70.

Leung, C. W., Laraia, B. A., Kelly, M., Nickleach, D., Adler, N. E., Kushi, L. H., & Yen, I. H. (2011). The influence of neighborhood food stores on change in young girls' body mass index. *American Journal of Preventive Medicine, 41*(1), 43–51.

Li, F., Fisher, K. J., Brownson, R. C., & Bosworth, M. (2005). Multilevel modelling of built environment characteristics related to neighbourhood walking activity in older adults. *Journal of Epidemiology and Community Health, 59*(7), 558–564.

Li, F., Harmer, P., Cardinal, B. J., Bosworth, M., & Johnson-Shelton, D. (2009). Obesity and the built environment: Does the density of neighborhood fast-food outlets matter? *American Journal of Health Promotion, 23*(3), 203–209.

Li, F., Harmer, P., Cardinal, B. J., Bosworth, M., Johnson-Shelton, D., Moore, J. M., . . . Vongjaturapat, N. (2009). Built environment and 1-year change in weight and waist circumference in middle-aged and older adults: Portland Neighborhood Environment and Health Study. *American Journal of Epidemiology, 169*(4), 401–408.

Lovasi, G. S., Hutson, M. A., Guerra, M., & Neckerman, K. M. (2009). Built environments and obesity in disadvantaged populations. *Epidemiology Reviews, 31,* 7–20.

Lovasi, G. S., Neckerman, K. M., Quinn, J. W., Weiss, C. C., & Rundle, A. (2009). Effect of individual or neighborhood disadvantage on the association between neighborhood walkability and body mass index. *American Journal of Public Health, 99*(2), 279–284.

Ludwig, J., Sanbonmatsu, L., Gennetian, L., Adam, E., Duncan, G. J., Katz, L. F., ... McDade, T. W. (2011). Neighborhoods, obesity, and diabetes: A randomized social experiment. *New England Journal of Medicine, 365*(16), 1509–1519.

Maes, M., Song, C., Lin, A., De Jongh, R., Van Gastel, A., Kenis, G., ... Smith, R. S. (1998). The effects of psychological stress on humans: Increased production of pro-inflammatory cytokines and a Th1-like response in stress-induced anxiety. *Cytokine, 10*(4), 313–318.

McDade, T. W., Hawkley, L. C., & Cacioppo, J. T. (2006). Psychosocial and behavioral predictors of inflammation in middle-aged and older adults: The Chicago Health, Aging, and Social Relations Study. *Psychosomatic Medicine, 68*(3), 376–381.

McEwen, B. S. (1998). Protective and damaging effects of stress mediators. *New England Journal of Medicine, 338*(3), 171–179.

Merten, M. J. (2010). Parental health and adolescent obesity in the context of community disadvantage. *Health Place, 16*(5), 1053–1057.

Miles, R., Panton, L. B., Jang, M., & Haymes, E. M. (2008). Residential context, walking and obesity: Two African-American neighborhoods compared. *Health Place, 14*(2), 275–286.

Mobley, L. R., Root, E. D., Finkelstein, E. A., Khavjou, O., Farris, R. P., & Will, J. C. (2006). Environment, obesity, and cardiovascular disease risk in low-income women. *American Journal of Preventive Medicine, 30*(4), 327–332.

Moore, L. V., & Diez Roux, A. V. (2006). Associations of neighborhood characteristics with the location and type of food stores. *American Journal of Public Health, 96*(2), 325–331.

Morland, K. B., & Evenson, K. R. (2009). Obesity prevalence and the local food environment. *Health Place, 15*(2), 491–495.

Morland, K., Wing, S., Diez Roux, A., & Poole, C. (2002). Neighborhood characteristics associated with the location of food stores and food service places. *American Journal of Preventive Medicine, 22*(1), 23–29.

Motl, R. W., Dishman, R. K., Ward, D. S., Saunders, R. P., Dowda, M., Felton, G., & Pate, R. R. (2005). Perceived physical environment and physical activity across one year among adolescent girls: Self-efficacy as a possible mediator? *Journal of Adolescent Health, 37*(5), 403–408.

Muennig, P., Sohler, N., & Mahato, B. (2007). Socioeconomic status as an independent predictor of physiological biomarkers of cardiovascular disease: Evidence from NHANES. *Preventive Medicine, 45*(1), 35–40.

Mujahid, M. S., Diez Roux, A. V., Borrell, L. N., & Nieto, F. J. (2005). Cross-sectional and longitudinal associations of BMI with socioeconomic characteristics. *Obesity Research, 13*(8), 1412–1421.

Mujahid, M. S., Diez Roux, A. V., Shen, M., Gowda, D., Sanchez, B., Shea, S., ... Jackson, S. A. (2008). Relation between neighborhood environments and obesity in the Multi-Ethnic Study of Atherosclerosis. *American Journal of Epidemiology, 167*(11), 1349–1357.

Myers, H. F. (2009). Ethnicity- and socio-economic status-related stresses in context: An integrative review and conceptual model. *Journal of Behavioral Medicine, 32*(1), 9–19.

Nordstrom, C. K., Diez Roux, A. V., Jackson, S. A., & Gardin, J. M. (2004). The association of personal and neighborhood socioeconomic indicators with subclinical cardiovascular disease in an elderly cohort: The cardiovascular health study. *Social Science and Medicine, 59*(10), 2139–2147.

Norman, G. J., Adams, M. A., Kerr, J., Ryan, S., Frank, L. D., & Roesch, S. C. (2010). A latent profile analysis of neighborhood recreation environments in relation to adolescent physical activity, sedentary time, and obesity. *Journal of Public Health Management and Practice, 16*(5), 411–419.

Ogden, C. L., Carroll, M. D., Kit, B. K., & Flegal, K. M. (2012). Prevalence of obesity and trends in body mass index among US children and adolescents, 1999–2010. *Journal of the American Medical Association, 307*(5), 483–490.

Pabayo, R., Belsky, J., Gauvin, L., & Curtis, S. (2011). Do area characteristics predict change in moderate-to-vigorous physical activity from ages 11 to 15 years? *Social Science and Medicine, 72*(3), 430–438.

Papas, M. A., Alberg, A. J., Ewing, R., Helzlsouer, K. J., Gary, T. L., & Klassen, A. C. (2007). The built environment and obesity. *Epidemiology Reviews, 29*, 129–143.

Powell, L. M., Auld, M. C., Chaloupka, F. J., O'Malley, P. M., & Johnston, L. D. (2007). Associations between access to food stores and adolescent body mass index. *American Journal of Preventive Medicine, 33*(4 suppl), S301–S307.

Powell, L. M., Slater, S., Mirtcheva, D., Bao, Y., & Chaloupka, F. J. (2007). Food store availability and neighborhood characteristics in the United States. *Preventive Medicine, 44*(3), 189–195.

Reidpath, D. D., Burns, C., Garrard, J., Mahoney, M., & Townsend, M. (2002). An ecological study of the relationship between social and environmental determinants of obesity. *Health Place, 8*(2), 141–145.

Robert, S. A., & Reither, E. N. (2004). A multilevel analysis of race, community disadvantage, and body mass index among adults in the US. *Social Science and Medicine, 59*(12), 2421–2434.

Rod, N. H., Gronbaek, M., Schnohr, P., Prescott, E., & Kristensen, T. S. (2009). Perceived stress as a risk factor for changes in health behaviour and cardiac risk profile: A longitudinal study. *Journal of Internal Medicine, 266*(5), 467–475.

Romero, A. J. (2005). Low-income neighborhood barriers and resources for adolescents' physical activity. *Journal of Adolescent Health, 36*(3), 253–259.

Ross, C. E. (2000). Walking, exercising, and smoking: Does neighborhood matter? *Social Science and Medicine, 51*(2), 265–274.

Ross, C. E., & Mirowsky, J. (1999). Disorder and decay: The concept and measurement of perceived neighborhood disorder. *Urban Affairs Review, 34*(3), 412–432.

Ruel, E., Reither, E. N., Robert, S. A., & Lantz, P. M. (2010). Neighborhood effects on BMI trends: Examining BMI trajectories for Black and White women. *Health Place, 16*(2), 191–198.

Rundle, A., Field, S., Park, Y., Freeman, L., Weiss, C. C., & Neckerman, K. (2008). Personal and neighborhood socioeconomic status and indices of neighborhood walk-ability predict body mass index in New York City. *Social Science and Medicine, 67*(12), 1951–1958.

Rundle, A., Neckerman, K. M., Freeman, L., Lovasi, G. S., Purciel, M., Quinn, J., ... Weiss, C. (2009). Neighborhood food environment and walkability predict obesity in New York City. *Environmental Health Perspectives, 117*(3), 442–447.

Rutt, C. D., & Coleman, K. J. (2005). Examining the relationships among built environment, physical activity, and body mass index in El Paso, TX. *Preventive Medicine, 40*(6), 831–841.

Sallis, J. F., Nader, P. R., Rupp, J. W., Atkins, C. J., & Wilson, W. C. (1986). San Diego surveyed for heart-healthy foods and exercise facilities. *Public Health Reports, 101*(2), 216–219.

Sampson, R. J. (2003). The neighborhood context of well-being. *Perspectives in Biological Medicine, 46*(3 suppl), S53–S64.

Sampson, R. J., Raudenbush, S. W., & Earls, F. (1997). Neighborhoods and violent crime: A multilevel study of collective efficacy. *Science, 277*(5328), 918–924.

Schell, L. M., & Gallo, M. V. (2012). Overweight and obesity among North American Indian infants, children, and youth. *American Journal of Human Biology, 24*(3), 302–313.

Slater, S. J., Ewing, R., Powell, L. M., Chaloupka, F. J., Johnston, L. D., & O'Malley, P. M. (2010). The association between community physical activity settings and youth physical activity, obesity, and body mass index. *Adolescent Health, 47*(5), 496–503.

Smith, G. D., Hart, C., Watt, G., Hole, D., & Hawthorne, V. (1998). Individual social class, area-based deprivation, cardiovascular disease risk factors, and mortality: The Renfrew and Paisley Study. *Journal of Epidemiology and Community Health, 52*(6), 399–405.

Stimpson, J. P., Nash, A. C., Ju, H., & Eschbach, K. (2007). Neighborhood deprivation is associated with lower levels of serum carotenoids among adults participating in the Third National Health and Nutrition Examination Survey. *Journal of the American Dietetic Association, 107*(11), 1895–1902.

Sturm, R., & Datar, A. (2005). Body mass index in elementary school children, metropolitan area food prices and food outlet density. *Public Health, 119*(12), 1059–1068.

Subramanian, S. V., Chen, J. T., Rehkopf, D. H., Waterman, P. D., & Krieger, N. (2005). Racial disparities in context: A multilevel analysis of neighborhood variations in poverty and excess mortality among Black populations in Massachusetts. *American Journal of Public Health, 95*(2), 260–265.

van Lenthe, F. J., & Mackenbach, J. P. (2002). Neighbourhood deprivation and overweight: The GLOBE study. *International Journal of Obesity Related Metabolic Disorders, 26*(2), 234–240.

Villarreal, A., & Silva, B. F. A. (2006). Social cohesion, criminal victimization and perceived risk of crime in Brazilian neighborhoods. *Social Forces, 84*(3), 1725–1753.

Wen, M., & Kowaleski-Jones, L. (2012). The built environment and risk of obesity in the United States: Racial-ethnic disparities. *Health Place, 18*(6), 1314–1322.

Wen, M., & Maloney, T. N. (2011). Latino residential isolation and the risk of obesity in Utah: The role of neighborhood socioeconomic, built-environmental, and subcultural context. *Journal of Immigrant and Minority Health, 13*(6), 1134–1141.

Wickrama, K. A. T., Wickrama, K. A. S., & Bryant, C. M. (2006). Community influence on adolescent obesity: Race/ethnic differences. *Journal of Youth and Adolescence, 35*(4), 647–657.

Williams, D. R., & Collins, C. (2001). Racial residential segregation: A fundamental cause of racial disparities in health. *Public Health Reports, 116*(5), 404–416.

Wilson, J. Q., & Kelling, G. L. (1989). Broken windows. In R. G. Dunham & G. P. Alpert (Eds.), *Critical issues in policing: Contemporary readings* (pp. 369–381). Prospect Heights, IL: Waveland Press.

Wilson, W. J. (1987). *The truly disadvantaged*. Chicago, IL: University of Chicago Press.

Wilson, W. J. (1996). *When work disappears*. New York, NY: Alfred A. Knopf.

Wolch, J., Jerrett, M., Reynolds, K., McConnell, R., Chang, R., Dahmann, N., ... Berhane, K. (2011). Childhood obesity and proximity to urban parks and recreational resources: A longitudinal cohort study. *Health Place, 17*(1), 207–214.

Yen, I. H., Michael, Y. L., & Perdue, L. (2009). Neighborhood environment in studies of health of older adults: A systematic review. *American Journal of Preventive Medicine, 37*(5), 455–463.

Zenk, S. N., Schulz, A. J., Hollis-Neely, T., Campbell, R. T., Holmes, N., Watkins, G., ... Odoms-Young, A. (2005). Fruit and vegetable intake in African Americans: Income and store characteristics. *American Journal of Preventive Medicine, 29*(1), 1–9.

Chapter 7

Crowded Living Conditions, Health, and Well-Being

Andrew S. London and Chantell B. Frazier

An emergent body of sociological, demographic, and public health research focuses on socioeconomic status as a fundamental cause of health disparities (Chang & Lauderdale, 2009; Link & Phelan, 1995, 1996, 2010; Rubin, Colen, & Link, 2010; Warren & Hernandez, 2007). Fundamental cause theory and empirical research articulate the notion that the causal association between economic constraint and a broad range of negative health outcomes persists over historical time and across disparate geographic, epidemiological, economic, and social contexts, even though the pathways that link socioeconomic status to health might change. Although this perspective underscores the importance of addressing socioeconomic status inequalities as a fundamental cause of health disparities, the specification of prevailing pathways linking economic constraint and poverty to health remains critically important.

In this chapter, we conceptualize the home as a place and focus on household crowding in relation to poverty and individual-level health and well-being. We begin with a discussion of the relationship between poverty and crowding, and illustrate the contemporary association between poverty and the experience of household crowding by presenting original analyses of 2008–2010 American Community Survey data.

We show that poverty is associated with increased levels of crowding. We then consider the processes by which household crowding is theorized to negatively affect physical and mental health, and we review the empirical literature that documents linkages between crowding and health among adults and children. Next, we briefly discuss how the effects of crowding may be moderated by or moderate other influences on health and well-being. A specific focus of our discussion is the effects of crowding on parent-child interactions and children's health, educational achievement, and behavior, all of which have potentially long-term consequences for health and well-being over the life course. Overall, we argue that crowding can best be understood as a mediator of the relationship between poverty and health; the negative association between poverty and health emerges in part because poverty increases crowding and crowding negatively affects health. The available evidence suggests that early-life crowding has the potential to be an engine of cumulating inequality over the life course; consistent with that proposition, we present results from an analysis of data from the American Community Survey indicating that the experience of crowding is particularly common early in the life course. We conclude with a call for more research at the nexus of poverty, household crowding, and health; the integration of life course and cumulative inequality perspectives into future research; additional efforts to conduct research using longitudinal data, representative samples, and more comprehensive measurement of the experience of crowding; and the evaluation of interventions developed on the basis of existing evidence and evidence emerging from future research.

Poverty and Household Crowding

Residential crowding occurs for various reasons (Gove & Hughes, 1983). Sometimes it occurs in college residence halls, where two young adults share a single room or a small off-campus apartment (Lepore, Evans, & Palsane, 1991). Sometimes it occurs with family growth; the birth of a child leads to a period of crowding until a new residence with more space can be found and afforded. More often, however, household crowding results from economic constraint; job loss, mortgage foreclosure, or a divorce or relationship change may lead people to move into new, smaller, and more-crowded living arrangements. Sometimes crowding is the result of such problems in the lives of others and the integration of family or friends into one's own household. Recent immigrants sometimes live in crowded conditions to pool limited economic resources and assist one another with the complexities of living in a foreign culture.

Overcrowding in the home is most prevalent among the poor, and this association is apparent at the household, family, and individual levels. For example, using 1990 Census data, focusing on households, and measuring crowding as more than one person per room, Myers, Baer, and Choi (1996) report that 12.81% of households with incomes less than 75% of the poverty threshold were crowded, compared to 9.39% of households with incomes 75–100% of the poverty level, 8.08% of households with incomes 100–199% of the poverty level, 4.09% of households with incomes 200–399% of the poverty level, and 1.10% of households with incomes 400% or more above the poverty threshold. At the family level, Meyers and Lee (2003) report that 34% of (working and nonworking) poor families in New York City in 1997 were living in households with less than one room per person, compared to only 6% of nonpoor families. At the individual level, Evans, Lepore, and Allen (2000) report a statistically significant correlation of –0.25 between income and crowding at the individual level; as income increases, the number of people per room decreases.

To illustrate the contemporary association between poverty and crowding, we present results from an original analysis of data from the American Community Survey. The American Community Survey is conducted continuously by the United States Census Bureau and provides annual demographic, social, economic, and housing data for the U.S. population. The public-use samples that we analyzed are very large; in each year, the American Community Survey includes information about more than 3 million Americans. Although standards for measuring crowding have changed over the course of the 20th century (Myers et al., 1996) and the Census Bureau does not have an official definition of crowded housing, the American Community Survey's public-use files contain a measure of occupants per room, which is derived by dividing the number of people enumerated in each occupied housing unit by the number of rooms enumerated in the housing unit. Consistent with the standard that has prevailed since the 1960s (Myers et al., 1996) and common practice in the contemporary research literature, we consider individuals living in housing units with more than one occupant per room to be living in crowded circumstances.

Figure 7.1 presents estimates of the percentage of the U.S. population living in crowded housing, overall and by poverty status, using 2008, 2009, and 2010 American Community Survey data. Several conclusions can be drawn from these data.

First, it is apparent that crowding is a common experience at the individual level in the United States. Overall, 15–16% of the population lived in crowded housing between 2008 and 2010. In other words, at the end of the first decade of the 21st century, approximately one out of every six Americans was living in a household in which there was less than one room per person.

Second, consistent with previous research, crowding is strongly associated with poverty, even though it is clear that not all people who live in poverty live in crowded circumstances. Among those who were living on incomes less than 50% of the poverty threshold between 2008 and

Figure 7.1
Trend in percentage of residents living in crowded housing, overall and by poverty status, 2008–2010.

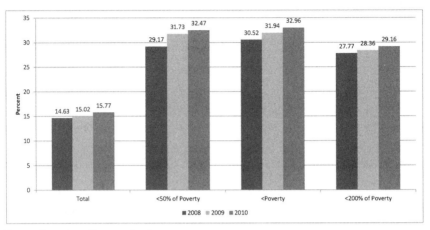

Source: American Community Surveys.

2010, the rate of crowding was substantially higher than the overall rate, ranging from 29.17% in 2008 to 32.47% in 2010. Among those living on incomes less than the poverty threshold, the crowding rate was similar to that among persons in deep poverty and exceeded 30% in each year. There was only a small drop in the percentage crowded when the population on which the estimate was derived included all those living on incomes less than 200% of the poverty threshold; the rate ranged from 27.77% in 2008 to 29.16% in 2010.

Third, the increasing rate of crowding over the 2008–2010 period suggests that the percentage crowded can change fairly rapidly in response to changing social and economic conditions. The period 2008–2010 encompasses what has come to be known as the Great Recession. During this period, housing values dropped, foreclosures increased substantially, and, it appears, households became more crowded generally, but especially among the poorest of the poor. Overall, the change in the rate of crowding for the population as a whole from 2008 to 2010 was 1.14 percentage points. Among those living on incomes less than 50% of the poverty threshold, the change was 3.30 percentage points, while it was 2.44 and 1.39 percentage points, respectively, among those living on incomes below the poverty threshold and on incomes less than 200% of the poverty threshold.

How Does Crowding Affect Health?

The extant literature suggests various mechanisms by which crowding might negatively affect physical and mental health and contribute to socioeconomic disparities in health. Household crowding involves close proximity to others for sustained periods of time, which facilitates the transmission of airborne infectious diseases. In contexts where airborne infectious diseases are common—such as historically in the United States and other developed countries, and today in many developing countries—household crowding is a substantial factor in the transmission of tuberculosis and other respiratory infections (Krieger & Higgins, 2002). Although the prevalence of tuberculosis has generally declined in the United States and other developed countries, ecological studies in low-incidence populations demonstrate that household overcrowding continues to be associated with tuberculosis occurrence and mortality, net of other factors, such as socioeconomic status and immigrant and ethnic concentration (Elender, Bentham, & Langford, 1998; Wanyeki et al., 2006).

More generally, the literature on crowding and health points to two interrelated processes that link crowding to individual-level physical and mental health: excess stimulation and lack of privacy (Gove, Hughes, & Galle, 1979). In the literature, crowding is increasingly conceptualized as an environmental stressor, which may interact with other environmental or social stressors to impair health and well-being (Lepore et al., 1991). From the perspective of the sociological stress process model (Pearlin, 1989; Pearlin, Menaghan, Lieberman, & Mullan, 1981), household crowding for many people who are exposed to it can be conceptualized as a chronic stressor. Exposure to crowded living conditions entails the potential for increased, often uncontrollable contact with others that usually demands some sort of a response or an accommodation and sometimes engenders conflict. For many, such circumstances produce stress and distress, especially when they persist. Because the structural circumstances that lead to crowding—such as poverty—are unlikely to change substantially over the short term, and because individuals often lack the social or economic resources that would allow them to live in alternative, more-spacious environments, it is conceivable that some individuals experience crowding over relatively long durations. Living in crowded circumstances is likely to be caused by poverty, rather than be a cause of poverty, although early-life crowding-related health, family relations, or school performance problems (Evans, Lepore, Shejwal, & Palsane, 1998; Guerrero et al., 2003; Maxwell, 2003; Solari & Mare, 2012) may increase the chances of being poor and living in crowded housing later in life. Taking all of these factors into consideration, when considered in close temporal proximity, crowding can best be understood as a potential mediator of the relationship between poverty and physical and mental health outcomes.

The literature provides additional theoretical insights that are useful for considering how crowding affects health. Regoeczi (2002) points to the literature on "fight versus flight" responses among crowded animals as a foundation for theorizing withdrawal versus aggression as responses to crowding among humans. In either case, there is a physiological response. In crowded households, the continual presence of demanding others may be distracting, may impede goal attainment, and could interfere with sleep; such chronic exposure to crowding may provoke feelings of frustration, anger, and stress or reduce the ability to cope with such feelings (Martimportigués-Goyenechea & Gómez-Jacinto, 2005). High levels of intensive, potentially unwanted, or ill-timed social interaction may exceed the individual's optimal level of engagement and coping resources, which could lead to withdrawal as an attempt to reduce exposure to demanding interactions and gain a sense of control. Both withdrawal and aggression in response to crowding may erode potentially stress-buffering social support resources, while the inability to control the level or timing of social interactions may erode the individual's sense of mastery. These social and psychological processes may, in turn, impair health and well-being.

Chronic exposure to stressors in circumstances of reduced or eroding coping resources can increase emotional distress in the short term and damage health in the long term. This mechanism is consistent with the notion of allostatic load, which Kahn and Pearlin (2006) have conceptualized as "the cumulative damage done to health and well-being under the burden of an unrelenting stressor in a critically important life domain" (p. 17). It is this increased allostatic load, as well as subjective feelings of being chronically stressed and exhausted, and impaired social support and coping resources, that are thought to connect household crowding to health and well-being.

What Is the Evidence Linking Crowding to Health?

Although there are sound theoretical reasons for hypothesizing that crowding affects health, to what extent does empirical evidence demonstrate that it does so? Periodically, in the literature, there have been debates about this very question. For example, Gove et al. (1979) introduced their path-breaking article by pointing to several recent reviews of the literature that concluded that the effects of density and crowding were minimal to nonexistent; they went on to challenge that claim by demonstrating substantial effects of crowding on a range of physical and mental health outcomes, as well as several health-related social outcomes, using more-rigorous methods than were typical up to that point. A debate between these authors and those they challenged was carried out in a series of published exchanges in the *American Sociological Review* (Booth, Johnson, & Edwards, 1980a, 1980b; Gove & Hughes, 1980a, 1980b).

More recently, Evans, Lepore, and Allen (2000) entitled one of their articles "Cross-Cultural Differences in Tolerance for Crowding: Fact or Fiction?" and addressed the commonly made, but under-researched, claim that the negative consequences of crowding do not occur among Asian-Americans and Latin-Americans because of cultural differences in interpersonal spacing norms and preferences—a claim that these authors termed "the myth of cultural heterogeneity in crowding tolerance" in the second paragraph of the introduction to their paper. Evans et al. went on to demonstrate that higher household density was similarly associated with higher levels of psychological distress among Anglo-Americans, African-Americans, Asian-Americans, and Latin-Americans, even though the latter two groups did perceive crowding differently than Anglo-Americans and African-Americans.

Emerging from the research brought about by these scientific debates is considerable evidence that crowding is associated with negative physical and mental health outcomes. Various studies suggest that crowded housing can act as a chronic stressor, and it is known that the experience of chronic stress can suppress immunity (Elender et al., 1998; Srinivasan, O'Fallon, & Dearry, 2003). Increased exposure to airborne infectious diseases coupled with stress-related immune system suppression may contribute to increased susceptibility to such illnesses among persons living in crowded housing. Beyond the association of crowding with tuberculosis and other airborne infectious diseases, which is well documented in the literature, other studies have identified associations between crowding and high blood pressure among boys (Evans, Lepore, & Allen, 2000), accumulated tiredness (Martim-portigués-Goyenechea & Gómez-Jacinto, 2005), inability to get good rest (Gove et al., 1979), and overall health (Gove et al., 1979). Recently, using data from the Child Development Supplement of the Panel Study of Income Dynamics (PSID) and the Los Angeles Family and Neighborhood Survey, Solari and Mare (2012) found that household crowding negatively affected children's health and well-being, net of socioeconomic characteristics. One ecological study associated crowded housing with infant mortality in the 1950s and 1960s, but not in the 1970s (Adamchak, 1979).

Although physical and mental health problems are often co-occurring, the existing literature pays considerably more attention to how crowding affects mental health. Crowded housing may affect emotional well-being by straining and disrupting interpersonal relationships and social support (Evans, Lepore, & Allen, 2000; Gove et al., 1979). Those living in crowded housing may also experience increased demands on their time, a lack of perceived space and privacy, and a loss of control over social interactions (Evans, Saegert, & Harris, 2001; Gove et al., 1979; Regoeczi, 2008). Overall, the available literature suggests that household crowding affects a number of social-psychological processes in ways that can be detrimental to mental health and well-being and indicates that crowding is associated negatively with various mental health outcomes. Crowded adults suffer more psychological distress compared to adults in households with adequate living space (Evans, Lepore, & Allen, 2000; Lepore et al., 1991).

Overcrowding has also been associated with an increase in various psychiatrically relevant symptoms and conditions, including nervous breakdowns, irritation, feelings of alienation, unhappiness, low self-esteem, obsessive-compulsive disorder, depression, anxiety, aggression, and withdrawal (Evans et al., 2001; Gabe & Williams, 1986; Gove et al., 1979; Guerrero et al., 2003; Regoeczi, 2008). Importantly, some of these associations between crowding and negative mental health outcomes have been demonstrated in different countries with different social and cultural contexts and varying levels of economic development (e.g., India and the United States) (Lepore et al., 1991), among various population groups, and in different historical time periods, which suggests that there is a generalizable negative association between crowding and mental health.

Crowding and Child Health and Well-Being

Although the bulk of the literature on crowding and health focuses on adults, some studies have paid particular attention to the consequences of household crowding for children's well-being (Solari & Mare, 2012). This research has focused both on health-related factors and on health. Some of this research has examined the home environment, suggesting that there is more conflict between parents and children in crowded homes (Booth & Edwards, 1976; Evans et al., 1998; Saegert, 1982). Gove et al. (1979) found that crowding was positively associated with parental reports that their children were a hassle, that parents were relieved when their children were out of the home, and that parents physically punished their children; conversely, crowding was negatively associated with being supportive of their children, knowing the children's playmates, and knowing the parents of their children's playmates. All of these associations persisted when controls for demographic variables were included in the models.

Some research has focused on school behavior, with children from crowded homes being found to have more behavioral problems in school and impaired academic achievement (Evans et al., 1998; Maxwell, 2003). Lower scores on standardized cognitive assessments have been reported for one- to three-year-old children who lived in crowded homes relative to those who did not (Wachs & Gruen, 1982), while elementary school-aged children from crowded households are slower to acquire reading skills than children from noncrowded homes (Murray, 1974; Saegert, 1982). Solari and Mare (2012) also found negative effects of living in crowded housing on children's math and reading achievement and external behavior problems. Conley (2001) reported that household crowding in childhood significantly reduced the number of years of completed schooling by age 25 years.

Relatively few studies have directly examined the consequences of household crowding for children's health. Evans et al. (1998) reported that crowding was associated with elevated blood pressure among 9- to 17-year-old boys in India, but not among girls. Among adolescents in Hawaii, crowding in the household was correlated positively with an increased prevalence of obsessive-compulsive disorder (Guerrero et al., 2003). In two different samples of college students, crowded living arrangements were associated with increased psychological distress as well as increased susceptibility to distress resulting from social hassles (Lepore et al., 1991). A recent study documented the negative effects of household crowding on a primary caregiver's (most often a parent's) report of the child's general health in a national sample (Solari & Mare, 2012). Taken together, these results suggest that crowding may have a range of negative consequences for children, youth, and those transitioning to adulthood across a range of contexts, which can have consequences for their health and well-being in the short and long terms.

Moderating Influences: What Mitigates or Compounds the Effects of Crowding on Health?

The available evidence suggests that there is an association between crowding and health and health-related outcomes for both adults and children. However, it is important to note that the literature also suggests that the effect of crowding on health and health-related outcomes may not be the same for all groups.

Sometimes researchers develop an argument for why the consequences of crowding may be particularly consequential for one group, and then they study that group only. For example, Gabe and Williams (1986) articulated an argument about why gender inequality might lead women to be particularly susceptible to the consequences of crowding, and then they examined the effects of crowding on depression among women only. They found a significant J-shaped association, with both low and high levels of crowding being detrimental to psychological health. Low crowding, in the extreme, is indicative of social isolation, which is distinct from high crowding and linked to health and well-being via different mechanisms.

Some research has directly tested for gender differences. For example, Regoeczi (2008) found that crowding increased depression among women, but not men, while it increased withdrawal, and withdrawal combined with aggression among men, but not women. Importantly, she also reported a J-shaped, nonlinear relationship between crowding and depression among women and used longitudinal data that allowed her to control for selection into crowding better than most studies.

One study sought to determine whether crowding—conceptualized as an environmental stressor—exacerbated the negative consequences of social hassles—conceptualized as a social stressor (Lepore et al., 1991). These authors tested main and interactive effects in three separate samples and found that crowding, but not social hassles, significantly increased psychological symptoms, and that there was a significant interaction between crowding and social hassles as well. In all three samples, individuals who experienced social hassles and lived in crowded conditions had the highest number of psychological symptoms.

These and other studies that have attempted to specify for whom crowding matters, and the circumstances under which crowding does and does not exert a negative influence on health and well-being, are important because they provide empirical guidance for further theorizing about the relationship between crowding and health, how it operates, and what might be done to mitigate its effects.

Life Course Perspectives on Crowding and Health

The available theoretical and empirical literature supports the conclusions that poverty is associated with living in crowded housing and that overcrowding is associated with a range of negative physical and mental health outcomes. As such, crowding can be conceptualized as a mediator of the poverty-health relationship, although it may not mediate that relationship fully or to the same degree for all subgroups of the population. The available literature also suggests that crowding affects both adults' and children's health and well-being, and that it may negatively affect parenting, social relations, school performance, and coping in ways that are relevant for health and well-being in the short term, and possibly over the long term.

To date, the literature that focuses on the consequences of crowding for health and well-being has tended to use cross-sectional studies that isolate the temporally proximate association between crowding and health or health-related outcomes, net of income and other factors, although some notable studies have used longitudinal data that allow for better control of selection (Conley, 2001; Regoeczi, 2008; Solari & Mare, 2012). Much of the existing research is based on small convenience samples, although some is based on laboratory research, as opposed to research in naturalistic settings. Taken together, the accumulated empirical evidence in the extant literature provides an ample basis to argue that there is a need for additional research on poverty, crowding, and health. As new research is undertaken, it would be useful for investigators to draw on the life course perspective as a guiding conceptual model, which is something that has not generally been done in studies of crowded housing and health (for exceptions, see Conley, 2001; Solari & Mare, 2012).

One of the main reasons that it is important to frame poverty, crowding, and health research in life course terms is that the experience of crowding is particularly prevalent among children, adolescents, and young adults. Figure 7.2 presents the percentages of Americans living in crowded housing, by single year of age, using 2008–2010 American Community Survey data. Although these data only provide a point-in-time snapshot of

Figure 7.2
Percentage of residents living in crowded housing, by age, 2008–2010.

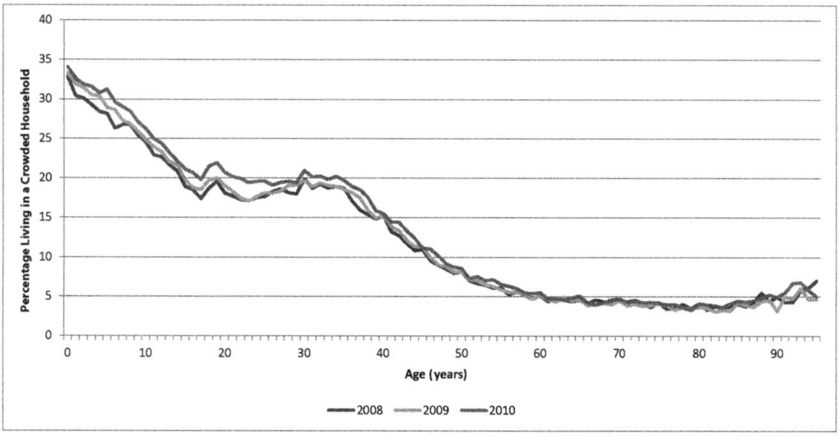

Source: American Community Surveys.

crowding and tell us nothing about the intensity or duration of the crowding that individuals experience, two patterns are particularly noteworthy.

First, across all three years, approximately the same pattern is observed—that is, crowding declines with age. It is notable that the rate of crowding peaks among the very youngest, although it declines by about 15 percentage points rapidly and linearly from ages 0 to 20 years. The rate of crowding plateaus around 20% for those aged 20–40 years, but then declines nonlinearly among those aged 40–60 years, leveling off around 5% among those aged 60 years and older. To the extent that crowding has consequences for children's health or educational performance and for parent-child interactions—which the available literature suggests it does—the influence of crowding has the potential to reverberate across the life course and affect later-life health trajectories or outcomes. That crowding has such long-term effects on health and well-being has not been well established in the literature and is not inevitable, as other factors may mitigate early-life influences on the life course that result from living in crowded circumstances. That said, such long-term influences are possible (Conley, 2001) and worth considering.

Second, there is some evidence of an increase in crowding among children, adolescents, and young adults over the 2008–2010 period that encompasses the Great Recession. This finding suggests that crowding is responsive to short-term changes in macroeconomic and other contextual circumstances (see also Figure 7.1).

Another reason to situate the study of poverty, crowding, and health within a life course framework is that socioeconomic disparities are a primary target of public health policy concern and intervention. There is ample evidence that it is critical to take early-life conditions into account when considering later-life health disparities and measures to ameliorate them. Disparities in child health outcomes by parental socioeconomic status have remained stable or increased in the past 50 years, despite steady improvements in average health among Americans and the creation of public health insurance programs for the poor (Case, Paxson, & Vogl, 2006; Chen, Martin, & Matthews, 2006a, 2006b; Duleep, 1989; Duncan, 1996; Stevens, 2006; Warren & Hernandez, 2007). By all measures—including insurance coverage, mortality, overall health, and chronic health problems—children of parents with low educational attainment, recent experience with welfare, and limited labor force experience fare worse than children whose parents have more social and economic resources (Aber, Bennett, Conley, & Li, 1997; Bauman, Silver, & Stein, 2006; Case & Paxon, 2006; DeNavas-Walt, Proctor, & Smith, 2007; Finch, 2003). Parental poverty and resource constraint is associated with poor child health, and crowding is a potential mediator of that relationship.

Childhood health is both an outcome of social and economic disadvantage and a factor in its reproduction over the life course and across generations (Haas, 2006; Willson, Shuey, & Elder, 2007). Disadvantage in early life relates to differences in health and socioeconomic attainment in adulthood, as well as childhood health disparities (Case, Lubotsky, & Paxson, 2002; Elman & O'Rand, 2004; Haas, 2006, 2007; Hayward & Gorman, 2004; O'Rand & Hamil-Luker, 2005; Palloni, 2006; Palloni & Milesi, 2006; Palloni, Milesi, White, & Turner, 2009; Preston, Hill, & Drevenstedt, 1998). Retrospective reports by adults indicate that lower parental socioeconomic status in childhood is associated with lower lifetime educational attainment and income, as well as higher rates of diabetes, high blood pressure, and functional limitations in adulthood (Haas, 2008; Hamil-Luker & O'Rand, 2007). In fact, childhood factors are more predictive of the rate of increased functional limitations in later life than is adult health or socioeconomic status (Haas, 2008). In a prospective study following a birth cohort into adulthood, Case, Fertig, and Paxson (2005) found that poor health in childhood not only predicted lower initial adult health and educational attainment, but also exerted a continuing negative effect on health into middle age.

The foregoing considerations suggest the utility of the life course perspective for conducting empirical studies at the nexus of poverty, crowding, and health. Although there are ongoing debates regarding the scope of life course scholarship and its relationship to such concepts as lifespan and life cycle (Alwin, 2012a, 2012b; O'Rand & Krecker, 1990), there is widespread agreement on five major principles of the life course perspective: lifelong development; linked lives; location in time and place; timing; and human agency (Elder & Johnson, 2002; Elder, Johnson, &

Crosnoe, 2003; Elder & Shanahan, 2006; George, 2003; Giele & Elder, 1998; Settersten, 1999, 2003). Each of these is relevant for research on poverty, crowding, and health.

First, the *life course perspective* emphasizes lifelong development and the notion that outcomes at any point in time result from cumulative, age-related developmental processes. Early-life experiences—such as living in crowded circumstances as a child—can influence, and sometimes fundamentally determine, what happens later. Second, the life course principle of *linked lives* focuses attention on the importance of social relationships and the interdependence of lives. The study of crowding is, fundamentally, about social relations and connection to others in a specific place—the home. The mechanisms by which crowding is thought to affect health and well-being operate to a large extent through stress associated with the quantity and quality of relationships with proximate others, in the form of overstimulation, lack of privacy, loss of control over social interactions, sleep deprivation resulting from the presence of others, and strained social relations.

Third, the study of crowded housing is, in part, about place—where one lives and spends a significant portion of one's childhood and non-working adult life. The life course principle of *location in time and place* embeds lives in specific geographical, historical, and institutional locations where various kinds of people are or are not encountered, certain kinds of interactions do or do not occur, and specific values are or are not emphasized. While crowded housing focuses our attention on the crowding in the home, this life course principle encourages us to think more broadly about place and the ways that crowding in the home might intersect with crowding in the classroom or neighborhood crowding. For example, are the consequences of household crowding greater among those living in unsafe urban neighborhoods that encourage, if not force, individuals to spend more time in the home? Some researchers have examined such issues, but they have not situated their work within or connected it to life course concepts. For example, Maxwell (2003) found that classroom crowding affected second- and fourth-grade girls' academic achievement and boys' behavior, and that household crowding increased psychological stress, although there was no apparent interaction between home and school crowding.

The focus on the effects of crowding on children as well as adults is consistent with the fourth life course principle of *timing* and is relevant to considerations of susceptibility to the effects of crowding during different periods of development. This life course principle focuses on when events and transitions occur in relation to age, and speaks to the importance of taking into account when personal life events occur, whether they trigger transitions, and how disruptive such transitions are to ongoing relationships, personal development, education, family patterns, and work. Research that links early-life conditions to later-life health trajectories and outcomes, and that considers how such conditions relate to socioeconomic status across the life course, underscores how important it is to take the dynamics, intensity, duration, and context of crowding over the life course into account in studies of poverty, crowding, and health.

Finally, the life course principle of *human agency* focuses on the role that individuals play in their own lives as they take action to pursue opportunities or address constraints that they encounter in various contexts. Not all people in objectively crowded circumstances experience negative outcomes, whereas some people in noncrowded circumstances do experience them. How individuals cope and accommodate to crowding partly shapes the consequences of crowding that they will experience, although it is likely that not all of the potential sequelae of crowding are under individual control.

The life course perspective is well suited to studying the relationships between poverty, crowding, and health disparities. Specifically useful, we argue, is a *cumulative exposure model* of the life course, in which adult social conditions mediate the effects of early-life social conditions on adult outcomes (Berkman, Ertel, & Glymour, 2011). According to this model, earlier-life social conditions can directly affect later-life outcomes; however, those influences may be offset or accentuated by various coping responses, participation in social institutions, exposure to formal public policies, and myriad other factors (Hendricks, 2012). What happens early in life—such as exposure to sustained crowding in childhood or adolescence—is central to subsequent processes of accumulating advantage and disadvantage. Recent research calls attention to the fact that household crowding is an understudied aspect of social inequality that has the potential to contribute to the intergenerational transmission of social inequality over the life course (Solari & Mare, 2012). Some research has documented long-term effects of childhood crowding on educational attainment, which is an important predictor of later-life health and a range of health-related trajectories and outcomes (Conley, 2001). Those deprived of resources in one domain often end up being deprived of resources in other domains, while those with access to resources are able to garner and command additional resources. This differential access to resources —perhaps especially when it occurs very early in the life course and affects health and educational performance—may accrue and accentuate inequalities across groups over time (Dannefer, 1987, 1988, 2003; Ferraro, Shippee, & Schafer, 2009; O'Rand, 1996, 2002). This kind of conceptual model underlays much contemporary research about health disparities; however, to date, crowding as a potential engine of cumulating inequality across the life course has not been systematically examined.

Looking to the Future

In this chapter, we have provided an overview of the theoretical and empirical research that links poverty, household crowding, and health. Persons living in crowded circumstances are vulnerable to a range of negative outcomes, some of which emerge early in life and may contribute to later-life socioeconomic and health disparities. The available, multidisciplinary research literature provides an ample conceptual and empirical basis on which investigators working in a range of disciplines and inter-disciplines might base future research. Additional research is warranted because there is much we still do not know about poverty, crowding, and health, even though the available literature provides many important findings and clues about fruitful directions for future research. To maximize the contribution of future research in this area, it would be useful for researchers to connect their investigations to the life course perspective, while remaining attentive to stress process and resource deprivation concepts and models. It will also be important for researchers to be attentive to a number of conceptual and methodological issues. We conclude this chapter by highlighting three such issues and by providing recommendations to help guide future research.

Much of the available literature on crowding and health is based on cross-sectional data. Consistent with our argument about the need for future research to draw on life course and cumulative inequality perspectives, it is critically important that future research draw on longitudinal data. This would enhance our understanding of the long-term effects of crowding and the mechanisms by which it affects health; it would also allow for greater control of selection into crowding. There is heterogeneity in experiences of crowding and crowding dynamics over time, and capturing that factor in investigations is important for advancing our understanding of when and how crowding matters for health. It may be the case that many existing longitudinal studies contain data that would allow for the derivation of an objective measure of household crowding that could be—but to date has not been—incorporated into the studies of health that have been done with those data. The recent study by Solari and Mare (2012) suggests just this possibility. Subjective measures of crowding may also be available. Perhaps measures of crowding have been included in surveys, but have not been analyzed. If such data exist, then there might be capacity for a relatively immediate, short-term gain in knowledge in this area. If such data do not exist, we encourage researchers who are designing new cross-sectional and, especially, longitudinal data collection efforts to incorporate measures of crowding into their surveys.

In general, the available literature on crowding and health is mostly based on convenience samples. Although the association between crowding and negative health and well-being outcomes across various contexts provides some support for claims about generalizability, it is important for future research to be based on more-representative samples of defined populations. There are many representative data sets publicly available. To the extent such data sets—both cross-sectional and longitudinal—include unanalyzed measures of household crowding, it may be possible for the research community to generate a set of generalizable research findings relatively quickly. Such findings can help guide future research and data collection, as well as contribute to the research base from which evidence-based interventions to mitigate crowding and its consequences can be developed.

To the extent that available data resources house data that can be used to measure crowding, they likely include only the most basic information (i.e., people per room, which requires only the number of people and the number of rooms in the household). To move the field forward, it will be important for researchers to develop a more complete set of indicators of exposure to crowding over the life course. For example, we need information about the dynamics of crowding (i.e., moves into and out of crowding over time) as well as the intensity of crowding, the ages and stages of development at which individuals experienced crowding, the context of crowding, and subjective appraisals of the consequences of crowding. Such complex data could be collected in prospective surveys more easily than in retrospective surveys, although there may be some information that can reliably be collected in retrospect. Developing valid, standard measures of crowding experiences that can regularly be incorporated into surveys is important as research in this area continues to evolve.

Overall, there is much to be learned from additional research on crowding and health over the life course that can inform the development of public policies that might mitigate some of the consequences of household crowding—and, therefore, some of the consequences of poverty—in peoples' lives. Housing problems and housing hardships are regularly raised in discussions of material deprivation and health and well-being; housing problems are a substantial focus of public health policy concern (Evans, Chan, Wells, & Saltzman, 2000; Krieger & Higgins, 2002; Saegert, Klitzman, Freudenberg, Cooperman-Mroczek, & Nassar, 2003; Srinivasan et al., 2003). Arguably, crowding is a form of material hardship (Heflin, 2006; Heflin, Sandberg, & Rafail, 2009), in that it represents the inability to attain a basic need—an adequate amount of living space to maintain healthy living. More research is necessary to provide a comprehensive understanding of the relationships among poverty, household crowding, and health and health-related outcomes over the life course. Such research will be necessary to inform the development of evidence-based interventions. Interventions aimed at mitigating the effects of poverty on crowding and the effects of crowding on health and health-related outcomes for children and adults have the potential to enhance the health and well-being of the poor both in the short term and over the life course.

References

Aber, J. L., Bennett, N. G., Conley, D. C., & Li, J. (1997). The effects of poverty on child health and development. *Annual Review of Public Health, 18*(1), 463–483.

Adamchak, D. J. (1979). Emerging trends in the relationship between infant mortality and socioeconomic status. *Social Biology, 26*(1), 16–29.

Alwin, D. F. (2012a). Integrating varieties of life course concepts. *Journals of Gerontology: Social Sciences, 67B*(2), 206–220.

Alwin, D. F. (2012b). Words have consequences. *Journals of Gerontology: Social Sciences, 67B*(2), 232–234.

Bauman, L. J., Silver, E. J., & Stein, R. E. (2006). Cumulative social disadvantage and child health. *Pediatrics, 117*(4), 1321–1328.

Berkman, L., Ertel, K., & Glymour, M. (2011). Aging and social intervention: Life course perspectives. In R. Binstock & L. George (Eds.), *Handbook of aging and the social sciences* (7th ed., pp. 337–351). San Diego, CA: Academic Press.

Booth, A., & Edwards, J. N. (1976). Crowding and family relations. *American Sociological Review, 41*(2), 308–321.

Booth, A., Johnson, D., & Edwards, J. (1980a). Reply to Gove and Hughes. *American Sociological Review, 45*(5), 870–873.

Booth, A., Johnson, D., & Edwards, J. (1980b). In pursuit of pathology: The effects of human crowding. *American Sociological Review, 45*(5), 873–878.

Case, A., Fertig, A., & Paxson, C. (2005). The lasting impact of childhood health and circumstance. *Journal of Health Economics, 24*(2), 365–389.

Case, A., Lubotsky, D., & Paxson, C. (2002). Economic status and health in childhood: The origins of the gradient. *American Economic Review, 92*(5), 1308–1334.

Case, A., & Paxson, C. (2006). Children's health and social mobility. *Future of Children, 16*(2), 151–173.

Case, A., Paxson, C., & Vogl, T. (2006, May). *Socioeconomic status and health in childhood: A comment on Chen, Martin and Matthews, K. A. (2006).* Center for Health and Wellbeing at Princeton University.

Chang, V., & Lauderdale, D. (2009). Fundamental cause theory, technological innovation, and health disparities: The case of cholesterol in the era of statins. *Journal of Health and Social Behavior, 50*(3), 245–260.

Chen, E., Martin, A. D., & Matthews, K. A. (2006a). Socioeconomic status and health: Do gradients differ within childhood and adolescence? *Social Science and Medicine, 62*(9), 2161–2170.

Chen, E., Martin, A. D., & Matthews, K. A. (2006b). Understanding health disparities: The role of race and socioeconomic status in children's health. *American Journal of Public Health, 96*(4), 702–708.

Conley, D. (2001). A room with a view or a room of one's own? Housing and social stratification. *Sociological Forum, 16*(2), 263–280.

Dannefer, D. (1987). Aging as intracohort differentiation: Accentuation, the Matthew effect, and the life course. *Sociological Forum, 2*(2), 211–236.

Dannefer, D. (1988). Age structure, the life course, and "aged heterogeneity": Prospects for research and theory. *Comparative Gerontology, 2*(1), 1–10.

Dannefer, D. (2003). Cumulative advantage/disadvantage and the life course: Cross-fertilizing age and social science theory. *Journals of Gerontology Series B—Psychological Sciences and Social Sciences, 58*(6), S327–S337.

DeNavas-Walt, C., Proctor, B. D., & Smith, J. (2007). *Income, poverty, and health insurance coverage in the United States: 2006.* Washington, DC: U.S. Census Bureau.

Duleep, H. O. (1989). Measuring socioeconomic mortality differentials over time. *Demography, 26*(2), 345–351.

Duncan, G. J. (1996). Income dynamics and health. *International Journal of Health Services, 26*(3), 419–444.

Elder, G. H. Jr., & Johnson, M. K. (2002). Perspectives on human development in context. In C. von Hofsten & L. Bergman (Eds.), *Psychology at the turn of the millennium. Volume 2: Social, developmental, and clinical perspectives* (pp. 153–175). East Sussex, UK: Psychology Press.

Elder, G. H., Johnson, M. K., & Crosnoe, R. (2003). The emergence and development of life course theory. In J. T. Mortimer & M. J. Shanahan (Eds.), *Handbook of the life course* (pp. 3–19). New York, NY: Kluwer Academic/Plenum.

Elder, G. H. Jr., & Shanahan, M. J. (2006). The life course and human development. In R. E. Lerner (Ed.), *Theoretical models of human development. Volume 1: The handbook of child psychology* (6th ed., pp. 665–715). New York, NY: Wiley.

Elender, F., Bentham, G., & Langford, I. (1998). Tuberculosis mortality in England and Wales during 1982–1992: Its association with poverty, ethnicity, and AIDS. *Social Science Medicine, 46*(6), 673–681.

Elman, C., & O'Rand, A. M. (2004). The race is to the swift: Socioeconomic origins, adult education, and wage attainment. *American Journal of Sociology, 110*(1), 123–160.

Evans, G. W., Chan, H. Y. E., Wells, N. M., & Saltzman, H. (2000). Housing quality and mental health. *Journal of Consulting and Clinical Psychology, 68*(3), 526–530.

Evans, G. W., Lepore, S. J., & Allen, K. M. (2000). Cross-cultural differences in tolerance for crowding: Fact or fiction? *Journal of Personal and Social Psychology, 79*(2), 204–210.

Evans, G. W., Lepore, S. J., Shejwal, B. R., & Palsane, M. N. (1998). Chronic residential crowding and children's well-being: An ecological perspective. *Child Development, 69*(6), 1514–1523.

Evans, G. W., Saegert, S., & Harris, R. (2001). Residential density and psychological health among children in low-income families. *Environment and Behavior, 33*(2), 165–180.

Ferraro, K. F., Shippee, T. P., & Shafer, M. H. (2009). Cumulative inequality theory for research on aging and the life course. In V. L. Bengtson, M. Silverstein, N. M. Putney, & D. Gans (Eds.), *Handbook of theories of aging* (2nd ed., pp. 413–434). New York, NY: Springer.

Finch, B. K. (2003). Early origins of the gradient: The relationship between socioeconomic status and infant mortality in the United States. *Demography, 40*(4), 675–699.

Gabe, J., & Williams, P. (1986). Is space bad for your health? The relationship between crowding in the home and emotional distress in women. *Sociology of Health and Illness, 8*(4), 351–371.

George, L. K. (2003). What life-course perspectives offer the study of aging and health. In R. A. Settersten, Jr. (Ed.), *Invitation to the life course: Toward new understandings of later life* (pp. 161–190). Amityville, NY: Baywood.

Giele, J. Z., & Elder, G. H. Jr. (Eds.). (1998). *Methods of life course research: Qualitative and quantitative approaches.* Thousand Oaks, CA: Sage Publications.

Gove, W. R., & Hughes, M. (1980a). The effects of crowding found in the Toronto Study: Some methodological and empirical questions. *American Sociological Review, 45*(5), 864–870.

Gove, W. R., & Hughes, M. (1980b). In pursuit of perceptions: A reply to the claim of Booth and his colleagues that household crowding is not an important variable. *American Sociological Review, 45*(5), 878–886.

Gove, W. R., & Hughes, M. (1983). *Overcrowding in the household: An analysis of determinants and effects.* Waltham, MA: Academic Press.

Gove, W. R., Hughes, M., & Galle, O. R. (1979). Overcrowding in the home: An empirical investigation of its possible pathological consequences. *American Sociological Review, 44*(1), 59–80.

Guerrero, A. P. S., Hishinuma, E. S., Andrade, N. N., Bell, C. K., Kurahara, D. K., Lee, T. G., . . . Stokes, A. J. (2003). Demographic and clinical characteristics of adolescents in Hawaii with obsessive-compulsive disorder. *Archives of Pediatrics and Adolescent Medicine, 157*(7), 665–670.

Haas, S. A. (2006). Health selection and the process of social stratification: The effect of childhood health on socioeconomic attainment. *Journal of Health and Social Behavior, 47*(4), 339–354.

Haas, S. A. (2007). The long-term effects of poor childhood health: An assessment and application of retrospective reports. *Demography, 44*(1), 113–135.

Haas, S. A. (2008). Trajectories of functional health: The "long arm" of childhood health and socioeconomic factors. *Social Science and Medicine, 66*(4), 849–861.

Hamil-Luker, J., & O'Rand, A. M. (2007). Gender differences in the link between childhood socioeconomic conditions and heart attack risk in adulthood. *Demography, 44*(1), 137–158.

Hayward, M., & Gorman, B. K. (2004). The long arm of childhood: The influence of early-life social conditions on men's mortality. *Demography, 41*(1), 87–107.

Heflin, C. M. (2006). Dynamics of different forms of material hardship in the Women's Employment Survey. *Social Service Review, 80*(3), 377–397.

Heflin, C. M., Sandberg, J., & Rafail, P. (2009). The structure of material hardship in U.S. households: An examination of the coherence behind common measures of well-being. *Social Problems, 56*(4), 746–764.

Hendricks, J. (2012). Considering life course concepts. *Journals of Gerontology: Social Sciences, 67*(2), 226–231.

Kahn, J. R., & Pearlin, L. I. (2006). Financial strain over the life course and health among older adults. *Journal of Health and Social Behavior, 47*(1), 17–31.

Krieger, J., & Higgins, D. L. (2002). Housing and health: Time again for public health action. *American Journal of Public Health, 92*(5), 758–768.

Lepore, S. J., Evans, G. W., & Palsane, M. N. (1991). Social hassles and psychological health in the context of chronic crowding. *Journal of Health and Social Behavior, 32*(4), 357–367.

Link, B. G., & Phelan, J. C. (1995). Social conditions as fundamental causes of disease. *Journal of Health and Social Behavior, 36*(Extra Issue), 80–94.

Link, B. G., & Phelan, J. C. (1996). Understanding sociodemographic differences in health: The role of fundamental social causes. *American Journal of Public Health, 86*(4), 471–473.

Link, B. G., & Phelan, J. C. (2010). Social conditions as fundamental causes of health inequalities. In C. E. Bird, P. Conrad, A. M. Freemont, & S. Timmermans (Eds.), *Handbook of medical sociology* (pp. 3–17). Nashville, TN: Vanderbilt University Press.

Martimportugués-Goyenechea, C., & Gómez-Jacinto, L. (2005). Simultaneous multiple stressors in the environment: Physiological stress reactions, performance, and stress evaluation. *Psychological Report, 97*(3), 867–874.

Maxwell, L. E. (2003). Home and school density effects on elementary school children: The role of spatial density. *Environment and Behavior, 35*(4), 566–578.

Meyers, M. K., & Lee, J. M. (2003). Working but poor: How are families faring? *Children and Youth Services Review, 25*(3), 177–201.

Murray, R. (1974). The influence of crowding on children's behavior. In D. Canter & T. Lee (Eds.), *Psychology and the built environment* (pp. 112–117). Chichester, UK: Wiley.

Myers, D., Baer, W. C., & Choi, S. Y. (1996). The changing problem of overcrowded housing. *Journal of the American Planning Association, 62*(1), 66–84.

O'Rand, A. M. (1996). The precious and the precocious: Understanding cumulative disadvantage and cumulative advantage over the life course. *Gerontologist, 3*(2), 230–238.

O'Rand, A. M. (2002). Cumulative advantage theory in life course research. *Annual Review of Gerontology and Geriatrics, 22*, 14–30.

O'Rand, A. M., & Hamil-Luker, J. (2005). Processes of cumulative adversity: Childhood disadvantage and increased risk of heart attack across the life course. *Journals of Gerontology Series B: Psychological Sciences and Social Sciences, 60B*(SI), 117–124.

O'Rand, A. M., & Krecker, M. L. (1990). Concepts of the life cycle: Their history, meanings, and uses in the social sciences. *Annual Review of Sociology, 16*(1), 241–262.

Palloni, A. (2006). Reproducing inequalities: Luck, wallets, and the enduring effects of childhood health. *Demography, 43*(4), 587–615.

Palloni, A., & Milesi, C. (2006). Economic achievement, inequalities and health disparities: The intervening role of early health status. *Research in Social Stratification and Mobility, 24*(1), 21–40.

Palloni, A., Milesi, C., White, R. G., & Turner, A. (2009). Early childhood health, reproduction of economic inequalities and the persistence of health and mortality differentials. *Social Science and Medicine, 68*(9), 1574–1582.

Pearlin, L. I. (1989). The sociological study of stress. *Journal of Health and Social Behavior, 30*(3), 241–256.

Pearlin, L. I., Menaghan, E. G., Lieberman, M. A., & Mullan, J. T. (1981). The stress process. *Journal of Health and Social Behavior, 22*(4), 337–356.

Preston, S. H., Hill, M. E., & Drevenstedt, G. L. (1998). Childhood conditions that predict survival to advanced ages among African-Americans. *Social Science and Medicine, 47*(9), 1231–1246.

Regoeczi, W. (2002). The impact of density: The importance of nonlinearity and selection on flight and fight responses. *Social Forces, 81*(2), 505–530.

Regoeczi, W. (2008). Crowding in context: An examination of the differential responses of men and women to high-density living environments. *Journal of Health and Social Behavior, 49*(3), 254–268.

Rubin, M., Colen, C., & Link, B. G. (2010). Examination of inequalities in HIV/AIDS mortality in the United States from a fundamental cause perspective. *American Journal of Public Health, 100*(6), 1053–1059.

Saegert, S. (1982). Environment and children's mental health: Residential density and low income children. In A. Baum & J. E. Singer (Eds.), *Handbook of psychology and health* (Vol. 2, pp. 247–271). Hillsdale, NJ: Lawrence Erlbaum.

Saegert, S., Klitzman, S., Freudenberg, N., Cooperman-Mroczek, J., & Nassar, S. (2003). Healthy housing: A structured review of published evaluations of US interventions to improve health by modifying housing in the United States, 1990–2001. *American Journal of Public Health, 93*(9), 1471–1477.

Settersten, R. A. (1999). *Lives in time and place: The problems and promises of developmental sciences.* Amityville, NY: Baywood Publishing.

Settersten, R. A. (Ed.) (2003). *Invitation to the life course: Toward new understandings of later life.* Amityville, NY: Baywood Publishing.

Solari, C., & Mare, R. (2012). Housing crowding effects on children's wellbeing. *Social Science Research, 41*(2), 464–476.

Srinivasan, S., O'Fallon, L. R., & Dearry, A. (2003). Creating healthy communities, healthy homes, healthy people: Initiating a research agenda on the built environment and public health. *American Journal of Public Health, 93*(9), 1446–1450.

Stevens, G. D. (2006). Gradients in the health status and developmental risks of young children: The combined influence of multiple social risk factors. *Maternal and Child Health Journal, 10*(2), 187–199.

Wachs, T. D., & Gruen, D. (1982). *Early experience and human development.* New York, NY: Plenum.

Wanyeki, I., Olson, S., Brassard, P., Menzies, D., Ross, N., Behr, M., & Schwartzman, K. (2006). Dwellings, crowding, and tuberculosis in Montreal. *Social Science Medicine, 63*(2), 501–511.

Warren, J. R., & Hernandez, E. M. (2007). Did socioeconomic inequalities in morbidity and mortality change in the United States over the course of the twentieth century? *Journal of Health and Social Behavior, 48*(4), 335–351.

Willson, A. E., Shuey, K. M., & Elder, G. H. Jr. (2007). Cumulative advantage processes as mechanisms of inequality in life course health. *American Journal of Sociology, 112*(6), 1886–1924.

Chapter 8

The Effects of Exposure to Neighborhood Violence

Margaret Hardy, David S. Kirk, and
Jeffrey M. Timberlake

Since the 1970s, there has been increasing attention paid to the plight of poor inner-city neighborhoods. The loss of blue-collar employment opportunities, coupled with the increasing settlement of middle-class residents in neighborhoods on the fringes of inner cities and in the suburbs, has led to dramatic growth in the concentration of poverty in many American cities (Jargowsky, 1998; Wilson, 1987, 1996). Although not all poor neighborhoods suffer from high rates of crime and violence, poverty contributes to higher rates of neighborhood crime and violence by undermining both formal social control (through a lack of institutional resources) and informal social control (through increased isolation and a weakening of social ties), and by contributing to the social and economic strain that often serves as a precursor to violence (Agnew, 2006; Warner, 1999). In turn, violence has both direct and indirect effects on a whole range of outcomes, particularly health and well-being. Research on the direct effects of violence victimization has revealed both short- and long-term physical and mental health effects, including injury, depression, and death. But what about the effects of violence on those individuals who merely witness a violent event? That is the question we seek to answer in this chapter.

Exposure to violence is a common occurrence in the everyday lives of many urban residents, including urban youth. For instance, a survey conducted in 2008 by the U.S. Office of Juvenile Justice and Delinquency Prevention revealed that more than 60% of youth younger than age 17 are directly or indirectly exposed to violence each year, with close to 40% suffering from exposure to multiple incidents of violence (Finkelhor, Turner, Ormrod, Hamby, & Kracke, 2009). Recent results from the Monitoring the Future Study, an ongoing survey of middle and high school-aged youth, reveal that more than 70% of those surveyed were concerned about violence in their neighborhoods, with the rates being much higher for African-American youth than for White youth (Esbensen, Peterson, Taylor, & Freng, 2010).

The consequences of exposure to neighborhood violence can be dire. For many urban residents, the threat of violence in their neighborhood has shaped "attitudes, perceptions, behavior, and social identity" (Wilkinson, 2003, p. 47). Violence in the neighborhood contributes to a sense of the unpredictable nature of daily life, in which merely walking down the street or waiting on the corner for a bus may be fraught with risk. For many urban neighborhoods, crime and violence are nothing new; however, over the past 30 years, violence in the inner city has become increasingly lethal due to the widespread availability of guns (Wilkinson, 2003). The prevalence of violence in a neighborhood can affect the socialization process for inner-city youth; in addition, as related to the topic of this chapter, it can affect internal and external health outcomes for all residents.

Youth and other urban residents need not be direct victims of a violent event to feel its effects; for example, simply hearing gunshots in the neighborhood can lead to changes in an individual's mental and physical health. Exposure to violence includes outcomes as diverse as post-traumatic stress disorder, anxiety, depression, low birth weight, sleep deprivation, obesity, attention-deficit/hyperactivity disorder (ADHD), asthma, and heart disease (Fitzpatrick & Boldizar, 1993; Graham-Bermann & Seng, 2005; Krug, Mercy, Dahlberg, & Zwi, 2002; Margolin & Gordis, 2000; Morenoff, 2003; Wright & Steinbach, 2001). In turn, the health consequences of exposure to violence, particularly those related to mental health, may impair cognitive development and hinder educational attainment (Grogger, 1997; Harding, 2010; Margolin & Gordis, 2000). Importantly, exposure to violence is unevenly distributed across race, ethnicity, and socioeconomic status. Thus the adverse consequences of repeated exposure to violence are largely concentrated among impoverished, minority households (Brennan, Molnar, & Earls, 2007; Fitzpatrick & Boldizar, 1993).

This chapter provides an overview of the effects of exposure to violence at the neighborhood level. We begin with a discussion of differences in exposure to violence according to demographic characteristics. We offer a theoretical rationale to explain the individual's reaction to exposure to violence, and provide an overview of the short- and long-term effects of exposure to violence on an individual's physical and mental health. We conclude by discussing avenues for future research and public policy initiatives.

Variations in Exposure to Violence

Studies of exposure to neighborhood violence have consistently found differences in the likelihood of exposure to violence based on the demographic characteristics of the neighborhood, including racial-ethnic composition and the poverty rate of the neighborhood. Rates of exposure to neighborhood violence are highest among individuals living in high-poverty urban neighborhoods with a predominantly African-American population. Many of the observed racial and ethnic differences in rates of exposure to violence are tied to conditions that are found in the neighborhood. Other structural factors, including poverty, social disorganization, and unemployment, are highly related to the risk of an individual being exposed to a violent event (Esbensen et al., 2010).

Economic restructuring of the U.S. economy is one root source of the race and socioeconomic differentials in exposure to violence. Over the past 40 years, large-scale macroeconomic changes, along with urban housing policy decisions, have contributed to an unequal distribution of poverty and unemployment by race and ethnicity. Wilson (1987, 1996) examined the effect of pervasive joblessness on urban African-American neighborhoods in the last decades of the 20th century. Deindustrialization in urban areas resulted in a loss of traditional blue-collar jobs, and a stratification between high- and low-wage jobs, with few opportunities found between them. Additionally, those low-skilled workers in urban neighborhoods who have retained employment have faced eroding opportunities within the workplace for economic advancement coupled with a drop in wages. These economic shifts have disproportionately affected low-skilled men. Low-skilled women have increasingly found opportunities within the growing service sector of the economy, as employment opportunities have increased in areas of employment that were traditionally dominated by women, including nursing and clerical work. The loss of goods-producing employment opportunities resulted in increasing numbers of men who are unemployed, working part-time, or in temporary jobs, as well as the growth of a class of men who are classified as habitually nonworking.

These economic changes have adversely affected the African-American population in urban areas. In 1970, roughly 70% of African-Americans in cities were working in blue-collar jobs; by 1987, however, fewer than 20% held similar jobs (Wilson, 1996). The number of African-American men employed in the service sector has increased in tandem with the growth of that sector; however, their annual earnings are below the earning potential found in manufacturing-sector jobs. Additionally, career advancement in service-sector jobs often requires secondary education, blocking additional paths for increasing earnings for those persons with only a high school diploma.

The depletion of job opportunities in the inner city, coupled with the out-migration of middle-class African-Americans and poor non-Blacks, has "removed an important social buffer that could potentially deflect the full impact of prolonged joblessness and industrial transformation" (Sampson & Wilson, 1995, p. 42). The viability of neighborhood institutions such as schools and churches is largely dependent upon the presence of stable families within the neighborhood. The loss of jobs and the exodus of middle-class families from the inner city have led to an erosion of these neighborhood institutions. Related to neighborhood violence, Sampson and Wilson (1995, p. 50) suggest that in disorganized, socially isolated slum communities, "a system of values emerges in which crime, disorder, and drug use are less fervently condemned." Hence, concentrated poverty and disadvantage lead to neighborhood violence because conventional norms and values that stand in opposition to violence are suspended in culturally isolated neighborhoods.

One of the consequences of the unequal distribution of poverty, primarily the concentration of poverty in inner-city African-American neighborhoods, is that the residents of these communities are disproportionately affected by crime and have a higher risk of exposure to crime and violence in the neighborhood (as apart from violence in the household). African-Americans and Latinos have been found to be more likely than Whites to be both victims and witnesses to violence, with African-Americans having higher rates of exposure than Latinos (Brennan et al., 2007; Fitzpatrick & Boldizar, 1993). Exposure to violence has also been found to vary by socioeconomic status (SES). Specifically, witnessing violence, violent victimization, and knowing of others who have been victimized are phenomena that disproportionately affect poor youth, particularly when compared with middle-class youth (Gladstein, Rusonis, & Heald, 1992).

Numerous surveys conducted over the past 20 years have revealed socioeconomic and racial differences in neighborhood exposure to violence. Sheidow, Gorman-Smith, Tolan, and Henry (2001) surveyed African-American and Latino teenagers living in inner-city neighborhoods in Chicago. More than 94% reported exposure to neighborhood violence at some point during their lifetime, and more than 86% reported witnessing neighborhood violence in the past year. A study conducted by Hill and Jones (1997) further supports the finding that neighborhood violence is concentrated in low-income minority neighborhoods. These researchers conducted a survey of 9- to 12-year-olds living in Washington, D.C., and found that more than 75% of low-income African-American children included in the study had witnessed an incident of neighborhood violence.

The Monitoring the Future Study provides evidence indicating that racial and ethnic differences in direct victimization and exposure to violence may be more subtle. In examining the high school seniors surveyed in the 1980s and 1990s, violent victimization and exposure to violence were not found to be dramatically different according to the race/ethnicity of the surveyed individual. However, when exposure to violence and victimization was broken down into specific categories, such as theft, mugging, and robbery, wide racial variations were reported. Incidents of exposure to the most violent types of crimes, such as robberies and aggravated assaults, were concentrated among the African-American youth in the study. Hence, while exposure to any type of violence was reported by youth regardless of race or ethnicity, the most violent forms uniquely affect African-American youth (Esbensen et al., 2010).

Health Consequences of Exposure to Violence

While victimization and exposure to violence have a well-documented link with future crime and delinquency, they produce important physical and mental health consequences as well. Research reveals that the effect of neighborhood violence extends beyond direct exposure to violence in the form of victimization, to nonfatal health problems grounded in indirect exposure—that is, witnessing violence (Buka, Stichick, Birdthistle, & Earls, 2001; Martinez & Richters, 1993). Witnessing violence has been found to affect both mental health and physical functioning.

One causal mechanism linking exposure to neighborhood violence and health is stress. Robert Agnew's general strain theory (1992, 2002) provides a theoretical framework for understanding how the stress brought on by exposure to violence can be detrimental to an individual's well-being. Agnew distinguishes three types of strain that a person can experience: a loss of something of value, a perceived negative experience, and failure to achieve a certain goal. There are numerous sources of each type of strain; two related types that Agnew specifically mentions as "negative" or "noxious" are residence in a violent neighborhood and witnessing violence (Agnew, 2002). According to general strain theory, an individual exposed to a strain such as neighborhood violence, for example, will experience a variety of negative emotions, including disappointment, fear, anxiety, and depression (Agnew, 2006).

Physical Health Consequences

The physiological effects of exposure to violence are not as extensively researched as mental health outcomes, yet exposure to violence may result in physical problems throughout the life course. Psychological stress from exposure to violence has been linked to biological changes in both the immune system and the hypothalamic-pituitary-adrenal (HPA) system (Wright & Steinbach, 2001). When these systems are operating under conditions of either overactivity or underactivity, the body is at an increased risk for many physical health problems, such as a decreased ability to fight infections (Wright & Steinbach, 2001). In a study conducted in Chicago, Morenoff (2003) found that neighborhood violence was significantly related to low birth weight, affecting not only incidence of low birth weight but also the reported health of the mother while pregnant. Neighborhood violence was found to be one of the strongest predictors of low birth weight, even when controlling for neighborhood structural characteristics such as poverty. The level of poverty and disadvantage in a neighborhood leads to differential exposure to stressors, including violence, which in turn influence physical health.

The influence of exposure to violence on the physical health of mothers was also identified in a study of Baltimore conducted by Johnson, Solomon, Shields, McDonald, McKenzie, and Gielen (2009). More than 50% of the predominantly African-American sample reported either medium or high levels of exposure to neighborhood violence in the past year. High levels of exposure to violence were linked to poor self-reported health, smoking, and a lack of exercise. Poor sleep behavior, such as frequently interrupted sleep, was significantly related to high exposure to violence. In addition to being linked to mothers' sleep behavior, exposure to neighborhood violence has been found to be positively related to sleep disturbance in adolescent youth (Cooley-Quille & Lorion, 1999).

Exposure to neighborhood violence appears to be highly influential in determining various health outcomes among children. In a sample of pre-school children living in poverty, children who reported symptoms of traumatic stress from witnessing violence experienced higher rates of asthma, allergies, and gastrointestinal problems than those youth who reported no traumatic stress (Graham-Bermann & Seng, 2005). Higher rates of asthma were also found in a sample of Boston youth exposed to violence, with many youth reporting an acute episode of asthma immediately following witnessing a violent event (Wright & Steinbach, 2001). Experiencing trauma related to witnessing violence may also produce biological responses similar to those found in youth with eating disorders or depression, including lower levels of testosterone and higher levels of cortisol (Buka et al., 2001; Putnam & Trickett, 1993). In addition to influencing physical health, exposure to neighborhood violence affects the level of compliance with medical follow-up for many of these disorders. Neighborhood violence has been linked to numerous negative health management outcomes, including fear of traveling to medical centers and pharmacies (Fong, 1995). Failure to fill prescriptions, or to engage with physicians who may monitor the continuation of care for physical health problems, may result in the unnecessary exacerbation of these health disorders.

Mental Health Consequences

The psychological stress related to exposure to neighborhood violence not only affects an individual's physical health, but has also been found to affect a variety of mental health outcomes, including depression and anxiety. Similar to many of the physical health outcomes, these mental health outcomes have been reported following exposure to a violent event, and most persist well past the point of initial exposure. The mental health outcomes, in particular, are interrelated and compound the consequences of exposure to violence (Margolin & Gordis, 2000).

Post-traumatic Stress Disorder.   Many of the physical effects related to exposure to violence, such as differential baseline levels of cortisol, are consistent with those found in studies of individuals with post-traumatic stress disorder (PTSD). In addition to the physical side effects of PTSD, the mental health symptoms of this disorder have been widely researched and documented in studies on exposure to violence. Children exposed to a single incident of violence at school reported measurable levels of symptoms of PTSD, such as flashbacks (Pynoos et al., 1987). Studies of chronic exposure to violence in the neighborhood have revealed similar results. In a survey of low-income African-American youth, being victimized and witnessing violence were found to be significantly related to reported symptoms of PTSD, with more than 25% of the sample meeting the diagnostic criteria for PTSD (Fitzpatrick & Boldizar, 1993).

Reports of symptoms of PTSD were also found in a study of lower-income adolescents who reported witnessing serious forms of violence, including homicide (Giaconia et al., 2005). More than 40% of the sample reported experiencing a traumatic event; of those youth who witnessed someone being hurt or killed, 64% met the criteria for a lifetime diagnosis of PTSD. The authors also found that receiving such a diagnosis was significantly related to an increased risk of experiencing other psychiatric disorders by the time the youth reached age 18. PTSD was associated with an increased risk of reporting major depression and serious substance use and dependence. Youth continued to report experiencing emotional and behavioral problems years past the initial traumatic experience, revealing the long-lasting effects of exposure to violence.

Depression.   While there exists a well-documented link between victimization and exposure to violence and PTSD, studies examining many of the other consequences of exposure to violence reveal the nuanced relationships among poverty, exposure to violence, and internalizing and externalizing behavior problems. Fitzpatrick (1993) examined low-income African-American youth residing in eight different neighborhoods within a single city. While violent victimization was related to increased depression, this relationship was not found for youth who reported just witnessing violence. In fact, older youth who were chronically exposed to violence actually reported fewer symptoms of depression. Fitzpatrick suggests that as youth age, they develop coping mechanisms that lead to an emotional insulation from the effects of exposure to violence. However, the physical and psychological costs of adapting to a chronically violent environment may ultimately result in "the once-insulated youth [becoming] the socially maladapted adult" (p. 531).

A study of inner-city youth in New York provides further evidence that youth who are exposed to violence may become desensitized as a way to cope with this form of stress. Moses (1999) examined various forms of neighborhood violence, including violence directed at the respondent's family or friends or directed at strangers. More than 60% of the sample reported at least one type of exposure to violence, and exposure to violence was found to be related to elevated reports of both depression and hostility. Moses also found that only violence against the respondent's family was significantly related to depression, whereas hostility was related only to violence against family and friends. Violence against strangers was thus unrelated to depression and hostility, and the lack of an emotional reaction to such violence given the overall prevalence of witnessing violence in the neighborhood indicates emotional desensitization.

Aggression and Violence.   In addition to physical and mental health concerns, increasing aggression and engagement in acts of violence have been found to result from exposure to violence. Heightened levels of depression and aggression were found among youth exposed to violence who participated in the Chicago Youth Development Study (Gorman-Smith & Tolan, 1998). In this study of African-American and Latino male youth residing in low-income communities, more than 60% of the sample reported witnessing at least one type of violence in the past year, with nearly 80% witnessing some form of violence in the neighborhood during their lifetime. The authors examined other potential sources of stress, such as health and family financial problems, and found that these sources of stress were not related to any changes in the youth's level of aggression. These results indicate that youth exposed to violence are at a heightened risk of perceiving violence and aggression as normative behavior.

The normalization thesis has been used to explain many of the negative outcomes related to aggression observed among those persons who are exposed to violence. According to this theory, individuals exposed to violence come to view violence as normative and, as a result, may perpetrate acts of violence or condone or tolerate violence in the future (Margolin & Gordis, 2000). Consistent with the normalization thesis, changes in aggressive behavior and cognitions were found in the Metropolitan Area Child Study. Of the first through sixth graders who were included in the sample, 80% were African-American or Latino, and all resided in neighborhoods with high levels of economic disadvantage. As the youth in the sample aged, reports of aggressive behavior increased, and the youth reported more normative beliefs that supported aggression as well (Guerra, Huesmann, & Spindler, 2003). Interestingly, as aggression increased, the youth in the study reported less exposure to violence. Guerra and colleagues caution that while this finding may represent an actual reduction in exposure to violence, given the high rates of violence in the neighborhoods in the study, it is also likely that as the youth aged, they became habituated to violence.

Surveys of middle and high school-aged youth (including the Monitoring the Future Study) have consistently found that youth who live in neighborhoods with high levels of violence, as well as ready access to guns and other weapons, are more likely to engage in future acts of violence than those youth who live in areas where these weapons are less available (Esbensen et al., 2010). In a survey of young adults, Paschall and colleagues (1998) found that past exposure to violence was one of the main risk factors for future violent behavior, with exposure to violence and subsequent delinquent behavior stratified along racial lines. In their sample of young adults in an urban area, 43% of all surveyed individuals reported having witnessed violence in the form of hearing a gun being shot, seeing another individual being stabbed or shot, or seeing gang activity, while 22% reported engaging in violent behavior. The low-SES African-American respondents were almost twice as likely as the low-SES White respondents to report having ever witnessed violence (85% compared to 49%). Additionally, the African-Americans in the study were also more likely to report perpetrating an act of violence in the year prior to the survey.

Implications for Public Policy and Future Research

Exposure to violence, whether in the form of direct victimization or witnessing violence in one's neighborhood, adversely affects individuals living in high-poverty areas. Exposure to violence has been revealed to have detrimental effects on both physical and mental health, and has also been linked to increased aggression, criminal acts, and changing normative beliefs about aggression. While exposure to violence does lead to heightened levels of depression and aggression immediately following the violent act, much of the more recent research suggests that the long-term effects of chronic exposure to violence may be the most damaging to the individual.

Few studies have examined the effects of sustained exposure to violence on an individual's health and behavioral outcomes. The effects of exposure to violence on long-term physical and mental health—particularly as discussed by Gorman-Smith and Tolan (1998), Guerra et al. (2003), and Giaconia et al. (1995)—persist beyond the point of initial exposure. Thus, in addition to any detrimental outcomes from the initial exposure to violence, an individual may develop heightened levels of mental health problems and increased aggression over time. The long-term effects of exposure to violence may also be amplified among those persons who are chronically exposed to violence. The changing cognitions related to aggression, as well as differential reported rates of depression among those exposed to violence, suggest that violence and aggression may become normative behavior for individuals living in these communities. This potential "desensitization" needs to be explored further in future research.

In addition to elucidation of the effects of the duration of exposure, a comprehensive understanding of the changing conditions of neighborhoods would enhance our understanding of the ways in which poverty interacts with an individual's exposure to violence in the neighborhood and the ability to cope with violence in the neighborhood. Research on neighborhood change has revealed that in tandem with changes in the concentration of poverty and affluence in many cities, many transitory working-class neighborhoods are undergoing processes of economic upgrading or downgrading according to these population changes (Morenoff & Tienda, 1997). Such changing conditions in neighborhoods have been shown to affect the residents of those areas. Brooks-Gunn and colleagues (1993) found that better childhood developmental outcomes occurred in neighborhoods as the proportion of moderate-income neighbors grew. Economic changes in neighborhoods, even if they do not directly influence the child's family's economic condition, may still influence childhood development, which could potentially include physical and mental health outcomes of witnessing violence.

The conditions of the neighborhood in which a person lives, particularly during childhood, may have long-term effects on an individual, even if he or she no longer lives in that area. Wheaton and Clarke (2003), using data from the National Survey of Children, found that when the conditions of the neighborhood in which an individual lived during childhood were controlled for, such as levels of poverty and violence, the current neighborhood conditions (in adulthood) had no significant effect on mental health. Thus, as suggested by the work of Guerra et al. (2003), early environmental conditions continue to influence individuals' mental health beyond the time they resided in a particular area. While an individual may live in a middle-class neighborhood with little crime in adulthood, childhood exposure to poverty and violence may have lasting consequences on mental health and social cognitions.

Evidence of the enduring consequences of poor, violent neighborhoods can be seen in evaluations of the Moving to Opportunity for Fair Housing Demonstration (MTO). Interim findings from the MTO experiment indicated that moving male youths out of impoverished neighborhoods had no effect on the psychological distress, depression, and anxiety. Moreover, moving out of poverty actually led to more risky behavior among males (i.e., drug and alcohol use, smoking, and arrest for property crime) (Kling, Leibman, & Katz, 2007; Kling, Ludwig, & Katz, 2005; Sanbonmatsu et al., 2011). For the adults in the families who changed neighborhoods, no significant improvement in physical health was reported and no significant change in employment status or income was found.

Given that simply moving away from a violent neighborhood is not a plausible solution for many individuals who are exposed to violence, and as even families who are able to move from high- to low-poverty neighborhoods may not experience positive benefits, strategies to lessen the impact of poverty and exposure to violence should also focus on increasing investment in neighborhood resources. Community empowerment theory argues that the more residents of a neighborhood are involved in the decision-making processes that influence the social conditions in which they live, the more those residents will take direct responsibility for and interest in their neighborhood (Welsh & Hoshi, 2002). Developing neighborhood social organizations and increasing involvement in existing programs or organizations may lessen both the impact of exposure to violence and the actual incidence of violence in the neighborhood.

While it remains imperative to focus on reducing violence in the neighborhood as a whole, other, more immediate strategies may potentially lessen the effects of exposure to violence on youth in particular. Youth have the benefit of interacting with an existing neighborhood institution—the school—on a daily basis; thus school-based programs provide a promising avenue toward lessening the impact of exposure to violence. Several school-based intervention programs, including social skills training programs and cognitive-behavioral therapy, have been found to be effective in reducing delinquency, substance use, and school dropout rates, along with other problem behaviors (Wilson, Gottfredson, & Najaka, 2001). For youth who may have been exposed to violence and are currently exhibiting problem behaviors, programs that include a cognitive-behavioral component may help to reduce current levels of aggression and provide youth with the skills they need to cope with future stressful events (Gottfredson,

Wilson, & Najaka, 2002). Other youth living in violent neighborhoods who may not have been exposed to violence yet will benefit from these programs as well, as the program will function as a preventive mechanism should the youth ever be exposed to violence. The availability of school-based prevention programs, however, is strongly tied to local economic conditions. As a result, many of the types of programs that have been shown to be effective in treating and reducing problem behaviors may not be available to those youth who are most in need of them.

Conclusion

Exposure to neighborhood violence remains a pervasive problem in many low-income urban areas despite the fact that aggregate levels of violence have declined in the United States for two decades. This problem persists because the decline in violence has been uneven. For instance, Weisburd and colleagues (2006) found that the overall crime rate in Seattle declined 24% from 1989 to 2002—yet the vast majority of street blocks in Seattle did not see any reduction in crime over the period, while a small percentage of blocks saw a significant uptick in crime. In many poor neighborhoods in the United States, more than half of all children and youth have reported witnessing violence, with this trend disproportionately affecting African-American youth (Esbensen et al., 2010). The consequences of exposure to violence range from increased rates of many physical health problems, such as asthma, heart disease, and low birth weight, to heightened symptoms of mental health conditions, such as depression and anxiety. Despite the various manifestations of exposure to violence, outcomes are linked to such exposure through the manner in which individuals cope with the stress related to neighborhood violence.

Is it tempting to think that by simply removing an individual from a dangerous or violent neighborhood, we would be able to eliminate the repercussions and stress that result from living in that environment. Unfortunately, that is not the case. The effects of exposure to violence very often persist beyond the point of initial exposure, and they may permanently alter an individual's level of aggression, anxiety, depression, and physical health. Exposure to violence also may increase the risk that an individual will commit future acts of violence. Because neighborhood effects endure, residential mobility programs such as MTO may have limited utility in offsetting the physical and mental health effects of exposure to neighborhood violence, at least in the short term. Clearly, then, additional policy interventions are needed that would provide individuals with the tools needed to cope with the stress related to violence exposure.

In addition to aiding individuals with stress management, interventions that focus on alleviating the effects of neighborhood poverty may lessen the incidence of violence. Rebuilding neighborhood institutions and increasing support for school-based intervention programs have a well-documented history of alleviating the negative effects of many neighborhood conditions, including poverty and violence. However, in an era where funding for new programs is scarce, it is up to researchers and practitioners to develop imaginative policy interventions that may not require the same degree of financial investment.

References

Agnew, R. (1992). Foundation for a general strain theory of crime and delinquency. *Criminology, 30*(1), 47–88.

Agnew, R. (2002). Experienced, vicarious, and anticipated strain: An exploratory study focusing on criminal victimization and delinquency. *Justice Quarterly, 19*(4), 603–632.

Agnew, R. (2006). *Pressured into crime: An overview of general strain theory.* Los Angeles, CA: Roxbury.

Brennan, R. T., Molnar, B. E., & Earls, F. (2007). Refining the measurement of exposure to violence (ETV) in urban youth. *Journal of Community Psychology, 35* (5), 603–618.

Brooks-Gunn, J., Duncan, G. J., Klebanov, P. K., & Sealand, N. (1993). Do neighborhoods influence child and adolescent development? *American Journal of Sociology, 99*(2), 353–395.

Buka, S. L., Stichick, T. L., Birdthistle, I., & Earls, F. J. (2001). Youth exposure to violence: Prevalence, risks, and consequences. *American Journal of Orthopsychiatry, 71*(3), 298–310.

Cooley-Quille, M. R., & Lorion, R. (1999). Adolescents' exposure to community violence: Sleep and psychophysiological functioning. *Journal of Community Psychology, 27*(4), 367–375.

Esbensen, F. A., Peterson, D., Taylor, T. J., & Freng, A. (2010). *Youth violence: Sex and race differences in offending, victimization, and gang membership.* Philadelphia, PA: Temple University Press.

Finkelhor, D., Turner, H., Ormrod, R., Hamby, S., & Kracke, K. (2009). *Children's exposure to violence: A comprehensive national survey. Juvenile Justice Bulletin.* Washington, DC: Office of Juvenile Justice and Delinquency Prevention.

Fitzpatrick, K. M. (1993). Exposure to violence and presence of depression among low-income African-American youth. *Journal of Consulting and Clinical Psychology, 61*(3), 528–531.

Fitzpatrick, K. M., & Boldizar, J. P. (1993). The prevalence and consequences of exposure to violence among African-American youth. *Journal of the American Academy of Adolescent Psychiatry, 32*(2), 424–430.

Fong, R. L. (1995). Violence as a barrier to compliance for the hypertensive urban African-American. *Journal of the National Medical Association, 87*(3), 203–207.

Giaconia, R. M., Reinherz, H. Z., Silverman, A. B., Pakiz, B., Frost, A. K., & Cohen, E. (1995). Traumas and posttraumatic stress disorder in a community population of older adolescents. *Journal of the American Academy of Child and Adolescent Psychiatry, 34*(10), 1369–1380.

Gladstein, J., Rusonis, E. J., & Heald, F. P. (1992). A comparison of inner-city and upper-middle class youths' exposure to violence. *Journal of Adolescent Health, 13*(4), 275–280.

Gorman-Smith, D., & Tolan, P. (1998). The role of exposure to community violence and developmental problems among inner-city youth. *Development and Psychopathology, 10*(1), 101–116.

Gottfredson, D. C., Wilson, D. B., & Najaka, S. S. (2002). School-based crime prevention. In L. W. Sherman, D. P. Farrington, B. C. Welsh, & D. L. Mackenzie (Eds.), *Evidence-based crime prevention* (pp. 56–164). New York, NY: Routledge.

Graham-Bermann, S. A., & Seng, J. (2005). Violence exposure and traumatic stress symptoms as additional predictors of health problems in high risk children. *Journal of Pediatrics, 146*(3), 349–354.

Grogger, J. (1997). Local violence and educational attainment. *Journal of Human Resources, 32*(4), 659–682.

Guerra, N. G., Huesmann, L. R., & Spindler, A. (2003). Community violence exposure, social cognition, and aggression among urban elementary school children. *Child Development, 74*(5), 1561–1576.

Harding, D. J. (2010). *Living the drama: Community, conflict, and culture among inner-city boys.* Chicago, IL: University of Chicago Press.

Hill, H. M., & Jones, L. P. (1997). Children's and parents' perceptions of children's exposure to violence in urban neighborhoods. *Journal of the National Medical Association, 89*(4), 270–276.

Jargowsky, P. A. (1998). *Poverty and place: Ghettos, barrios, and the American city.* New York, NY: Russell Sage Foundation.

Johnson, S. L., Solomon, B. S., Shields, W. C., McDonald, E. M., McKenzie, L. B., & Gielen, A. C. (2009). Neighborhood violence and its association with mothers' health: Assessing the relative importance of perceived safety and exposure to violence. *Journal of Urban Health, 86*(4), 538–550.

Kling, J. R, Leibman, J. B., & Katz, L. F. (2007). Experimental analysis of neighborhood effects. *Econometrika, 75*(1), 83–119.

Kling, J. R, Ludwig, J. O., & Katz, L. F. (2005). Neighborhood effects on crime for female and male youth: Evidence from a randomized housing voucher experiment. *Quarterly Journal of Economics, 120*(1), 87–130.

Krug, E. G., Mercy, J. A., Dahlberg, L. L., & Zwi, A. B. (2002). The world report on violence and health. *Lancet, 360*, 1083–1088.

Margolin, G., & Gordis, E. B. (2000). The effects of family and community violence on children. *Annual Review of Psychology, 51*, 445–479.

Martinez, P., & Richters, J. E. (1993). The NIMH community violence project: Vol. 2. Children's distress symptoms associated with violence exposure. *Psychiatry, 56*(1), 23–35.

Morenoff, J. D. (2003). Neighborhood mechanisms and the spatial dynamics of birth weight. *American Journal of Sociology, 108*(5), 976–1017.

Morenoff, J. D., & Tienda, M. (1997). Underclass neighborhoods in temporal and ecological perspective. *Annals of the American Academy of Political and Social Science, 551*, 59–72.

Moses, A. (1999). Exposure to violence, depression, and hostility in a sample of inner city high school youth. *Journal of Adolescence, 22*(1), 21–32.

Paschall, M. J., Flewelling, R. L., & Ennett, S. T. (1998). Racial differences in violent behavior among young adults: Moderating and confounding effects. *Journal of Research in Crime and Delinquency, 35*(2), 148–165.

Putnam, F., & Trickett, R. (1993). Child sexual abuse: A model of chronic trauma. *Psychiatry, 56*(1), 82–95.

Pynoos, R. S., Frederick, C., Nader, K., Arroyo, E., Steinberg, A., Eth, S., . . . Fairbanks, L. (1987). Life threat and posttraumatic stress in school-age children. *Archives of General Psychiatry, 44*(12), 1057–1063.

Sampson, R. J., & Wilson, W. J. (1995). Toward a theory of race, crime, and urban inequality. In J. Hagan & R. Peterson (Eds.), *Crime and inequality* (pp. 37–54). Stanford, CA: Stanford University Press.

Sanbonmatsu, L., Ludwig, J., Katz, L. F., Gennetian, L. A., Duncan, G. J., Kessler, R. C., . . . Lindau, S. T. (2011). *Moving to Opportunity for Fair Housing Demonstration Program: Final impacts evaluation.* Washington, DC: U.S. Department of Housing and Urban Development, Office of Policy Development and Research.

Sheidow, A. J., Gorman-Smith, D., Tolan, P. H., & Henry, D. B. (2001). Family and community characteristics: Risk factors for violence exposure in inner-city youth. *Journal of Community Psychology, 29*(3), 345–360.

Warner, B. D. (1999). Whither poverty? Social disorganization theory in an era of urban transformation. *Sociological Focus, 32*(1), 99–113.

Weisburd, D., Bushway, S., Lum, C., & Yang, S. (2006). Trajectories of crime at places: A longitudinal study of street segments in the city of Seattle. *Criminology, 42*(2), 283–321.

Welsh, B. C., & Hoshi, A. (2002). Communities and crime prevention. In L. W. Sherman, D. P. Farrington, B. C. Welsh, & D. L. Mackenzie (Eds.), *Evidence-based crime prevention* (pp. 165–197). New York, NY: Routledge.

Wheaton, B., & Clarke, P. (2003). Space meets time: Integrating temporal and contextual influences on mental health in early adulthood. *American Sociological Review, 68*(5), 680–706.

Wilkinson, D. L. (2003). *Guns, violence, and identity among African American and Latino youth.* New York, NY: LFB Scholarly Publishing.

Wilson, D. B., Gottfredson, D. C., & Najaka, S. S. (2001). School-based prevention of problem behaviors: A meta-analysis. *Journal of Quantitative Criminology, 17*(3), 247–272.

Wilson, W. J. (1987). *The truly disadvantaged.* Chicago, IL: University of Chicago Press.

Wilson, W. J. (1996). *When work disappears.* New York, NY: Vintage Books.

Wright, R. J., & Steinbach, S. F. (2001). Violence: An unrecognized environmental exposure that may contribute to greater asthma morbidity in high risk inner-city populations. *Environmental Health Perspectives, 109*(10), 1085–1089.

Chapter 9

Intersections of Development, Poverty, Race, and Space in the Mississippi Delta in the Era of Globalization: Implications for Gender-Based Health Issues

John J. Green and Debarashmi Mitra

Introduction

Globalization has led to development processes and practices across a variety of social and spatial contexts, resulting in differential impacts for various groups and affecting access to socioeconomic resources. The recent recession and labor market crisis have caused job losses and increased the number of working poor (United Nations, 2010) in both developed and less developed countries. Although economic restructuring programs are implemented primarily in the Global South (including the less-developed nations in the Southern Hemisphere and those with similar characteristics in the Northern Hemisphere), highly developed nations are also undergoing economic and social transformations. This includes the United States, with its high unemployment, pockets of deep poverty, and uneven economic growth.

Geographic differences in development programs (i.e., programs directed toward intentional social and economic change) adversely influence marginalized sections of the population, such as women and minority racial-ethnic groups, who are highly vulnerable to economic shocks and threats (Jensen, McLaughlin, & Slack, 2003; Nelson, 1999). Such groups are more likely to have limited human capital (e.g., education, labor force experience, advanced skills), causing them to be hit hard by economic restructuring, as jobs they formerly held are systematically transferred to other locales as part of the "race to the bottom" of wages, socioeconomic protections, and regulations. Under the free trade and limited government direction of economic restructuring programs and policies of the globalization project (McMichael, 2008), state-based social services are often cut—a trend that disproportionately affects women (Moghadam, 2007). Additionally, changes in the global economy have threatened the livelihoods of a growing number of women and their families, causing them to fall into poverty (Tickamyer et al., 1993) and compromising their health and well-being.

Through various local, national, and international initiatives, including the internationally agreed-upon Millennium Development Goals (MDGs), development programs have been implemented to respond to the impact of globalization. These programs address issues such as the eradication of poverty and the improvement of maternal health (United Nations, 2010). In the context of health disparities, prior research has documented that contextual factors such as neighborhoods and geographic locations influence the availability, affordability, and accessibility of socioeconomic resources, including health care services and recommended preventive care (Kirby & Kaneda, 2005). However, specific locations are rarely considered in the analyses of conventional development issues related to class, race, and gender-based inequalities and their effect on health disparities. Such development initiatives fail to illuminate the intersections of poverty, racial inequalities, and gender inequalities.

Race, ethnicity, and gender are dimensions of structured inequality—inequality that is inherent within various social institutions and arrangements—and they are often neglected in discussions of development. Nevertheless, the broader literature demonstrates that there are important intersections. As Moghadam (2007) notes, "Through institutions such as the transnational corporation and the state, the global economy generates capital largely through the exploitation of labor, but it is not indifferent to the gender and ethnicity of that labor" (p. 139). This chapter advances the argument that inclusion of geographic locations (i.e., spaces) in the analyses of development issues as they relate to racial and gender inequality in health outcomes is of critical importance.

The goal in this chapter is to synthesize intersectionality and livelihoods development perspectives with relevant health research conducted by the authors in the Mississippi Delta region. The intersections among assets and challenges within multiple systems of inequality are examined, and guidance is offered to practitioners and policymakers regarding their response to the health needs of women living in poverty. Taking the lead from the intersectionality approach and livelihoods framework, emphasis is directed toward construction of an integrated approach in development models to understand gender-based health outcomes, both generally and in the Mississippi Delta, particularly in the era of globalization.

The chapter begins by briefly reviewing "space" and "intersectionality" to prepare for the conceptual framework of "intersectional space." It then examines the intersections of development history, poverty, race, and gender in an actual physical location and employs the conceptual tool of "intersectional space." To explore the set of socioeconomic resources to which people have access, attention is then turned to assessment of how membership in multiple groups influences people's health status in a specific location. Next, an overview of uneven development in the Mississippi Delta is provided to illustrate the intersections of development models, race, poverty, and gender-based health outcomes. The final section offers some suggestions for policy formulation and further research.

Space and Intersectionalities in Context

In recent years, research on poverty and inequality has drawn on the analysis of spatiality (Lobao, Hooks, & Tickamyer, 2007; Tickamyer, 2000). The ways in which space is conceptualized and analyzed vary across studies, partly because of the complexity in spatial settings and dynamics. While an extensive review of "space" is beyond the scope of this chapter, space, as conceptualized by sociologists, geographers, and gender scholars, can be defined according to four key points.

First, space is not merely a geographic location, but is socially and culturally constructed and reconstructed (Soja, 1989) by different groups, through mutual, as well as conflicting, interests and power relations (Chandoke, 1993).

Second, the boundaries of any physical space may overlap with the boundaries of other physical spaces. For example, neighborhoods and school districts may have overlapping physical boundaries. Furthermore, a number of spaces may be embedded within the same physical location, such as counties nested in states, which are in turn nested in nations (Lobao, Rulli, & Brown, 1999). Similarly, nations in international regions, including the Global South and the Global North, and conglomerations of countries within a geographic region are often the by-products of other macro-level changes such as growth of knowledge economy at the global level and spread of "network society" (Castells, 1996).

Third, there is a recognition that space is shaped by other systems of inequality and macro-level processes, particularly uneven development processes. For instance, there are gaps between developed and less developed regions in terms of economic prosperity, employment opportunity, and per capita income. Furthermore, uneven development processes lead to spatial differences—differences in distribution of resources across physical locations—and unequal access to resources within a physical location. As Tickamyer (2000) notes, "spatial arrangements are both products and sources of other forms of inequality" (p. 806). Tickamyer argues that spatial arrangements "can be studied as the context for better scrutinized systems of race/ethnicity, class, gender, and sexual privilege (i.e. men have certain privileges based on their social group membership), as a formative factor in such systems and as their outcomes" (p. 806). Space, then, is simultaneously a source and an outcome of other forms of social inequality such as race-based inequality (Massey & Denton, 1993) and gender-based inequality (McCall, 2001) in different physical locations and institutions. Gotham (2003) posits that space can be analyzed as a connection between social institutions and individual actors who define and negotiate the physical boundaries and their own individual as well as group identities.

Fourth and finally, space can be conceptualized as a "multidimensional construct" that is "socially, culturally, economically, politically, and psychologically defined" (Fitzpatrick & LaGory, 2011, p. 8).

A review of the literature on space reveals that, with only a few exceptions focusing on rural regions and conditions of persistent poverty in the rural South (Duncan, 1999; Falk, Schulman, & Tickamyer, 2003), space (and the related concept, place) most often has been used in analyzing poverty, health, and other forms of inequality in cities, metropolitan areas, and urban areas. Furthermore, in studying spatial inequality related to poverty and health outcomes, researchers often use control variables coded in binary, either/or categories, such as "South/non-South region" or "metropolitan/ nonmetropolitan residence." Such dichotomous conceptualizations of space in terms of opposites offer a narrow perspective of spatial inequality and only partially capture the complex social, economic, and political processes operating within these areas (Tickamyer, 2000).

Another conceptual limitation in the analysis of spatial inequality arises from the use of singular and homogenous categories of class, race, or gender within a specific physical location. Such approaches typically see individuals in a minority group as homogenous, sharing the same life experiences including access to economic opportunities and well-being. Consequently, such approaches ignore the interlocking nature of hierarchical systems and the "multiplied effects of marginalizations" (Choo & Ferree, 2010) for individuals based on the multiplicity of class, race, and gender systems. To illustrate, Black upper-class men may be disadvantaged by race, but their opportunities and life experiences differ from those of Black working-class women, who are disadvantaged by multiple forms of inequalities, such as race, socioeconomic position, and gender. It is important to note, however, these hierarchical systems of inequality are produced in specific physical locations where these categories are created, maintained, and reproduced by sociocultural processes. Overall, even as the literature related to space has grown over the years, existing research studies have neglected to capture the connection between spatial locations and social processes of group formations shaped through multiple axes of inequality.

As a departure from the dichotomous framework of race and gender as binary categories that are assumed to exist in isolation from each other, an intersectionality approach emphasizes the ways that various systems of inequality overlap and shape one another (Collins, 1998; Crenshaw, 1991). As such, an intersectionality approach provides the context for understanding the complexities of social inequality and uneven development. This framework also contextualizes the construction of social difference as a multidimensional process of inequality based on socioeconomic position, race, gender, and other forms of structured inequality. While each hierarchical system can function independently, the systems work together and overlap with one another, creating multiple combinations of advantages and disadvantages for individuals and groups based on their social locations and memberships. Implicit in the intersectional approach is the argument that although class, race, and gender as hierarchical systems negatively influence the lived experiences of individual actors, they also have the potential to influence collective dynamics and group identity.

Although the intersectionality approach is not commonly used in empirical studies of development and health, this method provides a framework for identifying and analyzing disparities as they relate to the experiences of specific groups in specific spaces. The intersectional approach also provides a framework for analysis of other forms of inequality such as race- and gender-based health disparities. For example, economic empowerment of women not only impacts women's socioeconomic positions, but also influences their health status. Research studies demonstrate that women's economic power and political participation have positive effects on the health of their family (Varkey, Kureshi, & Lesnick, 2010). Other studies point to the complexity of social dynamics related to space by demonstrating that socioeconomic status, race, or gender identity alone may not account for variations in health outcomes (Hinze, Lin, Tanetta, & Andersson, 2012).

This chapter examines the linkages among development, poverty, race, and space to better understand gender-based health outcomes. Using the intersectional space theoretical framework to interpret uneven development in a specific regional location (i.e., Mississippi Delta), we ask two questions: (1) How might health outcomes in general and birth outcomes in particular vary by space and race? and (2) How might patterns of intersections and disparities in health status within a specific space be explored and explained?

Intersectional Space as a Conceptual Framework

As noted earlier, space, broadly defined as actual physical and geographic space, operates as the location for multiple intersectionalities based on class, race, gender, and other forms of inequality. While the intersectional approach focuses on the overlap between social groups and structural inequalities, it can also be used to demonstrate a wide variety of spatial inequalities. More specifically, the intersectional approach to space can illuminate multiple axes of social inequalities and overlapping categories of marginalization relevant to analyzing health outcomes across neighborhoods, communities, counties, cities, states, and regions.

"Intersectional space" is defined here as an actual physical space that is historically constructed and continuously shaped by the complex interactions of socioeconomic and cultural forces at the macro, meso, and micro levels. We employ the conceptual framework of intersectional space for analyzing the hierarchies, challenges, and opportunities embedded in a physical location by highlighting (1) intersectional space as it creates, recreates, and perpetuates social inequality through various large-scale developmental processes at the macro level; (2) intersectional space as it contains the contestations among social groups, communities, and institutional arrangements at the meso level; and (3) intersectional space as a site of social practices, everyday life experiences, and agency exercised by individuals and groups at the micro level.

At the macro level, the intersections of cultural forces, the global political economy, and historical processes of development create and re-create variations in socioeconomic status across spaces and regions. The decline in manufacturing-sector jobs and the growth of the service-sector economy have reconfigured economic institutions, affecting the available opportunities for various groups and causing persistent poverty in areas such as the rural southern region of the United States (Lobao, Hooks, & Tickamyer, 2008). In these regions, social inequality embedded in the space often influences other forms of inequalities such as disparities in well-being and health outcomes. For instance, studies show spatial patterning in mortality inequality in the United States (McLaughlin, Stokes, Smith, & Nonoyama, 2007). Research has also identified the link between socioeconomic resources and health, with the influence of these factors being mediated by race and gender (Williams & Sternthal, 2010).

Macro forces, such as open market economies, offer the potential to reduce gender- and race-based disparities by connecting women and other marginalized groups to markets and economic opportunities in an intersectional space. Without supportive public policies and socioeconomic safety nets, however, these opportunities can be ineffective or even detrimental. The findings from a cross-national study show that economic globalization has the potential to improve women's labor force status, their political and familial empowerment, and their maternal health (Mitra, 2007). Yet, the same study demonstrated that other macro-level forces, such as austerity programs and debt dependency of a country, negatively affect women's empowerment and access to economic opportunities. As global economic competition has increased, nation-states tend to focus on policies that cater to the demands of the privileged class more than the needs of vulnerable workers (Castells, 1997). As a result, globalization has marginalized many groups who are not equipped or underequipped to respond to changing economies, thereby creating further socioeconomic and spatial differences. This dynamic is particularly evident in knowledge-based economies. In the context of health disparities, macro-level changes need to be effectively analyzed to capture the variations in health outcomes across physical locations and within specific spaces.

At the meso level, within an intersectional space, institutional forces construct and articulate power relationships among groups. Inevitably, these forces afford unequal opportunities and consequently inhibit the well-being of different social groups. Spatial differences in institutional arrangements, labor laws, social practices, and programs implemented by states or civil society (Lobao et al., 2008) may either help or hinder the well-being of marginalized groups. Additionally, individuals, within and alongside broader institutions, can construct a space in which to effect change (Giddens, 1984). Examples of this dynamic are practices within the family and the workplace.

In many areas, symbolic boundaries between private space and public space separate homes from workplaces and often provide men with the privileges of employment, including access to health care (Ross & Mirowsky, 1995), while limiting such privileges for women, who are more likely to be expected to stay home or opt out of the labor market. Certainly there are exceptions to this dynamic. In many societies, women occupy dual roles as workers and caregivers (Ballantyne, 1999). Furthermore, changes in the economic structure and lack of institutional support make balancing work and family a major challenge for women, especially for single mothers (Burris, 1991), who remain especially vulnerable to poverty. Although their participation in the formal labor market has increased, rates of compensation remain inequitable for women. As Cotter, Hermsen, and Vanneman (2007) argue, changes in opportunity structure in specific locations may lead to higher risks of poverty. Such risks of poverty are amplified for specific groups, including racial and ethnic minorities, women, and single mothers, who often lack adequate safety nets and access to resources in a physical location.

Existing policies and programs directed toward poverty and developmental issues have spatially uneven impacts because they are frequently implemented through a combination of federal-, state-, and county-level offices (Lobao & Hooks, 2003) as well as community-based organizations, which are unevenly located within an intersectional space. Similar patterns have been identified in studies outside of the United States (Bebbington, 2004). More generally, cultural norms and local practices influence policies designed to address poverty (Henderson & Tickamyer, 2009). Within an intersectional space, access to such pathways is determined by physical location, socioeconomic position, race and ethnicity, and gender, all of which affect access to health care services.

In industrialized countries, health care responsibility has shifted from state-funded efforts to informal, less-centralized caregivers, including voluntary organizations and the family (Milligan, 2003). This shift has affected individuals' ability to maintain healthy lifestyles by disrupting access to regular health care providers, especially in rural areas where there is a lack of sufficiently comprehensive community-based care systems (Chalifoux, Neese, Buckwalter, Litwak, & Abraham, 1996). This trend in rural areas illustrates the uneven development patterns and limited access to community-based health care across spatial units.

In the context of uneven development within an intersectional space, scholarship focusing on livelihood systems may be instructive. Individuals, households, organizations, and communities use a mix of livelihood strategies in an attempt to meet and secure a certain standard of living, negotiating social, economic, and political relations within communities and broader institutions in the process (Bebbington, 1999; De Haan, 2000; Ellis, 1998; Hall & Midgley, 2004). Of major interest are the opportunities and threats posed by economic restructuring. The processes of globalization pose particularly challenging opportunities and threats to those who live at the margins of society, because access to resources influences people's capacity to handle changes taking place within the broader society (Bebbington, 1999; De Haan, 2000; De Haan & Zoomers, 2005). Thus the resource mix shapes people's vulnerability and resiliency in the face of change, within an intersectional space.

Organizations and institutions mediate an individual's access to the assets necessary for coping with change by opening and closing pathways for development (De Haan & Zoomers, 2005) in ways that may be spatially uneven (Bebbington, 2004). Local, national, and global processes and policies influence which pathways are available in specific spaces to particular groups. Access to resources provides people with the capacity to respond to broad-based change. Conversely, limited access to these assets results in greater vulnerability for individuals and families. Thus changes in political and economic structures have the potential to influence the livelihood strategies of various social groups.

Finally, at the micro level, opportunities and challenges shape the quality of life in an intersectional space of different groups and individual actors as they attempt to gain control over their own lives and contribute to the development of their families, households, and communities. Within an intersectional space, individual actors maintain social networks and use those ties to both access resources and build support systems for themselves and, in turn, for the groups in which they are members. Intersectional space offers a sociospatial setting in which individuals and groups develop social networks and exercise decision making about their everyday lives and the ways in which they might bring about transformative changes in their communities. Although highly structured on one side, intersectional space, as an ever-evolving concept with fluid and flexible social practices, has openings for collective action and resistance to inequality by local and marginalized groups.

In sum, the intersectional space framework provides an important point of departure for an investigation of how the relations among people belonging to different groups (e.g., based on socioeconomic position, race, and gender) in specific locations enable or constrain access to various resources and how that access affects other forms of inequality, particularly health disparities. While much of the analysis within the development framework is grounded in the context of modernization and globalization processes in the global periphery, we bring together these intersections in livelihood perspectives and development processes in the Mississippi Delta Region in the United States—an intersectional space and rural region that is considered a "periphery within the core," with hierarchical systems based on class, race, and gender (Hyland & Timberlake, 1993). It is to that region that we now turn.

The Context: Uneven Development in the Mississippi Delta

In exploring intersectional space and the connections between geographic space, poverty, race, gender, and health outcomes, the region known as the Mississippi Delta serves as an illustrative case. The region may be conceived at a variety of spatial levels, including one encompassing 252 counties/parishes across an eight-state region unified under the Delta Regional Authority (n.d.). This chapter focuses on the "Core" Delta, consisting of 11 counties in the Yazoo-Mississippi Rivers floodplain located in the northwest region of Mississippi. Also of interest are the similarities and differences among this area, the state of Mississippi as a whole, and the lower section of the Mid-South Region (Arkansas, Louisiana, and Mississippi) (see Figure 9.1).

Figure 9.1
Lower Mid-South and Core Delta regions of the United States.

Source: Map produced by the Center for Population Studies, University of Mississippi.

Extensive ports were built along the Mississippi River in the 1800s, followed by construction of railroad tracks across the region and draining of bottomlands for agriculture. With the rise in production agriculture, especially cotton, the Delta was directly connected with the world economic system. Highly fertile land, an abundant water supply, and a warm climate supported what first began as a plantation-based agricultural economy (for an environmental history, see Saikku, 2005). The highly intensive plantation structure of agriculture brought great wealth to the region, but it was distributed unequally and resulted in little local investment in other economic sectors. The plantation system first used slave labor. After the Civil War, sharecropping and tenant systems predominated, and the Core Delta became more widely settled—an economic system causing future underdevelopment in the region much as it did in other countries with similar plantation-style economies (Beckford, 1999). When industrialization began, it tended to offer low-wage jobs, which gave little relief to oppressed workers.

As noted by Jones, Thornell, and Hamon (1992), multiple factors have contributed to the low levels of education endemic to the Delta. Because the Delta is largely dependent on agriculture, there has historically been little investment in education in this region. In the 1960s, the quality of education was further compromised when residents established a system of private schools for Whites in response to court-ordered racial integration. With recent economic declines and shifting population demographics, fewer resources have been invested in public education (Jones et al., 1992). Overall, wealthy landowners and other elites showed little interest in educating minorities and the poor; the unfortunate result was and is a high number of undereducated workers, which further perpetuates the array of problems associated with poverty. This legacy is one of the reasons the region continues to have struggling schools. Not only does the Delta region have limited employment opportunities, but the jobs also tend to be below the occupational status level expected by those who achieve postsecondary education. Hence, many college-educated youth leave in search of better employment opportunities elsewhere.

Agriculture continues to be an important yet vulnerable sector in the economy. Recent conflicts within the World Trade Organization over U.S. agricultural subsidies do not bode well for the dominant system of agriculture in the Delta, which is dependent on high-tech, capital-intensive row crop production and is largely supported by government subsidies. Beyond cotton and rice, soybeans and corn have proved financially rewarding with the boom in biofuels, but they are also vulnerable because of their status as subsidized commodities traded globally. The farm-raised catfish industry, once considered the future hope for the Delta region, faces global pressures. Small-scale vegetable, fruit, and livestock producers do exist, but they must deal with major challenges in accessing local and regional markets (Kleiner & Green, 2008) flooded by produce from national and multinational companies.

In manufacturing, global pressures are equally challenging. Originally marketing itself on the basis of cheap labor, low taxes, and few regulations, the Delta is no longer a prime target for capital in its search for low wages, low tax rates, and limited environmental regulations. Some local firms have gone out of business, while other internationally connected corporations have left the region in search of even lower operating costs. This phenomenon is shaping the whole of the American rural southern economy, as starkly exemplified in the textile industry (Glasmeier & Leichenko, 1999).

As the discussion of the intersectional space framework presented previously noted, the overlap of poverty and race in the rural American South negatively impacts residents of the region (Swanson, Harris, Skees, & Williamson, 1995) and particularly those in the Delta (Duncan, 1999). The population of the Delta region numerically comprises a majority of Black/African-American residents (U.S. Census Bureau, 2010). Poverty rates are high in the Delta when compared to Mississippi, the broader Mid-South Region, and the United States as a whole (U.S. Census Bureau 2006–2010). Furthermore, racial disparities are stark. For instance, five-year estimates from the American Community Survey suggest that 44.8% (±1.6%) of individual Blacks were living on incomes at or below the poverty line in 2006–2010 compared to 12.5% (±1.5%) of Whites in the Core Delta. Furthermore, there were differences in poverty rates between males (31.3%, ±1.3%) and females (39.0%, ±1.4%).

Several areas in the Delta have undergone significant economic changes due to increased suburbanization around urban areas and development of tourism and casino gambling. For instance, De Soto County, Mississippi—a buffer between Memphis, Tennessee, and the Core Delta—is one of the fastest-growing areas in the United States in terms of percent change in population (U.S. Census Bureau, 2010). Furthermore, Tunica County—which borders De Soto County—was only one of two counties in the region to increase its population between 2000 and 2010, as documented by the U.S. Census Bureau's Decennial Census. Even so, studies show the Delta has continued high unemployment and poverty rates similar to previous documented trends (see Cosby, Brackin, Mason, & McCulloch, 1992; Kersen, 2002). Employment and earnings are racially stratified, with Whites having higher employment rates and lower poverty rates than Blacks (U.S. Census Bureau, 2006–2010).

Uneven Development and Health in the Mississippi Delta

Simply stated, the trajectory of uneven development in the Delta is not good for the health of people in the region (Cosby & Green, in press). In addition to reflecting the influences of poverty and inequality, the physical availability of health care is complicated by its rural character and debilitating shortage of health care providers (Butts & Cossman, 2008). The limited availability of insurance continues to present a challenge to

Mississippi and the Delta region, further limiting access to affordable health care for many Delta residents. Whereas the national median was nearly 82% among states and the District of Columbia, the portion of Mississippians 18–64 years of age covered by health insurance (private and government) was approximately 74% in 2010 (Centers for Disease Control and Prevention [CDC], 2010). According to the Delta Rural Poll, a telephone survey of residents from the 11 Core Delta counties, the estimated share of the population with health insurance was 74% for 2011 as well, with approximately 19% of the respondents relying on means-tested government programs (Center for Community and Economic Development [CCED], 2011). If national programs, such as the Patient Protection and Affordable Care Act, in addition to state-level health care reforms, are implemented, discrepancies in health care coverage are expected to decrease dramatically. However, with these policies under political attack, the future remains uncertain.

National and regional research demonstrates that health outcomes are unequally distributed across space and by race, and a series of studies shows the Mississippi Delta among the spatial clusters of low life expectancy identified in the United States (Cosby, 2005; Cossman, Blanchard, James, Jackson-Belli, & Cosby, 2002; Cossman, Cossman, Jackson-Belli, & Cosby, 2003; Cossman, Cossman, James, Blanchard, & Cosby, 2004). The history and demographics of the Delta are typical of unhealthy regions, which are characterized by distinctive histories that include poverty, discrimination, and a high proportion of people in a minority racial status.

Using self-rated health as an indicator of the population's overall well-being, the U.S. CDC (2010) reports that the percentage of adults reporting poor/fair health in Mississippi was nearly 23.7% in 2010 (Table 9.1), a rate in line with other states in the Mid-South but much higher than the national median of 14.7%. The estimate for the Delta region in 2011 was 34.8% (CCED, 2011).

Racial disparities are pronounced for self-rated health across these geographic spaces. In the Mid-South, Mississippi, and the Core Delta spaces, a larger percentage of Blacks report fair/poor health when compared to Whites at the national level (Table 9.2).

Utilizing specific measures of birth outcomes to assess global health, the United Nations Development Program (UNDP) provides quantitative data to assess variations and disparities in access to health care relative to race and space. Preterm births (i.e., births occurring at less than 37 weeks' gestation) and low birth weights (i.e., babies born weighing less than 2500 grams) are major contributors to infant mortality and morbidity (Williamson et al., 2008). According to researchers from the CDC's National Center for Health Statistic (NCHS), 12.2% of all live births in

Table 9.1
Self-Rated Health Status by Spatial Location

Spatial Location*	Percentage in Poor/Fair Health**
National (Median)	
Fifty states and District of Columbia	16.9%
	(n = 51)
Lower Mid-South Region	
Arkansas	19.1%
	(±1.7%)
	(n = 1,012)
Louisiana	21.1%
	(±1.2%)
	(n = 1,805)
Mississippi	23.7%
	(±1.4%)
	(n = 2,484)
Core Delta	34.8%
	(±3.1%)
	(n = 981)

*National and statewide estimates are from the Centers for Disease Control and Prevention's 2010 Behavioral Risk Factor Surveillance System (BRFSS). The Core Delta estimate is from the 2011 Delta Rural Poll (DRP).

**Self-rated health was originally measured in the BRFSS on a five-point scale ranging from excellent to poor. Self-rated health in the DRP was originally measured on a four-point scale. Health status was recoded into poor or fair health compared to all other options for both data sets. Margins of error are based on the 95% confidence level.

the United States were premature in 2009 (Martin et al., 2011). The rates were lower for non-Hispanic Whites (10.9%) and higher for non-Hispanic Blacks (17.5%). Total preterm rates were higher in the Mid-South Region (13.1% in Arkansas, 14.7% in Louisiana, and 14.5% in Mississippi), again with racial disparities being noted. Consistent patterns were identified with low birth weights. Of total live births, 8.2% were delivered preterm in 2009. Of those births, 8.2% were non-Hispanic Whites and 13.6% were non-Hispanic Blacks. Total rates of preterm births were somewhat higher in the Mid-South (8.9% in Arkansas, 10.6% in Louisiana, and 12.2% in Mississippi), with notable racial disparities between Whites and Blacks (Martin et al., 2011).

Investigating multiyear (2006–2010) patterns within Mississippi and the Core Delta region more directly, geographic and racial disparities become more evident. As shown in Table 9.3, the Delta region and Blacks in particular are overrepresented in poor birth outcomes as measured through preterm births and low birth weights.

Table 9.2
Self-Rated Health Status by Spatial Location and Race

	Percentage in Poor/Fair Health**	
Spatial Location*	White	Black
National (Median)		
Fifty states and District of Columbia	12.9%	20.7%
	(n = 51)	(n = 36)
Lower Mid-South Region		
Arkansas	17.9%	24.2%
	(±1.9%)	(±7.0%)
	(n = 730)	(n = 162)
Louisiana	18.8%	26.3%
	(±1.4%)	(±2.7%)
	(n = 1,110)	(n = 585)
Mississippi	20.5%	29.8%
	(±1.5%)	(±2.7%)
	(n = 1,396)	(n = 992)
Core Delta	29.5%	36.9%
	(±5.6%)	(±3.8%)
	(n = 308)	(n = 651)

*National and statewide estimates are from the Centers for Disease Control and Prevention's 2010 Behavioral Risk Factor Surveillance System (BRFSS). Core Delta estimate is from the 2011 Delta Rural Poll (DRP).

**Self-rated health was originally measured in the BRFSS on a five-point scale ranging from excellent to poor. Self-rated health in the DRP was originally measured on a four-point scale. Health status was recoded as poor or fair health compared to all other options for both data sets. Margins of error are based on the 95% confidence level.

Table 9.3
Birth Outcomes by Spatial Location and Race of Mother

	Core Delta		Mississippi	
Birth Outcomes (2006–2010)*	White	Black	White	Black
Live births	3,754	16,252	117,749	98,360
Percentage of total live births (all racial groups)	18.7%	80.9%	53.5%	44.7%
Percentage of births born preterm (<37 weeks' gestation)	15.2%	22.9%	14.1%	21.8%
Percentage of births born low-weight (<2,500 grams)	9.0%	16.0%	8.7%	16.5%

*Data are from the Mississippi Department of Health's Mississippi Statistically Automated Health Resource System for the years 2006 through 2010.

Socioeconomic Position, Poverty, Gender, and Health

Interpreted through the intersectional space framework, the socioeconomic resources most important for people's health vary by geographic
space and race. Findings demonstrate the importance of education,
employment, income, and insurance, among other factors, and these
insights lead to critical policy implications (Acevedo-Garcia, Osypuk,
McArdle, & Williams, 2008).

Education is crucial for good health (Green, Kerstetter, & Nylander,
2008; Schnittker, 2004). Because they possess greater awareness of health
issues, educated persons are more likely to engage in beneficial health
behaviors. Also, education provides people with the means to achieve
more rewarding occupations and higher incomes. Those who have higher
education are more likely to occupy positions where they can earn
adequate incomes and enjoy the benefits of insurance. By comparison,
lower levels of formal education are associated with higher levels of poor
self-rated health, life-threatening illness, and early mortality (Link,
Phelan, Miech, & Westin, 2008), the consequences of which are exacerbated by poverty.

Employment and income influence access to socioeconomic resources
that are important for health (Åhs & Westerling, 2006; Burgard, Brand,
& House, 2009; Green et al., 2008; Ross & Mirowsky, 1995). Employment influences health along two pathways. First, employment
increases income and decreases hardship. Second, healthy people have
a higher likelihood of obtaining and keeping jobs (Ross & Mirowsky,
1995). Employment and adequate income both increase the chances that
a person will be able to afford to live in a healthy place and follow a
healthy lifestyle. In addition, adequate income influences the quality
of care a person can afford, and often the employee receives health
insurance.

The United States is well known for its high-cost health care system,
and insurance is largely responsible for determining who receives
adequate care in this country. Research demonstrates that insurance
coverage influences health, because it serves as the means of access to
the system (Quesnel-Vallée, 2004). Some employers provide health
insurance to their workers, and individuals who are not covered by
an employer or who own small businesses can purchase insurance.
However, these policies are expensive. For those who cannot obtain
insurance coverage through such mechanisms and who have low
enough incomes to meet means-tested thresholds or are elderly,
government programs—Medicaid and Medicare—provide some access
to health care.

Inevitably, people slip through the cracks and are not eligible for these
different options. Perhaps their employers do not provide insurance or

they cannot afford to purchase it for themselves, yet they do not qualify for or do not participate in government programs because they are not poor enough. Such individuals are often labeled the "uninsured working poor." The South tends to have lower levels of insurance coverage compared to the United States as a whole (DeNavas-Walt, Proctor, & Lee, 2005; U.S. Census Bureau, 2012), and research from the Delta shows that having employer-provided health insurance is associated with better self-rated health, especially among Blacks (Green et al., 2008). Although insurance coverage is projected to expand dramatically under the Patient Protection and Affordable Care Act (2010), the future of this policy is far from secure.

Navigating the complex U.S. health care system and accessing health care is a complicated endeavor. This effort may be even more problematic for low-income families, including pregnant women and mothers. A series of focus groups conducted among women who were pregnant or had children revealed a shared concern over limited health care facilities in the region, a severe lack of women's health specialists, and the ever-increasing cost of care (Leonard, 2008). Recent participatory public meetings held in three Delta communities identified similar concerns in regard to factors associated with preterm births (Community Foundation of Northwest Mississippi [CFNM], 2012).

Studies of inequality show that race influences health status. From a sociological perspective, racial categories can be approached as features of ascribed status and socially constructed categories. One's status influences which pathways one finds open and which pathways are closed in the pursuit of higher education, better employment, and higher incomes. The previously cited research from the Delta found that—when disaggregated by racial group—education, employment, and insurance status influenced health somewhat differently for Whites and Blacks (Green et al., 2008).

On a sexual biology level, there are similarities between males and females in terms of health problems and steps to prevent them. At the same time, there also are differences, largely related to sexual reproduction. For example, some diseases are fairly unique to males, whereas others are more specific to females. More important to the present study is the point that as a social category, gender may also be addressed as a socially ascribed status, with pathways for accessing resources and health being partially determined by the different roles and power provided to men and women.

Connecting race and gender, research evidence is accumulating in support of the argument that beyond socioeconomic characteristics, including poverty and inequality, Black women continue to have higher rates of poor birth outcomes owing to the ways in which racism and stress permeate U.S. society (Alio et al., 2010). The "weathering hypothesis" attributed to Geronimus (1992; Holzman et al., 2009) suggests that social inequalities facilitate a faster decline in health among Black women, thereby leading to disparities in health outcomes with increased age. This premature decline in health (i.e., "weathering") leads to greater risk for poor birth outcomes (e.g., preterm births, low birth weights, infant deaths).

With expanded migration of labor searching for employment opportunities during the global era, old assumptions of men leaving their families to find work, while still accurate to some degree, do not tell the full story. Many women move within their country as well as across national borders, either alone or with their families. As shown in a recent qualitative study of Latina immigrants living in the Delta region (Rosas, 2008), moving to a new area puts women in a vulnerable situation as they try to navigate an unfamiliar health system, especially when they also encounter cultural, language, and legal barriers.

So far, a generally negative picture of women's health status has been portrayed. There is an upshot, however. Despite challenges to women's health, just as with men's, many situations have been improving over time. Beyond increasing access to services and advances in technology, the improvements in women's health appear to be a result of increases in education, at least in part. Based on longitudinal analysis of national data over a 30-year time span, Hill and Needham (2006) demonstrated that educational gains have been important for improvements in self-rated health. The improvements they noted were greater and more linear for women than they were for men.

In explaining advances and problems in women's health, Garcia et al. (2010) argue that access to health care is an important indicator of women's health and empowerment at the individual, community, and institutional levels. However, such access to health care and actual physical and mental well-being of women varies along poverty and racial dimensions. Racial inequality influences patterns of economic inequality and, consequently, one's chance of a longer and healthier life. For example, racial gaps are observed in the higher percentages of preterm births, low birth weights, and infant deaths previously discussed. Clifton et al. (2009) noted that medically at-risk women, including low-income and minority individuals, often experience frequent marginalization and face barriers with implications for accessing services within health care system. These barriers include limited social support, fewer income-earning opportunities, and restricted information about the health care system. Clifton et al. argue that such problems must be analyzed within "specific cultural, socioeconomic, ethnic, and relational contexts" (p. 144) to determine which interventions might be sustainable.

In the Mississippi Delta, the links between socioeconomic resources and health are clearly evident. Key-informant interviews and focus groups (Green, Nylander, Harbin, & Edwards, 2003) and public forums

(CFNM, 2012) asked participants to identify what they perceive as the important issues influencing health. Participants identified several problems in need of attention. Limited education and lack of good jobs were viewed as contributors to prolonged poverty, and concern was expressed over the short- and long-term health consequences of persistent poverty.

Many people in the Delta face socioeconomic challenges and associated poor health outcomes. However, women face a specific set of challenges that should be accounted for in discussions of development and livelihood strategies. In the Core Delta, women have lower rates of employment and higher rates of poverty than men (U.S. Census Bureau, 2006–2010). Consequently, it is plausible that women in the Mississippi Delta are less likely to receive employment-related health benefits. Women's growing impoverishment may be partially a result of their concentration in the service-sector economy, which is associated with low incomes and fewer secure employment opportunities. These inequalities are particularly important for women who are single and raising children, as demonstrated in the poverty rates discussed earlier.

In the global context, the relative importance of socioeconomic resources for health status is likely to increase. Health needs will, in turn, influence broader social and economic development. The Delta region continues to have poor-performing schools and restricted employment opportunities. Families face the stress of making ends meet given a limited resource base and rural isolation. Additionally, the Delta hosts minimal health facilities and professionals. Deltans face an array of health risks and actual problems, including poor diet, obesity, hypertension, cardiovascular disease, and diabetes. In the quickly changing and competitive global economy, it appears that the Delta region must overcome not only its past but also its contemporary situation to achieve a higher standard of living.

Community and Health Development
Efforts in the Mississippi Delta

Bebbington (2004) notes the importance of accounting for the intentional development initiatives of government agencies and nongovernmental organizations when exploring and trying to explain patterns of uneven development. In the Delta, building from a vibrant history of community organizing and development to overcome structural inequality, there are numerous examples of grassroots action combined with state and federal public health initiatives. Some of this work dates back to the founding of the nation's first rural community health center in Mound Bayou, Mississippi, located in the heart of the Core Delta (National Library of Medicine, n.d.). Several community and health development interventions have been established in the region in contemporary times. They illustrate the kinds of actions being undertaken to address uneven development, improve health outcomes, and reduce racial disparities in the Delta Region.

Among the efforts to improve health conditions in the Delta is the Delta Healthy Start Program, a maternal and child health program operated by the Tougaloo College Health and Wellness Center and Delta Health Partners. Incorporating case management teams consisting of nurses and social workers who make home visits and coordinate in-school educational/support activities, the program is part of a national Healthy Start initiative to reduce the impact of poor birth outcomes.

Connecting education, workforce development, employment, and health in the Core Delta counties of Bolivar, Coahoma, and Quitman, the Tri-County Workforce Alliance developed and implemented a program for young people to improve their academic skills and learn about health and health care professions. Beginning in the first year with only high school students, the program recently completed its second year in 2012, having expanded its scope to include both middle and high school students. The students participated in workshops, field trips, and summer institutes. Middle school participants were involved with health disparity action research studies with family members and other people in their communities, while high school participants had opportunities for mentoring and job shadowing. Evaluation of this program has shown it to be very popular among participants and their parents, and it appears that youth are changing their confidence and aspirations concerning college and careers in the health sector (Phillips & Green, 2012).

Additionally, a collaborative program between the Mississippi Office of Nursing Workforce and the Dreyfus Health Foundation has engaged college students in community colleges and bachelor-level university programs to promote nursing education, career ladder advancement, and community service around health. In a program combining traditional education with advances such as dual enrollment courses and dedicated educational units at health care facilities, the students are offered unique and state-of-the-art opportunities to learn and practice nursing skills. In addition, through use of the Dreyfus Health Foundation's Problem Solving for Better Health methodology for community engagement, students receive the tools needed to connect the classroom and the community.

The School-Based Asthma Management (SAM) Program is operated through Delta State University's Center for Community and Economic Development with resources from the CDC, Mississippi Department of Health, and other funding partners. It works with school nurses and health organizations to provide education, training, and capacity building to help schools better serve children with asthma and other health problems.

The Aaron E. Henry Community Health Center and the North Central Area Health Education Center, both longtime partners with the organizations previously mentioned, are leading a team effort with community health centers in the region to increase education and training opportunities for health center employees. This program seeks to improve employee recruitment and retention and to help employees prepare for advancement up the career ladder in these centers. The program prepares employees, no matter what their specific occupations may be, to better serve patients, families, and communities in terms of the pressing health issues the Delta now faces.

These examples of community and health development efforts highlight recognition of the intersections of poverty, race, and health in the space of the Mississippi Delta. Furthermore, such efforts point toward the types of innovations being pursued in the face of historically uneven development and longstanding livelihood challenges. Although these efforts are taking place on a relatively small scale and operate only at the local and regional levels, there is much to be learned from them in terms of how community and health development may reshape the intersections of poverty, race, and health in the region.

Conclusion

By employing the intersectional space conceptual framework, we draw attention to contemporary development issues at multiple scales from the institutional to the individual levels within a specific space. Our conceptual framework highlights socioeconomic position, poverty, race, gender, and space, which are intricately intertwined through intersectional processes at the macro level, institutions and group conflict at the meso level, and formation of identities and agency at the micro level. Intersectional space critically analyzes the multiple identities of individuals and the interlocking advantages (or disadvantages) available to them based on their group memberships, thereby making it possible to examine health outcomes across various social groups in a physical location. Poverty and race drawn on intersectional space can provide valuable insights into how key development issues emerge and intersect to influence uneven developmental outcomes such as health disparities.

First, intersectional spaces with diverse sets of processes and practices not only vary over time, but also are subject to change at the intersections of the global political economy and local forces, as evidenced in the case of the Mississippi Delta. The Delta region's geographic location, historical legacy, and the current global economic crisis pose challenges to livelihood diversification and women's access to socioeconomic resources. Delta women and other marginalized groups in the region face vulnerabilities and challenges to their livelihood systems that warrant attention. The situation is not new, but rather extends from a history of uneven development and socioeconomic exclusion. In analyzing gender-based

health issues, the linkages between the intersectional approach from gender scholarship and the livelihoods framework in development studies
highlights poverty, race, and other structural inequalities in an intersectional space, the Mississippi Delta. Within the context of broader changes
in global developmental processes, ascribed social group memberships in
an intersectional space impact health status in general, and health outcomes of women in particular.

Many attempts have been made to help marginalized people, with
efforts ranging from churches providing food to families in times of need
to federal policies and assistance programs. Laudable for their many successes, these initiatives may be critiqued for their overly generalized
understanding of poverty and poor health, simplistic clinical models,
and their tendency to blame impoverished people for their situation. The
favorite target tends to be the single mother.

Institutional arrangements, involving government-level organizations
and community- and faith-based programs, are often used to fill the service gaps in an intersectional space. As Bebbington (2004) rightly notes,
these organizational interventions influence uneven development. The
argument is that these organizations are closer to the people they serve,
offer tailored services, and can mix government funds with support from
foundations and private contributions. These organizations do provide
much needed assistance in their specific locations. In some isolated communities, they may be the only local providers. Even so, local efforts are
not immune from some of the same challenges faced by traditional
church-based relief programs and government poverty alleviation—
especially blaming the victim. There tends to be an infatuation with who
is truly "deserving" of help.

Criticisms aside, numerous organizations are attempting to assess and
address women's needs in regard to employment and health care in the
Delta. In effect, they are working to counter the uneven trajectory of
broader political economic development in the region. The Tri-County
Workforce Alliance brings together people who are unemployed with
educators, businesses, and government agencies to address educational
improvement, job training, and employment. In terms of health, community health centers, first organized as part of civil rights movement activism, continue to provide access to affordable health services. Groups are
also working to improve maternal and child health. As previously discussed, the Delta does not suffer from a lack of committed people and
organizations working to improve quality of life. What they need is for
development policy to follow suit.

Second, generic efforts to improve education and employment and
thereby overcome poverty, although helpful, are likely to fall short for
many women, especially those with family responsibilities. From a livelihoods perspective, it is critical that development initiatives take the

traditional role of women as caregivers, the feminization of labor, and rapid changes through globalization into account within an intersectional space. If a woman is going to college, working at a casino, and trying to take care of young children, she will face numerous challenges. For many women, especially those who are the sole providers for the family, these demands may prove overwhelming, leading to greater stress, lower quality of life, and poorer health outcomes. Providing a woman in this situation with financial assistance to go to school is important, but by itself it will do little to secure her overall livelihood. Even the diverse array of assistance programs are troubling, given that they are handled by a complex mix of local organizations and government agencies, which require lengthy application processes and are consumed with determining who "deserves" assistance. These problems, along with the feminization of poverty and the commercialization of women's health clinics (Thomas & Zimmerman, 2007), have serious consequences for women in the Delta. Because social inequality is complex and ever evolving in the contemporary era of globalization, a focus on intersectional space can be applied to explore and analyze the multiple dimensions of development issues and the social differences arising in specific locations. The findings from such investigations may help to inform education, workforce development, and assistance policies and programs.

Third, intersectional space informs how health disparities are created, reproduced, and contested in a specific location. Understanding the intersections between assets and challenges allows better insight into development processes and provides guidance to practitioners and policymakers for how to respond to the identified needs. Focusing on intersectional space, it was argued that women's access to economic resources and their ability to address health-based needs are simultaneously couched in their local communities, global processes, and diverse social identities in specific locations. Inevitably, intersectional spaces are social constructions— yet they have measurable physical boundaries and structured inequalities and, as such, can be employed as conceptual tools within and across countries to explore local, regional, and global patterns of inequality.

Although improvements in health and access to health care have been made for various groups in specific locations, some places within the United States, such as the Delta region, persistently show up on the negative side of most health indicators. Given the uneven development patterns and physical location of the Mississippi Delta, Deltans do not have easy access to the state-of-the-art health facilities and the myriad options in health care services that may be available in other physical locations in the United States. This problem is further compounded for marginalized groups such as women and racial minority groups, who are less able to access employment and employment benefits such as health insurance, pension, paid sick leave, and maternity leave. Exploration of these issues may benefit from application of an intersectional space framework that allows for simultaneous foci on development, poverty, race, gender, and health, thereby addressing the problems and better informing possible solutions.

This chapter has addressed a limited number of indicators of general health status and maternal health. However, intersectional space as a conceptual framework offers the explanatory power to examine a wide range of health-based issues related to poverty, race, and gender in a variety of spatial units. Here, the focus was on differences in health status identified by comparing the data available for the Blacks and Whites who make up the majority of the population in the Core Mississippi Delta. However, using the framework of intersectional space, it is possible to expand this study to find the relationships between health status and poverty among other racial and ethnic groups across spatial locations.

Fourth and finally, gender-based health disparities in an intersectional space call for a more holistic set of responses to development issues at the macro, meso, and micro levels. Although livelihood strategies and development interventions include access to material resources through negotiations and participation in cultural practices within specific social contexts, such practices and negotiations may affect both men and women differently based on other structured inequalities, including race-based hierarchies that are embedded in particular locations. Efforts at local, state, national, and global levels need to focus on supportive systems and policies that provide the basis for resiliency as well as agency for individual actors and marginalized groups in facing the challenges of uneven spatial development and the resultant health disparities.

References

Acevedo-Garcia, D., Osypuk, T. L., McArdle, N., & Williams, D. R. (2008). Toward a policy-relevant analysis of geographic and racial/ethnic disparities in child health. *Health Affairs, 27*(2), 321–333.

Åhs, A., & Westerling, R. (2006). Self-rated health in relation to employment status during periods of high and low levels of unemployment. *European Journal of Public Health, 16*(3), 294–304.

Alio, A. P., Richman, A. R., Clayton, H. B., Jeffers, D. E., Wathington, D. J., & Salihu, H. M. (2010). An ecological approach to understanding Black-White disparities in perinatal mortality. *Maternal and Child Health Journal, 14*(4), 557–566.

Ballantyne, P. J. (1999). The social determinants of health: A contribution to the analysis of gender differences in health and illness. *Scandinavian Journal of Public Health, 27*(4), 290–295.

Bebbington, A. (1999). Capitals and capabilities: A framework for analyzing peasant viability, rural livelihoods, and poverty. *World Development, 27*(12), 2021–2044.

Bebbington, A. (2004). NGOs and uneven development: Geographies of development intervention. *Progress in Human Geography, 28*(6), 725–745.

Beckford, G. L. (1999). *Persistent poverty: Underdevelopment in plantation economies of the Third World*. Kingston, Jamaica: University of the West Indies Press.

Burgard, S. A., Brand, J. E., & House, J. S. (2009). Perceived job insecurity and worker health in the United States. *Social Science and Medicine, 69*(5), 777–785.

Burris, B. H. (1991). Employed mothers: The impact of class and marital status on the prioritizing of family and work. *Social Science Quarterly, 72*(1), 50–66.

Butts, C. C., & Cossman, J. S. (2008). *Mississippi's primary labor force: Assessing primary care providers*. Mississippi State, MS: Mississippi Health Policy Research Center, Social Science Research Center.

Castells, M. (1996). *The rise of network society*. London, UK: Blackwell.

Castells, M. (1997). *The power of identity*. London, UK: Blackwell.

Center for Community and Economic Development (CCED). (2011). *Delta Rural Poll data set*. Cleveland, MS: Delta State University.

Centers for Disease Control and Prevention (CDC). (2010). *Behavioral Risk Factor Surveillance System Survey data*. Atlanta, GA: U.S. Department of Health and Human Services. http://apps.nccd.cdc.gov/brfss/

Chalifoux, Z., Neese, J., Buckwalter, K., Litwak, E., & Abraham, I. (1996). Mental health services for rural elderly: Innovative service strategies. *Community Mental Health Journal, 32*(5), 463–480.

Chandoke, N. (1993). On the social organization of urban space: Subversions and appropriations. *Social Scientist, 21*(5–6), 63–73.

Choo, H. Y., & Ferree, M. F. (2010). Practicing intersectionality in sociological research: A critical analysis of inclusions, interactions, and institutions in the study of inequalities. *Sociological Theory, 28*(2), 129–149.

Clifton, A., Cadzow, B. W., & Rowe, J. (2009). The Priscilla project: Facilitating equality and the self-empowerment of at-risk women in healthcare encounters. *Gender Issues, 26*(2), 141–151.

Collins, P. H. (1998). It's all in the family: Intersections of gender, race, and nation. *Hypatia, 13*(3), 62–82.

Community Foundation of Northwest Mississippi (CFNM). (2012). *Premature births in the Mississippi Delta*. Public meetings.

Cosby, A. (2005). *The wealth and health of the Delta*. Presentation at the Delta in Global Context Workshop, Delta State University, Cleveland, MS. http://ntweb.deltastate.edu/vp_academic/abarton/Delta%20in%20Global%20Context/Slides/Cosby.pdf

Cosby, A. G., Brackin, M. W., Mason, T. D., & McCulloch, E. R. (Eds.). (1992). *A social and economic portrait of the Mississippi Delta*. Mississippi State, MS: Social Science Research Center and Mississippi Agriculture and Forestry Experiment Station.

Cosby, A. G., & Green, J. J. (In press). A framework for development in the Mississippi Delta: Exploring education, income, and health in the global context. In A. W. Barton & P. Meikle (Eds.), *The Mississippi Delta in a global context*. Jackson, MS: University Press of Mississippi.

Cossman, R. E., Blanchard, T. C., James W. L., Jackson-Belli, R., & Cosby, A. G. (2002). Healthy and unhealthy places in America: Are there really spatial clusters? *Proceedings of the 22nd Annual ESRI International User Conference*. http://gis.esri.com/library/userconf/proc02/pap1064/p1064.htm

Cossman, R. E., Cossman, J. S., Jackson-Belli, R., & Cosby, A. G. (2003). Mapping high or low mortality places across time in the United States. *Health and Place, 9*(4), 361–369.

Cossman, R. E., Cossman, J. S., James, W. L., Blanchard, T. C., & Cosby, A. G. (2004). Mortality rates across time: Does persistence suggest "healthy and unhealthy places" in the United States? In D. G. Janelle, B. Warf, & K. Hansen (Eds.), *World minds: Geographical perspectives on 100 problems* (pp. 87–92). Amsterdam, Netherlands: Kluwer Press.

Cotter, D. A., Hermsen, J. M., & Vanneman, R. (2007). Placing family poverty in area contexts: The use of multilevel models in spatial research. In L. M. Lobao, G. Hooks, & A. R. Tickamyer (Eds.), *The sociology of spatial inequality* (pp. 163–188). Albany, NY: State University of New York.

Crenshaw, K. (1991). Mapping the margins: Intersectionality, identity politics, and violence against women of color. *Stanford Law Review, 43*(6), 1241–1299.

De Haan, L. J. (2000). Globalization, localization, and sustainable livelihood. *Sociologia Ruralis, 40*(3), 339–365.

De Haan, L., & Zoomers, A. (2005). Exploring the frontier of livelihoods research. *Development and Change, 36*(1), 27–47.

Delta Regional Authority. (n.d.). Delta Regional Authority counties and parishes. http://www.dra.gov/about-us/eight-state-map.aspx

DeNavas-Walt, C., Proctor, B. D., & Lee, C. H. (2005). *Income, poverty, and health insurance coverage in the United States: 2004.* Washington, DC: Current Population Reports, U.S. Census Bureau.

Duncan, C. (1999). *Worlds apart: Why poverty persists in rural America.* New Haven, CT: Yale University Press.

Ellis, F. (1998). Household strategies and rural livelihood diversification. *Journal of Development Studies, 35*(1), 1–38.

Falk, W., Schulman, M., & Tickamyer, A. (Eds.). (2003). *Communities of work: Rural restructuring in local and global contexts.* Athens, OH: Ohio University Press.

Fitzpatrick, K., & LaGory, M. (2011). *Unhealthy cities: Poverty, race, and place in America.* New York, NY: Routledge Press.

Garcia, F. A. R., Freund, K. M., Berlin, M., Digre, K. B., Dudley, D. J., Fife, R. S., . . . Trott, J. A. (2010). Progress and priorities in the health of women and girls: A decade of advances and challenges. *Journal of Women's Health, 19*(4), 671–680.

Geronimus, A. T. (1992). The weathering hypothesis and the health of African-American women and infants: Evidence and speculations. *Ethnic Disparities, 2*(3), 207–221.

Giddens, A. (1984). *The constitution of society.* Cambridge, MA: Polity Press.

Glasmeier, A. K., & Leichenko, R. M. (1999). What does the future hold? What globalization might mean for the rural South. *Southern Rural Sociology, 15,* 59–83.

Gotham, K. F. (2003). Toward an understanding of the spatiality of urban poverty: The urban poor as spatial actors. *International Journal of Urban and Regional Research, 27*(3), 723–737.

Green, J. J., Kerstetter, K., & Nylander, A. B. (2008). Socioeconomic resources and self-rated health: A study in the Mississippi Delta. *Sociological Spectrum, 28* (2), 194–212.

Green, J., Nylander, A. B., Harbin, T., & Edwards, A. (2003). *Delta health system assessment: An overview of perceptions obtained from focus groups and key-informant interviews.* Cleveland, MS: Center for Community and Economic Development.

Hall, A., & Midgley, J. (2004). *Social policy for development*. Thousand Oaks, CA: Sage Publications.

Henderson, D., & Tickamyer, A. (2009). The intersection of poverty discourses: Race, class, culture and gender. In B. T. Dill & R. E. Zambrana (Eds.), *Emerging intersections: Race, class, and gender in theory, policy, and practice* (pp. 50–72). New Brunswick, NJ: Rutgers University Press.

Hill, T. D., & Needham, B. L. (2006). Gender-specific trends in educational attainment and self-rated health, 1972–2002. *American Journal of Public Health, 96*(7), 1288–1292.

Hinze, S. H., Lin J., Tanetta, E., & Andersson, T. E. (2012). Can we capture the intersections? Older Black women, education, and health. *Women's Health Issues, 22*(1), e91–e98.

Holzman, C., Eyster, J., Kleyn, M., Messer, L. C., Kaufman, J. S., Laraia, B. A., ... Elo, I. T. (2009). Maternal weathering and risk of pre-term delivery. *American Journal of Public Health, 99*(10), 1864–1871.

Hyland, S., & Timberlake, M. (1993). The Mississippi Delta: Change or continued trouble. In T. A. Lyson & W. W. Falk (Eds.), *Forgotten places: Uneven development in rural America* (pp. 76–101). Lawrence, KS: University Press of Kansas.

Jensen, L., McLaughlin, D. K., & Slack, T. (2003). Rural poverty: The persisting challenge. In D. L. Brown & L. E. Swanson (Eds.), *Challenges for rural America in the twenty-first century* (pp. 118–131). University Park, PA: Pennsylvania State University Press.

Jones, R., Thornell, J., & Hamon, G. (1992). Educational attainment in the Delta. In A. G. Cosby, M. W. Brackin, T. D. Mason, & E. R. McCulloch (Eds.), *A social and economic portrait of the Mississippi Delta* (pp. 90–103). Mississippi State, MS: Social Science Research Center and Mississippi Agriculture and Forestry Experiment Station.

Kersen, T. M. (2002). *The changing Delta, 1990–2002*. Mississippi State, MS: Social Science Research Center, Mississippi State University.

Kirby, J. A., & Kaneda, T. (2005). Neighborhood socioeconomic disadvantage and access to health care. *Journal of Health and Social Behavior, 46*(1), 15–31.

Kleiner, A., & Green, J. J. (2008). Expanding the marketing opportunities and sustainable production potential for minority and limited resource agricultural producers in Louisiana and Mississippi. *Southern Rural Sociology, 23*(1), 149–169.

Leonard, S. (2008). *Participant evaluation of the Tougaloo College/Delta health partners Healthy Start program in the Mississippi Delta*. Institute for Community-Based Research. Cleveland, MS: Delta State University.

Link, B. G., Phelan, J. C., Miech, R., & Westin, E. L. (2008). The resources that matter: Fundamental social causes of health disparities and the challenge of intelligence. *Journal of Health and Social Behavior, 49*(1), 72–91.

Lobao, L., & Hooks, G. (2003). Public employment, social welfare, and local well-being: Does a lean and mean government benefit the masses? *Social Forces, 82*(2), 519–556.

Lobao, L. M., Hooks, G., & Tickamyer, A. R. (Eds.) (2007). *The sociology of spatial inequality*. Albany, NY: State University of New York.

Lobao, L. M., Hooks, G., & Tickamyer, A. R. (2008). Poverty and inequality across space: Sociological reflections on the missing-middle subnational scale. *Cambridge Journal of Regions, Economy, and Society, 1*(1), 89–113.

Lobao, L., Rulli, J., & Brown, L. A. (1999). Macrolevel theory and local-level inequality: Industrial structure, institutional arrangements, and the political economy of redistribution. *Annals of the Association of American Geographers*, *89*(4), 571–601.

Martin, J. A., Hamilton, B. E., Ventura, S. J., Osterman, M. J., Kirmeyer, S., Mathews, T. J., & Wilson, E. C. (2011). Births: Final data for 2009, supplemental tables. *National Vital Statistics Reports, 60*(1), I8–I9.

Massey, D., & Denton, N. (1993). *American apartheid.* Cambridge, MA: Harvard University Press.

McCall, L. (2001). *Complex inequality: Gender, class, and race in the new economy.* New York, NY: Routledge.

McLaughlin, D. K., Stokes, C. S., Smith, P. J., & Nonoyama, A. (2007). Differential mortality across the United States: The influence of place-based inequality. In L. M. Lobao, G. Hooks, & A. R. Tickamyer (Eds.), *The sociology of spatial inequality* (pp. 141–162). Albany, NY: State University of New York.

McMichael, P. (2008). *Development and social change: A global perspective.* Los Angeles, CA: Pine Forge Press.

Milligan, C. (2003). Location or dis-location: From community to long-term care—the caring experience. *Journal of Social and Cultural Geography, 4*(4), 455–470.

Mitra, D. (2007). *Globalization, women's labor force status and empowerment: A cross-national study.* Doctoral dissertation, Department of Sociology, University of Connecticut, Storrs, CT.

Moghadam, V. M. (2007). Gender and the global economy. In J. T. Roberts & A. B. Hite (Eds.), *The globalization and development reader: Perspectives on development and global change* (pp. 135–151). Malden, MA: Blackwell Publishing.

National Library of Medicine (NLM). (n.d.). Against all odds: On common ground. http:// apps.nlm.nih.gov / againsttheodds / exhibit / community_health / common_ground.cfm

Nelson, M. K. (1999). Economic restructuring, gender, and informal work: A case study of a rural county. *Rural Sociology, 64*(1), 18–43.

Patient Protection and Affordable Care Act, Pub. L. No. 111-148, §2702, 124 Stat. 119, 318–319 (2010).

Phillips, M., & Green, J. J. (2012). *Tri-County Workforce Alliance program evaluation: High school mentorship program for nursing and middle school summer academy in science, mathematics and reading. Evaluation report submitted to the W. K. Kellogg Foundation.* University, MS: Center for Population Studies.

Quesnel-Vallée, A. (2004). Is it really worse to have public health insurance than to have no insurance at all? Health insurance and adult health in the United States. *Journal of Health and Social Behavior, 45*(4), 376–392.

Rosas, M. (2008). *Exploring health status and barriers to health care access among Mexican immigrants in the Yazoo-Mississippi Delta.* MS thesis, Division of Social Sciences, Delta State University, Cleveland, MS.

Ross, C. E., & Mirowsky, J. (1995). Does employment affect health? *Journal of Health and Social Behavior, 36*(3), 230–243.

Saikku, M. (2005). *This delta, this land: An environmental history of the Yazoo-Mississippi floodplain.* Athens, GA: University of Georgia Press.

Schnittker, J. (2004). Education and the changing shape of the income gradient in health. *Journal of Health and Social Behavior, 45*(3), 286–305.

Soja, E. (1989). *Post-modern geographies: The reassertion of space in critical social theory.* London, UK: Verso.

Swanson, L. E., Harris, R. P., Skees, J. R., & Williamson, L. (1995). African Americans in the southern rural regions: The importance of legacy. In J. B. Stewart & J. E. Allen-Smith (Eds.), *Blacks in rural America* (pp. 103–118). New Brunswick, NJ: Transaction Publishers.

Thomas, J. E., & Zimmerman, M. K. (2007). Feminism and profit in American hospitals: The corporate construction of women's health centers. *Gender and Society, 21*(3), 359–383.

Tickamyer, A. R. (2000). Space matters: Spatial inequality in future sociology. *Contemporary Sociology, 29*(6), 805–813.

Tickamyer, A. R., Bokemeier, J., Feldman, S., Harris, R., Jones, J. P., & Wenk, D. (1993). Women and persistent rural poverty. In Rural Sociological Society Task Force on Persistent Rural Poverty (Ed.), *Persistent poverty in rural America* (pp. 200–229). Boulder, CO: Westview Press.

United Nations. (2010). The Millennium Development Goals report. http://mdgs.un.org/unsd/mdg/Resources/Static/Products/Progress2010/MDG_Report_2010_En. pdf

U.S. Census Bureau. (2006–2010). American Community Survey five-year estimates. http://factfinder2.census.gov/faces/nav/jsf/pages/index.xhtml

U.S. Census Bureau. (2010). Decennial Census. http://factfinder2.census.gov/faces/nav/jsf/pages/index.xhtml

U.S. Census Bureau. (2012). Health insurance coverage status by state for all people: 2011. http://www.census.gov/hhes/www/cpstables/032012/health/toc.htm

Varkey, P., Kureshi, S., & Lesnick, T. (2010). Empowerment of women and its association with the health of the community. *Journal of Women's Health, 19*(1), 71–76.

Williams, D. R., & Sternthal, M. (2010). Understanding racial-ethnic disparities in health: Sociological contributions. *Journal of Health and Social Behavior, 51*(suppl 1), S15–S27.

Williamson, D. M., Abe, K., Bean, C., Ferré, C., Henderson, Z., & Lackritz, E. (2008). Current research in preterm birth. *Journal of Women's Health, 17*(10), 1545–1549.

Chapter 10

Health and the Stress Process in Rural America

Karen T. Van Gundy and Meghan L. Mills

Background

Despite steady health improvements in recent decades, rural Americans still fare worse than their non-rural counterparts on most physical health indicators, and the most rural areas tend to experience the worst health outcomes (Eberhardt et al., 2001; Eberhardt & Pamuk, 2004; Gamm, Hutchison, Dabney, & Dorsey, 2003; Ricketts, 1999). Such variations have been attributed, in part, to the relatively lower socioeconomic status (SES) observed in rural areas; however, SES differences do not fully explain rural/non-rural health differences (Jackson, Doescher, Jerant, & Hart, 2005; Joens-Matre et al., 2008; Mcmurray, Harrell, Bangdiwala, & Deng, 1999; Reis et al., 2004; Tai-Seale & Chandler, 2010; Wang, 2001). Moreover, with few exceptions, rural residents do *not* suffer poorer mental health outcomes than non-rural residents, even though low-SES populations average higher levels of psychological distress and disorder (Gamm, Stone, & Pittman, 2010; Kessler et al., 2005; Kessler et al., 1994; Mogatt, Bradley, Adams, & Morris, 2005). As such, observed place-based differences in health patterns cannot be explained by SES alone.

In this chapter, we examine these anomalous interrelationships among rural/non-rural residency, SES, and health. We draw on the sociological "stress process" framework (Pearlin, 2010) to explore the mechanisms underlying recent rural/non-rural trends in mortality, physical health, and mental health. We use data from two national surveys—the Behavioral Risk Factor Surveillance Survey (*2010 Behavioral Risk Factor Surveillance System Codebook Report*, 2011) and the National Survey on Drug Use and Health (*National Survey on Drug Use and Health: Public Use Codebook*, 2011)—and two local youth surveys (see Van Gundy, Stracuzzi, Rebellon, Tucker, & Cohn, 2011)—the Rural Youth Study (RYS) and the New Hampshire Youth Study (NHYS)—to highlight demographic, socioeconomic, and community-linked characteristics that contribute to health and well-being in rural America. We describe the reasons typically offered to explain rural/non-rural health patterns, and we highlight ways in which "stress process" approaches can extend current understandings of residency-based health patterns. We conclude with suggestions for future health-related research, practice, and policy.

Key Terms and Trends

We follow the World Health Organization (WHO, 2012) and define health as "a state of complete physical, mental and social well-being and not merely the absence of disease and infirmity." We consider three categories of health: mortality (e.g., life expectancy, infant mortality), physical health (e.g., chronic disease, weight), and mental health (e.g., mood disorders, substance abuse). Given the age-graded distribution of most health outcomes over the life course (Elder, Johnson, & Crosnoe, 2003; Mcleod & Almazan, 2003; Pearlin, Schieman, Fazio, & Meersman, 2005), our presentation of health and well-being includes estimates that are disaggregated by age. Unless specified otherwise, we categorize age into the following four groups: youth (ages 12–17), young adults (ages 18–25), middle adults (ages 26–59), and older adults (60 or more years of age).

We also consider the role and significance of SES, which involves interconnected positions of social, economic, and political power in society. Following Conger, Conger, and Martin (2010), our definition incorporates various dimensions, including income, education level, employment status, and occupational prestige. To define rural residency, we use the Office of Management and Budget's (OMB) definition of rurality as it contrasts with non-rural (urban and suburban) metropolitan statistical areas (MSAs; see OMB, 2003). According to this definition, non-rural areas are defined as MSAs, or densely developed core counties containing a large population, along with adjacent communities, which have a high degree of social and economic integration with that urban core. Unless specified otherwise, "rural" areas include those counties that are not included in

MSAs, whereas "non-rural" areas refer to counties that are included in such metropolitan statistical areas (OMB, 2003; U.S. Census Bureau, 2009).

As of 2010, approximately 20% of the U.S. population resided in a rural area, and nearly 75% of all U.S. counties were classified as rural ("2010 Census Urban and Rural Classification and Urban Area Criteria," 2010). The sociodemographic makeup of rural populations differs by region (e.g., Northeast, Midwest, South, West), yet clear national trends are evident (Eberhardt et al., 2001; Eberhardt & Pamuk, 2004). In particular, rural counties experience higher poverty rates than their non-rural counterparts; in fact, rural poverty rates are almost twice as high as suburban rates (Eberhardt et al., 2001; Johnson, 2006). In addition, rural areas are often referred to as "graying areas" due to the large percentage of older adults in residence there. The "graying" of rural America is due to the combination of out-migration of young adults in search of better educational and occupational opportunities and in-migration of older adult retirees seeking natural amenities, lower population densities, and cheaper living expenses (Carr & Kefalas, 2009; Eberhardt et al., 2001; Johnson, 2006; Roger, 2000; Sherman & Sage, 2011). On average, rural areas also are less racially and ethnically diverse than large urban cores (Kirschner, Berry, & Glasgow, 2006).

The Stress Process in Rural America

The "stress process" framework (Pearlin, 1989, 1999, 2010) is the dominant model for the sociological study of health and well-being. This model purports that health is socially patterned by interrelationships among social statuses, environmental stressors, and important psychosocial or coping resources. In this chapter, we apply the stress process to understand patterns of health and well-being in rural and small town America.

Social statuses include social and economic population categories—such as rural/non-rural residency, SES, or age—which serve as proxies for common group experiences (Pearlin, 1999). Here we focus on rural/non-rural residency and SES as interrelated social statuses that have implications for exposure to social stress, the availability of psychosocial or coping resources, and physical and mental health outcomes. According to this framework, differences by social status group, such as poorer physical health in rural versus non-rural areas, can be attributed partially to group variations in social stress exposure and in access to psychosocial resources.

Stress exposure refers to one's contact with noxious environmental strains that can affect health. Stress experiences are structured by social statuses, such that some groups (e.g., low-SES individuals) are more likely than others (e.g., high-SES individuals) to experience hardship and adversity. Generally speaking, stress exposure includes recent and traumatic life events, such as a serious accident or the death of a parent, and chronic strains, which "emerge more insidiously and [are] more persistent" (Pearlin, 1999, p. 400).

Stress proliferation, or the interplay among multiple levels and types of stressors, can be particularly harmful. Thus residency-based health disparities may derive, in part, from combinations of proximate stressors with broader, place-based economic and sociohistorical conditions. Rural contexts may be especially problematic for their impoverished inhabitants, who confront higher levels, and qualitatively different types, of strains than their higher-SES counterparts (Turner & Avison, 2003; Turner, Wheaton, & Lloyd, 1995).

Rural/non-rural health patterns also may stem from place-based variations in the presence or utility of psychosocial resources. *Psychosocial resources* are personal and social attributes "having the capacity to hinder, prevent, or cushion the development of the stress process and its outcomes" (Pearlin, 1999, p. 405). Social contexts influence the extent to which such resources are available, acquirable, or effective for reducing or buffering stress effects. Levels of health-promoting resources such as social support, personal mastery, and self-esteem are lower among poor and otherwise disadvantaged groups (Thoits, 1995; Turner, Taylor, & Van Gundy, 2004).

As a group, rural residents tend to possess attitudes, beliefs, and values that discourage some health-promoting actions, such as seeking treatment for mental health problems (Jones, Cook, & Wang, 2011; Komiti, Judd, & Jackson, 2006). Yet rural areas tend also to foster community loyalty, cohesion, and attachment (Hofferth & Iceland, 1998; Jacob, Bourke, & Luloff, 1997; Romans, Cohen, & Forte, 2011), which can reduce risk for health-related troubles (e.g., Van Gundy et al., 2011). Therefore, a better comprehension of the detriments *and* benefits that characterize rural lives can offer crucial insights into rural health problems and solutions.

Rural Health Outcomes

Consistent with prior research on rural/non-rural health (Eberhardt et al., 2001; Eberhardt & Pamuk, 2004), this chapter focuses on three crucial health dimensions: mortality, physical health, and mental health. To avoid the confounding of rural health effects with correlates of health and well-being, where possible we account for sociodemographic, environmental, and community-linked variations in effects. For instance, given the general tendency for older adults, women, and the impoverished to show higher rates of chronic physical illness, we adjust for these correlates in our estimates of rural/non-rural health trends. When possible, we also call attention to important rural/non-rural variations *within* demographic groups (e.g., age, sex, SES).

Mortality

An important measure of health that is critical to the understanding of rural and non-rural health disparities is mortality (Mansfield, Wilson, Kobrinski, & Mitchell, 1999; Senior, Williams, & Higgs, 2000). At the national level, the United States has relatively high life expectancy rates and low infant mortality rates ("Mortality Tables," 2012), yet life expectancy at birth for those living in rural counties is significantly lower than the national average, even when controlling for other factors known to affect life expectancy, such as sex, race/ethnicity, and SES (Crossman, James, Cosby, & Cossman, 2010; Eberhardt et al., 2001; Mansfield et al., 1999; Senior et al., 2000).

Research reveals that rates of premature mortality or death before age 75 are significantly greater among rural than non-rural residents. The most pronounced mortality disparity is among youth. Infant mortality rates in the United States are 20% lower in suburban areas compared to rural areas. Rates of death before reaching age 24 in youth and young adults living in the most rural counties are 31% higher than the comparable rates in the most urban counties, and 65% higher than the comparable rates in suburban counties. With regard to working-age adults (ages 25–64), in the Northeast and Midwest the highest mortality rates are in large urban cores, but in the South the highest rates are in rural areas. For older adults (ages 65 and older), the rural/non-rural mortality gap is the smallest: compared to their non-rural counterparts, the rural mortality rates are only 7% higher (Eberhardt et al., 2001; Eberhardt & Pamuk, 2004).

Rural/non-rural disparities in mortality originate from differences in fatal chronic diseases, injuries, and suicides. That is, Americans living in rural U.S. counties are more likely to die from heart disease, chronic obstructive pulmonary disease (COPD), unintentional injury, and suicide. Rural adults are 20% more likely to die of heart disease, and rural adult men are 30% more likely to die of COPD, than their non-rural counterparts. Most significantly, the number of premature deaths due to unintentional injury increases as a county becomes more rural. At any age, mortality resulting from unintentional injury is 86% higher in the most rural counties than in suburban areas for men and 80% higher for women (Eberhardt et al., 2001; Eberhardt & Pamuk, 2004; Peek-Asa, Zwerling, & Stallones, 2004).

Higher mortality rates among rural young adults are attributed largely to the greater likelihood of fatal motor vehicle accidents for rural young men (Maio, Green, Becker, Burney, & Compton, 1992; Muelleman & Mueller, 1996). In addition, rural populations, especially White rural males ages 15 years and older, have an 80% higher suicide rate than their non-rural counterparts (Eberhardt et al., 2001; Hirsch, 2006). Such patterns illustrate the social complexity of rural/non-rural heath patterns and underscore the importance of exploring and understanding rural/non-rural health patterns *within* sociodemographic groups (e.g., by age, race/ethnicity, sex).

Physical Health

Understanding the disparities in physical health morbidities between rural and non-rural residents is important because there are direct links between a person's physical health, ability to perform everyday activities, life expectancy, and overall quality of life (Eberhardt et al., 2001; Eberhardt & Pamuk, 2004). Recent evidence shows that rural Americans are at a higher risk for physical inactivity, obesity, cardiovascular disease, COPD, and periodontal disease. Rural residents also report relatively higher levels of chronic physical health conditions and limitations in everyday activities (Ahn, Burdine, Smith, Ory, & Phillips, 2011; Eberhardt et al., 2001; Eberhardt & Pamuk, 2004; Esch & Hendryx, 2011; Patterson, Moore, Probst, & Shinogle, 2004; Ricketts, 1999). As data from the 2010 Behavioral Risk Factor Surveillance Survey (BRFSS) illustrate, rural residents suffer higher rates of coronary heart disease, diabetes, heart attack, obesity, periodontal disease, physical inactivity, and stroke (see Table 10.1).

Regarding physical inactivity and obesity—both critical risk factors for the leading causes of death in the United States (Mcmurray et al., 1999; "Mortality Tables," 2012; U.S. Department of Health and Human Services, 2000)—research reveals that rural Americans report lower rates of leisure-time physical activity and higher rates of obesity. Self-reported obesity is 28% higher among adults in the most rural counties than among adults who live in suburban counties (Eberhardt et al., 2001; Jackson et al., 2005; Sobal, Troiano, & Frongillo, 1996). Additionally, some research indicates that the rural/non-rural disparity in obesity may be even greater when measuring height and weight directly as opposed to relying on self-reports (Befort, Nazir, & Perri, 2012).

Controversy exists in the literature regarding whether actual rural/non-rural differences in physical health exist, or whether the purported differences are instead artifacts of sociodemographic variations, such as differences by age and SES (Bethea, Lopez, Cozier, White, & Mcclean, 2012; Phillimore & Reading, 1992; Smith, Humphreys, & Wilson, 2008). With respect to obesity, research shows that high rates of obesity in rural areas are partially attributable to the lower SES positions of those who live in rural locations; however, such patterns are still apparent when statistical controls for age and SES are applied (Jackson et al., 2005; Joens-Matre et al., 2008; Mcmurray et al., 1999; Reis et al., 2004; Tai-Seale & Chandler, 2010; Wang, 2001). In addition, relatively high obesity rates in rural areas have been linked to time spent watching television and playing video

Table 10.1
Physical Health Outcomes by Age and Rural/Non-rural Residency

	Rural	p	Non-rural
Asthma	13.20		13.41
18–25 years old	19.02		18.67
26–59 years old	13.86		13.89
60 or older	12.16		12.39
Cancer	14.16		13.70
18–25 years old	2.78	* * *	0.30
26–59 years old	8.27	*	7.21
60 or older	21.47		22.91
Coronary Heart Disease	6.55	* * *	7.77
18–25 years old	0.34		0.25
26–59 years old	3.62	* * *	2.37
60 or older	12.49	* * *	11.61
Diabetes	14.82	* * *	12.88
18–25 years old	2.10		1.93
26–59 years old	10.31	* * *	8.77
60 or older	20.19	* * *	18.87
Exercise (past month)	68.40	* * *	74.32
18–25 years old	71.62	* * *	81.93
26–59 years old	71.19	* * *	77.19
60 or older	65.05	* * *	70.14
Heart Attack	7.77	* * *	5.92
18–25 years old	0.20		0.25
26–59 years old	3.61	* * *	2.51
60 or older	12.46	* * *	10.64
Obesity	31.19	* * *	27.18
18–25 years old	22.75	* * *	18.28
26–59 years old	34.57	* * *	29.03
60 or older	28.36	* * *	25.62
Periodontal Disease	62.97	* * *	53.23
18–25 years old	19.52		14.82
26–59 years old	51.49	* * *	41.46
60 or older	77.72	* * *	71.36
Stroke	5.08	* * *	4.06
18–25 years old	0.65		0.33
26–59 years old	2.49	* * *	1.88
60 or older	7.98	* * *	7.07

Notes: Presented are weighted percentage estimates based on data from the 2010 Behavioral Risk Factor Surveillance Survey (*2010 Behavioral Risk Factor Surveillance System Codebook Report*, 2011). The data include 444,927 respondents. Asterisks denote statistically significant differences between rural and non-rural respondents (* $p < .05$; ** $p < .01$; *** $p < .001$).

games, lack of sidewalks, higher rates of physical inactivity, lack of health education, and less access to health care (Felton et al., 2002; Jackson et al., 2005; Patterson et al., 2004).

Another potential source of greater obesity among rural residents involves tendencies toward "food insecurity" or the lack of "consistent, dependable access to enough food for active, healthy living" in rural America; that is, "food deserts," or areas with limited or no access to fresh and nutritious foods at affordable prices, predominate in rural areas (Morton & Blanchard, 2007, p. 1; Nord, Coleman-Jensen, Andrews, & Carison, 2010). Of particular concern, food insecurities can elevate obesity rates among low-SES rural residents who lack financial resources and must choose to purchase unhealthy high-caloric foods with low nutritional values to make the most of their meager food budgets (Dinour, Bergen, & Yeh, 2007).

With regard to leisure-time physical inactivity, both men and women in the most rural areas report approximately 50% higher prevalence rates than their counterparts in suburban areas (Eberhardt et al., 2001; Patterson et al., 2004; Reis et al., 2004). This discrepancy may arise because persons who have occupations that require some degree of physical activity are less likely to be physically active in their leisure time, and such occupations are more common in rural areas (Eberhardt et al., 2001; Hendryx, 2011; Reis et al., 2004). Due in part to such risk factors, rural Americans, especially men, have significantly higher rates of cardiovascular disease even when accounting for rural/non-rural age and SES differences (Barnett, Halverson, Elmes, & Braham, 2000; Eberhardt et al., 2001; Esch & Hendryx, 2011; Taylor, Hughes, & Garrison, 2002).

Research suggests that rural residents also report higher rates of diabetes, hypertension, arthritis, stroke, and certain types of cancers, and these differences persist even after statistical adjustments for SES are made (Eberhardt & Pamuk, 2004; Huang et al., 2002; Mainous, King, Garr, & Pearson, 2004; Obisesan, Vargas, & Gillum, 2000; Ricketts, 1999). In addition, a clear trend between urbanization and the prevalence of COPD is evident; as urbanization level decreases, the prevalence of COPD increases. The most important risk factors for COPD are cigarette smoking and exposure to airborne pollutants. Thus higher rates of COPD in rural areas can be attributed, in part, to relatively higher smoking rates and greater exposure to airborne pollutants via employment in coal mining, auto manufacturing, or pulp and paper industries (Doescher, Jackson, Jerant, & Garyhart, 2006; Eberhardt et al., 2001; Hendryx, 2011; Veitch, 2009).

In addition, age- and SES-adjusted rates of periodontal disease and edentulism are higher among rural as compared to non-rural residents (Ahn et al., 2011; Eberhardt et al., 2001; Eberhardt & Pamuk, 2004). Edentulism (complete tooth loss) can diminish one's quality of life, resulting in severe psychological, social, and physical adverse effects

(Allen, 2003). Edentulism has declined over the past half century in the United States, but its burden still falls disproportionately on seniors (ages 65 and older) living in the most rural counties. Approximately 47% of rural seniors report complete tooth loss, as compared to only 34% of suburban seniors (Ahn et al., 2011; Eberhardt et al., 2001; Eberhardt & Pamuk, 2004; Vargas, Dye, & Hayes, 2002).

Finally, recent research has examined rural/non-rural differences in subjective (self-reported) physical health (Bethea et al., 2012; Nummela, 2008). Rural residents show poorer self-rated health and more often report chronic physical health conditions that limit their ability to engage in everyday activities than do non-rural residents. Even when examining the age- and SES-adjusted rates of self-reported activity limitations, 18% of rural men and 19% of rural women report chronic conditions that limit their everyday activity, as compared to only 12% of non-rural men and 14% of non-rural women (Eberhardt et al., 2001; Eberhardt & Pamuk, 2004). Such work further supports the physical health disparities noted in official medical and death records; it indicates that rural/non-rural health differences are not simply artifacts of the relatively low SES in rural America and shows that rural/non-rural health patterns vary within groups (e.g., by sex).

Mental Health

Although clear rural/non-rural disparities in physical health exist, research has revealed few rural/non-rural differences in mental health outcomes—despite the tendency for mental health problems to predominate in low-SES populations (Gamm et al., 2010; Kessler et al., 2005; Kessler et al., 1994; Mogatt et al., 2005). As such, rural/non-rural mental health patterns are not attributable to SES. As data from the 2010 National Survey on Drug Use and Health (NSDUH) show, except for anxiety disorder, whose prevalence is elevated among rural women aged 26–59, rural and non-rural residents show similar rates of affective disorders (see Table 10.2).

Suicide rates, however, tell a different story. Although no rural/non-rural differences in suicide rates are apparent for females, the rate of rural male suicide is considerably elevated, especially among young males (ages 15–25). Even though U.S. suicide attempts are more prevalent among females, males are four to six times more likely to complete suicide. "Gendered" suicidal behaviors may place males at greater risk than females (Maris, Berman, & Silverman, 2000). For instance, males more often use reliably lethal methods (e.g., firearms), which are both more readily available and a more common means of suicide in rural areas (Booth, Briscoe, & Powell, 2000; Judd, Cooper, Fraser, & Davis, 2006; Maris et al., 2000).

In addition, there are no clear differences between rural and non-rural areas with regard to substance abuse, with one exception: rural Americans

Table 10.2

Mental Health Outcomes by Age, Sex, and Rural/Non-rural Residency

	Rural			Non-rural	
	Males	**Females**	**p**	**Males**	**Females**
Anxiety Disorder	3.45	8.43		3.16	6.72
12–17 years old	0.38	4.40		1.12	2.87
18–25 years old	2.31	7.27		2.60	7.45
26–59 years old	4.99	11.93	*	4.30	8.28
60 or older	3.37	6.61		2.66	5.84
		$p < .001$			$p < .001$
Major Depressive Episode	5.53	7.67		5.04	8.45
12–17 years old	5.17	14.09		4.12	11.89
18–25 years old	6.85	10.55		5.05	11.74
26–59 years old	5.56	7.94		5.67	9.14
60 or older	5.22	6.73		4.32	6.67
		ns			$p < .001$
Alcohol Abuse	6.07	1.59		5.44	2.27
12–17 years old	2.20	4.66		2.91	2.88
18–25 years old	13.76	5.15		12.09	6.38
26–59 years old	6.51	1.52		6.56	2.51
60 or older	4.90	0.16		2.21	0.53
		$p < .001$			$p < .001$
Marijuana Abuse	0.61	0.33		0.89	0.40
12–17 years old	1.89	1.35		1.88	1.29
18–25 years old	1.66	1.20		2.54	1.23
26–59 years old	0.73	0.23		0.63	0.25
60 or older	0	0		0.25	0.05
		ns			$p < .001$
Illicit Drug Abuse (Excluding Marijuana)	0.41	0.25		0.56	0.31
12–17 years old	0.69	2.66		0.62	1.16
18–25 years old	1.69	0.04		1.13	0.73
26–59 years old	0.49	0.03		0.74	0.28
60 or older	0	0		0.10	0
		ns			$p < .01$
Tobacco Dependence	18.05	17.42	* * *	13.79	11.70
12–17 years old	5.41	5.05	* * *	2.84	2.49
18–25 years old	24.64	25.04	* * *	14.93	12.80
26–59 years old	25.05	26.71	* * *	17.62	14.79
60 or older	14.73	10.32		12.05	10.44
		ns			$p < .001$

Notes: Presented are weighted percentage estimates based on data from the 2010 National Survey on Drug Use and Health (*National Survey on Drug Use and Health: Public Use Codebook*, 2011). The data include 57,873 cases. Mental health outcomes are based on DSM-IV criteria (American Psychiatric Association, 1994) for each disorder in the past 12 months. Asterisks denote statistically significant differences between rural and non-rural areas (* $p < .05$; ** $p < .01$; *** $p < .001$), and "ns" denotes statistically nonsignificant sex differences within rural and non-rural samples at $p < .05$.

are significantly more likely to abuse tobacco (Coomber et al., 2010; Cronk & Sarvela, 1997; Doescher et al., 2006; Hartley, Bird, & Dempsey, 1999; Hutchison & Blakely, 2003; Lambert, Gale, & Hartley, 2008; Pruitt, 2009; Van Gundy, 2006). Youth living in the most rural counties are approximately 19% more likely to report smoking, and rural adults are approximately 32% more likely to do so, compared to their respective non-rural counterparts (Doescher et al., 2006; Eberhardt et al., 2001; Eberhardt & Pamuk, 2004; Rahilly & Frarwell, 2007; Sarvela, Cronk, & Isberner, 1997; Smith & Fiore, 1999). As Table 10.2 shows, rural and non-rural residents exhibit similar rates of alcohol, marijuana, and other illicit drug abuse across age. Tobacco dependence rates, however, are much higher for rural youth and adults.

The most rural areas tend to demonstrates the lowest levels of education and the highest levels of unemployment, both of which are correlated with an increased prevalence of tobacco use and delayed or lack of access to medical and media resources designed to deter and curtail cigarette abuse (Eberhardt et al., 2001; Eberhardt & Pamuk, 2004; Sarvela et al., 1997; Smith & Fiore, 1999). Yet again, rural/non-rural tobacco use patterns persist even after adjustments for SES are made. In addition, elevated tobacco use rates coincide with an absence of smoke-free laws and restrictions in rural areas; there is a direct negative correlation between the degree of urbanization and the extensiveness of anti-cigarette smoking laws (Eberhardt et al., 2001; York et al., 2010).

Variations by rural/non-rural residency in other "risky" alcohol- and drug-related behaviors also are evident. Research shows that rural youth are more likely to begin using illicit drugs at earlier ages; to be more accepting of substance use, especially underage drinking; and to have easier access to substances such as alcohol, marijuana, and methamphetamines. More so than non-rural residents, rural residents drive under the influence of alcohol or drugs, and they more often turn to drug manufacturing or sales as a means of economic survival (Hartley et al., 1999; Hutchison & Blakely, 2003; Lambert et al., 2008; Pruitt, 2009; Van Gundy, 2006).

In fact, the relationship between urbanization and substance abuse is more complex when considering demographic factors—such as age, sex, and SES—that may influence this relationship (Substance Abuse and Mental Health Services Administration, 2008). Most research finds that rural residency does not increase substance abuse, even when sociodemographic factors are controlled (Hartley et al., 1999; Hutchison & Blakely, 2003; Lambert et al., 2008; Pruitt, 2009; Van Gundy, 2006). Yet, just as rural/non-rural mortality and physical health trends vary by group (e.g., by age, sex, or SES), within-group mental health disparities require careful scrutiny.

As Table 10.2 shows, a "gender gap" in affective and substance use disorders is less apparent in rural areas: while non-rural residents show sex differences for every mental health outcome presented, rural sex differences emerge only for anxiety disorder and alcohol abuse, with respectively higher rates being observed for women and men in these geographic areas. Moreover, the rate of stimulant abuse among the rural unemployed is *seven times* the corresponding rate among the urban unemployed (Van Gundy, 2006). Such findings beg the question, "Why are these health patterns different in rural America?"

Explanations for Rural Health Patterns

Reasons for rural/non-rural variations in mortality, physical health outcomes, and mental health outcomes are complex. Often, the origins of rural health inequities are ascribed to SES, geography, and "rural culture" (Auchincloss & Hadden, 2002; Hendryx, 2008; Murimi & Harpel, 2010; Peterson & Litaker, 2010; Veitch, 2009). SES-based explanations derive from the lower educational attainment, lower income, and lower rates of employment associated with rural residency (Eberhardt et al., 2001; Hartley, Quam, & Lurie, 1994; Johnson, Brems, Warner, & Roberts, 2006; Larson & Hill, 2005; Lu, Samuels, Kletke, & Whitler, 2010; Rowland & Lyons, 1989; Smith et al., 2008). As data from 2010 BRFSS show (see Figure 10.1), rural adults are significantly less educated and less likely to be employed on a full-time basis.

Some scholars have suggested that because rural Americans are less educated, they may not possess sufficient knowledge about healthy practices, such as preventive care, timely help-seeking, and the avoidance of

Figure 10.1
Adult socioeconomic and preventive health care indicators by rural/non-rural residency.

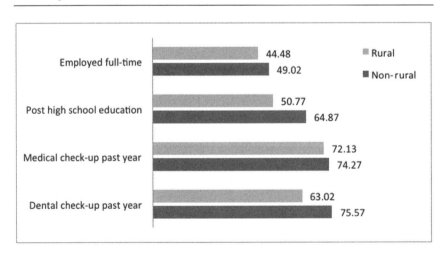

"risky" behaviors that compromise health (Bryant & Mah, 1992; Casey, Thiede, & Klingner, 2001; Eberhardt et al., 2001; Harju, Wuensch, Kuhl, & Cross, 2006; Probst, Moore, Baxley, & Lammie, 2002). In addition, higher unemployment rates in rural areas decrease the likelihood that residents will have health insurance (Larson & Hill, 2005), and low-paying work, coupled with geographically linked job opportunities (e.g., mining, chemical industries), increases work-related injuries and exposure to toxic environments (Esch & Hendryx, 2011; Hendryx & Fedorko, 2011; Luo & Hendryx, 2010; Merchant, Kross, Donham, & Pratt, 1989; Veitch, 2009; Zwerling, Miller, Lynch, & Torner, 1996). The geographic isolation of rural areas also makes it difficult to achieve regular access to health care due to long travel distances to obtain care and an ever-growing shortage of health professionals in rural America (Brade & Beauregard, 1994; Hendryx, Borders, & Johnson, 1995; Hicks, 1990). As Figure 10.1 shows, rural adults are significantly less likely than their urban counterparts to have had medical or dental checkups in the prior year.

Geographic isolation also may cultivate a "rural culture" that includes the mistrust of health professionals and other "outsiders." Part of the rural/non-rural gap in mortality and physical health morbidity, for instance, may be connected to rural beliefs and values. For example, rural dwellers more often ignore, disregard, or disbelieve warnings about the risks associated with reckless or intoxicated driving, unhealthy diets, physical inactivity, and preventive health and dental care (Biola & Pathman, 2009; Hendryx, 2008; Maio et al., 1992; Muelleman & Mueller, 1996; Murimi & Harpel, 2010; Patterson et al., 2004). Moreover, self-reliance, community ties, and religious beliefs may contribute to a rural emphasis on health-related self-responsibility, reliance on informal and nonprofessional sources of health care, and the avoidance of professional help-seeking (Hoyt, Conger, & Valde, 1997; Komiti et al., 2006; Macintyre, Ellaway, & Cummins, 2002; Murimi & Harpel, 2010; Wrigley, Jackson, Judd, & Komiti, 2005).

Yet beneficial health effects of a "rural culture" also are possible. While the preceding explanations provide some evidence that rural hardships and local cultural messages contribute to some poorer health outcomes in rural America, they fail to explain completely rural/non-rural physical health disparities, and they do little to explain why rural residents do not suffer poorer mental health outcomes (excluding tobacco use disorders) than their non-rural counterparts. As discussed earlier, "stress process" approaches (e.g., Pearlin, 2010) consider the stresses and strains on the one hand, and the personal and social resources on the other hand, that combine to affect health for social status groups (e.g., low-SES groups, rural residents). Qualities such as self-reliance and community cohesion, which reduce timely help-seeking or other health-promoting practices, also may reduce risk for some health problems or buffer the harmful effects of stress on health.

Applying the Stress Process

As an example, recent work (Van Gundy et al., 2011) applies the stress process in an attempt to clarify some of the advantages and disadvantages of a rural context for youth health and well-being. Van Gundy and colleagues use data from youth in rural and non-rural New Hampshire to examine the utility of stress process explanations for two very different community contexts in the same U.S. state. The rural youth data come from the ongoing Rural Youth Study (RYS), which includes the population of 7th and 11th graders in spring 2008 who attended public schools in New Hampshire's poorest and most rural county (Stracuzzi, 2009). The urban youth data come from the ongoing New Hampshire Youth Study (NHYS), which included 7th and 10th graders during the 2007–2008 school year who attended public schools in southern New Hampshire counties, where nearly one-third of the state's population resides (Johnson & Macieski, 2009).

Despite the relatively low SES of the RYS participants, results indicate *lower* rates of depressed mood and problem substance use (excluding tobacco) among these youth compared to the non-rural sample (Van Gundy et al., 2011). Although the rural youth report higher levels of stress, they also show higher levels of self-esteem and personal mastery, both of which reduce risk for depression. When statistical controls are applied for the rural youths' tendencies toward higher stress exposure, self-esteem, and mastery, differences by rural/non-rural residency in depressed mood disappear, but problems with alcohol and drugs remain significantly lower for the rural sample.

Not surprisingly, rural youth show higher levels of community attachment than non-rural youth; for rural and non-rural youth alike, community attachment buffers the effects of stressful events on problem substance use (Van Gundy et al., 2011). For youth with high levels of community attachment, the harmful effects of stress exposure on substance use problems are less severe. Yet community attachment reduces risk for depressed mood among rural youth only; that is, rural youth not only experience more community attachment, but this sense of community attachment is also more beneficial to them.

Recent Findings and Future Directions

As stated earlier, rural American adversities, beliefs, and values contribute to fluctuations in health in complex ways. Using again the RYS and NHYS data sets (Van Gundy et al., 2011), considerations about how social strains and community messages shape health from early in the life course are possible. These data contain insights into rural/non-rural youths' perceptions about the risks related to substance use, the availability of illicit

Figure 10.2
Perceptions about substance availability/risk by sample.

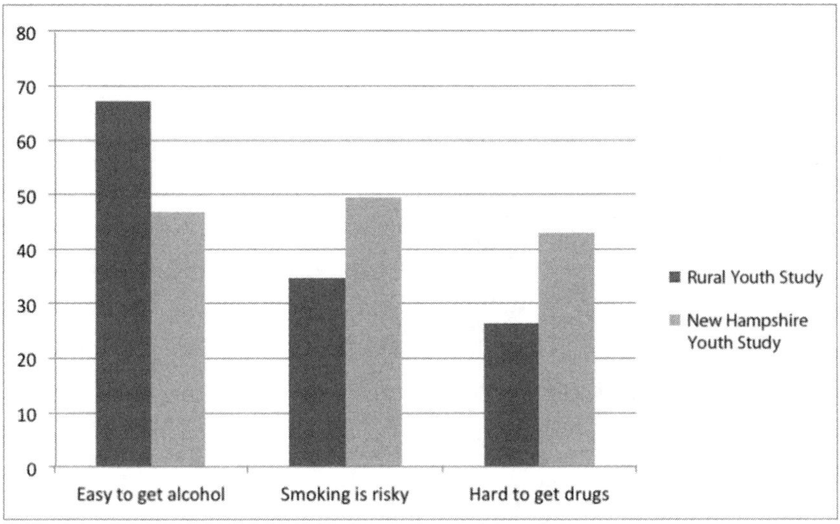

substances, the types of stressors confronted by youth, and the pros and cons of strong community cohesion in rural areas.

As Figure 10.2 shows, the rural youth surveyed in New Hampshire tend to perceive greater availability of substances than their non-rural counterparts; that is, relative to non-rural youth, the rural youth are significantly more likely to agree that it is "easy to get alcohol" and that it is not "hard to get drugs" in their neighborhoods or communities. Interestingly, perceived availability in this rural context does not seem to influence problem substance use. In fact, the rural youth in the New Hampshire surveys experience alcohol and other drug problems at lower rates than non-rural youth. However, Figure 10.2 also shows that the rural youth are less likely to perceive that tobacco use is risky. Compared to the non-rural youth, rural youth disagree more often that "smoking is risky." Separate analyses of these data sets show that, as is true for national rural/non-rural trends, the rural youth in New Hampshire use tobacco at significantly higher rates. In fact, when controlling for age, sex, and SES, the RYS youth are three times more likely than the NHYS youth to smoke cigarettes daily.

As noted earlier, Van Gundy et al. (2011) find that, on average, rural sample respondents report higher rates of stressful life events; however, differences in types of stressors are not clear from that work. As Figure 10.3 shows, there are rural/non-rural differences in the experience of some types of stressful life events. Specifically, the RYS youth more often

Figure 10.3
Stressful life events experienced by rural/non-rural youth.

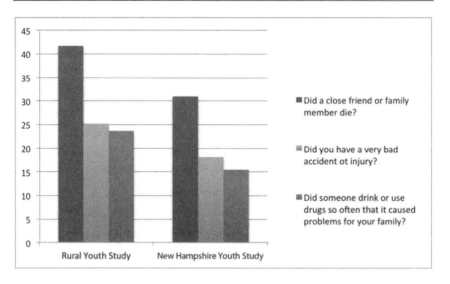

report the death of a close friend or family member, a serious accident or injury, and the presence of someone who drank or used drugs "so often that it caused problems for [her/his] family." Notably, rural/non-rural gaps in these life events persist even after applying statistical controls for age, sex, and SES. The first two events (death of a close friend/family member and a serious accident/injury) presumably derive from two sources discussed previously: the tendency for rural workers to be employed in dangerous occupations and variations in "risky" health behaviors, such as intoxicated driving, that predominate in rural areas. The tendency for rural youth to report chronic life conditions more often, such as the strain associated with friends' or family members' problem substance use, is important to explore in future research.

As discussed earlier, strong community ties serve as important resources for rural residents, and higher levels of community cohesion are found in rural areas (Van Gundy, 2006; Van Gundy et al., 2011). As Figure 10.4 shows, compared to the NHYS youth, the RYS youth are more likely to agree that they live in a close-knit community, that their neighbors are helpful, and that people in their communities or neighborhoods get along. Such patterns exist even with adjustments for age, sex, and SES. Community attachment can offset the harmful effects of stress exposure on problem substance use and may be especially important for boys in rural America. As Van Gundy and Mills (2011) find, highly stressed RYS girls who do not care about their communities are twice as likely as highly

Figure 10.4
Community cohesion by rural/non-rural sample.

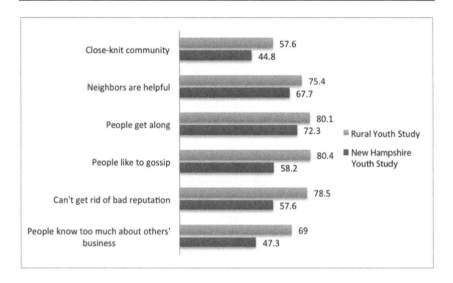

stressed girls who care about their communities to report substance use problems; by comparison, highly stressed RYS boys who do not care about their communities are nearly *four times* as likely to report substance use problems as are highly stressed boys who care about their communities. Thus "gendered" and place-linked stress processes require further study.

The potential harms associated with close-knit rural communities also require further consideration. As Figure 10.4 shows, the RYS youth are more likely than the NHYS youth to agree that people like to gossip, that "once you get a bad reputation you can't get rid of it," and that people in their communities "know too much about other people's business." Again, these patterns are observed even after implementing statistical adjustments for age, sex, and SES. As Van Gundy and colleagues (2011) have observed, "the same strong ties that present benefits for some may exclude others, demand conformity, and thwart positive social and personal development" (p. 297; also see Portes, 1998). In fact, this sense of rejection by, or detachment from, the local community increases risk for both depressed mood and problem substance use in the RYS and NHYS youth. As such, social programs aimed at fostering mental health should include strategies that not only promote community attachment, but also address the needs of detached or "disconnected" (Brown & Emig, 1999) members of rural *and* non-rural communities.

In addition, applying the stress process to inequalities within rural contexts is crucial. In particular, the consideration of social statuses,

psychosocial resources, and multiple social and health outcomes is warranted. As an example, using the RYS data, Mills and Van Gundy (2012)
find that stressful life events and community attachment explain significant portions of the SES-mental health disparity in rural youth; however,
neither stress nor social attachments appreciably affect the SES-
overweight disparity. Instead, the tendency for low-SES youth in this rural
context to be overweight can be explained by, or attributed to, SES variations in self-esteem. Thus practitioners seeking to reduce the SES health
gap within rural communities might consider approaches that increase
psychosocial resources such as self-esteem and community attachment.

Finally, careful attention should be paid to rural/non-rural inequalities
in the access to, and utilization of, professional health services. Geographic hurdles and the social stigma attached to mental health services
may discourage rural Americans from seeking care when needed. Analyses of the RYS and NHYS data reveal that rural and non-rural youth are
equally likely to have been prescribed medications for their emotions,
nerves, learning, or behavior, yet the rural youth are significantly less
likely than the non-rural youth to have used such medications in the preceding six months (7.2% for rural youth versus 11.6% for urban youth).
This difference is statistically significant even after applying controls for
age, sex, SES, stressful life events, and community attachment. Whether
this difference reflects the underutilization of, or a lack of access to, mental
health services is unclear. Future work should explore this topic more
closely.

Conclusion

More than a decade ago, Eberhardt et al. (2001) observed that "communities at different urbanization levels also differ in their demographic,
environmental, economic, and social characteristics, and these characteristics greatly influence the magnitude and types of health problems communities face" (p. 7). Indeed, key demographic, socioeconomic, and
community features have shaped rural health experiences in meaningful
ways. Inhabitants of rural areas tend to occupy lower-SES positions relative to non-rural residents; on average, rural residents are less educated,
earn a lower income, are more likely to be unemployed, and are less likely
to have health insurance than non-rural residents (Eberhardt et al., 2001;
Hartley et al., 1994; Johnson, 2006; Larson & Hill, 2005; Lu et al., 2010).
Rural populations also tend to be significantly older than non-rural populations; this difference is due partly to the out-migration of rural families
in search of educational or employment opportunities in more urbanized
areas and partly to the in-migration of older adult retirees to rural towns
and communities (Carr & Kefalas, 2009; Sherman & Sage, 2011). Together,
these sociodemographic trends render the tendency for rural residents to

suffer relatively poorer physical health than their non-rural counterparts somewhat unsurprising.

It is surprising, however, that rural/non-rural physical health differences remain even when accounting for age, sex, and SES; thus sociodemographic factors alone cannot explain rural/non-rural health differences. Moreover, rural residents show similar or *lower* rates of most mental health outcomes. That is, rural/non-rural Americans show little to no variation in anxiety, depression, and substance use disorders (excluding tobacco use), despite the general tendency for mental health problems to predominate among low-SES groups. Such patterns are fairly stable despite the fact that rural Americans report that many illicit drugs are "easy to obtain" and despite the tendency for rural areas to lack formal support services that address alcohol- and drug-related problems (Hartley et al., 1999; Hutchison & Blakely, 2003; Mills, 2010; Substance Abuse and Mental Health Administration, 2008; Van Gundy, 2006).

To better understand rural/non-rural patterns of health, this chapter considered both the harms and the benefits associated with rural life. We drew on work from the sociology of mental health and applied the "stress process" (e.g., Pearlin, 2010) to examine rural/non-rural patterns of health and well-being. We submit that the stresses felt by rural residents can erode the physical health of those residents, and suggest that those stresses derive only partly from the relatively low SES associated with rural residency. Of particular concern are chronic strains, such as persistent financial or family troubles, that are insidious, enduring, and highly damaging. The coalescence of chronic strains with other rural hassles (e.g., limited access to healthy foods or services) can exacerbate the effects of stress exposure and thwart short- and long-term health and well-being.

However, the informal social ties and other psychosocial resources that characterize rural communities offer a support structure that can offset stress effects and mitigate psychological harm. As prior research has revealed, rural Americans possess strong personal and social resources to cope with stress. The same "rural culture" that rewards "unhealthy" qualities, such as self-reliance and community loyalty (Hoyt et al., 1997; Komiti et al., 2006; Macintyre et al., 2002; Murimi & Harpel, 2010; Wrigley et al., 2005), also equips its residents with the mental health benefits of such attributes. As recent research shows, community attachment, self-esteem, and a sense of personal mastery in rural youth may reduce or counter risks for outcomes such as depression, problem substance use, and obesity (Mills & Van Gundy, 2012; Van Gundy & Mills, 2011; Van Gundy et al., 2011). As such, health policies and practices informed by "stress process" approaches hold great promise.

Indeed, "stress process" approaches can identify, clarify, and address the mechanisms that underlie SES- and residency-based health disparities. For instance, explanations concerning "gendered" patterns of mental health require elucidation. Of particular interest here are the processes that yield elevated rates of suicide for rural young males (Booth et al., 2000; Judd et al., 2006; Maris et al., 2000), the tendency for community attachment to be especially protective against problem substance use for rural young males (Van Gundy & Mills, 2011), and the tendency for fewer sex differences in substance use disorders among rural residents. Concerning the last point, the dangerously high risk for tobacco use disorders among both rural women and men (Doescher et al., 2006; Eberhardt et al., 2001; Eberhardt & Pamuk, 2004; Rahilly & Frarwell, 2007; Sarvela et al., 1997; Smith & Fiore, 1999) calls for especially urgent attention.

In conclusion, an appreciation of the resources and detriments embedded within residential contexts is critical. Rather than blaming a "rural culture" for rural health disparities, a systematic search for ways of combating the stressful realities of rural lives is needed. While we may not be able to eliminate all rural life strains, we can work to build upon those resources that buffer the harmful effects of stress exposure in rural areas. To tackle the unique challenges present in rural and small-town America and to eradicate rural/non-rural inequalities in health, an emphasis on the development and maintenance of personal, social, and community resources is vital.

Acknowledgments

Support for the Rural Youth Study is provided by the Social and Economic Sciences (SES) program of the National Science Foundation (NSF #155797), the Neil and Louise Tillotson Fund of the New Hampshire Charitable Foundation, and the Carsey Institute at the University of New Hampshire. Support for the New Hampshire Youth Study is provided by the NSF Law and Social Sciences (LSS) and SES programs (#0550145, #0833271, and #1026803). We thank Drs. Ellen S. Cohn, Eleanor M. Jaffee, Cesar J. Rebellon, Erin Hiley Sharp, Nena F. Stracuzzi, and Corinna Jenkins Tucker for their contributions to this work. We also thank Ben Bullock, Kirstie Kemmerer, and Michael Staunton for their comments on an earlier draft of this chapter.

References

2010 behavioral risk factor surveillance system codebook report. (2011). Atlanta, GA: Centers for Disease Control and Prevention.
2010 Census urban and rural classification and urban area criteria. (2010). http://www.census.gov/geo/www/ua/2010urbanruralclass.html
Ahn, S., Burdine, J. N., Smith, M. L., Ory, M. G., & Phillips, C. D. (2011). Residential rurality and oral health disparities: Influences of contextual and individual factors. *Journal of Primary Prevention*, 32(1), 29–41.

Allen, P. F. (2003). Assessment of oral health related quality of life. *Health and Quality of Life Outcomes, 1*(1), 40–48.

Auchincloss, A. H., & Hadden, W. (2002). The health effects of rural-urban residence and concentrated poverty. *Journal of Rural Health, 18*(2), 319–336.

Barnett, E., Halverson, J. A., Elmes, G. A., & Braham, V. E. (2000). Metropolitan and non-metropolitan trends in coronary heart disease mortality within Appalachia 1980–1997. *Annuals of Epidemiology, 10*(6), 370–379.

Befort, C. A., Nazir, N., & Perri, M. G. (2012). Prevalence of obesity among adults from rural and urban areas of the United States: Findings from NHANES (2005–2008). *Journal of Rural Health, 28*(4), 392–397.

Bethea, T. N., Lopez, R. P., Cozier, Y. C., White, L. F., & Mcclean, M. D. (2012). The relationship between rural status, individual characteristics, and self-rated health in the Behavioral Risk Factor Surveillance System. *Journal of Rural Health, 28*(4), 327–338.

Biola, H., & Pathman, D. E. (2009). Are there enough doctors in my rural community? Perceptions of the local physician supply. *Journal of Rural Health, 25*(2), 115–123.

Booth, N., Briscoe, M., & Powell, R. (2000). Suicide in the farming community: Methods used and contact with health services. *Occupational and Environmental Medicine, 57*(9), 642–644.

Brade, N. J., & Beauregard, K. (1994). *Health status and access to care of rural and urban populations.* Agency for Health Care Policy and Research Publication No. 94–0031. Rockville, MD: U.S. Department of Health and Human Services.

Brown, B. V., & Emig, C. (1999). Prevalence, patterns, and outcomes. In D. J. Besharov (Ed.), *America's disconnected youth: Toward a preventive strategy* (pp. 101–116). Washington, DC: American Enterprise Institute for Public Policy Research.

Bryant, H., & Mah, Z. (1992). Breast cancer screening attitudes and behaviors of rural and urban women. *Preventative Medicine, 21*(4), 405–418.

Carr, P., & Kefalas, M. J. (2009). *Hollowing out the middle: The rural brain drain and what it means for America.* Boston, MA: Beacon Press.

Casey, M. M., Thiede, C. K., & Klingner, J. M. (2001). Are rural residents less likely to obtain recommended preventive healthcare services? *American Journal of Preventative Medicine, 21*(3), 182–188.

Conger, R. D., Conger, K. D., & Martin, M. J. (2010). Socioeconomic status, family processes, and individual development. *Journal of Marriage and Family, 72*(3), 685–704.

Coomber, K., Tournbourou, J. W., Miller, P., Staiger, P. K., Hemphill, S. A., & Catalano, R. F. (2010). Rural adolescent alcohol, tobacco, and illicit drug use: A comparison of students in Victoria, Australia, and Washington State, United States. *Journal of Rural Health, 27*(4), 409–415.

Cronk, C. E., & Sarvela, P. D. (1997). Alcohol, tobacco, and other drug use among rural/small town and urban youth: A secondary analysis of the monitoring the future data set. *American Journal of Public Health, 87*(5), 760–764.

Crossman, J. S., James, W. L., Cosby, A. G., & Cossman, R. E. (2010). Underlying causes of the emerging non-metropolitan mortality penalty. *American Journal of Public Health, 100*(8), 1417–1419.

Dinour, L. M., Bergen, D., & Yeh, M. C. (2007). The food insecurity-obesity paradox: A review of the literature and the role food stamps may play. *Journal of the American Dietetic Association, 107*(11), 1952–1961.

Doescher, M. P., Jackson, J. E., Jerant, A., & Garyhart, L. (2006). Prevalence and trends in smoking: A national rural study. *Journal of Rural Health, 22*(2), 112–118.

Eberhardt, M. S., Ingram, D. D., Makuc, D. M., Pamuk, E. R., Freid, V. M., Harper, S. B., ... Xia, H. (2001). *Urban and rural health chartbook.* Hyattsville, MD: National Center for Health Statistics.

Eberhardt, M. S., & Pamuk, E. R. (2004). The importance of place of residence: Examining health in rural and nonrural areas. *American Journal of Public Health, 94*(10), 1682–1686.

Elder, G. H., Johnson, M. K., & Crosnoe, R. (2003). The emergence and development of life course theory. In J. T. Mirtimer & M. J. Shanahan (Eds.), *Handbook of the life course* (pp. 3–19). New York, NY: Kluwer Academic/Plenum Publishers.

Esch, L., & Hendryx, M. (2011). Chronic cardiovascular disease mortality in mountaintop mining areas of central Appalachian states. *Journal of Rural Health, 27*(4), 350–357.

Felton, G. M., Dowda, M., Ward, D. S., Dishman, R. K., Trost, S. G., Saunders, R., & Pate, R. R. (2002). Differences in physical activity between Black and White girls living in rural and urban areas. *Journal of School Health, 72*(6), 250–255.

Gamm, L., Hutchison, L., Dabney, B., & Dorsey, A. (2003). *Rural healthy people 2010: A companion document to healthy people 2010.* College Station, TX: Texas A&M University System Health Science Center, School of Rural Public Health, Southwest Rural Health Research Center.

Gamm, L., Stone, S., & Pittman, S. (2010). *Mental health and mental disorders: A rural challenge: A literature review.* College Station, TX: Texas A&M University System Health Science Center, School of Rural Public Health, Southwest Rural Health Research Center.

Harju, B. L., Wuensch, K. L., Kuhl, E. A., & Cross, N. J. (2006). Comparison of rural and urban residents' implicit and explicit attitudes related to seeking medical care. *Journal of Rural Health, 22*(4), 359–363.

Hartley, D., Bird, D. C., & Dempsey, P. (1999). Rural mental health and substance abuse. In T. C. Ricketts (Ed.), *Rural health in the United States* (pp. 231–265). New York, NY: Oxford University Press.

Hartley, D., Quam, L., & Lurie, N. (1994). Urban and rural differences in health insurance and access to care. *Journal of Rural Health, 10*(2), 98–108.

Hendryx, M. (2008). Mental health professional shortage in rural Appalachia. *Journal of Rural Health, 24*(2), 179–182.

Hendryx, M. (2011). Introduction to special section: Environmental health for rural populations. *Journal of Rural Health, 27*(4), 339–341.

Hendryx, M., Borders, T., & Johnson, T. (1995). The distribution of mental health providers in a rural state. *Administration and Policy in Mental Health, 23*(2), 153–155.

Hendryx, M., & Fedorko, E. (2011). The relationship between toxic release inventory discharges and mortality rates in rural and urban areas of the United States. *Journal of Rural Health, 27*(4), 358–366.

Hicks, L. L. (1990). Availability and accessibility of rural health care. *Journal of Rural Health, 6*(4), 485–505.

Hirsch, J. K. (2006). A review of the literature on rural suicide: Risk and protective factors, incidence, and prevention. *Crisis, 27*(4), 189–199.

Hofferth, S. L., & Iceland, J. (1998). Social capital in rural and urban communities. *Rural Sociology, 63*(4), 574–598.

Hoyt, D. R., Conger, R., & Valde, J. (1997). Psychological distress and help seeking in rural America. *American Journal of Community Psychology, 25*(4), 449–470.

Huang, B., Wyatt, S. W., Tucker, T. C., Bottorff, D., Lengerich, E., & Hall, H. I. (2002). Cancer death rates, Appalachia, 1994–1998. *Morbidity and Mortality Weekly Report, 51*(24), 527–529.

Hutchison, L., & Blakely, C. (2003). *Substance abuse: Trends in rural areas: A literature review.* College Station, TX: Texas A&M University System Health Science Center, School of Rural Public Health, Southwest Rural Health Resource Center.

Jackson, E. J., Doescher, M. P., Jerant, A. F., & Hart, L. G. (2005). A national study of obesity prevalence and trends by type of rural county. *Journal of Rural Health, 21*(2), 140–148.

Jacob, S., Bourke, L., & Luloff, A. E. (1997). Rural community stress, distress, and well-being in Pennsylvania. *Journal of Rural Studies, 13*(3), 275–288.

Joens-Matre, R. R., Welk, G. J., Calabro, M. A., Russell, D. W., Nicklay, E., & Hensley, L. D. (2008). Rural-urban differences in physical activity, physical fitness, and overweight prevalence of children. *Journal of Rural Health, 24*(1), 49–54.

Johnson, K. (2006). *Demographic trends in rural and small town America. Reports on Rural America, 1*(1). Durham, NH: Carsey Institute, University of New Hampshire.

Johnson, K., & Macieski, R. (2009). *Demographic trends in the Manchester-Nashua metropolitan area.* New England Issue Brief No. 16. Durham, NH: Carsey Institute, University of New Hampshire.

Johnson, M., Brems, C., Warner, T., & Roberts, L. (2006). Rural-urban health care provider disparities in Alaska and New Mexico. *Administration and Policy in Mental Health, 33*(4), 504–507.

Jones, A. R., Cook, T. M., & Wang, J. (2011). Rural-urban differences in stigma against depression and agreement with health professionals about treatment. *Journal of Affective Disorders, 134*(1), 145–150.

Judd, F., Cooper, A. M., Fraser, C., & Davis, J. (2006). Rural suicide: People or place effects? *Australian and New Zealand Journal of Psychiatry, 40*(3), 208–216.

Kessler, R. C., Berglund, P., Demler, O., Jin, R., Koretz, D., Merikangas, K. R., . . . Wang, P. S. (2005). The epidemiology of major depressive disorder: Results from the National Comorbidity Survey Replication (NCS-R). *Journal of the American Medical Association, 289*(23), 3095–3105.

Kessler, R. C., Mcgonagle, K. A., Zhao, S., Hughes, M., Eshleman, S., Wittchen, H. U., & Kendler, K. S. (1994). Lifetime and 12–month prevalence of DSM-III-R psychiatric disorders in the United States. *Archives of General Psychiatry, 51*(1), 8–19.

Kirschner, A. E., Berry, H., & Glasgow, N. (2006). The changing faces of rural America. In W. A. Kandel & D. L. Brown (Eds.), *Population change and rural society* (pp. 53–74). Dordrecht, Netherlands: Springer.

Komiti, A., Judd, F., & Jackson, H. (2006). The influence of stigma and attitudes on seeking help from a GP for mental health problems: A rural context. *Social Psychiatry and Psychiatric Epidemiology, 41*(9), 738–745.

Lambert, D., Gale, J. A., & Hartley, D. (2008). Substance abuse by youth and young adults in rural America. *Journal of Rural Health, 24*(3), 221–228.

Larson, S. L., & Hill, S. C. (2005). Rural-urban differences in employment-related health insurance. *Journal of Rural Health, 21*(1), 21–30.

Lu, N., Samuels, M. E., Kletke, P. R., & Whitler, E. T. (2010). Rural-urban differences in health insurance coverage and patterns among working-age adults in Kentucky. *Journal of Rural Health, 26*(2), 129–138.

Luo, J., & Hendryx, M. (2010). Environmental carcinogen releases and lung cancer mortality in rural-urban areas of the United States. *Journal of Rural Health, 27*(4), 342–349.

Macintyre, S., Ellaway, A., & Cummins, S. (2002). Place effects on health: How can we conceptualise, operationalise and measure them? *Social Science and Medicine, 55*(1), 125–139.

Mainous, A. G., King, D. E., Garr, D. R., & Pearson, W. S. (2004). Race, rural residence and control of diabetes and hypertension. *Annuals of Family Medicine, 2*(6), 563–568.

Maio, R. F., Green, P. E., Becker, M. P., Burney, R. E., & Compton, C. (1992). Rural motor vehicle crash mortality: The role of crash severity and medical resources. *Accident Analysis and Prevention, 24*(6), 631–642.

Mansfield, C. J., Wilson, J. L., Kobrinski, E. J., & Mitchell, J. (1999). Premature mortality in the United States: The roles of geographic area, socioeconomic status, household type, and availability of medical care. *American Journal of Public Health, 89*(6), 893–898.

Maris, R. W., Berman, A. L., & Silverman, M. M. (2000). *Comprehensive textbook of suicidology.* New York, NY: Guilford Press.

McLeod, J. D., & Almazan, E. P. (2003). Connections between childhood and adulthood. In J. T. Mortimer & M. J. Shanahan (Eds.), *Handbook of the life course* (pp. 391–411). New York, NY: Kluwer.

McMurray, R. G., Harrell, J. S., Bangdiwala, S. I., & Deng, S. (1999). Cardiovascular disease risk factors and obesity of rural and urban elementary school children. *Rural Health Research, 15*(4), 365–374.

Merchant, J. A., Kross, B., Donham, K. J., & Pratt, D. S. (1989). *Agriculture at risk: A report to the nation.* Kansas City, MO: National Coalition for Agricultural Safety and County Health, National Rural Health Association.

Mills, M. L. (2010). *Help in a haystack: Youth substance abuse and mental health services in the North Country.* New England Issue Brief No. 20. Durham, NH: Carsey Institute, University of New Hampshire.

Mills, M. L., & Van Gundy, K. T. (2012). Socioeconomic status and the stress process in rural youth: The role of social attachments. In *Proceedings from the Annual Meeting of the American Sociological Association.* Denver, CO, August 20, 2012.

Mogatt, D. F., Bradley, M. M., Adams, S. J., & Morris, C. D. (2005). *Mental health and rural America: 1994–2005.* Washington, DC: U.S. Department of Health and Human Services, Health Resources and Service Administration, Office of Rural Health Policy.

Mortality tables. (2012). National Vital Statistics System.

Morton, L. W., & Blanchard, T. C. (2007). Starved for access: Life in rural America's food deserts. *Rural Realities, 1*(4), 1–10.

Muelleman, R. S., & Mueller, K. (1996). Fatal motor vehicle crashes: Variations of crash characteristics within rural regions of different population densities. *Journal of Trauma, 41*(2), 315–320.

Murimi, M. W., & Harpel, T. (2010). Practicing preventive health: The underlying culture among low-income rural populations. *Journal of Rural Health, 26*(3), 273–282.

National Survey on Drug Use and Health: Public use codebook. (2011). Research Triangle Park, NC: RTI International.

Nord, M., Coleman-Jensen, A., Andrews, M., & Carison, S. (2010). *Household food security in the United States, 2009.* Economic Research Report No. 108. Washington, DC: U.S. Department of Agriculture, Economic Research Service.

Nummela, O. (2008). Social participation, trust and self-rated health: A study among ageing people in urban, semi-urban and rural settings. *Health and Place, 14*(2), 243–253.

Obisesan, T. O., Vargas, C. M., & Gillum, R. F. (2000). Geographic variation in stroke risk in the United States: Region, urbanization, and hypertension in the Third National Health and Nutrition Examination Survey. *Stroke, 31*(1), 19–25.

Office of Management and Budget (OMB). (2003). *Revised definitions of metropolitan statistical areas, new definitions of micropolitan statistical areas and combined statistical areas, and guidance on use of the statistical definitions of these areas.* OMB Bulletin No. 03–04. Washington, DC: Author.

Patterson, P. D., Moore, C. G., Probst, J. C., & Shinogle, J. A. (2004). Obesity and physical inactivity in rural America. *Journal of Rural Health, 20*(2), 151–159.

Pearlin, L. I. (1989). The sociological study of stress. *Journal of Health and Social Behavior, 30*(3), 241–256.

Pearlin, L. I. (1999). Stress and mental health: A conceptual overview. In A. V. Horwitz & S. L. Scheid (Eds.), *A handbook for the study of mental health: Social contexts, theories, and systems* (pp. 161–175). New York, NY: Cambridge University Press.

Pearlin, L. I. (2010). The life course and the stress process: Some conceptual comparisons. *Journal of Gerontology Series B: Psychological Sciences and Social Sciences, 65B*(2), 207–215.

Pearlin, L. I., Schieman, S., Fazio, E. M., & Meersman, S. C. (2005). Stress, health and the life course: Some conceptual perspectives. *Journal of Health and Social Behavior, 46*(2), 205–219.

Peek-Asa, C., Zwerling, C., & Stallones, L. (2004). Acute traumatic injuries in rural populations. *American Journal of Public Health, 94*(10), 1689–1693.

Peterson, L. E., & Litaker, D. G. (2010). County-level poverty is equally associated with unmet health care needs in rural and urban settings. *Journal of Rural Health, 28*(4), 373–382.

Phillimore, P., & Reading, R. (1992). A rural advantage? Urban-rural health differences in northern England. *Journal of Public Health, 14*(3), 290–299.

Portes, A. (1998). Social capital: Its origins and applications in modern sociology. *Annual Review of Sociology, 24*, 1–24.

Probst, J. C., Moore, C. G., Baxley, E. G., & Lammie, J. J. (2002). Rural-urban differences in visits to primary care physicians. *Family Medicine, 34*(8), 609–615.

Pruitt, L. (2009). The forgotten fifth: Rural youth and substance abuse. *Stanford Law and Policy Review, 20*, 101–148.

Rahilly, C. R., & Frarwell, W. R. (2007). Prevalence of smoking in the United States: A focus on age, sex, ethnicity, and geographic patterns. *Current Cardiovascular Risk Reports, 1*(5), 379–383.

Reis, J. P., Bowles, H. R., Ainsworth, B. E., Dubose, K. D., Smith, S., & Laditka, J. N. (2004). Nonoccupational physical activity by degree of urbanization and U.S. geographic region. *Medicine and Science in Sports and Exercise, 36*(12), 2093–2098.

Ricketts, T. C. (Ed.). (1999). *Rural health in the United States.* New York, NY: Oxford University Press.

Roger, C. C. (2000). The graying of rural America. *Forum for Applied Research and Public Policy, 15*(4), 52–55.

Romans, S., Cohen, M., & Forte, T. (2011). Rates of depression and anxiety in urban and rural Canada. *Social Psychiatry and Epidemiology, 46*(7), 567–575.

Rowland, D., & Lyons, B. (1989). Triple jeopardy: Rural, poor, and uninsured. *Health Services Research, 23*(6), 975–1004.

Sarvela, P. D., Cronk, C. E., & Isberner, F. R. (1997). A secondary analysis of smoking among rural and urban youth using the Monitoring the Future data set. *Journal of School Health, 67*(9), 372–375.

Senior, M., Williams, H., & Higgs, G. (2000). Urban-rural mortality differentials: Controlling for material deprivation. *Social Science and Medicine, 51*(2), 289–305.

Sherman, J., & Sage, R. (2011). Sending off all your good treasures: Rural schools, brain-drain, and community survival in the wake of economic collapse. *Journal of Research in Rural Education, 26*(11), 1–14.

Smith, K. B., Humphreys, J. S., & Wilson, M. G. A. (2008). Addressing the health disadvantage of rural populations: How does epidemiological evidence inform rural health policies and research? *Australian Journal of Rural Health, 16*(2), 56–66.

Smith, S. S., & Fiore, M. C. (1999). The epidemiology of tobacco use, dependence and cessation in the United States. *Primary Care, 26*(3), 433–461.

Sobal, J., Troiano, R. P., & Frongillo, E. A. (1996). Rural-urban differences in obesity. *Rural Sociology, 61*(2), 289–305.

Stracuzzi, N. (2009). *Youth aspirations and sense of place in a changing rural economy: The Coos Youth Study.* New England Issue Brief No. 1. Durham, NH: Carsey Institute, University of New Hampshire.

Substance Abuse and Mental Health Services Administration. (2008*). Results from the 2007 National Survey on Drug Use and Health: National findings.* NSDUH Series H-34. DHHS Publication No. 08-4343. Rockville, MD: Office of Applied Studies.

Tai-Seale, T., & Chandler, C. (2010). *Nutrition and overweight concerns in rural areas: A literature review.* College Station, TX: Texas A&M University System Health Science Center, School of Public Health, Southwest Rural Health Science Center.

Taylor, H. A., Hughes, G. D., & Garrison, R. J. (2002). Cardiovascular disease among women residing in rural America: Epidemiology, explanations, and challenges. *American Journal of Public Health, 92*(4), 548–551.

Thoits, P. A. (1995). Stress, coping, and social support: Where are we? What next? *Journal of Health and Social Behavior,* Extra issue, 53–79.

Turner, R. J., & Avison, W. R. (2003). Status variations in stress exposure: Implications for the interpretation of research on race, socioeconomic status, and gender. *Journal of Health and Social Behavior, 44*(4), 488–505.

Turner, R. J., Taylor, J., & Van Gundy, K. (2004). Personal resources and depression in the transition to adulthood: Ethnic comparisons. *Journal of Health and Social Behavior, 45*(1), 34–52.

Turner, R. J., Wheaton, B., & Lloyd, D. A. (1995). The epidemiology of social stress. *American Sociological Review, 60*(1), 104–125.

U.S. Census Bureau. (2009). Rural definitions. www.ers.usda.gov/data/ruraldefinitions/NH.pdf

U.S. Department of Health and Human Services. (2000). *Tracking healthy people 2010.* Washington, DC: Government Printing Office.

Van Gundy, K. (2006). *Substance abuse in rural and small town America. Reports on Rural America, 1*(2). Durham, NH: Carsey Institute, University of New Hampshire.

Van Gundy, K. T., & Mills, M. L. (2011). *Teen stress and substance use problems in Coös: Survey shows strong community attachment can offset risk.* New England Issue Brief No. 29. Durham, NH: Carsey Institute, University of New Hampshire.

Van Gundy, K. T., Stracuzzi, N. F., Rebellon, C. J., Tucker, C. J., & Cohn, E. S. (2011). Perceived community cohesion and the stress process in youth. *Rural Sociology, 76*(3), 293–318.

Vargas, C. M., Dye, B. A., & Hayes, K. L. (2002). Oral health status of rural adults in the United States. *Journal of the American Dental Association, 133*(12), 1672–1681.

Veitch, C. (2009). Impact of rurality on environmental determinants and hazards. *Australian Journal of Rural Health, 17*(1), 16–20.

Wang, Y. (2001). Cross-national comparison of childhood obesity: The epidemic and the relationship between obesity and status. *International Journal of Epidemiology, 30*(5), 1129–1136.

World Health Organization (WHO). (2012). Definition of health. https://apps.who.int/aboutwho/en/definition.html

Wrigley, S., Jackson, H., Judd, F., & Komiti, A. (2005). Role of stigma and attitudes toward help-seeking from a general practitioner for mental health problems in a rural town. *Australian and New Zealand Journal of Psychiatry, 39*(6), 514–521.

York, N. L., Rayens, M. K., Zhang, M., Jones, L. G., Casey, B. R., & Hahn, E. J. (2010). Strength of tobacco control in rural communities. *Journal of Rural Health, 26*(2), 120–128.

Zwerling, C., Miller, E. R., Lynch, C. F., & Torner, J. (1996). Injuries among construction workers in rural Iowa: Emergency department surveillance. *Journal of Occupational Environmental Medicine, 38*(7), 698–704.

Chapter 11

Improving Health: Asset-Based Community Development

Kathleen T. Grimm, Jessica Bauer Walker, and Deborah L. Puntenney

Introduction

The increasing gap between those who enjoy good health and those who struggle significantly has been described in terms of the complexity of the public health domain—that is, in terms of access to the opportunity for health based on social condition, employment, education, safety, and an ecology that supports health. The milieu of public health recognizes the complex interaction of many factors that work in concert to improve health, especially in the realm of population health. In 1998, the Institute of Medicine (IOM) defined the public health domain this way: "Public health is what we, as a society, do collectively to assure the conditions in which people can be healthy." Health is a contextual, community-based reality, while disease is treated in institutions and systems designed to deliver health care. The socioecologic construct of health highlights the preeminence of the social determinants of health—the environment where one is born, lives, goes to school, recreates, works, shops, and builds relationships and social connectivity. Although a collective group of factors that contribute to health status is recognized and well researched, a significant root cause of unequal health opportunity for communities is poverty.

Simply stated, "Income is a significant contributor to health" (Woolf, 2007). There is ample evidence in both the medical and social science literature that the link between poverty and disease is strong (Government Accounting Office [GAO], 2007; Lynch et al., 1998; Woolf, 2007), and that income inequality worsens health outcomes (Lynch et al., 1998). Low socioeconomic status itself contributes to premature mortality and excess morbidity. While researchers continue to sift through the multiple known contributors to poor health status—including job insecurity, poor housing, low educational status, and relationship insecurity—a factor that stays constant within all these examinations of poor health outcome is the element of poverty (Blacksher, 2009).

A view of health using the larger framework of the social determinants of health will challenge research, policy, and funding streams that currently are constrained and narrow and that do not address the socioecologic factors of health beyond health care delivery. This chapter presents the argument that one-dimensional health initiatives that are not placed in the context of the physical, mental, emotional, spiritual, economic, educational, and social well-being of individuals and communities can be unsustainable and costly. The paradigm-shifting concept explored in this chapter views populations and communities as "assets," rather than as entities defined by a deficiency view as "diseased" or "needy." These human and neighborhood assets have capabilities to build health in their neighborhoods when significant resources are redirected to the root causes of disease, through both community-based investment and grassroots change. The required change in thinking contrasts with current methodologies that view outside experts working alone, in a top-down manner, as being able to create change by "delivering" health to people. Sustainable change happens when communities have the power to utilize asset-based mobilization and community organizing principles to attain the foundation for better health. This achievement requires a shift in the distribution and structure of power that exists within current hierarchical, expert-driven processes to make changes that work toward the coproduction of health that combines professional and/ or institutional efforts with community-based, grassroots efforts. Differences in health between populations and groups are due to the structure and characteristics of society, not just to differences in health care (Marmot, 2006).

This shift in focus, which entails moving away from the traditional "disease-based focus," necessitates reorganization of current funding streams and other resource investments that have been made in the interest of health promotion. We will explore the following issues:

1. Changes needed in conceptualization of health and poverty, and how poverty is predictive of poor health outcomes

2. Changes in research methodology and measurement of community health
3. Changes in policy and leadership to produce a sustainable infra-structure for asset-based community development and health

Changing the View of "Health"

A traditional view of health is often described as an absence of disease sufficient to maintain a long life. In this view, health is reduced to a process of treating illness and extending life. We are familiar with the numerous indicators of health in the population, such as low incidence of infant mortality and low rates of heart disease (Centers for Disease Control and Prevention [CDC], 2011; U.S. Department of Health and Human Services, 2010, 2011). Traditional views tend to examine the quantity of life (lifespan) but consider the quality of life only in terms of disease prevention and treatment. This approach fails to take into account many dimensions of good health and quality of life, in particular those related to the dynamics of health that are not measured in current evaluative methodologies. The measures and evaluative tools of "risk" and "health" have been developed as part of this model of medicine and scientific analysis, where accountability for health outcome does not consider public health and the social determinants of health, or strategies for recognition of the impact of factors such as poverty and the *opportunity* for better health status (Childress et al., 2002).

When health is defined as the absence of disease, one approach to achieving that outcome is simply to treat diseases as they appear. Our current health care delivery system operates mostly in this reactive mode, and we have invested billions in creating the systems that provide such treatment. At the same time, however, we have largely ignored the role of individuals and communities in the proactive creation of healthy environments and the concept of prevention. This systemization of health has reduced the capacity of individuals and communities to take action toward building health through the very process of creating professional health delivery systems (McKnight, 1995). Health begins with neighborhoods that are safe, children who are secure, and adults who can age without fear of isolation. Health begins in homes and neighborhoods that are supportive of residents, in jobs and incomes that are secure, and in ecologies that allow for persons to attain health status. Health that starts at home spreads to the larger community, within the structures that keep people at work, in school, and free from drugs, alcohol, and trauma.

One example that currently exists when viewing health as synonymous with health care delivery systems is the language and understanding in mainstream American culture that views age as "disease." Policy positions have been developed and resource investments made to care for the large wave of aging Americans, who are widely recognized as having more health needs. Health care delivery systems have positioned them-selves as an answer to caring for aging Americans, with more resource investment required to support this service-based industry. The approach suggesting that age is a disease, requiring more health care infrastructure, is not congruent with many societies around the world, where aging com-munity members are considered "elders" who are held in high esteem and provided neighborhood and family-based supports to assist them navigate the physical, mental, and emotional changes associated with aging. Indeed, life expectancy and quality of life are much higher and associated health care costs much lower in societies that do not view age as equivalent to disease (Organization of Economic Cooperative Develop-ment [OECD], 2011). The real need will be for communities that support healthy aging—communities with walkable and safe neighborhoods, home settings that are compatible with the "aging in place" environments that lessen social exclusion of our aging, and recognition of the vital con-tributions that aging citizens can provide. The placement of "oldness" within a framework of disease and deficiency disenfranchises the aging population from redefining its own competencies, skills, and capacities to be healthy (McKnight, 1995).

Institutions and programs of health delivery that work with vulnerable or marginalized populations (e.g., seniors, children, immigrants and refu-gees, those of low socioeconomic status), but do not support this inclusive framework of health, will continue to fail to secure better health status for communities, particularly those in poverty (IOM, 2012). Communities of poor health are enmeshed in the poverty of dependency on systems for their health, as they have been educated through social media and power-ful marketing campaigns to "ask" for "coaching" on how to be well. Research suggests that the power differential that is created by systems of health impedes even those who have been thought to be powerful and educated enough to work with health systems to coproduce health—not just those who may come from backgrounds that provide little formal education or opportunities—from developing self-efficacy. A recent study of educated, socioeconomically secure Californians, in a position thought to facilitate copartnering with health systems to meet their personal health needs, demonstrated the barriers between "patient" and "doctor" in regard to collaborative decision making toward better health outcomes (Frosch, May, Rendle, Tietbohl, & Elwyn, 2012). If we accept the current thinking that the power differential between systems and persons seeking health care is of little consequence, then we may create larger systems, yet have no impact on health outcomes. In shifting current research and funding streams, the pre-viously unchallenged assumptions of "educated consumerism" by health systems as a way to secure improved health need closer examination. Com-munities of health are those that have been able to shift the distribution of power from "top-down" work to a "bottom-up" process that merges health initiatives with the larger, more powerful systems. Partnership in this way allows for community voice and choice in the distribution of resources to allow for protection of vulnerable members living within the community.

The definition of health we use here encompasses the traditional definition in that it includes a lack of disease so that the person can live a long life. Our definition goes further, however, by suggesting that to overcome the interdependency and causality associated with poverty and neighborhood environment, a more equitable society must emerge. The only way for that to happen is for people to become involved in both the definition and the creation of their own healthy communities, in partnership with larger systems. Improved health outcomes will happen at the community level when individuals, families, and whole communities actively engage in altering the conditions in the places where they live (changing their relationship to the places), altering the way they live (changing their own health behavior), and working together to demand an equitable distribution of resources (changing policies) such that their combined efforts produce greater opportunities to live healthy lives. Thus health is the product of individual and community investment, partnership with agencies and institutions, and active engagement on policy issues that can help pave the way for good health. Health is something that can be built, not something that someone else delivers. There is a need for greater support for resources invested in the process of health determination and opportunity for health at the community level, with better recognition of widening income inequality and poverty gaps and the impact of poverty on all other social determinants of health.

The ability to impact the sociocultural ecology that is the largest contributor to a person's health eludes many who provide care in the current delivery system of health care. A recent survey of 1,000 American physicians found that physicians "reported that if they had the power to write prescriptions to address social needs, such prescriptions would represent approximately 1 out of 7 prescriptions they write" (Robert Wood Johnson Foundation, 2011). The same survey also found that 82% of physicians said patients frequently express health concerns caused by unmet social needs that are beyond their control as physicians. In addition, 74% of doctors reported that these unmet needs often prevent them from providing quality medical care. These unmet needs were reported as affecting patients of all income levels (Moyer, 2012).

The Role of the Community in Health Promotion

The definitional perspective of "community" must be nuanced to recognize that "community" is difficult to define for every process and policy. It cannot be interpreted to be homogeneity of thinking or doing. In neighborhoods and families, however, community recognizes the informal network of relationships that builds community capacity. In community organizing and community building, two basic principles are key—namely, relationship building and the creation of networks and collective identities. This collective action builds on assets that are shared "asset capital": locally invested in building collective strength and power to change policy and build change (Warren & Mapp, 2011). Through local asset building, communities are organized to be politically active and assertive, and they learn to work against pervasive distrust and fatalism (Praxis Project, 2012).

This participatory model directs action and policy not based on assumptions made by researchers alone, but rather by valuing community partners in such a way that the product of health and community development is a shared product, from design to implementation. Health-directed research in this model reduces stigmatizing assumptions of populations, which in turn allows for translation of research into better health because of community participation and the shared responsibility inherent in coproduction (Burklow & Mills, 2009; Dickert & Sugarman, 2005). Moreover, when trusted community members are architects for change and leaders in the creation of better health in neighborhoods, the personal investment of community members directly impacted creates viability and sustainability for health. Leadership and change at this local level have been phenomena that the United States has seen in social movements toward civil, women's, and worker's rights, as well as in rights-based issue campaigns organized around voting, reproductive health, HIV/AIDS, and environmental health. While racial and socioeconomic health disparities continue to worsen in communities across the United States (Link, Northridge, Phelan, & Ganz, 1998; National Center for Health Statistics, 2006; Wilkinson and Marmot, 2003), a solution has evaded the many systems charged with increasing equity because there has been little collective action to link health systems with community development and capacity at the local level. Without the active involvement of those residents who are most affected by the problems, fixes that are wholly or largely dependent on an outside entity such as charity are rarely sustainable. Creating health, therefore, cannot be a one-dimensional pursuit, but rather must be viewed as the confluence of the people and systems existing in and responsible for that space working together. Health can be built and maintained in a community that is competent "when each person knows that their own success, personally and economically, is dependent on the success of their neighbors" (McKnight & Block, 2010).

Social connectivity and grassroots change that build on community organizing have worked in other sectors, and examples can be found within the health arena as well. Notably, many communities have organized around environmental health issues such as pollution or toxic waste as they identified them to be root causes of disease and poor health, and have been able to collectively mobilize toward positive change. For example, grassroots citizen action brought significant change in environmental policy and industry standards in the Love Canal demonstrations in upstate New York (Center for Health, Environment, and Justice, 2012). Civic engagement and participatory democracy can be a primary tool used to create better health outcomes in communities if built in a way that is organized with strategy and sustainability in mind, and with a high degree of civic engagement and leadership from those who are directly affected. In fact, research shows that indicators of citizen participation, such as voter engagement, are directly linked to quality of life and health status (Navarro, 2004). Often in communities, issues or campaigns for change create short-term, heavily resourced strategies to produce results. Outside resources and experts are "parachuted in" to mobilize a community. The results are also short term, however. When the experts who have converged to solve a problem leave, the community is left without the tools, the leadership, or the support for sustainable change, with limited advocacy skills (Praxis Project, 2012). This "parachute politics" principle is analogous to health care systems "delivering" health to community members, without taking into account the importance of community members' active participation in designing and coproducing individual and community health.

Community health that is sustainable should move away from the reactive, disease-based view that is highly dependent on experts and outside resources. A different approach would be to locate "expert" voices of community within the community itself and to require partnership beyond inserting outside experts to prescribe solutions.

Community Context and Community Assets

Authors McKnight and Block (2010) use this descriptor of community:

A neighborhood is the place where you live or sleep. It could be your block or the square mile surrounding where you live. It may or may not have a name.

The word community is more difficult, because we use the general term to describe what happens outside systems and institutions. It also refers to an aggregation of people or neighborhoods that have something in common. It is both a place and an experience of connectedness. (p. 5)

Communities and populations viewed as deficient give policymakers and researchers the view that change needs to be directed *at* the community, rather than being built *with* the community. Health in a strengths-based context recognizes the person's ability to feel valued as an asset and to reduce his or her stress based on dependence and the charity of others. Competent communities are built on the recognition that citizens who live within the community recognize and build on the value of local assets (McKnight & Block, 2010).

A healthy community functions as the local context for individuals' experience of well- being as well as being the result of healthy behaviors and investments. For a disadvantaged community, building a healthier place depends on a cycle of gradual transitions on both sides of this equation. In other words, healthier behavior and investment can gradually produce a better context for living, and a better context for living can in turn increase opportunities for healthy behaviors and investments. Building community health must happen with residents (often referred to by institutions as patients, clients, or consumers) as coproducers, instead of simply being delivered to residents as recipients (Zappia & Puntenney, 2010). When health is placed in a community-based context, every component of a community represents an asset; moreover, when the majority of assets are deployed toward making a healthier place, a more realistic, sustainable kind of health can be achieved (Kretzmann & McKnight, 1993; Turner, McKnight, & Kretzmann, 1999).

Current financing for health in the United States is not aligned with the asset-based, community-driven process we describe here, but rather on the disease- and deficiency-based paradigm (IOM, 2012). This perspective complicates the ability and capacity of communities to build health, as an integrated approach based on assets, community building, and social determinants of health is severely under-resourced. This capacity-building principle for health has value in a community's own human resources as foundational. These human resources are threefold: (1) *social capital*—changes in relations that facilitate action; (2) *human capital*—changes in persons and acquisition of skills that enable action; and (3) *moral capital*—investment of personal and collective resources for justice (Stokols, Grzywacz, McMahan, & Phillips, 2003). Socially connected communities strengthen the environment for health opportunity through interconnected, intergenerational, and culturally competent constructs. Without support for strong neighborhoods based on these principles, the power differential of control and economic investment in resources for health will continue to be misaligned and detrimental to community health (Hofrichter, 2003). These can be difficult ideas for institutions to integrate, as they run contrary to the conventional wisdom that those entities with greater expertise and resources can do more to alter undesirable conditions than those entities who are victimized by them. However, a growing research base increasingly reflects the notion that detriment to society is created by the enormous investments in clinical care and delivery systems (IOM, 2012).

If the root causes of poor health outcomes are to be understood, we must drill down to factors that are neighborhood and community based, and that focus on human and social capital. When examining disease incidence rates in the context of neighborhoods and populations, and when observing the strong correlation between health outcomes and education, housing, food access, and incarceration rates, we see that public health and health care initiatives that focus on individual responsibility to "take charge of your health" are limited in their scope due to their lack of consideration of community context. The community structure and the support of community strategies in health have been the most influential in the sustainability of the creation of healthy lives (McKnight, 1995; Warren, 2001).

Informal neighborhood and community networks can play a significant role in helping individuals keep their health, or get it back when health is lost. This endeavor involves investment in and recognition of the social capital within a community. Community and social structure have historically provided what we could refer to as primary care or prevention. Root-cause views of disease will challenge long-held views and require new investment strategies. For example, eradication of violence in households and neighborhoods may be a key factor in reducing obesity, as such violence is as much a significant contributor to obesity as any other environmental restructuring or dietary changes (Felitti & Anda, 2010). Similarly, adverse childhood experiences, including poverty and educational level, lead to a trajectory of adult disease (Lawlor, Sterne, Tynelius, Davey Smith, & Rasmussen, 2006).

The choice to direct revenue streams at institutions or service delivery systems alone under-resources the integrated construct that involves community, focusing on deficits and needs rather than assets, and ignoring the root causes of disease. For example, preventive health efforts have often been directed by institutions and systems toward interventions at earlier stages of disease (i.e., "upstream interventions"). One example is the process currently in place to reduce lead toxicity in children, which has focused on conducting blood tests for lead levels in toddler-age children. While valuable, this testing occurs *after* a child may have already been exposed to a toxic level of environmental lead sources and suffered irreparable harm. Innovative upstream interventions move outside the health care system and work in the community to identify homes where pregnant women live and test these homes for lead *before* a baby's brain has ever had a toxic exposure (Berg, Eckstein, Steiner, Gavard, & Gross, 2012). Lead exposure can affect IQ and behavior, having long-lasting effects on educational achievement and health outcomes. The problem of lead toxicity is disproportionately felt in communities of poverty, where children living in these communities live in homes that are older and more likely to be contaminated with lead (CDC, 2012).

Resource reinvestment and reorganization does not imply that institutional health and resources are unnecessary, but rather posits that they should be complementary to community efforts and capacity building. Decentralizing service provision, with a focus on health (not disease), and investment in collaborations between the institutional and community sectors could significantly build community strength and efficacy. Community capacity building is an inherently broad and integrative endeavor, in the sense that it subsumes many different resources toward improved population health. The MacArthur Foundation, for example, defines community capacity as "the ability to mobilize the energy and talents of its members and to secure outside resources, such as capital investment and public services, to foster individual growth and improve the quality of life" (Stokols et al., 2003). Capacity building creates a cadre of individuals who both understand the needs and values of the community as only members can and understand the theories and methods of public health that can help meet those community needs appropriately (Heitman & McKieran, 2003).

Poverty's Complexities

The health impacts of poverty, social environment, and class have been researched and well documented in both the medical and social sciences literature (Marmot 2004, 2006; Rank, 2004). In the simplest terms, poverty has often been understood in the context of the most obvious of acquisitions—money and wealth. Poverty in a more complex analysis involves realms that extend beyond enumeration of one's wealth in terms of socioeconomic status (SES) alone. It encompasses not merely poverty of economics, but also poverty of opportunity and individual and community efficacy that correlates with poor health (Marmot, 2004, 2006; Satcher & Higginbotham, 2008). When considering poverty and health, the sphere of poverty's influence is wider and has an impact reaching well beyond monetary measures. "Poverty as disease" risks placing SES in the medical model, as if there were a one-dimensional approach or "cure" for low SES. Populations living in poverty are then imagined as homogeneous, without exploration of the confluence of factors that create and perpetuate poverty (Hodari, 2008). Poverty, when cast as such a one-dimensional concept, reflects neither the intensity of this phenomenon nor its duration. For example, poverty's influence on human development, particularly on the human brain, illustrates how poverty experienced at a critical phase of life has an impact that lasts a lifetime.

Additionally, as generations of American children are born into poverty, we now see systemic and intergenerational poverty that prevents family and community health from being actualized. Reports of poverty's impact on health status affect all age groups, but for the first time in history, children in some geographic areas of the United States will not live as long as their parents. The promise of the "American dream" is becoming increasingly out of reach for families experiencing persistent and long-term poverty (Sanders, 2011). Complicating this bleak picture is the documented reality that the opportunity to "close the gap" of inequality economically will not be available to a large majority of poor people, at least not without significant policy change (Bradbury, 2012). There have always been persons living in poverty; however, upward mobility was a possibility for large numbers. A recent OECD report paints a different reality of the world in which we now live. The report noted that the United States has the fourth highest inequality level in the OECD, after Chile, Mexico, and Turkey (OECD, 2011).

Poverty defined by SES alone, although a significant factor in achievement of those factors that define better health—better job security, a higher educational status, better neighborhood conditions—must be examined through a lens viewing poverty in a larger context. This understanding acknowledges systematic failure to recognize the personal value of an individual living in poverty as well as the individual's ability to contribute to solution creation. Disparities arise from poverty of representation in the political system, lack of representation in the power base of institutions, and the disenfranchisement of individuals or groups because of the lack of asset recognition of individuals and persons living in poverty.

Populations that cycle through intergenerational poverty persist in dependency because they lack power and the tools of self-efficacy: income, education, and other indicators of SES. This lack of power and the power differential created contribute to a lack of political capital and influence (i.e., voting in democratic elections processes) as well as a poverty of self-importance, self-expression, and self-fulfillment. In Sir Michael Marmot's lecture given to the Royal College of Physicians in 2006, and published subsequently, this contextual poverty is described in terms of a person's lack of autonomous expression, which creates a lack of empowerment, lack of control, limited opportunities for social engagement, and ultimately lack of freedom that leads to poor health (Marmot, 2006). The power dynamics associated with lack of power and control and associated stress, in addition to the impact of racism, have been identified as contributors to the disparate health status of African-Americans who have achieved greater SES, but whose health outcomes remain lower than their White counterparts at the same level of economic status. Issues such as heart disease, stroke, and chronic kidney disease occur in larger numbers among African-Americans who have SES in higher income brackets (Gee & Payne-Sturges, 2004).

Neighborhoods in which a high percentage of minorities live are also likely to be places where the local population experiences health disparities when compared to the population as a whole. Clearly, certain factors—low levels of employment, low income, and high density of minorities—are interrelated, making the reduction of health disparities a highly complex undertaking. Disparities and poor health are also associated with what has been described as neighborhood "psychosocial hazards" (Augustin, Glass, James, & Schwartz, 2008). These psychosocial hazards consist of "visible characteristics of neighborhoods such as violent crime, abandoned buildings, and signs of incivility" (Augustin et al., 2008, 1664) that activate a stress response in individuals and can lead to disease. Such hazards complicate neighborhoods characterized by concentrations of residents living in poverty. While the relationships among these variables are enormously complex, some of the factors that must be considered for a holistic response include issues associated with neighborhood environments:

1. The quality of the physical environment (e.g., housing, sidewalks and streets, green space, environmental hazards)
2. The quality of the economic environment (e.g., local economy, availability of jobs, affordability of housing)
3. The quality of the social environment (e.g., knowledge of and trust of one's neighbors, ability to take collective action)

Neighborhood environments that fare poorly when assessed on these issues may also fail to provide or support the development of the following opportunities for healthy choices and good health outcomes:

1. Access to resources (e.g., healthy food, health care, quality schools)
2. Safe, high-quality public and private space (e.g., low crime and violence, quality housing, limited noise, safe transit, opportunities for exercise)
3. Social connectedness (e.g., social capital, collective efficacy)

In contrast, communities that do offer a healthy context—physically, economically, and socially—are more likely to have healthy populations (Ellaway, Macintyre, & Bonnefoy, 2005)—yet we do not as a society ensure that every community provides this environment. This failure occurs through a combination of institutional policies that allow resources and investment to be delivered in an inequitable manner and a national ethos that does not question such inequity. For a community, the downward spiral is usually self-perpetuating. Because there is no clear mandate for all communities to be healthy, some drift into decline; fewer and fewer resources are then invested, so that the decline accelerates. For people living in such neighborhoods, hope also declines, and as the community context worsens, people withdraw from their neighbors and their belief in the efficacy of collective action disappears. Often the act of receiving charity, though it may alleviate immediate problems that individuals or families may face, is perceived as confirming that they are not entitled to earn the resource for themselves and that they must rely on others to give them. Once withdrawal occurs, the only way to address the problems facing a community appears to be the deployment of experts and outside ideas—charity in another form. The community is no longer viewed as the expert on its own health issues; instead, the larger system assumes the expertise, and those experts and their ideas may further erode the ability of communities to act. The current large-system approaches to public health and community wellness have contributed to a web of disparities, distrust, and dependency. Ongoing, intergenerational poor health status fosters collective fatalism that has been recognized in disempowered communities (Gee & Payne-Sturges, 2004). Generations of joblessness, poor education, and disempowerment have made it more difficult for the community to create its own platform to move toward asset building.

This interdependent reality of health complexity and poverty requires a shared approach toward achieving health, with the community playing a much more significant role in designing and developing solutions—not a larger and more complex health delivery system and top-down approaches that are justified using data sets based on one-dimensional indicators of health. A larger system is necessary only if we continue to believe that disease is the value we should invest in, not health. Innovative institutions could reexamine their role in reorganizing to address the social, institutional, and organizational constraints that impede good health. These issues of health will be best attended to within the social structure of the family, the neighborhood, and the community. Institutions created to deliver care cannot restore health in this complexity of context and ecology; institutions alone cannot eradicate diseases of poverty and lack of health status.

Policy is an important tool to create a framework for the broad and complex health improvement and promotion that values the role of community and addresses the role of poverty as a primary factor impacting health. Policy change needs to work from a platform that does not define poverty as a condition experienced by the individual, but rather as a sociocultural and systemic phenomenon. Health policies that are individually oriented in a linear fashion, with causality for poor health proscriptively assigned to individual vulnerability or fault, ignore the social and political structures that work against health determination. Whether in rich countries or poor, higher disease rates experienced by disadvantaged populations are not a naturally occurring phenomenon, but rather occur because of the way societies are organized and policies made (Marmot, 2006).

Research Gaps and Policy Change

Society's need for health opportunity and health justice entails not just greater investment in financially based reform alone, but will require payment restructuring that invests in social and human capital as well as community strength. More importantly, a shared philosophy needs to be created that shifts the focus to and starts conversations about health opportunity as a societal imperative. Currently, the agenda for change in health advances the mantra of quality and reduction of disparities in health outcome. As health systems work to reduce disparity, accountability for action and impact must be measured. Policy and resource distribution will need to account for the root causes of disease and the social determinants of health. Reframing the argument for all citizens to "have the opportunity for health" rather to "have more and more health care" will necessitate reorganization of the societal investment where foundational health occurs: in human and social capital and in community and neighborhood assets.

Moving the discussion away from health care delivery and toward health is a societal challenge. The current system has evolved to occupy a space in the collective social and societal consciousness such that when a change in the system is discussed, the system weighs in, as a stakeholder. When policy development for change and health reform is undertaken, we hear the voice of system and institutional leadership.

Current funding streams have been constrained by a narrow view of health as one issue. The contextual concept of health does not always fit the "logic model" as proposed by major funders in health care. The socioecologic model is dynamic and complex. Creating health, therefore, cannot be a one-dimensional pursuit, but rather must be viewed as the confluence of the many people and systems existing in and responsible for that space working together. Evidence that organizing around assets rather than needs can result in positive changes in the physical, social, and economic contexts of a neighborhood has been generated by a number of asset-based community development (ABCD) practitioners (e.g., Kretzmann & McKnight, 1993; Kretzmann & Puntenney, 2010; McKnight & Block, 2010; Puntenney & Moore, 1998; Puntenney & Zappia, 2010). It has also been demonstrated that, from this approach, community mobilization can increase the capacity of residents to address community issues and participate in partnerships with policymakers and institutions (Blejwas, 2010; Green, 2010; Puntenney & Zappia, 2010; Snow, 2001). Conventional wisdom and funding streams support a need-based, problem-specific, reactive approach. Needs assessments are primary tools in determining resources allocation and, in turn, shape how the work that is funded is oriented. As such, health care and social service systems see helping as "fixing"—that is, they focus on problems that need to be addressed by professionals within the system. A differing approach would view the person/community as having the ability and dignity to make the needed change if given the opportunity. An asset-based approach that respects individuals, families, and communities as resources for themselves and for one another fosters a sense of responsibility, ownership, and competency. This perspective will ultimately foster sustainability and stability because the success of a neighborhood-based initiative relies more on the internal resources of a community than on outside professionals.

WHO, through its Commission on the Social Determinants of Health, underscored yet another essential shift that must occur when speaking of the poor health of those living in poverty—a shift away from the thinking that poor health and poverty are part of a natural social order: "This unequal distribution of health-damaging experiences is not in any sense a 'natural' phenomenon but is the result of a toxic combination of poor social policies and programmes" (Commission on the Social Determinants of Health, 2008, 1). The paradigm shift that must occur in policy development will recognize the community as the expert in designing programs aimed at the creation of competent communities and recognize health as a large, intersectoral, multidimensional phenomenon.

The research methodologies and financing that have heretofore driven resource investment and health promotion practice now need to address the social ecology of communities, which represents a dynamic interface with a person's health. Traditional research and evaluation methodology, such as randomized controlled trials, ignores the importance of external influences, participant choice, qualitative research methods, and the complexity of human behavior and social interactions (Burklow & Mills, 2009).

The poorly aligned financing of a holistic view of health in context creates barriers and obstructs the ability and capacity of connected communities to build health in a neighborhood construct. A new body of evidence must be generated by using qualitative research methodologies and being informed by the community, but more importantly by building health infrastructure with community leadership and capacity building processes. Social structure and communities need to critically examine how many of their own resources are being reinvested in their ability to create wellness versus being paternalistically allocated toward what a system refers to as "health community programs." Research has thus far been driven in a linear process, aimed at identifying one outcome that can be tracked and reproduced. Community development and health are linked, and community health contributes in a direct way to community development. Unfortunately, the research on intersectoral approaches to health and community development requires an approach that is currently underdeveloped in health literature. Because this approach is so complex, it has proved difficult to evaluate using current quantitative methodologies (Erickson & Andrews, 2011).

One qualitative research method that facilitates community members as social change agents for health is community-based participatory research (CBPR). CBPR is a joint effort that involves researchers and community representatives in all phases of the research process. The joint effort engages community members, employs local knowledge in the understanding of health problems and the design of interventions, and invests community members in the processes and products of research (Burklow & Mills, 2009). A CBPR project might examine the overall health of a neighborhood or populations by considering various and multifaceted indicators such as the number of people employed, the percentage of youth graduating from high school, venues to access fresh and healthy foods, incarceration/reentry rates, and emergency room admissions. This approach can allow for a deeper analysis as to whether an initiative is affecting health and well-being at a systemic level and considers whether a specific targeted program might actually be either counterproductive or complementary to overall well-being. CBPR allows the community to actively become involved in the design of the intervention.

CBPR is not synonymous with creating "focus groups" as a method for inputting community voice. Marketers have used focus group reflections as a way to create products and services that meet the needs expressed by a group of consumers. Focus groups have been a common methodology in designing interventions aimed at the "consumer." This commonly used research component has allowed for community members to voice concerns or needs, but has not translated into either community control of the agenda or building of community capacity for health promotion. The reality that programs and interventions have been designed to appeal to the community by using their input toward framing and marketing—but without allowing the community to build its own capacity for change and growth—has played a part in creating distrust of the research findings in communities living in poverty. This distrust has occurred due to the experience of communities consistently "having their reality reinterpreted, devalued, ignored, or otherwise disrespected. Indeed, in many communities, it is almost impossible to overstate the amount of distrust" (Ferman & Hill, 2004).

CBPR makes it easier to measure key indicators of success based on individual, family, and neighborhood self-sufficiency, stability, and safety. Multidimensional outcomes can be placed in the context of the physical, mental, emotional, spiritual, and social well-being of individuals and communities. As populations are studied, they also build community capacity for change. This stands in contrast to focus group research, which is commonly conducted as a first step toward making change in a community. Ethical community-based practice and research depend not only on a clear understanding of community and identification of the community's interests, but also on the way in which community participation and representation are understood. Community-based participatory research is a

> collaborative approach to research that equitably involves all partners in the research process and recognizes the unique strengths that each brings. CBPR begins with a research topic of importance to the community and has the aim of combining knowledge with action and achieving social change to improve health outcomes and eliminate health disparities. (W. K. Kellogg Foundation, 2005)

Asset-based community development is known across the United States, and increasingly around the world, as a method for engaging diverse groups around what is positive in a community. ABCD is defined by principles and practices that emphasize assets. The principles on which it is based include (1) being people centered or resident driven, (2) being asset or strength based, (3) being locally focused or place based, and (4) having a bottom-up or grassroots orientation. The practices associated with ABCD include asset mapping (simply a mechanism for identifying different types of local assets) and asset mobilization (the organizing of residents to use the assets they identify to effect change). This approach delineates six types of assets present in every neighborhood, no matter how disadvantaged or disinvested it may appear to be (Kretzmann & McKnight, 1993):

Actors

1. Individuals: the talents and skills of local people
2. Associations: local informal groups and the network of relationships they represent
3. Institutions: agencies, professional entities and the resources they hold

Context

4. Infrastructure and physical assets: land, property, buildings, equipment
5. Economic assets: the productive work of individuals, consumer spending power, the local economy, local business assets
6. Cultural assets: the traditions and ways of knowing and doing of the groups living in the community

Asset-based community development is place based and resident driven, and does not provide a single method or model for implementing the approach. Instead, each group designs its asset mapping tools and mobilization strategies according to its own vision for community improvement. In the ABCD process, grassroots resident engagement works most effectively when people take regular small-scale steps that produce small but noticeable changes in the community. When used to address the social determinants of health, asset-based community development considers the relationship between neighborhood assets, health improvement, and social change. A few examples of funders that have invested in the community building aspects of health creation include the following:

1. The W. K. Kellogg Foundation was an early funder of community building through its support of such programs as Healthy Community Partners. This effort used an asset-based approach to engage residents in generating a vision for community health in a neighborhood in Saginaw, Michigan. Partnering with two universities engaged in health professions training and a local hospital, the project utilized local residents as "health educators." The residents taught the professionals in training about community-defined health and well-being and explained how they could—as health professionals—collaborate with local associations, organizations, and institutions on local healthy community initiatives (Puntenney, 1999).

2. Using a nontraditional model, the Health Action Fund in Dayton, Ohio, encouraged neighborhood community groups to develop strategies for health promotion and prevention. With the funds going directly to community groups, the groups were able to address the neighborhood health needs they had identified. Leadership roles were assumed by community members, and through this project, residents were empowered to identify and meet their own needs. They also developed relationships with academics, who learned that the community can be an essential partner in the promotion of health. The natural leaders identified also offered academics a point of access into the community (Maurana & Clark, 2000).

3. Partnering with the Chicago Community Trust, the Community Memorial Foundation and other local stakeholders outside Chicago developed strategies to develop a community that would be friendly to older adults. Using an asset-based approach, older adults came together to identify local assets that could be mobilized toward creating a community that was friendly to people as they aged. Forming a 100-person-strong community council, residents actively engaged in articulating and advocating for the kinds of amenities and services they thought would help them age successfully in place. Their ideas included healthy and appropriately sized and configured housing, safe public spaces, and access to public spaces and activities, among others (Puntenney, 2004).

4. The Boston Health Public Housing Project was supported by the W. K. Kellogg Foundation on a four-year project in which research

universities, public housing residents, and Boston health and housing agencies addressed issues of asthma and pest control in Boston public housing. Residents assumed central roles in the project, well beyond that of research subjects. They helped to set the priorities for the environmental issues that should be tackled first, and they were compensated for their time participating in the project (W. K. Kellogg Foundation, 2005).

5. In Chicago, state, local, and federal funding streams helped support the West Side Health Authority (WHA) to organize the West Garfield and Austin neighborhoods. Through the project, local residents were mobilized, along with associations and institutions. All were focused on improving the health and well-being of the residents of the neighborhoods. Working with Every Block a Village (a partner group), WHA promoted health through four related programs: Healthy Lifestyles; Junior Healthy Lifestyles; Healthy Babies for Healthy Communities; and a research project aimed at better understanding the community's health challenges. Accomplishments are many, including lead testing for approximately 240 children and 350 homes and "community medicine" training for more than 400 Cook County physicians (Kretzmann & Puntenney, 2010).

6. The Robert Wood Johnson Foundation (2011) has funded numerous initiatives through its "vulnerable populations portfolio," which focuses on social determinants of health such as playgrounds and recess for schoolchildren to create healthier and higher-achieving students, utilization of ex-offenders to mitigate street violence, and a "Roadmaps to Health" program that will fund policy and systems changes around education, employment and income, family and social support, and community safety as the key drivers of community health.

7. Harlem Children's Zone has established a "do whatever it takes" approach to support children from birth to college through broad community collaboration in Harlem, New York. The immutable platform upon which the Harlem Children's Zone was built consists of the value of children, the principle of community building, and the need to overcome "limits of traditional approaches" (*Whatever It Takes: A White Paper of the Harlem Children's Zone*). Community capacity for sustainable action is built into actions taken, and the community works together to create a "culture of success," reorganizing the community to build a better future for children.

8. Southern Echo, in the Mississippi Delta, established in 1989, is an intergenerational model of community organizing, education, and leadership development, working at a grassroots level in African-American communities to transform individuals, and the communities in which they live. The mission statement of Southern Echo is as follows:

Southern Echo's underlying goal is to empower local communities through effective community organizing work, in order to create a process through which community people can build the broad-based organizations necessary to hold the political, economic, educational and environmental systems accountable to the needs and interest of the African-American community. (www.southernecho .org)

Working from an asset- or strength-based foundation is essential for mobilizing residents toward positive action, as residents themselves can be powerful agents of change to improve their community and thereby improve opportunities for health. This plays out in several different ways. First, residents of under-resourced neighborhoods are often alienated from or marginalized within other local assets, in particular the institutions charged with serving them (e.g., schools, medical centers). The lack of trust contributes to a lack of quality partnerships, which can impact how the institution is able to "deliver" its product. For example, if families are marginalized within schools, the educational "product" is almost impossible to deliver. Likewise, an individual receiving health services who is unable or unwilling to implement the recommendations of the health provider will thwart the ability of the health "product" to be delivered. Without involvement on both sides, progress will not be achieved. Second, in disadvantaged communities, there is a strong tendency to describe and define that community only in terms of its problems, needs, and failings. In such places—and in an era of economic limitations—it is critical to refocus our perspective on *what does exist and what is possible*, rather than solely considering what is lacking and seems impossible.

The determinants of health include the physical, social, and economic environments in which people live; personal behavior and access to medical care contribute to health as well. Because altering the physical, social, and economic environments of poor communities is such an enormous and multidimensional task, we tend to reduce our approach to health to the two determinants over which we feel we have more control: health care and personal behavior. Yet in doing so, we ignore the fact that estimates suggest that the majority of health disparities are actually attributable to the other factors (Satcher & Higginbotham, 2008). To change health outcomes, we cannot continue to address health in this manner. Without people being engaged in the creation of their own health, including making their neighborhood contexts appropriate for supporting health, health disparities will not be overcome.

Conclusion

Policies and projects to eliminate poverty and create better health have been driven in unidirectional ways that have delivered services to populations in need, in large part by professionals within large organizations in health care and social service sectors. Asset-based strategies, in contrast, start with the creative capacities of the population and community itself. Health care systems working outside the contextual reality of communities, especially those in poverty, have contributed to the erosion of community capacity to care for itself. In moving toward a reinvestment and reorganization of both institutional and community roles and responsibilities, investment should be aligned to support and build the asset-based community and social capital that has been foundational to healthy and equitable societies and communities throughout history. A road map toward improving community health will benefit from the incorporation of principles and practices that build on community assets and strengths—such as community organizing and community building, community-based participatory research, and the development of collaborative partnerships between health care delivery systems and those individuals and communities who are living in poverty or experiencing the most significant health disparities.

Moreover, a fundamental shift in policy and resource expenditure toward health creation must take place. Poor communities can be strengthened through an asset-based, socioecological approach to promote and sustain health equity. To address the complexity of poverty and community building, institutions must be reorganized and resources reallocated to create large-scale change to significantly improve community health and reduce health disparities. Much of this reinvestment will need to be in the form of human capital investment and recognition of the assets of individuals, neighborhoods, and communities. The Institute of Medicine report released in April 2012 speaks to many of the paradigm shifts suggested in this chapter that will be necessary to sustain health initiatives at a community level. Community health improvement plans must mobilize multiple community stakeholders and foster sustainable partnerships. The IOM report recognizes the complexity of interactions at the community level and acknowledges that the root causes of poor health outcomes need to be addressed, including the view that accounts for the role of poverty, income inequality, and the determinants of health that are outside the current health care delivery systems. This approach to change necessitates the recognition and inclusion of community as a partner, and the acceptance of community leadership as an asset for planning meaningful interventions for better health.

The deliberate strategy that must be developed will acknowledge the imperative to address fundamental social structure inequalities and the social determinants of health to reduce the impact of poverty on health. Health cannot be separated from economic stability and social structure— the socioecologic model. In policy, partnership with the community—and recognizing the assets a neighborhood and community have—cannot be divorced from health initiatives or health projects.

References

Augustin, T., Glass, T., James, B., & Schwartz, B. (2008). Neighborhood psychosocial hazards and cardiovascular disease: The Baltimore Memory Study. *American Journal of Public Health, 98*(9), 1664–1669.

Berg, D. R., Eckstein, E. T., Steiner, M. S., Gavard, J. A., & Gross, G. A. (2012). Childhood lead prevention through prenatal housing inspection and remediation in St. Louis, MO. *American Journal of Obstetrics and Gynecology, 206*(3), 199.e1–4.

Blacksher, E. (2009). Health: The value at stake. *Hastings Center Report*, (suppl), 27–29.

Blejwas, E. (2010). Asset-based community development in Alabama's black belt: Seven strategies for building a diverse community movement. In G. Green & A. Goetting (Eds.), *Mobilizing communities: Asset building as a community development strategy* (pp. 48–67). Philadelphia, PA: Temple University Press.

Bradbury, K. (2012). *Long-term inequality and mobility. Public Policy Briefs*, No.12–1:1–12. Federal Reserve Bank of Boston.

Burklow, K., & Mills, L. (2009). Giving voice to underserved and culturally diverse groups using community-based participatory research. *Open Medical Education Journal, 2*, 75–79.

Center for Health, Environment, and Justice. (2012). Love Canal. http://chej.org/about/our-story/love-canal/

Childress, J. F., Faden, R. R., Gaare, R. D., Gostin, L. O., Kahn, J., Bonnie, R. J., . . . Nieburg, P. (2002). Public health ethics: Mapping the terrain. *Journal of Law, Medicine & Ethics, 30*(2), 170–178.

Commission on Social Determinants of Health. (2008). *Closing the gap in a generation: Health equity through action on the social determinants of health. Final report of the Commission on Social Determinants of Health.* Geneva, Switzerland: World Health Organization.

Dickert, N., & Sugarman, J. (2005). Ethical goals of community consultation in research. *American Journal of Public Health, 95*(7).

Ellaway, A., Macintyre, S., & Bonnefoy, X. (2005). Graffiti, greenery, and obesity in adults: Secondary analysis of European cross sectional survey. *British Medical Journal, 331*(7517), 611–612.

Erickson, D., & Andrews, N. (2011). Partnerships among community development, public health, and health care could improve the well-being of low-income people. *Health Affairs, 30*(11), 2056–2063.

Felitti, V., & Anda, R. (2010). The relationship of adverse childhood experiences to adult health, well-being, social function, and healthcare. In R. A. Lanius, E. Vermetten, & C. Pain (Eds.), *The impact of early life trauma on health and disease: The hidden epidemic* (pp. 77–86). New York, NY: Cambridge University Press.

Ferman, B., & Hill, T. L. (2004). The challenges of agenda conflict in higher-education community research partnerships: Views from the community side. *Journal of Urban Affairs, 26*(2), 241–257.

Frosch, D., May, S., Rendle, K., Tietbohl, C., & Elwyn, G. (2012). Authoritarian physicians and patients' fear of being labeled "difficult" among key obstacles to shared decision making. *Health Affairs, 31*(5), 1030–1038.

Gee, G., & Payne-Sturges, D. C. (2004). Environmental health disparities: A framework integrating psychosocial and environmental concepts. *Environmental Health Perspectives, 112*(17), 1645–1653.

Government Accounting Office (GAO). (2007). Poverty in America. GAO-07-344. www.gao.gov/new.items/d07344.pdf

Green, G. (2010). Natural amenities and asset-based development in rural communities. In G. Green & A. Goetting (Eds.), *Mobilizing communities: Asset building as a community development strategy* (pp. 130–145). Philadelphia, PA: Temple University Press.

Harlem Children's Zone. (2009). Whatever It Takes: A White Paper on the Harlem Children's Zone.

Heitman, E., & McKieran, L. (2003). *Community-based practice and research: Collaboration and sharing power.* Ethics and Public Health Curriculum: A project funded through HRSA, ASPH and the Hastings Center, Module 4.

Hodari, J. (2004). Poverty and control: George Bush and the Millennium Challenge Account. *Journal of Politics and Society, XIV*, 109–115.

Hofrichter, R. (2003). The politics of health inequities: Contested terrain. In R. Hofrichter (Ed.), *Health and social justice: Politics, ideology, inequity in the distribution of disease* (pp. 1–56). San Francisco, CA: John Wiley & Sons.

Institute of Medicine (IOM). (1998). *The future of public health.* Washington, DC: National Academies Press.

Institute of Medicine (IOM). (2012). *For the public's health: Investing in a healthier future.* Washington, DC: National Academies Press.

Kretzmann, J., & McKnight, J. (1993). *Building communities from the inside out.* Evanston, IL: Northwestern University.

Kretzmann, J., & Puntenney, D. (2010). Neighborhood approaches to asset mobilization: Building Chicago's West Side. In A. Goetting & G. P. Green (Eds.), *Mobilizing communities: Asset building as a community development strategy* (pp. 112–129). Philadelphia, PA: Temple University Press.

Lawlor, D. A., Sterne, J. A., Tynelius, P., Davey Smith, G., & Rasmussen, F. (2006). Association of childhood socioeconomic position with cause-specific mortality in a prospective record linkage study of 1,839,384 individuals. *American Journal of Epidemiology, 164*(9), 907–915.

Link, B., Northridge, M. E., Phelan, J. C., & Ganz, M. L. (1998). Social epidemiology and the fundamental cause concept: On the structuring of effective cancer screens by socioeconomic status. *Milbank Quarterly, 76*(3), 375.

Lynch, J., Kaplan, G. A., Pamuk, E. R., Cohen, R. D., Heck, K. E., Balfour, J. L., & Yen, I. H. (1988). Income inequality and mortality in metropolitan areas of the United States. *American Journal of Public Health, 88*(7), 1074–1080.

Marmot, M. (2004). *The status syndrome: How social standing affects our health and longevity.* New York, NY: Henry Holt and Company.

Marmot, M. (2006). Health in an unequal world. *Lancet, 368*(9552), 2081–2094.

Maurana, C., & Clark, M. (2000). The Health Action Fund: A community-based approach to enhancing health. *Journal of Health Communication, 5*(3), 243–254.

McKnight, J. (1995). *The careless society: Community and its counterfeits.* New York, NY: Basic Books.

McKnight, J., & Block, P. (2010). *The abundant community: Awakening the power of families and neighborhoods.* San Francisco, CA: Berrett-Koehler Publishers.

Moyer, C. S. (2012, Jan. 2). Unmet social needs worsen health. *American Medical News.* http://www.amednews.com/article/20120102/health/301029952/4/

National Center for Health Statistics. (2006). Health, United States. http://www.cdc.gov/nchs/data/hus/hus06.pdf

Navarro, V. (Ed.). (2004). *The political and social contexts of health.* Amityville, NY: Baywood.

Organization for Economic and Cooperative Development (OECD). (2011). Divided we stand: Why inequality keeps rising. http://www.oecd.org/els/socialpoliciesanddata/dividedwestandwhyinequalitykeepsrising.htm

Praxis Project (2012). How we make a difference. http://www.thepraxisproject.org/about/our-vision/how-we-make-difference

Puntenney, D. (1999). *Organizational development and health professions curriculum.* Saginaw, MI: Center for Health Professions of St. Mary's Medical Center.

Puntenney, D. (2004). *Aging well in greater Lyons township: A report to project funders.* Evanston, IL: Northwestern University.

Puntenney, D., & Moore, H. (1998). *City-sponsored community building: Savannah's Grants for Blocks story.* Evanston, IL: Asset-Based Community Development Institute, Northwestern University.

Puntenney, D., & Zappia, B. (2010). *Grassroots activism and community health improvement.* Unpublished manuscript presented at the annual meeting of the Society for the Study of Social Problems.

Rank, M. R. (2004). *One nation, underprivileged: Why American poverty affects us all.* New York, NY: Oxford University Press.

Robert Wood Johnson Foundation. (2011). Report: Health care's blind side: The overlooked connection between social needs and good health. http://www.rwjf.org/content/dam/farm/reports/surveys_and_polls/2011/rwjf71795

Sanders, B. (2011). Is poverty a death sentence? The human cost of socioeconomic disparities. A report from Chairman Bernie Sanders, Subcommittee on Primary Health and Aging, US Senate Committee on Health, Education, Labor & Pensions. Washington, DC: US Senate. http://www.sanders.senate.gov/imo/media/doc/IsPovertyADeathSentence.pdf.

Satcher, D., & Higginbotham, E. J. (2008). The public health approach to reducing disparities in health. *American Journal of Public Health, 98*(3), 400–403.

Snow, L. (2001). *The organization of hope: A workbook for rural asset-based community development.* Evanston, IL: Northwestern University.

Stokols, D., Grzywacz, J., McMahan, S., & Phillips, K. (2003). Increasing the health promotive capacity of human environments. *American Journal of Health Promotion, 18*(1), 4–13.

Turner, N., McKnight, J. L., & Kretzmann, J. P. (1999). A guide to mapping and mobilizing the associations in local neighborhoods. Chicago, IL: ACTA Publications. http://www.abcdinstitute.org/docs/MappingAssociations(2).pdf.

U.S. Department of Health and Human Services. (2010). Healthy people 2020. http://www.healthypeople.gov/2020/about/default.aspx

U.S. Department of Health and Human Services. (2011). Final review: Healthy people 2010. http://www.cdc.gov/nchs/healthy_people/hp2010/hp2010_final_review.htm

Warren, M. R. (2001). *Dry bones rattling: Community building to revitalize American democracy.* Princeton, NJ: Princeton University Press.

Warren, M. R., & Mapp, K. L. (2011). *A match on dry grass: Community organizing as a catalyst for school reform.* New York, NY: Oxford University Press.

Wilkinson, R., & Marmot, M. (Eds.). (2003). *Social determinants of health: The solid facts* (2nd ed.). Geneva, Switzerland: World Health Organization. http://www.euro.who.int/document/e81384.pdf

W. K. Kellogg Foundation. (2005). The Boston healthy public housing project: Partnership transforms community. *Health Programming Update, 562,* 4.

Woolf, S. H. (2007). Future health consequences of the current decline in US household income. *American Journal of Public Health, 298*(16), 1931–1933.

Zappia, B. J., & Puntenney, M. D. L. (2010). Grassroots activism and community health improvement.

Chapter 12

Place-Based Strategies for Addressing Health Disparities

Barbara J. Zappia and Deborah L. Puntenney

American society has always exhibited disparities in power, social status, and economic status, but the gaps separating the advantaged from the less advantaged are now widening and taking on new dimensions. The relationships among the unequal distribution of income, education, health, and longevity in the United States are well known and broadly accepted. Health disparities have been examined through a number of lenses, including a focus on access to health care and the influences of race and poverty on the differential health outcomes experienced by different groups. The relationship between socioeconomic status (SES) and health outcomes is understood, and SES is considered to be a reliable predictor of mortality, morbidity, and disability in the United States as well as in most industrialized nations (Adler, Boys, Chesney, Folkman, & Syme, 1993). A large body of evidence has demonstrated health inequalities associated with income levels; these findings are consistent and persistent over time (Marmot, 2005; McDonough, Duncan, Williams, & House, 1997; Mustard, Derksen, Berthelot, Wolfson, & Roos, 1997; Wilkinson & Marmot, 2003). The most disadvantaged members of society—the poor, less educated, and racial and ethnic minorities—have simply experienced shorter lifespans and more ill health than the more affluent segments (Link & Phelan, 1995).

It is also true that SES largely dictates the sorts of neighborhoods individuals will live in over the course of their lives. In recent years, the research spotlight has focused on neighborhoods and the impact they can have on health outcomes. Scholars increasingly consider "place" (i.e., the physical, social, economic, and cultural environments in which people live, work, and play) to be an important factor when investigating how socioeconomic disparities translate into health disparities. The concept that where one lives might influence one's health is hardly novel; a rich body of literature has highlighted the association of community contexts and their physical and social environmental makeup with health outcomes (Diez Roux & Mair, 2010; Ludwig et al., 2011; Steptoe & Feldman, 2001). Affluent communities tend to support healthy development of children and adults, whereas places of concentrated poverty, along with their attendant characteristics (e.g., distressed housing, poor-performing schools, low social capital), are associated with considerable health concerns, including low-birth-weight babies, violence, and high infant mortality (Sampson & Morenoff, 2000).

As awareness of the impact that place can have on health outcomes has expanded, efforts to address health disparities have increasingly focused on this consideration. This chapter addresses the kinds of strategies for addressing health disparities that are oriented, at least in part, to the context in which the disparities exist—that is, place-based strategies. We begin by discussing what is known about health disparities, emphasizing the relationships between poverty and health as well as the relationships between neighborhoods (place) and health. We describe several theoretical frameworks for understanding how place and health interact, and we propose a comprehensive model that combines several of these and incorporates community-based action as a central component. Next, we review a selection of programs aimed at building healthier communities by addressing the intersection of health and place, including several in which community organizing is deployed as a key strategy. We follow with a discussion of how different interest groups might think about engaging in place-based efforts to reduce health disparities in ways that reach beyond the provision of care to incorporate health disparity populations in the creation of solutions. Included in this discussion are reviews of two programs we consider to hold promise because of their innovative approaches. The chapter concludes with an argument that supports the idea that the most promising place-based strategies take a comprehensive approach, emphasizing the physical place, acknowledging the social relationships existing in the place, and taking a life course view of altering neighborhood arrangements at the individual, organizational/institutional, and structural/policy levels that inhibit good health.

Poverty and Health

In the 21st century, health disparities are pervasive across the United States. The National Longitudinal Mortality Study found a negative association between mortality and education, income, and occupation—all common measures of socioeconomic standing (Institute of Medicine, 2004). Further illustrations of health inequalities—in terms of both morbidity and mortality—are found in the following areas:

1. *Infant mortality and children's health.* Children born to mothers with less than a high school diploma are nearly twice as likely to die in their first year of life as those children whose mothers have 16 years or more of education (Mathews & MacDorman, 2007). Overall, children in affluent families are seven times more likely to be in good health than low-income children (Braveman & Egerter, 2008).
2. *Childhood overweight and obesity.* Children in poverty are more likely than their more affluent counterparts to be overweight. Almost one-fourth of children living below the federal poverty line are overweight, and prevalence rates decline as families rise above the poverty line (U.S. Department of Health and Human Services, 2006).
3. *Poverty and health.* Poor adults are five times more likely to rate their health as fair or poor as compared to those with greater wealth (Braveman & Egerter, 2008).
4. *Activity and chronic disease.* Chronic illness limits the work activity and personal care of poor adults at three times the rate it impacts wealthy adults. The prevalence of diabetes—a major cause of illness, disability, and death—is twice as great in poor adults; heart disease is 50% more prevalent (Braveman & Egerter, 2008).
5. *Life expectancy.* Adults who have not finished their high school education can expect a life five years shorter than adults who have gone on to complete their college education (Braveman & Egerter, 2008).

Link and Phelan (1995) posit that more affluent groups enjoy power, prestige, and social connections that they can utilize effectively to the benefit of their health and increased longevity, such that socioeconomic status is a "fundamental cause" of health disparities (p. 81). Those persons with greater resources are able to more easily live a healthy lifestyle, choose healthy neighborhoods in which to live, obtain safe and fulfilling jobs, and surround themselves with an effective social network. Health disparities associated with poverty and other socioeconomic variables affect children, adults, and families, compelling some health experts to refer to social class as "the ignored determinant of the nation's health" (Isaacs & Schroeder, 2004, p. 1137).

Neighborhoods and Health

Neighborhoods are particularly useful settings for examining socioeconomic inequality and concomitant health disparities, as they provide a
milieu in which to explore the physical, social, economic, and cultural
environments that can impact the health of individuals and families.
Neighborhood place of residence is "strongly patterned by social position
and ethnicity" (Diez Roux & Mair, 2010, p. 125) and, therefore, could be a
vital contributor to social inequalities in health. For low-income individuals with limited mobility, neighborhoods may exert a particularly strong
influence on life and health (Bernard et al., 2007).

Research on neighborhoods and health, which surfaced in the 1980s,
relied primarily on secondary data linking individual health status to a
census tract area. The seminal Alameda County study, for example, considered social and physical environments to be determinants for excess
mortality in low-SES populations (Haan, Kaplan, & Camacho, 1987). The
study identified a powerful effect of place of residence on health above
and beyond individual SES; the authors found a 50% higher risk of death
for individuals living in poor neighborhoods, even after controlling for
other sociodemographic factors such as age, race, employment, social isolation, access to medical care, health status, and individual income.

Diez Roux and Mair (2010) note the limited ability to make cross-
comparisons among early studies due to varied use of census tracts as
neighborhood proxies and the variable strengths of associations across
studies. Much of this early research supported the premise that neighborhoods impact health beyond the influence of individual characteristics.
Living in under-resourced or low-SES neighborhoods, Diez Roux and
Mair noted, is "generally associated with poor health outcomes including
greater mortality, poorer self-reported health, adverse mental health outcomes, greater prevalence of chronic disease risk factors, greater incidence
of diseases such as cardiovascular disease and diabetes, and adverse child
health outcomes" (p. 127).

A more recent longitudinal study used data from Moving to Opportunity (MTO), a project sponsored by the U.S. Department of Housing and
Urban Development and conducted from 1994 to 1998, to investigate the
association between neighborhoods of residence on specific health outcomes, concentrating on obesity and diabetes. MTO randomly assigned
women and children living in high-poverty public housing into one of
three groups: a group receiving housing vouchers agreeing to move to
low-poverty areas; a traditional voucher group; and a control group. Survey data gathered as part of a follow-up to MTO in 2008–2010 included
health outcomes data. The study found that those women who moved to
low-poverty regions exhibited a decreased risk for extreme obesity and

diabetes, further supporting the importance of neighborhood environments on health behaviors and health outcomes (Ludwig et al., 2011).

The influence of place may begin in childhood and confer lasting effects through adulthood. Johnson, Schoeni, and Rogowski (2011) investigated adult health trajectories in relationship to neighborhood environments experienced as children. They write: "Living in a neighborhood with concentrated poverty may have consequences above and beyond those of growing up in a poor family because of social isolation, crime, weakened social institutions, unrelenting stress, inferior health care accessibility and other factors" (p. 626). Using longitudinal data from the Panel Study of Income Dynamics (PSID), their study found a relationship between living conditions during early childhood and adult health status. Adults who lived in high-poverty neighborhoods during their childhood were found to have spent 45% of their adult years in fair or poor health. By comparison, those growing up in nonpoor neighborhoods spent a much smaller proportion (15%) of their adult years in fair or poor health, indicating the lasting effects of growing up in a high-poverty neighborhood (Johnson et al., 2011).

These studies point to the contribution of neighborhood place of residence to health disparities. Macintrye and Ellaway (2003) suggest five aspects of neighborhoods thought to promote or hinder good health: (1) neighborhood physical attributes such as air and water that all residents share; (2) healthy environments for home, work, and play; (3) services such as education systems and public transportation that families need to support their everyday activities; (4) social and cultural aspects of the neighborhood; and (5) residents' and other stakeholders' perception of the neighborhood. Each of these five domains is socially determined, and each may be either health promoting or health deterring. Therefore, it is suggested that as health is in some part the result of the extent to which these aspects are present in a neighborhood, the most effective health interventions may be those that take them on directly.

In the next section, we explore several mechanisms through which neighborhood environments exert an influence on health. These mechanisms include (1) effects on physical activity; (2) access to healthy food; (3) norms, social capital, cohesion, and collective efficacy; and (4) social relationships and perceptions of safety and violence.

Effects on Physical Activity

The potentially serious effects of physical inactivity—including heart disease, diabetes, hypertension, obesity, and premature mortality—are well documented and have generated a high degree of concern within public health systems. Despite this grim association, the 2000 Behavioral

Risk Factor Surveillance System found that only 26% of adults engage in the recommended amount of physical activity (Macera, Jones, Ham, Kohl, & Buchner, 2003). Personal characteristics such as motivation and self-efficacy are often used to explain inactivity in a population (Sherwood & Jeffery, 2000). Individual-level recommendations are then applied to increase physical activity, with little attention paid to the limitations and supports for physical activity provided by the social and physical environments in which one lives. According to McNeill, Krueter, and Subramanian (2006), such interventions are unlikely to produce the behavior change desired. They argue that addressing the underlying reasons people may be inactive (e.g., social norms related to exercise or safe and pleasant opportunities for being physically active) is a necessary part of supporting an increase in physical activity.

The study of environmental impacts on physical activity has focused primarily on how neighborhoods promote walking not only for exercise but also as part of the typical experience of living in the community. Ross (2000) found that both lower-income and more-affluent neighborhoods influenced walking, but in distinctly different ways. After controlling for individual factors such as SES, race, and education, this study found that residents of both high-poverty and affluent areas walked in their neighborhoods. In lower-income neighborhoods, even when residents expressed fear of crime and victimization, the density of housing encouraged greater walking than in nonpoor neighborhoods, although it is unclear whether the known health rewards of walking are realized when fear of crime and victimization overshadows this "healthy" action. Ross conjectures that individuals in economically disadvantaged neighborhoods would likely walk even more if they were less afraid when leaving their homes. In contrast, more-affluent neighborhoods create a culture that supports walking for good health. An after-dinner walk or a walk to school is visible to others in the neighborhood and creates the impetus for those observing the behavior to do the same.

A number of studies have demonstrated that the quality of the environment influences the extent to which residents are physically active. In a study of eight European communities, Ellaway and colleagues (2005) used data collected as part of the Large Analysis and Review of European Housing and Health Studies (LARES). Health questionnaires were used to obtain self-reports of health, including height and weight measures that were subsequently used to calculate body mass index (BMI). Trained surveyors then assessed through direct observation such things as litter, graffiti, and the amount of green space and open areas. Residents of neighborhoods with more graffiti and litter and less open green space were 50% less likely to be physically active and three times more likely to be obese than their counterparts in more inviting communities (Ellaway et al., 2005).

Macintrye (2000) describes a pattern that she refers to as "deprivation amplification" (p. 6) found over a decade of research in Glasgow, Scotland. In under-resourced places where low-income individuals reside, local facilities for physical activity are substandard. Tennis courts and sports facilities, for example, were less frequently found in Macintyre's study, as were green spaces to walk or play with children. Research in the United States demonstrates similar findings. Using data from the Multiethnic Study of Atherosclerosis (MESA) study, Diez Roux et al. (2007) found an association between adults living in close proximity to recreational and sports facilities and participation in physical activities.

McCormack, Rock, Toohey, and Hignell (2010) reviewed qualitative studies that investigated urban parks and their associations with physical activity. Their review of 21 such studies revealed the importance of both the physical conditions of parks and social attributes toward encouraging physical activity. As anticipated, parks that are perceived as safe and well maintained support children and youth in their use of the space for physical activity. In an analogous fashion, perception of neighborhood safety can influence physical activity and health of children. In the United States, parents' perceptions of their neighborhoods as less safe were associated with increased risk for their children being overweight by age seven (Lumeng, Appugliese, Cabral, Bradley, & Zuckerman, 2006).

Access to Healthy Food

Like physical activity, nutritional practices are associated with a host of health concerns. Diets high in fat and calories have been associated with numerous health problems, including heart disease and obesity, while diets rich in wholesome and nutritious food are seen as prerequisites for good health. In 2005, the diets of less than one-fourth of Americans included the recommended servings of fruits and vegetables. Furthermore, chronic diseases related to poor diets and nutrition cost the United States more than $33 billion in medical expenditures (Bovell-Benjamin, Hathorn, Ibrahim, Gichuhi, & Bromfield, 2009).

In their study of food environments and obesity, Cummins and Macintyre (2006) argue that poor people with less education are more likely to be obese, with "living in a low-income or deprived area independently associated with the prevalence of obesity and the consumption of a poor diet" (p. 100). Unhealthy diets may be influenced, in part, by the ease with which healthy and nutritious foods are available and affordable. Focus-group participants in Schulz and Lempert's (2004) study voiced their concerns that the quality of food in their local convenience stores was poor, yet riding two buses to access a higher-quality market outside of their neighborhoods was challenging. The result, according to one woman, is "it's always easier to do the wrong thing than it is to do the right thing when it comes to nutrition" (p. 447). A number of studies support this assertion.

Access to healthy food has profound implications for diet and nutrition. When supermarkets are available in African-American neighborhoods, residents are more likely to reduce the amount of fat in their diets and eat more fruits and vegetables (Morland, Wing, Diez Roux, & Poole, 2002). Low-income neighborhoods and neighborhoods with predominately African-American residents are less likely to enjoy an abundance of reasonably priced produce and other fresh products due to a paucity of nearby supermarkets. The lack of healthy choices at the local corner market and limited transportation to reach larger grocers compound matters (Altschuler, Somkin, & Adler, 2004; Macintyre & Ellaway, 2003; Morland et al., 2002).

The prevalence of obesity has been demonstrated to be associated with the location of convenience stores, supermarkets, and fast-food chains (Morland & Evenson, 2009). Moreland and her colleagues (2002) discovered in a number of U.S. cities that supermarkets are four times more likely to be found in White neighborhoods than in African-American neighborhoods, and that fast-food restaurants, which are not known for serving healthy fare, are more likely to be present in middle- and low-income areas than in more affluent communities. Similarly, healthy foods were less available in Black and low-income neighborhoods in Baltimore than in White and high-income neighborhoods. This study used a healthy food availability index in a cross-sectional study of 159 census tracts (Franco, Diez Roux, Glass, Caballero, & Brancati, 2008).

Two qualitative studies attempted to gain insight on the ways residents take action to obtain food within their environment despite neighborhood conditions. First, Rose (2010) demonstrated how residents engage in food practices in Detroit. This study found that residents of low-income neighborhoods faced numerous struggles to obtain healthy, nutritious food at a cost that was affordable. Residents displayed resourcefulness obtaining food, despite the challenge of finding food locally available. For example, fear for personal safety when walking to stores and limited availability of food banks nearby were cited as constraints. Nonetheless, residents shared transportation costs to find food sources outside of the area and carefully examined food purchased in nearby stores known for poor-quality provisions. In the second study, Altschuler et al. (2004) captured residents' activism targeting securing a supermarket for their low-income neighborhood. This community achievement was not merely about obtaining healthy food, but also signaled a neighborhood moving toward recovery from crime and drugs. As with the Rose study (2010), this example of engagement represents a type of activism that illustrates how people can act within and upon their neighborhood environments to secure better health.

Each of these studies provides evidence for the ways that the physical environment promotes or hinders individual behaviors—specifically, physical activity and the consumption of healthy foods. The studies do not, however, fully explain how and to what extent individuals act within and upon the physical environment and how such actions result in healthy or unhealthy developmental trajectories. The assertion that the environment causes lack of physical activity and unhealthy food consumption is overly simplistic. Instead, the complex interplay of individuals reacting to and acting on their environment shapes healthy behaviors and, ultimately, health. Moreover, efforts to change health outcomes by changing aspects of the environment without consideration of personal and collective agency are likely to be, at best, partial solutions.

Norms, Social Capital, Cohesion, and Collective Efficacy

Research on social environments acknowledges that people are interconnected and, therefore, that their health and well-being are interconnected. According to Sampson (2003), social processes that occur within collective neighborhood life mediate health outcomes and must be explored to understand neighborhood impacts on health. Putnam (1995) refers to social capital as those "features of social organization such as networks, norms, and social trust that facilitate coordination and cooperation for mutual benefit" (p. 67). Social supports and positive relationships—both between individuals and across a community—are important contributors to health. Strong social networks and high levels of social cohesion are protective of good health, whereas individuals who experience less social support are more likely to experience illness and premature death. Social isolation is more commonly experienced by those living in poverty, and communities with the widest income gaps separating the rich from the poor exhibit less social cohesion, more violent crime, and higher rates of heart disease (Wilkinson & Marmot, 2003).

Social capital and a related concept, collective efficacy, are considered somewhat intangible, yet highly influential factors within a neighborhood. Sampson, Raudenbush, and Earls (1997) define collective efficacy as "social cohesion among neighbors combined with their willingness to intervene on behalf of the common good" (p. 918). These authors found that tight-knit communities with high collective efficacy are more likely to act in union against crimes in the community. Social capital and collective efficacy influence the quality of life in a neighborhood such that in places with higher levels of these assets, neighbors can trust each other and rely on each other more. Knowing that a neighbor can be relied upon for help is theorized to reduce stress and worry. An alternative notion is that collective efficacy is an indicator of political power, such that neighborhoods with high collective efficacy work together to maintain or improve neighborhood conditions (Cohen, Finch, Bower, & Sastry, 2006).

Altschuler et al. (2004) also investigated how neighborhood residents could be agents of change—mobilizing and acting in response to neighborhood threats. In lower-SES neighborhoods, these threats took the forms of graffiti, crime, and violence. In contrast, more prosperous neighborhoods bonded together against new retail stores entering the neighborhood or against streetlights that might destroy the peaceful darkness of their wooded street. Again, while not explicitly conceptualizing this action in terms of human agency, this study demonstrates the ways that social cohesion can be transformed into collective efficacy. Altschuler et al.'s study concludes that "becoming involved in one's community and organizing for its improvement involves the development of ties with others in the neighborhood, becoming more involved citizens, and possibly the provision of affective support and self-esteem" (p. 1228).

Using state-level data, Kawachi, Kennedy, Lochner, and Prothrow-Stith (1997) explored the connections between levels of social capital (measured by perceived levels of fairness, trust, helpfulness of others, and levels of civic engagement) and overall mortality rates. After controlling for income and poverty, a strong correlation was discovered between social capital and lower rates of mortality. Additionally, states with the greatest income disparities had very low levels of social trust and civic engagement. Large gaps separating the rich from the poor were "powerfully and negatively related to level of investment in social capital" (p. 1495). In subsequent work, Kawachi, Kennedy, and Glass (1999) investigated the relationship between individual factors such as low income, education, smoking, and self-rated health using data from the Behavioral Risk Factor Surveillance System. Their study revealed that these individual factors were associated with self-reports of poorer health. After controlling for these individual factors, the researchers demonstrated that where people lived and levels of trust and cohesion within their place of residence made a difference in their self-reported health status. This relationship was intact for all income levels, while those in the lowest-income groups saw the largest effects of social capital on health.

Lochner, Kawachi, Brennan, and Buka (2003) examined social capital on a smaller scale, extending previous research on social capital to the neighborhood level. This study used a cross-sectional design using data from the Project on Human Development in Chicago. Data linked deaths for persons between the ages of 45 and 64 years, race, sex, and neighborhood social capital across more than 300 neighborhoods to explore the association between social capital and mortality rates. Using perceived reciprocity and trust and organizational membership as indicators of social capital, this study found that higher neighborhood social capital was associated with lower death rates for total mortality. For Whites, a similar relationship was seen for death from heart disease and from other causes, while this relationship was weaker for African-Americans.

Comparable research attempted to distinguish between two types of social capital—bonding and bridging social capital—and their distinct relationships with self-reported health status. Bonding social capital was conceptualized as relationships between persons similar to each other, while bridging social capital is that observed among dissimilar persons. Modest levels of protective health mechanisms for both forms of social capital—again greater for Whites than for African-Americans—were identified in this study as well (Kim, Subramanian, & Kawachi, 2006).

Cohen et al. (2006) investigated collective efficacy not only in relationship to self-reports of health, but also in terms of a specific intermediate health indicator—namely, overweight in youth. Youth overweight was chosen as the focus of this study in part because youth generally do not choose the neighborhoods in which they live and are reliant on their social environments. Measures of height and weight were used to calculate BMI with data from the Los Angeles Family and Neighborhood Survey (LAFANS), and items relating to collective efficacy were collected based on the work of Sampson et al. (1997). After controlling for neighborhood SES and other individual-level factors, this study demonstrated significant relationships between collective efficacy, BMI, risk for overweight, and overweight status in youth. Youth in neighborhoods with low efficacy demonstrated 64% higher odds of being at risk for overweight than those youth living in neighborhoods with average levels of efficacy. Social relationships among adults are, therefore, associated with overweight status of neighborhood children (Cohen et al., 2006).

In neighborhoods where many neighbors know and trust each other, innovative health ideas such as preventive health measures are more likely to be accepted and implemented. In such communities, healthy behaviors such as walking for exercise are more likely to become normal, accepted, everyday activities (Kawachi et al., 1999). Likewise, when neighborhoods provide walkable designs, residents are more likely to know their neighbors and be involved socially—building greater social capital (Leyden, 2003).

For women in Detroit, social interactions were found to be vital to health and paramount to the maintenance of social relationships and roles in the neighborhood. For the women in this study (Schulz & Lempert, 2004), relationships and health were clearly situated within the context of their neighborhood. For example, women spoke easily of the importance of social relationships to their health, and they clearly saw the contradiction when they hesitated to open their doors or invite others into their homes out of fear that someone would intrude on their personal matters or that young people might steal from them. They saw neighborhood conditions as the source of worry, leading to the subsequent closing of their doors to others. They recognized that this action undermined the social relationships that otherwise might provide connections and supports integral to good health as they defined it. Similarly, women in the study spoke of the ways that they limited the outdoor activity of their children in the neighborhood to protect them—again fully recognizing that constraining the social relationships of children might also impact their health negatively (supporting the findings from the 2006 study by Lumeng et al.). These women did make attempts to remain socially connected to good friends and family and to be physically active for their health and wellness, including active participation with younger generations and maintaining valued social positions through cooking and sharing meals.

Social Relationships and Perceptions of Safety and Violence

Geis and Ross (1998) found that living within neighborhood conditions lacking social control—places where violence, graffiti, crime, and drug use are common—produces feelings of powerlessness among residents, especially when connections to neighbors have frayed. According to these authors, this sense of powerlessness is what links individuals' lived experiences and their emotional/behavioral responses. When a lack of control becomes a regular feature of daily life, individuals come to believe that their actions have little impact on desired outcomes (Geis & Ross, 1998). Social bonds formed between neighbors provide a level of protection against neighborhood disorder and subsequent feelings of powerlessness. Unfortunately, those individuals who need these social connections the most due to their neighborhood conditions are least likely to attain them (Geis & Ross, 1998). Broken social bonds, therefore, might help explain study results demonstrating that residents of neighborhoods with high levels of stressors in the forms of crime, violence, traffic, and noise are more likely to self-report poorer health and physical functioning (Steptoe & Feldman, 2001).

A qualitative study by Altschuler et al. (2004) considered how the concept of social capital and residents' perception of their neighborhoods might impact health. Through a series of interviews and focus groups in diverse neighborhoods in a large city in California, the authors identified three main themes relevant to neighborhoods and health: meaning of "neighborhood," amenities and liabilities, and mobilization and activism in neighborhoods. When speaking about the meaning of "neighborhood," residents mentioned their block-level relationships with neighbors and what the authors identify as bonding social capital and trust and reciprocity between families. Personal safety and the safety of neighbors were very important to residents and related to feelings of belonging. In lower-income neighborhoods, higher levels of crime and feeling unsafe were a bigger problem than in middle-income communities, and perceptions of safety were somewhat relative to neighborhood norms (Altschuler et al., 2004). Fear for personal safety, especially when walking in the neighborhood, was cited as a stressor for some residents in working-class and low-income neighborhoods. This contrasts to the financial stress that residents of middle-income neighborhoods expressed as being associated with the cost of living in their neighborhood. Residents who felt a sense of belonging in their neighborhood stated that their place of residence contributed to good health or alleviated some of the stress that they experienced. Perceptions of beauty also differed between neighborhoods. Prosperous neighborhoods valued the natural splendor of their neighborhood, which included woods and streams. Residents of lower-SES communities mourned the absence of the most basic green spaces such as lawns and medians (Altschuler et al., 2004).

Models for Understanding Place and Health

As early place-based research developed, a number of conceptual paradigms for the spatial patterning of health emerged. Individual-level, compositional explanations (who you are) propose that individuals living in a neighborhood share characteristics that explain, in part, the connection of health to place of residence. Compositional models require individual-level interventions to improve health status. In contrast, structural-level or contextual models (where you are) contend that the environment has effects on groups of residents living within it over and above the contribution made by individual characteristics (Macintyre & Ellaway, 2003). Macintrye and Ellaway (2003) claim "the distinction between people and places, composition and context, is somewhat artificial. People create places, and places create people" (p. 26), a notion closely aligned with an ecological framework.

Bernard et al. (2007) provide a compelling conceptualization of neighborhoods and the local production of health, with an emphasis on resource distribution and individuals as active agents in acquiring resources. They posit that health disparities are in large part the result of access to resources—both positive resources such as good schools and green space and negative resources such as liquor stores and broken social ties. Those more dependent upon neighborhood resources—often the poorest, sickest, or those without transportation—experience the impact of neighborhood influence to a greater degree than do more mobile groups. Building on the work of Galster (2001), these authors propose the notion of users and producers and resources—individuals who influence the movement of neighborhood resources.

Through their consumption, service use, political processes and social connection patterns, these neighborhood actors reproduce and transform their context, while the lifestyle and health of individuals are affected by the goods consumed, the services used, and the social relationships built. This collective lifestyle heuristic is an attempt to capture this dialectical relationship between individuals and places. (Bernard et al., 2007, p. 1840)

Considerable emphasis is placed not merely on the number and types of resources that are available within a neighborhood, but also on the systems by which those resources are distributed across different neighborhood families and individuals (Bernard et al., 2007).

This kind of explanation moves away from the simplistic contextual versus compositional analysis of neighborhood health and instead presents a more dynamic model that explores the relationships between people and environments (how you interact with your environment), a concept proving more useful in understanding the complexities of spatially distributed health outcomes.

Ecological Frameworks, Life Course Theory, and Health Disparities

Health research and health promotion have often located personal responsibility at the nexus of efforts to improve health. This strategy is predicated on the assumption that personal health behaviors (e.g., exercise, diet, medication adherence) are infinitely modifiable given adequate education and motivation. Such an individual focus is consistent with Western ideology and the American tenet that "we are masters of our own fate." Nevertheless, firm attachment to these principles fails to acknowledge the ways that health behaviors are socially acquired within groups, and it ignores the roles of the physical and social environment in creating opportunities to engage in a healthy lifestyle. Becker (1993) challenges public health systems to widen their perspective:

But to turn our attention beyond the individual—to recognize the social and economic determinants of disease, health, and wellness—is complex and threatening. Doing something about poverty, racism, unemployment, inequitable access to education and other resources, and quality of environment involves notions of planned social and economic change. (p. 4)

Capturing "upstream" determinants of health and "the processes through which the social structure shapes the social circumstances and health experiences of different socioeconomic groups" is unachievable with an individualistic focus alone (Pearce & McKinlay, 1998). Thus, as socioeconomic disparities in health cannot be understood or remedied by the application of an individualistic, personal-behavior paradigm, the systems and structures that generate and reproduce health inequities must also be in focus.

Life course theory provides a lens for studying health inequalities occurring within social pathways and across diverse developmental trajectories. Five principles of life course theory are helpful to place current research in context and to guide both future studies and the development of health interventions. The first principle, *lifespan development*, acknowledges that development is a lifelong process and can be applied to better understand the intersection of health, place, and SES over the life course as cohorts live and develop in different contexts over time (Elder, Johnson, & Crosnoe, 2004). The second principle, *agency*, encompasses the ways that choices made and actions taken across the lifespan promote or hinder the attainment of a healthy life: "Children, adolescents, and adults are not passively acted upon by social influence and structural constraints. Instead, they make choices and compromises based on the alternatives that they perceive before them" (p. 11). Individuals are active agents who not only mediate the influence of social structure, but also shape social structure via the choices they make and the goals that they set. The third principle, *time and place*, reflects that lives are embedded in and shaped by the historical times and places experienced over a lifetime. The fourth principle, *timing*, can be applied to help understand how the "developmental antecedents and consequences of life transitions, events, and behavior patterns that vary according to their timing in a person's life" are related to health inequalities (p. 12). The fifth principle, *linked lives*, suggests that lives are interdependent and reliant on social relationships. The presence and quality of social relationships, created within and shaped by one's environment, have increasingly been linked to health status (Wilkinson & Marmot, 2003). Collectively, these five principles suggest the need to understand human lives and health outcomes within a social and historical context, with consideration to relationships with significant others (Elder et al., 2004).

Graham (2002) applies life course theory to build three explanatory models for health disparities. The "critical periods model" (p. 2007) posits that SES disparities in health are determined by exposures (e.g., poor fetal nutrition, childhood deprivation, family disruptions and disadvantage) that occur at critical periods of development to influence physical and mental health status in adulthood. In contrast, the "pathways model" (p. 2007) proposes that conditions early in life form a conduit toward adult health, with disadvantage early in life affecting future trajectories such as school and future employment. Finally, "accumulation models" (p. 2007) view advantage and disadvantage to have both a cumulative impact and a dose impact on health. Cumulative advantage is the "systemic tendency for interindividual divergence in a given characteristic (e.g., money, health, or status) with the passage of time" (Dannefer, 2003, p. 237).

Cumulative impacts of disadvantage, when endured consistently over the life course, pose the greatest likelihood for development of poor health as an adult. Thus improvement in socioeconomic position at a later stage in life can ameliorate—though not eliminate—health risks associated with early hardship (Graham, 2002).

According to Elder (1985), uncovering the social, physical, and economic life trajectories of groups of individuals, the stability or change in lives over time, and the relationships between life trajectory and transitions can help researchers to better understand health inequalities and better shape responses. Nevertheless, despite the passing of nearly 25 years since the public health field has drawn attention to social-ecological models of health improvement, leaders in control of policy and funding continue to be often stifled by short-term visions for achievement within narrow time frames. As Glanz and Bishop (2010) state,

> Because social norms and the physical environment of a community can take years to show meaningful change, ecological models that account for a long, often slow chain of events are necessary both to program design and to help decision makers understand the need for patience and continued support. (p. 410)

A Comprehensive Model

What we learned from our broad review of the literature encourages us to propose a comprehensive framework for understanding and addressing health disparities. We incorporate concepts associated with life course theory and build upon the work of Cummins et al. (2007), Diez Roux and Mair (2010), Bernard et al. (2007), and Macintrye and Ellaway (2003). Our framework, illustrated in Figure 12.1, recognizes what is clearly a complex pathway from the health disparities associated with poverty and place to improvements in the health status indicators we typically use to measure well-being. It begins with the acknowledgment that low-income and segregated neighborhoods are under-resourced to the degree to which they fail to provide residents with physical and social environments that foster good health. What differentiates our model from its predecessors is the recognition that residents of low-income neighborhoods are not simply passive victims of the effects of their neighborhood environment, though they may indeed be victimized by it. Instead, individuals are understood to exert agency in two distinct ways—*within* and *upon* the environment in which they live.

In this model, individual agency is applied within the constraints and opportunities existing in the environment, and the interaction moves the individual/family along a health trajectory—good or bad—that reaches into the future. The choices individuals make help shape their attitudes,

Figure 12.1
A comprehensive framework for understanding and addressing health disparities.

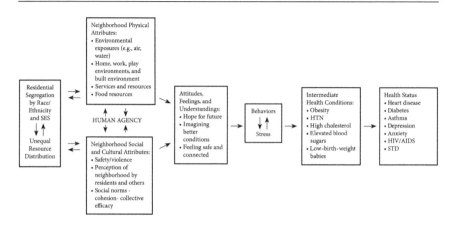

feelings, and understandings about their neighborhood and the possibilities for their future there. The cumulative stress of living in a low-income neighborhood also influences residents' behaviors; those behaviors, in turn, help perpetuate or reduce the experience of stress. When residents individually and collectively exert agency, their potential to transform the surrounding physical and social environment, for better or worse, emerges. Over time, these behaviors and decisions may have contributed to the development of the health conditions typically associated with low SES, but they also have the potential to derail these negative health conditions and begin to alter the future health trajectory of individuals and the community. It is in working toward this potential that we think interventions targeting both the physical and social contexts for health via the mechanism of human agency hold the most promise for success. Engaging residents in altering the conditions in which they make choices can produce a "snowball effect" in which more involvement and action produce more confidence to change the future, and more confidence produces behaviors and decisions that are more likely to promote health. Given that the social determinants of health are primarily structural in nature, this engagement is a critical aspect of communities' ability to ultimately confront the systems and policies that originally contributed to the development of an unhealthy context.

Place-Based Strategies for Health Improvement

Despite growing substantiation for health inequalities, little measurable reduction in health disparity measures has been demonstrated at the national level in the United States. *Healthy People 2010*, the Centers for Disease Control and Prevention's strategy to create a healthy nation for all, failed to demonstrate progress in 84% of targeted health disparities between racial and ethnic groups over 10 years (Centers for Disease Control and Prevention, n.d.). In addition, "health disparities among income groups, as well as by geographic location and disability status did not change, with the exception of a few objectives" (p. ES-22). Interventions designed to impact health disparities usually emerge from health provider organizations or academic medical institutions and strive to apply or create evidence-based interventions for established disease-specific disparities (e.g., asthma, heart disease). Many programs of this sort frame themselves as community-based interventions, but the community referred to is often vastly larger than a neighborhood; in addition, while interventions may be delivered within neighborhoods, an overarching focus on the place as the context for health is rarely evident (e.g., Carleton, Lasater, Assaf, Feldman, & McKinlay, 1995; Morgan et al., 2004).

Other initiatives considered to be place based do not focus explicitly on health, but rather frame their interventions around improvements in the community that could potentially foster better health outcomes via enhancements to systems in the neighborhood environment. These include such strategies as Promise Neighborhoods (Jean-Louis, Farrow, Schorr, Bell, & Fernandez, 2010; Lester, 2009) and community schools (Bookmyer & Niebuhr, 2011), both of which engage an array of community-based nonprofit organizations and agencies to wrap programs and services around community residents in ways that attempt to transform the educational, economic, or other outcomes of individuals and families. This type of strategy often attempts to engage residents in some part of the process, but residents' main role in these initiatives tends to be as recipients of the programs and services offered, rather than as agents of community change.

Some interventions offer both a community orientation and a focus on improving health. Increasing children's play and physical activity in the face of an obesity epidemic has become the focus of many programs, such as KaBOOM!—a national nonprofit that advocates for school recess and assists communities to build their own playgrounds. Results from a study of the impact of the KaBOOM! community build approach on children's play have been uniformly positive, with 100% of surveyed adult participants reporting that the new community playground had a positive impact on the quality and quantity of children's play (Puntenney, 2008). Other efforts, such as Healthy in a Hurry corner stores in Louisville, Kentucky, work to increase the accessibility and availability of healthy food in neighborhoods considered to be food deserts. Still other initiatives combine approaches—for example, Healthi Kids, a Monroe County, New York, community-based coalition, promotes policies that support healthy food in schools and child care centers, more physical activity and safe play areas, and breastfeeding for a healthy start in life (Healthi Kids, 2010).

A somewhat different array of programs have sought to improve neighborhood environments through the development of policies that support safer, more livable environments. One example is Complete Streets, in which urban planners use ordinances designed to ensure safe and attractive access to and through communities to individuals of all abilities and ages (McCann & Rynne, 2010). Several studies show that implementation of a Complete Streets policy has contributed to healthy change. For example, in Boulder, Colorado, the policy led to residents driving less and opting for transport by bike, bus, and foot instead (National Research Center, 2010). A more comprehensive example is the Port Towns Community Health Partnership in Maryland, which works to change community conditions associated with health disparities "by encouraging sustainable practices, policies and neighborhood conditions that enable a healthy and active environment" (Port Towns Community Health Partnership, 2011). This multisector approach includes targeting obesity through creating opportunities for healthy eating and supporting policies that help improve the larger environment for active living.

A prominent example in 2012 was First Lady Michelle Obama's Let's Move program, which explicitly targets childhood obesity through multi-faceted interventions. While neighborhoods are not the primary focus for Let's Move, several of its strategies for taking action target groups of people in neighborhoods acting together—for example, community and faith organizations. Let's Move offers an array of ideas and numerous how-to guides for such health-promoting activities as planting a community garden and creating opportunities for physical exercise. It also includes ideas for elected officials related to policy change that can support healthy behaviors, such as enhancing public safety near parks and other public spaces where children are likely to be. The program has supported legislation at the national level, including the Healthy, Hunger Free Kids Act, that is expected to contribute to the future success of Let's Move by providing guidance and funding to school-based feeding programs (Healthy Hunger Free Kids Act of 2010, 2010). Let's Move is partnered with the President's Task Force on Childhood Obesity, and it represents a framework for addressing this issue across a variety of domains, including families, schools, and communities. The materials provided through the program bring together an impressive number of ideas for action as well as resources that community groups and organizations can use to implement their plan. Interestingly, while the research undergirding the findings of the task force clearly associates the issue of obesity with the social determinants of health (White House Task Force on Childhood Obesity, 2010), this connection is much less visible in the Let's Move toolkit or on the website, which suggests that "just a few lifestyle changes" will help children lead healthier lives. It remains to be seen whether Let's Move will provoke the kinds of broad change in families and communities it hopes to achieve.

Community Engagement and Organizing

How people are engaged in these interventions matters a great deal, as the literature on community engagement and health demonstrates. Community engagement and organizing strategies represent a general approach to community building and have been used to engage people on myriad issues at the global, national, regional, local, and neighborhood levels. The manner of engagement, meaning the ways that specific people are encouraged to participate, looks very different depending on the level at which the organizing takes place and the purposes of the entity deploying the strategy. For example, community engagement can occur at the grassroots level (among residents of a place) or at the organizational or institutional level (among professionals serving a place). Much of the literature that describes engaging the community to improve physical and social health refers to building coalitions with agency and institutional membership, while very little attention has been paid to grassroots, neighborhood-based coalitions (Kegler & Wyatt, 2003). In addition, the community change addressed by these coalitions is usually explored through the lens of service delivery such as new programs, services, or practices for needy community members as opposed to grassroots efforts to engage community members in changing the physical, social, and economic environments of a neighborhood. Additionally, when coalitions of professionals attempt to engage and mobilize residents at the neighborhood level, those efforts often proceed in a top-down manner organized around the health interests of institutional leaders. For example, Kegler and Wyatt (2003) explored factors integral to mobilizing neighborhoods around teen pregnancy prevention. Both the specific health focus and the formation of a neighborhood coalition were driven by grant funding from the Centers for Disease Control and Prevention, as opposed to representing a health concern and action plan identified by neighborhood residents. Their findings address why top-down approaches to engaging community members often fail, and these lessons are clearly pertinent to agencies considering health interventions at the neighborhood level. In particular, the authors note that "sitting in meetings, reviewing data, and developing action plans may represent a professional approach to addressing problems that has little relevance to low-income families trying to make ends meet" (Kegler & Wyatt, 2003, p. 167).

Stokols, Grzywacz, McMahan, and Phillips (2003) identify three key elements to creating community capacity to improve health. First, assets (including individuals) must be engaged and mobilized toward action to improve health. Next, assets must be expanded and diversified as time passes, bringing new energy and resources to bear. Third, community efforts must be sustained over time to allow for improvements in health status. Underscoring the success of community engagement and mobilization is the privileging of health concerns most important to neighborhood residents over those of medical experts or institutional partners.

Organizing efforts with demonstrated success in engaging residents to improve neighborhood and community environments are, for the most part, not explicitly oriented to the goal of reducing health disparities. However, because they do produce results on some of Macintrye and Ellaway's (2003) five health-promoting neighborhood characteristics (in particular, healthy environments, social and cultural aspects, and resident/stakeholders' perception of the neighborhood), they are worthy of consideration. If improvements in these areas function as foundational changes that support larger individual and community change, then community engagement and organizing strategies may be a critical starting place for place-based strategies for health improvement. Indeed, authentic engagement of the people most impacted by health disparities is the one variable that has been consistently ignored in health improvement programs.

Horowitz and Lawlor (2008) cite a number of reasons why public health efforts have failed to embrace community development processes. First, engaging neighborhood residents involves a sometimes lengthy process of relationship development, forming partnerships, and helping people develop the power to envision and craft their own course of action. This is often at odds with the intent to intervene on a disparity related to a particular health outcome. In fact, the health disparities of greatest concern to public health professionals may be of little interest to neighborhood residents. Resident action to improve such neighborhood characteristics as safety, education, or income may not directly impact the health concern of top priority for medical experts. Rather, the connection may be less direct, or at least comprise more intermediate steps than direct interventions involve.

Where Do We Go from Here?

With very little improvement in health disparities at the national level being achieved after years of investment in reducing them, it is clear that more innovation is required. Yet in spite of the great need for more inventive programs that take a comprehensive approach, such strategies have proved difficult to find. We now consider several innovative approaches currently under way and examine how various actors interested in place-based health improvements—funders, researchers, activists, and community members—might take up different and more pioneering approaches in their work.

Innovation for Funders

We first explore how two forward-thinking funders are supporting community-based efforts to reduce health disparities in ways we believe offer promise for reducing health disparities and that, once fully evaluated, may prove to be effective models for other communities and funders. These examples reflect the categories incorporated in the comprehensive framework for understanding and addressing health disparities illustrated in Figure 12.1; indeed, they represent much of the basis on which the framework was developed. They emphasize changing how people engage and interact around a particular issue or opportunity within the place in question. In each case, the place tends to be relatively small and to be defined in a manner closely associated with the relationships existing—or potentially existing—there. The examples also define people living in the place as actors/agents on their own behalf, unlike more traditional approaches in which residents are viewed as recipients of professional knowledge and services, exerting agency only in their choice to follow or disregard the health improvement advice they are given.

The grants illustrated in these examples support efforts that (1) focus on one or more of the social determinants of health *within a specific place*, (2) keep health status—as measured by specific disease indicators—in the frame as a long-term objective while evaluating progress toward intermediate outcomes along the way, (3) recognize individual and collective human agency as important intermediaries between neighborhood context and health outcomes, and (4) include residents as authentic actors in the design and implementation of health improvement strategies. In both cases, these efforts are in relatively early stages, and though they may not currently be able to demonstrate results on specific disease indicators or actual health disparities, they do show positive movement on some of the foundational changes we think necessary to achieve larger health objectives.

Building Healthy Communities, California.   Through its Building Healthy Communities program, the California Endowment has engaged with residents and organizations in 14 communities to undertake 10 years of work toward improving health outcomes. After significant investment in research on health disparities (e.g., Bell & Lee, 2011; Healthy Eating Active Communities, 2007), the Endowment has undertaken a set of long-term strategic investments across the state to support the creation of healthy communities. Anthony Iton (2008), a senior member of the Healthy Communities team, describes the assumptions on which the program is based in his critique of using a medical model to address the root causes of health disparities. He argues that ignoring what he calls *upstream* conditions (i.e., the social-ecological contexts that create health inequities) in favor of using a medical model to focus on *downstream* factors (i.e., genetics, access to health knowledge and care) eliminates the possibility of overcoming health disparities. Instead, Building Healthy Communities emphasizes starting at the community level and engaging the individuals who are most impacted by health disparities in altering the community landscape and creating opportunities for better health outcomes. The Building Healthy Communities program has identified 10 outcomes for community health that include (1) place-based items (e.g., "residents live in communities with health-promoting land use, transportation and community development"); (2) health services items (e.g., "all children have health coverage"); and (3) attitude items (e.g., "California has a shared vision of community health") (California Endowment, n.d.). The 14 participating communities completed a one-year planning process that brought together multisector alliances to define a vision for community health for 2020 and craft a plan for getting there. The communities have been especially interested in three areas of action: (1) children require safe peaceful communities in which they can be contributors, (2) children need access to quality health care, and (3) everyone needs to live in places that promote good health.

The California Endowment takes a long-term perspective on the Building Healthy Communities program. The planning year was the first of 10 years of support the Endowment has committed to, and the 14 partnerships are expected to innovate and create new strategies for change as they move through the process. The design of these grants encourages changes in the physical context of the neighborhood, sees residents as essential actors in the process, and focuses on specific health improvements over the long term. In additional to financial resources, the Endowment provides extensive capacity building support to all of the communities involved in this program. It has a strong orientation to asset-based community development (see Kretzmann & McKnight, 1993), and those project activities that utilize an asset-based approach— that is, focusing on positives and possibilities, engaging residents as assets—and that are resident driven will have a high priority for additional funding.

Neighborhood Health Status Improvement Initiative, New York.

Through its Neighborhood Health Status Improvement Initiative (NHSII), the Greater Rochester Health Foundation is supporting local groups to design and implement community-based interventions to improve the health status of people living in neighborhoods challenged by poverty and health disparities (Zappia & Puntenney, 2010). This program is grounded in the idea that place matters, and it emphasizes the need for community stakeholders to identify and mobilize local assets that can be deployed toward community health improvement. Through the program, residents and organizations are expected to work together to improve an array of environmental conditions, create public spaces and places where healthy behaviors are an option, and help ensure that residents' health care needs are met. Each of the grantees has created mechanisms for residents to take a central role in mapping and mobilizing assets, defining local health priorities, and designing and implementing activities that will alter one or more of the social determinants of health.

There is ample evidence that when communities organize around their assets rather than their needs, neighborhood improvements can result in numerous areas, including the physical, environmental, social, and economic contexts (e.g., Blejwas, 2010; Green, 2010; Kretzmann & McKnight, 1993; Kretzmann & Puntenney, 2010; McKnight & Block, 2010; Puntenney & Moore, 1998; Snow, 2001). Building on this research, the Greater Rochester Health Foundation provides technical support in community engagement to its grantees through the Asset-Based Community Development Institute (ABCD) at Northwestern University.

The Foundation views improving neighborhood health status as a long-term investment. To assess the value of this investment and accumulate knowledge at every step along the way, it supports a program evaluation that is examining an array of short-, medium-, and long-term outputs and outcomes. While some differences in the progress made by individual grantees have been noted, some reasons to be optimistic are also emerging from the evaluation. Examples from two of the projects illustrate accomplishments to date.

The first example involves an inner-city neighborhood with approximately 2,247 residents, more than half living below the federal poverty line (Project HOPE, n.d.). Groups of residents in this community identified (1) drugs and alcohol, (2) youth development, (3) public safety, and (4) personal lifestyle and healthy opportunities as their four focus areas for work under the NHSII grant. While their activities in these categories are too numerous to mention, a few basic facts help illustrate the group's progress:

1. Six community gardens and a local produce stand were developed; a community playground was built (literally) by residents and partners; locally created public art was installed on streets throughout the neighborhood; 40 neighborhood walks against local drug trade were undertaken; three block clubs were formed and 60 resident meetings were held; and 15 neighborhood events were held, including a neighborhood summit.

2. More than 380 residents actively participated in some aspect of the project; more than 1,100 attended project activities.
3. Eight active partnerships were developed with local nonprofits in place; strong partnerships were forged with the local government agencies (e.g., police, district attorney, city departments); and community participation, partnerships, and commitment to eliminating local drug markets were recently leveraged in the receipt of significant additional funding from a prominent national health funder.
4. In their fourth year of the project, 41% of residents said that the relationship between residents and the police had improved; 70% were proud to live on their street; 70% said they believed they had at least some ability to make a positive difference in their neighborhood; and 61% expected things to improve in their community. All indicators are moving in a positive direction.

This project has started to alter the neighborhood context for health and has actively moved into the realm of policy change to support its work. The group recently received additional funding for policy change work. Residents are actively involved and are increasing their collective capacity to undertake work at the local level and to partner with all sorts of agencies and entities interested in working with them on their health objectives.

The second example involves a rural community with approximately 5,041 residents, almost 20% living below the federal poverty line (Our Town Rocks, n.d.). Groups of residents in this community identified (1) improving personal health behaviors such as eating healthier and increasing exercise, (2) adding healthy activities and foods to community events, (3) increasing economic health and stimulating small business growth, (4) improving the look of the main street in the central village, and (5) boosting available services and access to services as their five health improvement priorities under the NHSII grant. Again, while the group's activities are too extensive to mention, some basic facts illustrate their progress:

1. Small business grant/loan program were established; a new store featuring resident arts and crafts is in its third year; a farmer's market served an average of 70 people per week in its third season; walking and exercise programs, a pet therapy program, an alcohol-free high school graduation program, and a K–6 reading program are all ongoing.
2. More than 100 residents actively participated in some aspect of the project; many more attended project events; monthly community meetings were attended by 30–35 residents; and 15 resident champions coordinated project activities.

3. Active partnerships were established with local nonprofits, municipalities, housing organizations, media outlets, and local associations
   (e.g., Rotary Club).
4. In the fourth year of the project, 83% of residents said that their quality of life in the community was good or better; 85% said they had
   visited the main street once a week or more; 50% reported having
   engaged in physical exercise on five or more days of the past week;
   and 41% reported having eaten four or more fruits and vegetables
   on the previous day. All indicators are moving in a positive
   direction.

This project has also started to alter the neighborhood landscape in
ways that promote health. Residents are actively involved and regularly
contribute to, as well as manage, many of the activities the project is
implementing. The project is now considered the "go to" entity for all
sorts of local agencies for both input and action on community improvement activities.

These examples illustrate that it is possible to address health disparities
in multidimensional ways that more comprehensively tackle the multiple
factors associated with them. Each example is based in a specific place;
residents of the place are engaged as actors in the transformation of the
place and their own health behaviors; transformation is addressed at the
individual, community, and policy levels; and the investment is made
over time, with the long-term objectives being health improvement and
reduction in disparities.

Innovation for Researchers, Activists, and Communities

According to Horowitz and Lawlor (2008), innovative health-
improvement strategies have been less likely to gain the attention of
researchers interested in SES disparities, and research on approaches
and policies that address the social determinants of health are quite limited (Horowitz & Lawlor, 2008; Roussos & Fawcett, 2000). This dearth of
research is unsurprising given the widespread attention paid by scholars
to health delivery systems and access to health care, and the fact that comprehensive, place-based approaches to addressing health disparities are
relatively new on the scene. However, as funders and communities
experiment with such new approaches, a real opportunity opens up for
researchers whose interests span the domains of health disparities, poverty, and place. They can target their work at the cutting edge of defining
and elucidating a whole new area of study, and, if they are activist scholars, they can do so in a proactive manner that helps to move the field forward. Researchers can be valuable partners for funders and other
supporters of this work in helping to craft logic models; develop

appropriate short-, medium-, and long-term outcomes; and create measures and instruments that can effectively track progress over a period of years. They can also be valuable partners for community residents in helping them understand, value, and participate in the research process. Other community activists can contribute as well, particularly in terms of encouraging organizing that focuses on community assets and opportunities for health, and by incorporating community members of all kinds as equal actors in the definition and implementation of place-based strategies for reducing health disparities. Finally, community residents can activate themselves around the social determinants of health. Taking action with others expands the power a community may have in advocating for policies and practices that have an impact on community members' health, and it enhances the residents' own role as an integral part of the equation for reducing health disparities in the place they live.

None of these groups alone will be successful at reducing health disparities, and cooperation and collaboration are required to achieve any degree of success. As a consequence, each group needs to recognize the importance of the potential contributions made by the others, and to value what each party has to offer.

Conclusion

In this chapter, we have sought to present a compelling argument for the importance of a new approach to eliminating health disparities. Decades of public investment in population health, including the reduction of disparities, have failed to yield the desired results. In spite of what we know about the treatment of specific diseases, we actually know relatively little about how to effectively untangle the complex and interconnected causes of poor health, in particular those related to place. In narrowly targeting our interventions, we may have missed the opportunity to actually alter the outcomes we seek to improve.

We suggest that more comprehensive approaches to improving health disparities are necessary, and we offer the following considerations for adopting place-based approaches for health improvement. First, with respect to the complexity of the relationships between health and place, health promotion efforts should embrace an ecological framework for understanding and intervening effectively within these intricate and messy associations between health, health behaviors, and neighborhoods in which families live, work, and play. An ecological approach (Bronfenbrenner, 1977) to health promotion attends to individuals and families nested within the context of a neighborhood or community setting, and it considers behavior as something that both is affected by and affects the environment. In addition, an ecological lens assists in thinking about interventions across multiple levels or domains within a neighborhood context, such as homes, schools, places of worship, community agencies, or on the block. Fitzpatrick and LaGory (2011) point to the importance of this multilevel approach when considering ways to mitigate risk or enhance health protective factors for youth. We concur that health promotion, within the boundaries of a neighborhood or community, should consider the multiple, interconnected, and overlapping opportunities to improve health.

Next, we see the engagement of community residents as integral to the success of health improvement measures at the neighborhood level. At the most basic level, the meaningful engagement of neighborhood residents means that interventions can be prioritized to reflect what residents care most about, as opposed to what policymakers and other health experts deem most important. Local residents and their local knowledge are assets that should be acknowledged, validated, and incorporated into health improvement efforts in the context where they live. As we have demonstrated in previous sections, neighborhood residents can be powerful agents of transformation in neighborhoods, creating changes with the potential to impact personal health and the health of others. As residents become mobilized to improve neighborhood health, working in concert with others on their street or block, they develop relationships with others—former strangers—who can provide reciprocal social supports and social resources. This reinvigorated social organization and subsequent social support offer some protection from neighborhood risk and may reduce the negative effects of chronic stress (Thoits, 1995). In addition, the collective efficacy and subsequent improvements in the neighborhood context (e.g., reduction in violence, cleaner streets) resulting from community engagement and action can lead to a direct reduction of factors contributing to neighborhood-level stress. The element of human agency, when nurtured by community engagement and organizing efforts, is a powerful force for action within and upon neighborhoods. It can provide residents with subtle opportunities to make choices and decisions that break the constraints of their social and economic circumstances.

Finally, place-based approaches to health improvement must consider the policies and structures that contribute to the creation of neighborhoods that fail to support healthy developmental trajectories for residents. Those interested in health promotion and reduction of health disparities must look "upstream" to the systems that perpetuate inequities in health. This examination is not limited to health policy, however, but also includes housing policies that fail to disrupt neighborhood segregation, transportation policies that make it more difficult for some to access living-wage employment, and education policies that perpetually leave some children behind their peers. Future health promotion efforts should not passively accept the policies of the past as an inevitable characteristic of the future. New approaches must be both place based and focused upon the social determinants of health to ensure that the environments in which people live provide the possibility of, and supports for, healthy living. These approaches must recognize that individual and collective human agency are important intermediaries between neighborhood context and health outcomes, and include residents as authentic actors in the design and implementation of health improvement strategies. Health promotion efforts must keep health status and improvements on specific disease indicators in focus as long-term objectives. Nevertheless, it will also be critical to define a clear, logical pathway from changing neighborhood contexts and conditions, to building human agency and expanding empowerment, to changing health behaviors and outcomes, and to assess progress on short- and medium-term outcomes along the way.

References

Adler, N. E., Boys, W. T., Chesney, M. A., Folkman, S., & Syme, S. L. (1993). Socioeconomic inequalities in health. *Journal of the American Medical Association*, *269*(31), 3140–3145.

Altschuler, A., Somkin, C. P., & Adler, N. E. (2004). Local services and amenities, neighborhood social capital, and health. *Social Science & Medicine*, *59*(6), 1219–1229.

Becker, M. H. (1993). A medical sociologist looks at health promotion. *Journal of Health and Social Behavior*, *34*(1), 1–6.

Bell, J., & Lee, M. (2011). *Why race and place matter.* Oakland, CA: Policy Link.

Bernard, P., Charafeddine, R., Frohlich, K. L., Daniel, M., Kestens, Y., & Potvin, L. (2007). Health inequalities and place: A theoretical conception of neighbourhood. *Social Science & Medicine*, *65*(9), 1839–1852.

Blejwas, E. (2010). Asset-based community development in Alabama's black belt: Seven strategies for building a diverse community movement. In G. Green & A. Goetting (Eds.), *Mobilizing communities: Asset building as a community development strategy* (pp. 48–67). Philadelphia, PA: Temple University Press.

Bookmyer, J., & Niebuhr, D. (2011). California healthy start. http://partnerfor children.org/press-room#publications

Bovell-Benjamin, A. C., Hathorn, C. S., Ibrahim, S., Gichuhi, P. N., & Bromfield, E. M. (2009). Healthy food choices and physical activity opportunities in two contrasting Alabama cities. *Health & Place*, *15*(2), 429–438.

Braveman, P. A., & Egerter, S. (2008). *Overcoming obstacles to health: Report from the Robert Wood Johnson Foundation to the Commission to Build a Healthier America.* Princeton, NJ: Robert Wood Johnson Foundation.

Bronenbrenner, U. (1977). Toward an experimental ecology of human development. *American Psychologist*, *32*(7), 513–531.

California Endowment. (n.d.). *Building healthy communities: Ten outcomes for community health* [Brochure]. Los Angeles, CA: Author.

Carleton, R. A., Lasater, T. M., Assaf, A. R., Feldman, H. A., & McKinlay, S. (1995). The Pawtucket Heart Health Program: Community changes in cardiovascular risk factors and projected disease risk. *American Journal of Public Health, 85*(6), 777–785.

Centers for Disease Control and Prevention. (n.d.). Healthy people 2010: Final review, executive summary. http://www.cdc.gov/nchs/healthy_people/hp2010/hp2010_final_review.htm

Cohen, D., Finch, B. K., Bower, A., & Sastry, N. (2006). Collective efficacy and obesity: The potential influence of social factors on health. *Social Science & Medicine, 62*(3), 769–778.

Cummins, S., Curtis, S., Diez Roux, A. V., & Macintyre, S. (2007). Understanding and representing "place" in health research: A relational approach. *Social Science & Medicine, 65*(9), 1825–1838.

Cummins, S., & Macintyre, S. (2006). Food environments and obesity: Neighborhoods or nation? *International Journal of Epidemiology, 35*(1), 100–104.

Dannefer, D. (2003). Cumulative advantage/disadvantage and the life course: Cross-fertilizing the age and social science theory. *Journal of Gerontology, 58B*(6), S327–S337.

Diez Roux, A. V., Evenson, K. R., McGinn, A. P., Brown, D. G., Moore, L., Brines, S., & Jacobs Jr, D. R. (2007). Availability of recreational resources and physical activity in adults. *American Journal of Public Health, 97*(3).

Diez Roux, A. V., & Mair, C. (2010). Neighborhoods and health. *Annals of the New York Academy of Sciences, 1186*(1), 125–145.

Elder, G. H. (1985). *Life course dynamics: Trajectories and transitions, 1968–1980.* Ithaca, NY: Cornell University Press.

Elder, G. H., Johnson, M. K., & Crosnoe, R. (2004). The emergence and development of life course theory. In J. T. Mortimer & M. J. Shanahan (Eds.), *Handbook of the life course* (pp. 3–19). New York, NY: Springer.

Ellaway, A., Macintyre, S., & Bonnefoy, X. (2005). Graffiti, greenery, and obesity in adults: Secondary analysis of European cross sectional survey. *British Medical Journal, 331*(7517), 611.

Fitzpatrick, K., & LaGory, M. (2011). *Unhealthy cities: Poverty, race, and place in America.* New York NY: Routledge.

Franco, M., Diez Roux, A. V., Glass, T. A., Caballero, B., & Brancati, F. L. (2008). Neighborhood characteristics and the availability of healthy food in Baltimore. *American Journal of Preventive Medicine, 36*(6), 561–567.

Galster, G. (2001). On the nature of neighborhood. *Urban Studies, 38*(12), 2111–2124.

Geis, K. J., & Ross, C. E. (1998). A new look at urban alienation: The effect of neighbourhood disorder on perceived powerlessness. *Social Psychology Quarterly, 61*(3), 232–246.

Glanz, K., & Bishop, D. B. (2010). The role of behavioral science theory in development and implementation of public health interventions. *Annual Review of Public Health, 31*(1), 399–418.

Graham, H. (2002). Building an inter-disciplinary science of health inequalities: The example of lifecourse research. *Social Science & Medicine, 55*(11), 2005–2016.

Green, G. (2010). Natural amenities and asset-based development in rural communities. In G. Green & A. Goetting (Eds.), *Mobilizing communities: Asset building as a community development strategy* (pp. 130–145). Philadelphia, PA: Temple University Press.

Haan, M., Kaplan, G. A., & Camacho, T. (1987). Poverty and health: Prospective evidence from the Alameda County study. *American Journal of Epidemiology, 125*(6), 989–998.

Healthi Kids. (2010, December). *Recess report 2010*. Rochester, NY: Author.

Healthy Eating Active Communities. (2007). *Key lessons from California schools working to change school food environments*. Los Angeles, CA: Author.

Healthy Hunger Free Kids Act of 2010, Pub. L. no. 111-296, 124 Stat. 3183 (2010). Print.

Horowitz, C., & Lawlor, E. F. (2008). Community approaches to addressing health disparities. In J. A. Cohen (Ed.), *Challenges and successes in reducing health disparities: Workshop summary* (pp. 161–192). Washington, DC: National Academies Press.

Institute of Medicine. (2004). *The future of the public's health in the 21st century.* Washington, DC: National Academies Press.

Isaacs, S. L., & Schroeder, S. A. (2004). Class: The ignored determinant of the nation's health. *New England Journal of Medicine, 351*(11), 1137–1142.

Iton, A. (2008). The ethics of the medical model in addressing the root causes of health disparities in local public health practice. *Journal of Public Health Management & Practice, 14*(4), 335–339.

Jean-Louis, B., Farrow, F., Schorr, L., Bell, J., & Fernandez, K. (2010). *Focusing on results in Promise Neighborhoods*. New York: Harlem Children's Zone, Center for the Study of Social Policy, & PolicyLink.

Johnson, R. C., Schoeni, R. F., & Rogowski, J. A. (2011). Health disparities in mid-to-late life: The role of earlier life family and neighborhood socioeconomic conditions. *Social Science & Medicine, 74*(4), 625–636.

Kawachi, I., Kennedy, B. P., & Glass, R. (1999). Social capital and self-rated health: A contextual analysis. *American Journal of Public Health, 89*(8), 1187–1193.

Kawachi, I., Kennedy, B. P., Lochner, K., & Prothrow-Stith, D. (1997). Social capital, income inequality, and mortality. *American Journal of Public Health, 87*(9), 1491.

Kegler, M. C., & Wyatt, V. H. (2003). A multiple case study of neighborhood partnerships for positive youth development. *American Journal of Health Behavior, 27*(2), 156–169.

Kim, D., Subramanian, S. V., & Kawachi, I. (2006). Bonding versus bridging social capital and their associations with self rated health: A multilevel analysis of 40 U.S. communities. *Journal of Epidemiology and Community Health, 60*(2), 116–122.

Kretzmann, J., & McKnight, J. (1993). *Building communities from the inside out.* Evanston, IL: Northwestern University.

Kretzmann, J., & Puntenney, D. (2010). Neighborhood approaches to asset mobilization: Building Chicago's West Side. In A. Goetting & G. P. Green (Eds.), *Mobilizing communities: Asset building as a community development strategy* (pp. 112–129). Philadelphia, PA: Temple University Press.

Lester, P. (2009). *Tipping neighborhoods to success*. Alliance for Children and Families and United Neighborhood Centers of America.

Leyden, K. M. (2003). Social capital and the built environment: The importance of walkable neighborhoods. *American Journal of Public Health, 93*(9), 1456–1558.

Link, B. G., & Phelan, J. C. (1995). Social conditions as fundamental causes of disease. *Journal of Health and Social Behavior, 36*, 80–94.

Lochner, K. A., Kawachi, I., Brennan, R. T., & Buka, S. L. (2003). Social capital and neighborhood mortality rates in Chicago. *Social Science & Medicine, 56*(8), 1797–1805.

Ludwig, J., Sanbonmatsu, L., Gennetian, L., Adam, E., Duncan, G., Katz, L., ... McDade, T. (2011). Neighborhoods, obesity, and diabetes: A randomized social experiment. *New England Journal of Medicine, 365*(16), 1509–1519.

Lumeng, J. C., Appugliese, D., Cabral, H. J., Bradley, R. H., & Zuckerman, B. (2006). Neighborhood safety and overweight status in children. *Archives of Pediatrics & Adolescent Medicine, 160*(1), 25–31.

Macera, C. A., Jones, D. A., Ham, S. A., Kohl, H. W., & Buchner, D. (2003). Prevalence of physical activity, including lifestyle activities among adults —United States, 2000–2001. Centers for Disease Control and Prevention. *Morbidity and Mortality Weekly Review, 52*(32), 764–766.

Macintyre, S. (2000). The social patterning of exercise behaviours: The role of personal and local resources. *British Journal of Sports Medicine, 34*(1), 6.

Macintyre, S., & Ellaway, A. (2003). Neighborhoods and health: An overview. In I. Kawachi & L. F. Berkman (Eds.), *Neighborhoods and health* (pp. 20–42). New York, NY: Oxford University Press.

Marmot, M. (2005). Social determinants of health inequalities. *Lancet, 365*(9464), 1099–1104.

Mathews, T. J., & MacDorman, M. F. (2007). *Infant mortality statistics from the 2004 period linked birth/infant death dataset* (Vol. 55). Hyattsville, MD: National Center for Health Statistics.

McCann, B., & Rynne, S. (2010). Complete streets: Best policy and implementation practices. American Planning Association Advisory Service. http://www.planning.org/apastore/search/Default.aspx?p=4060

McCormack, G. R., Rock, M., Toohey, A. M., & Hignell, D. (2010). Characteristics of urban parks associated with park use and physical activity: A review of qualitative research. *Health & Place, 16*(4), 712–726.

McDonough, P., Duncan, G. J., Williams, D., & House, J. (1997). Income dynamics and adult mortality in the United States, 1972 through 1989. *American Journal of Public Health, 87*(9), 1476–1483.

McKnight, J., & Block, P. (2010). *The abundant community.* San Francisco, CA: Berrett-Koehler Publishers.

McNeill, L. H., Krueter, M. W., & Subramanian, S. V. (2006). Social environment and physical activity: A review of concepts and evidence. *Social Science & Medicine, 63*(4), 1011–1022.

Morgan, W. J., Crain, E. F., Gruchalla, R. S., O'Connor, G. T., Kattan, M., Evans, R., ... Mitchell, H. (2004). Results of a home-based environmental intervention among urban children with asthma. *New England Journal of Medicine, 351*(11), 1068–1080.

Morland, K., & Evenson, K. (2009). Obesity prevalence and the local food environment. *Health & Place, 15*(2), 491–495.

Morland, K., Wing, S., Diez Roux, A. V., & Poole, C. (2002). Neighborhood characteristics associated with the location of food stores and food service places. *American Journal of Preventive Medicine, 22*(1), 23–29.

Mustard, C. A., Derksen, S., Berthelot, J. M., Wolfson, M., & Roos, L. L. (1997). Age-specific education and income gradients in morbidity and mortality in a Canadian province. *Social Science & Medicine, 45*(3), 383–397.

National Research Center, Inc. (2010). *Modal shift in the Boulder Valley.* Boulder, CO: Author. http://completestreets.org/webdocs/resources/boulder-modes hift09.pdf

Our Town Rocks. (n.d.). *Bringing country neighbors together for good: A rural area builds on its strengths and inspires healthy action* [Brochure]. Dundee, NY: Author.

Pearce, N., & McKinlay, J. (1998). Back to the future in epidemiology and public health: Response to Dr. Gori. *Journal of Clinical Epidemiology, 51*(8), 643–646.

Port Towns Community Health Partnership. (2011, March). *Port Towns Community Health Partnership community action plan.* Edmonston, MD: Author.

Project HOPE. (n.d.). *Helping people lead with their strengths: The new way forward for a healthier neighborhood* [Brochure]. Rochester, NY: Author.

Puntenney, D. (2008). *KaBOOM! Building community one playground at a time.* Washington, DC: KaBOOM! http://kaboom.org/about_kaboom/reports _and_studies

Puntenney, D., & Moore, H. (1998). *City-sponsored community building: Savannah's Grants for Blocks story.* Evanston: IL: Northwestern University.

Putnam, R. D. (1995). Bowling alone: America's declining social capital. *Journal of Democracy, 6*(1), 65–78.

Rose, D. J. (2010). Captive audience? Strategies for acquiring food in two Detroit neighborhoods. *Qualitative Health Research* [Epub ahead of print].

Ross, C. E. (2000). Walking, exercising, and smoking: Does neighborhood matter? *Social Science & Medicine, 51*(2), 265–274.

Roussos, S. T., & Fawcett, S. B. (2000). A review of collaborative partnerships as a strategy for improving community health. *Annual Review of Public Health, 21*(1), 369–342.

Sampson, R. J., Raudenbush, S. W., & Earls, F. (1997). Neighborhoods and violent crime: A multilevel study of collective efficacy. *Science, 277*(5328), 918–924.

Sampson, R. J. (2003). Neighborhood-level context and health: Lessons from sociology. In I. Kawachi & L. F. Berkman (Eds.), *Neighborhoods and health* (pp. 132–146). New York, NY: Oxford University Press.

Sampson, R. J., & Morenoff, J. D. (2000). Public health and safety in context: Lessons from community-level theory on social capital. In B. D. Smedley & S. L. Syme (Eds.), *Promoting health: Intervention strategies from social and behavioral research* (pp. 366–389). Washington, DC: National Academies Press.

Sampson, R. J., Raudenbush, S. W., & Earls, F. (1997). Neighborhoods and violent crime: A multilevel study of collective efficacy. *Science, 277*(5328), 918–924.

Schulz, A. J., & Lempert, L. B. (2004). Being part of the world: Detroit women's perceptions of health and the social environment. *Journal of Contemporary Ethnography, 33*(4), 437–465.

Sherwood, N., & Jeffery, R. W. (2000). The behavioral determinants of exercise: Implications for physical activity interventions. *Annual Review of Nutrition, 20*(1), 21–44.

Snow, L. (2001). *The organization of hope: A workbook for rural asset-based community development.* Evanston, IL: Northwestern University.

Steptoe, A., & Feldman, P. J. (2001). Neighborhood problems as sources of chronic stress: Development of a measure of neighborhood problems, and associations with socioeconomic status and health. *Annals of Behavioral Medicine, 23*(3), 177–185.

Stokols, D., Grzywacz, J. G., McMahan, S., & Phillips, K. (2003). Increasing the health promotive capacity of human environments. *American Journal of Health Promotion, 18*(1), 4–13.

Thoits, P. A. (1995). Stress, coping, and social support processes: Where are we? What next? *Journal of Health and Social Behavior, 35*(Extra Issue), 53–79.

U.S. Department of Health and Human Services. (2006). Child health USA 2006. http://www.mchb.hrsa.gov/chusa_06/index.htm

White House Task Force on Childhood Obesity. (2010). Solving the problem of childhood obesity within a generation. http://www.letsmove.gov/white -house-task-force-childhood-obesity-report-president

Wilkinson, R., & Marmot, M. (Eds.). (2003). *Social determinants of health: The solid facts* (2nd ed.). Geneva, Switzerland: World Health Organization. http:// www.euro.who.int/document/e81384.pdf

Zappia, B., & Puntenney, D. (2010, August). *Grassroots activism and community health improvement.* Paper presented at the meeting of the Society for the Study of Social Problems, Atlanta, GA.

Index

About the Editor and Contributors

KEVIN M. FITZPATRICK, PhD, is Professor and Jones Chair in Community, Department of Sociology and Criminal Justice at the University of Arkansas. As the Jones Chair and the Director of the Community and Family Institute, Dr. Fitzpatrick continues his work on homelessness, the health of special populations, and obesity and food insecurity among at-risk school-age youth. His work in community and urban sociology focuses on the role of "place" in our understanding of a variety of health, crime, and quality of life outcomes.

RALEIGH BAILEY, PhD, is founding director of the Center for New North Carolinians (CNNC) at the University of North Carolina at Greensboro (UNCG) and a senior research scientist in the Office of Research and Economic Development at UNCG. In 2003, Dr. Bailey received the Lifetime Achievement Award from the North Carolina Department of Health and Human Services Refugee Program for service to refugees, and in 2008 he received the Outstanding Leadership Award from the North Carolina Commission on Volunteerism and Community Service. In March 2010, the Office of the Governor of the State of North Carolina awarded him the Order of the Long Leaf Pine. Dr. Bailey has worked as an educator and practitioner in the field of cultural anthropology, immigrants, and refugees for more than 30 years. His doctoral work at Hartford Seminary Foundation was in anthropology of religion.

GEORGIANA BOSTEAN is currently a postdoctoral fellow at the University of California at Los Angeles in the Fielding School of Public Health. Her research addresses health issues across the life course among minority and vulnerable populations, particularly migrants. She has published book chapters and peer-reviewed articles in the *Journal of Immigrant and Minority Health* and *Research in the Sociology of Health Care*, among others. Her research has been supported by the National Science Foundation, the University of California Office of the President, and the University of California-Irvine Center for Study of Latinos in Global Society. She is an active committee member on the American Sociological Association's Section on Aging and Life Course.

ERNESTO CASTAÑEDA, PhD, is assistant professor in the Department of Sociology and Anthropology at the University of Texas at El Paso. He holds a bachelor's degree from the University of California-Berkeley and MA, MPhil, and PhD degrees in sociology from Columbia University. Dr. Castañeda was a visiting scholar at the Sorbonne and the Institute of Political Studies (Sciences Po) in Paris. His research compares Latino and Muslim immigrants in the United States and Europe. Dr. Castañeda has conducted surveys and ethnographic fieldwork in the United States, France, Spain, Switzerland, Mexico, Algeria, and Morocco. He is interested in the relationship between the contexts of immigrant reception, including the avenues available for political voice, and the political inclusion of immigrants and minorities. His ongoing research projects look into migration, homelessness, mental health, and health disparities along the U.S.-Mexico border. He has published on the complex relationship between remittances and development; hometown associations and diaspora organizations; urban exclusion; and transnational families and the children of migrants left behind in their places of origin.

SHARON WARREN COOK, PhD, is the interim chair in the Department of Sociology and Social Work at North Carolina A&T State University. Dr. Cook has managed community-based mental health programs and served as a social work educator for nearly three decades. Her research and publications focus on the implementation of empowerment activities with underrepresented populations, health disparities, and cultural competence in community practice. She is actively involved in community engagement projects that reflect her research interests.

AKILAH DULIN KEITA, PhD, is an assistant professor in the Department of Behavioral and Social Sciences at Brown University and the Institute for Community Health Promotion. Dr. Dulin Keita obtained a PhD in medical sociology from the University of Alabama at Birmingham in 2007. Her current research examines neighborhood contexts of diet, physical activity, obesity-related comorbidities, and biomarkers of stress among racial/ethnic minorities. She has particular interests in processes of neighborhood-level changes resulting from urban revitalization policies and public health interventions and the potential effects on the aforementioned behavioral and health outcomes.

CHANTELL B. FRAZIER is a PhD candidate in sociology at Syracuse University's Maxwell School of Citizenship and Public Affairs. She holds a master's degree in sociology, received her bachelor's degrees in sociology and biology from DePaul University in Chicago, and is a member of the American Sociological Association and the Sociology Honor Society, Alpha Kappa Delta. Her research interests include quantitative methodology, medical sociology, women's health inequalities, and reproductive health. She is currently working on her dissertation, which is an analysis of health care access and other socioeconomic factors that influence women's reproductive health outcomes in the United States.

BRIAN JOSEPH GILLESPIE is currently a postdoctoral fellow with the Social Science Research Network at the University of California, Irvine, and a lecturer at California State University, Channel Islands. His primary research interests are in demography, family, and the life course. He has several papers currently in press and under review on the impact of residential mobility on individuals, families, and communities. His research has been supported by the National Science Foundation, the American Sociological Association Section on Methodology, and the Center of Expertise on Migration and Health.

JOHN J. GREEN, PhD (University of Missouri-Columbia), is director of the University of Mississippi Center for Population Studies, where he also serves as associate professor of sociology. He serves as the founding director of the Institute for Community-Based Research, a multi-institutional collaborative. Much of his own research focuses on development and health in community and regional contexts. Dr. Green is currently the editor of *Community Development*, the official journal of the Community Development Society.

KATHLEEN T. GRIMM, MD, MHSc, graduated from the State University of New York-Buffalo medical school in 1993, and completed a four-year residency in combined internal medicine/pediatrics in Buffalo, New York. After completion of her residency, she worked in private practice for more than a decade, before working for some time in the University Medicine/Pediatrics clinic site, where she actively participated in teaching of residents and medical students. Dr. Grimm completed a master's program in bioethics at the University of Toronto in 2008. Her current position as a physician is working in palliative care, under the umbrella of the Center for Hospice and Palliative Care in Buffalo. Her interest in advocacy and policy has been a part of her professional life since graduation from residency. Dr. Grimm has served in leadership positions including terms as president of the Erie County Medical Society, president of the Kaleida Medical-Dental Staff, members of professional organizations policy committees at a national level, and past chair of a number of committees, including a local collaborative formed between the University of Buffalo and United Way of Buffalo and Erie County, addressing the prevention of childhood obesity. Her advocacy and passion for community work have led to her current position as co-chair of the Community Health Worker network of Buffalo, a network of public health workers focused on the social determinants of health and health justice. Dr. Grimm is a graduate of the Community Health Foundation of WCNY's Fellows program, working collaboratively to address the needs of children living in poverty. Recently, her work with the Community Health worker network of Buffalo, New York, was presented in Vancouver, Canada, at the "Priorities in International Health" conference and at the National Physicians Alliance conference in 2012.

LONNIE HANNON, PhD, has engaged in study of socioeconomic factors and life quality that has evolved into a theoretical approach that uses macroeconomic transitions and structural inequality as root factors associated with health disparities, neighborhood disadvantage, and economic stagnation. As a significant component of his personal mission, Dr. Hannon believes that student development and service to the community are critically important to the future of the United States. Dr. Hannon regularly teaches Urban Society, Statistics, and Introduction to Sociology courses. He ensures that each student receives the care and personal development needed to function at the highest level. He also serves as a mentor to students and neighborhood youth with the goal of helping them achieve their most positive selves.

MARGARET HARDY is a PhD candidate in the Department of Criminology and Criminal Justice at the University of Maryland, College Park. Her research interests include criminal sentencing, immigration, and neighborhood effects.

HANNA JOKINEN-GORDON is a doctoral candidate at Florida State University in the Department of Sociology. She is a medical sociologist and a social demographer. Her broad interests include how social inequalities in health and well-being emerge, and are maintained, through life course processes. Specifically, her research interests are in immigrant and minority health, maternal and child health, and neighborhoods.

DAVID S. KIRK is associate professor in the Department of Sociology and a faculty research associate of the Population Research Center at the

University of Texas at Austin. His current research explores the effects of neighborhood change, residential mobility, and neighborhood culture on behavior. His recent research has appeared in *American Journal of Sociology, American Sociological Review, The Annals of the American Academy of Political and Social Science*, and *Criminology*.

JOSUÉ GILBERTO LACHICA is a graduate student in the Department of Sociology and Anthropology at the University of Texas at El Paso. He has completed an ethnographic study addressing the transnational aspects of homelessness on the U.S.-Mexico border. His current research uses a combination of nonparticipant observation, semi-structured interviews, and surveys to document homeless experiences of internal migrants, veterans, migrant agricultural workers, and Hispanic populations living in public housing.

MARY T. LEWIS, PhD, MSW, LICSW, is an associate professor of social work at North Carolina A&T State University. She has practiced in the field of social work for more than 30 years, mainly with individuals, families, and communities who are economically and financially disenfranchised. After living and working overseas, she began her current research and course development, which seeks to enhance the internationalization of social work courses and researching student capacity building when working with diversity. Dr. Lewis is a research fellow with the Center for New North Carolinians at the University of North Carolina at Greensboro and a member of the board of directors for the Refugee and Immigrant Network of Greensboro (RING) in North Carolina.

ANDREW S. LONDON is chair and professor of sociology and a senior research associate in the Center for Policy Research in the Maxwell School of Citizenship and Public Affairs at Syracuse University. He is also a senior fellow in the Institute for Veterans and Military Families and a faculty affiliate in the Aging Studies Institute. From 2006 to 2012, he was a founding co-director of the Lesbian, Gay, Bisexual, and Transgender (LGBT) Studies Program. His research focuses on the health, care, and well-being of stigmatized and vulnerable populations, including persons living with HIV, informal caregivers, welfare-reliant and working-poor women and their children, the previously incarcerated, veterans, and LGBT persons and their families.

A. B. MAYFIELD-CLARKE, PhD, CCC/SLP, and Fellow of the American Speech-Language-Hearing Association, is a private practitioner in the field of speech/language pathology with a specialization in corporate speech/language pathology for government employees and non-English speakers (i.e., refugees and immigrants). She previously served as an associate dean for research and graduate studies, associate professor, and program director of Speech/Language Pathology and Audiology at North Carolina A&T State University in Greensboro, North Carolina. With more than 35 years of experience, Dr. Mayfield-Clarke continues to serve as a faculty mentor for undergraduate students in preparation for their entry into graduate programs. She is actively involved in research specializing in issues in multicultural linguistically diverse populations, low-level lead poisoning and its impact on speech and language behavior, quality of service delivery to the 0- to 5-year-old population, and preprofessional training programs.

YOLANDA McDONALD is a Graduate Diversity Fellow in the College of GeoSciences, Department of Geography at Texas A&M University. She received a BA in multidisciplinary studies and an MA in sociology from the University of Texas at El Paso. She has been the recipient of two Hispanic Health Disparities Research Center Graduate Student Research Grants funded by the National Institute on Minority Health Disparities. She has published in the areas of environmental justice and health disparities. Her research interests include medical geography, social and environmental justice, political ecology, human dimensions of environmental change, water governance and injustices, and the role of race, ethnicity, and socioeconomics on exposure to environmental hazards and health disparities.

MEGHAN L. MILLS is a doctoral candidate in sociology at the University of New Hampshire (UNH) concentrating in health and illness. Her current work, which is funded by the National Science Foundation and the Carsey Institute at UNH, involves an ongoing longitudinal study of rural youth. Her dissertation (in progress) examines how socioeconomic status and goal-striving stress contribute to the well-being of rural youth over time. Her recently published work on racial disparities in mental health treatment appears in *Psychiatric Services*.

DEBARASHMI MITRA, PhD, is assistant professor of sociology and community development at Delta State University. She received her PhD in sociology from the University of Connecticut. Dr. Mitra's research focuses on gender and development, globalization, and social change in national and international contexts. In particular, she is interested in examining issues related to state and labor, women and work, and development and health. Her scholarship has appeared in journals such as *Mobilization* and *International Journal of Contemporary Sociology*.

MAURA NSONWU, PhD, MSW, LCSW, is the assistant chair and interim BSW director at North Carolina A&T State University in the Department of Sociology and Social Work. She has practiced as a clinician, educator, and researcher in the areas of refugee resettlement, human trafficking, health care, child welfare, and social work education for more than 25 years. Dr. Nsonwu is a research fellow with the Center for New North Carolinians at the University of North Carolina at Greensboro, where her research has focused on working with refugee and immigrant communities and issues of human trafficking.

DEBORAH L. PUNTENNEY holds the title of Research Associate Professor in the School of Education and Social Policy at Northwestern University, where she conducts community research and teaches courses in social policy, the family, and gender. Dr. Puntenney also operates a consulting firm specializing in the areas of community research and evaluation, social justice strategies for philanthropic and nonprofit organizations, and asset-based community development. For the last 20 years, she has been associated with the Asset-Based Community Development Institute at Northwestern University and authored many of the institute's workbooks. All of her direct community work emphasizes the design and implementation of asset-oriented strategies toward social justice goals. Beyond her work with the ABCD Institute, her research and writing emphasize themes related to community, gender, and social policy.

JEFFREY M. TIMBERLAKE is associate professor of sociology at the University of Cincinnati. His research interests are in the sociology of population, urban sociology, race and ethnicity, and quantitative research methods. His current research focuses on causes and consequences of urban inequality. Recent projects include analyses of racial and ethnic residential segregation, exposure of children to neighborhood poverty and violence, attitudes of Ohioans toward immigrants and immigration, and urban demographic change from 1970 to 2010. He has recently published papers in *Demography, Social Science Quarterly, Journal of Urban Affairs,* and *Urban Affairs Review.*

KAREN T. VAN GUNDY is associate professor of sociology at the University of New Hampshire (UNH) and a faculty fellow at the Carsey Institute at UNH. Her work applies stress and life course perspectives to examine variations in health, emotional, and behavioral outcomes across the life course. Her current work, which is funded by two National Science Foundation grants and by the New Hampshire Charitable Foundation, considers the effects on health and well-being of family, school, work, and community contexts for rural and urban youth and emerging adults. Her recent publications appear in the *Journal of Health and Social Behavior, Social Science & Medicine,* and *Rural Sociology.*

JESSICA BAUER WALKER has been a community advocate and front-line worker in local, national, and international contexts. She has served as an AmeriCorps volunteer in Montana and a Peace Corps volunteer in Jamaica, as an organizer for two presidential campaigns and for Rock the Vote, and as a project manager for several community-based organizations and initiatives targeting issues such as youth development, environmental health, and HIV/AIDS. Ms. Walker is currently the director of the Community Health Worker Network of Buffalo, where she works to provide opportunities for the residents of vulnerable neighborhoods to realize their full potential for health and well-being through empowerment and asset-building strategies for individuals and communities. She has a passion for creating positive change for her local community of urban Buffalo and beyond to foster a more just and sustainable world for our children and all future generations.

BARBARA J. ZAPPIA is a senior program officer at the Greater Rochester Health Foundation (GRHF) in Rochester, New York, where she oversees the Neighborhood Health Status Improvement Initiative—an asset-based, grassroots effort to improve the health status of residents in Rochester neighborhoods. Ms. Zappia joined GRHF in 2006, bringing with her nearly 20 years of professional experience as a physical therapist, along with development and program evaluation roles in community agencies and higher education. She holds a BS from Ithaca College, has an MPA from State University of New York at Brockport, and is a doctoral student at the University of Rochester.